AMERICAN MERCHANT SHIPS

Series II

"GREAT ADMIRAL," 1497 TONS, BUILT IN 1869, AT EAST BOSTON
From the oil painting by Charles R. Patterson, owned by
the late William Dunning Sewall

AMERICAN MERCHANT SHIPS

1850–1900

Series II

by

FREDERICK C. MATTHEWS

DOVER PUBLICATIONS, INC.

NEW YORK

Published in Canada by General Publishing Company, Ltd., 30 Lesmill Road, Don Mills, Toronto, Ontario.

Published in the United Kingdom by Constable and Company, Ltd., 10 Orange Street, London WC2H 7EG.

This Dover edition, first published in 1987, is an unabridged republication of the work in two "series" originally published as publications 21 (1930) and 23 (1931) by the Marine Research Society, Salem, Massachusetts. The 1931 publication bore the subtitle "Series Two"; the title page of the 1930 publication had no series indication. The frontispiece of the first series, printed in color in the original edition, is here reproduced in black and white.

Manufactured in the United States of America

Dover Publications, Inc., 31 East 2nd Street, Mineola, N.Y. 11501

Library of Congress Cataloging-in-Publication Data

Matthews, Frederick C.
American merchant ships, 1850–1900 / by Frederick C. Matthews.
   p.   cm.
Reprint. Originally published: Salem, Mass. : Marine Research Society, 1930–1931.
Includes index.
ISBN 0-486-25538-7 (pbk. : v. 1). ISBN 0-486-25539-5 (pbk. : v. 2)
1. Merchant ships—United States—History.   I. Title.
VM378.M38   1987
387.2'24'0973—dc19   87-16623
                                       CIP

In Loving Memory of
My Wife
Who Unselfishly Aided Me
To Realize My Life-Long Ambition
Yet Did Not Live to See Its Consummation
This Volume is Dedicated

PORTRAITS OF SHIPS

PORTRAITS OF SEA CAPTAINS

AMERICAN MERCHANT SHIPS

Series II

AMERICAN MERCHANT SHIPS

ABNER COBURN

THE three skysail-yard ship *Abner Coburn*, named after the Governor of Maine, whose term of office was 1862-1863, was built by William Rogers at Bath, Maine, and was launched in October, 1882. She was 223 feet, by 43, by 26:8 feet and registered 1878 tons. She hailed from Bath and for over ten years was managed by her builder although much of her ownership was vested in residents of Searsport. Later the management passed to Pendleton, Carver & Nichols. In 1900, while the ship was on a passage from New York to Hong Kong, she was purchased by the California Shipping Co. of San Francisco and they, some twelve years later, sold her to Libby, McNeill & Libby.

Prior to 1900 the *Coburn* was engaged in trade principally between Atlantic ports and the Orient although she made several Cape Horn passages to San Francisco. The California Shipping Co. chartered her mostly for offshore lumber carrying on the Pacific, and Libby, McNeill & Libby used her in connection with their salmon canneries in Alaska. While owned on the Pacific coast she was laid up idle for quite lengthy periods, at times. A year or so ago she was burned at Puget Sound for the metal used in her construction.

The *Coburn's* passages were made in fair average time and from what can be learned her career was rather uneventful. However, in May, 1886, when bound from New York to San Francisco with general cargo including a quantity of kerosene, she narrowly escaped being destroyed by fire. When off the Brazilian coast some cargo stowed in the between decks was found to be burning but prompt and energetic action on the part of Captain Nichols and his crew prevented the fire from gaining much headway and it was finally got under control and subdued. On another occasion the ship put into Montevideo with her coal cargo badly heated but fortunately she was able to make port in time to prevent material damage being done.

3

The *Coburn* was built to be commanded by Capt. Geo. A. Nichols of Searsport and prior to his death on board, in 1897, he was continuously in her with the exception of a passage made from New York to Seattle by Capt. Jas. C. Gilmore and two round voyages to the Orient made by Capt. Jas. P. Butman. After the death of Captain Nichols, Captain Butman made another voyage to the Orient when Capt. Benj. F. Colcord succeeded and was in command until the ship changed hands. While owned on the Pacific coast the *Coburn* had many different masters.

Prior to taking command of the *Coburn*, Capt. Geo. A. Nichols had been master of the barks *Joshua Loring* and *S. W. Swazey* and the ship *Phineas Pendleton*. On the voyage during which he met his death, the ship had left New York, Mar. 24, 1897, with case oil for Hong Kong. On June 20th, while the ship was running before a heavy gale under two lower topsails and a reefed foresail and being then about midway between the Cape of Good Hope and Australia, she took a very heavy sea over the stern. The watch was just being changed at 4 P.M. when the wave broke aboard and carried away the wheelhouse. Captain Nichols was coming out of the companionway and was caught and crushed against the ladder, having both legs broken and receiving severe injuries internally. He expired some seven hours later. First officer Melvin L. Park was badly hurt and unable to do duty for a number of weeks. Morning revealed the two lower yards on the foremast loose and threshing about dangerously, the lee rail some ten feet under water, and all the running rigging of the ship in such a mess that after she was finally hove to, it required two days to straighten out the tangle. The body of Captain Nichols was committed to the deep in the midst of very stormy weather with a high, confused sea running and all hands were much affected by the scene. The navigation of the ship then devolved on the second mate, Jos. F. Nichols, son of her former commander, who, though then under nineteen years of age, successfully took her to her destination by way of Anjer. By the time Hong Kong was reached, chief officer Park had recovered and he took the ship back to New York, the passage occupying six months, fourteen days, a call having to be made at

St. Helena for a supply of provisions. Young Nichols made the following voyage as mate under Captain Butman after which he entered the service of the New York & Porto Rico Steamship Co. Later on he went as mate on the steamer *Texan* of the American Hawaiian Steamship Co.'s fleet, afterwards becoming her commander and continuing as master of different steamers in that employ for some twenty years. At present Captain Nichols is marine superintendent for a large San Francisco company.

Capt. Geo. A. Nichols was but forty-eight years of age at the time of his death. He came from an old seafaring family, his father being Capt. Amos Nichols, managing owner of the ship *Matilda*, and his brothers, Amos Nichols, Jr., and Wilfred V. Nichols, well-known shipmasters. Hugh Nichols, son of Capt. Geo. A., was chief officer of the *Coburn* on the voyage to Japan, made in 1896, when Captain Butman was in command. The ship left New York February 12th and four days later Mr. Nichols was washed overboard during a heavy gale and drowned.

The career of Capt. J. P. Butman as a shipmaster is contained in account of the ship *E. B. Sutton*, in the present volume, while that of Capt. Benj. F. Colcord is in that of the ship *Wm. H. Connor*, in "American Merchant Ships," Series I.

ADAM M. SIMPSON

THE ship *Adam M. Simpson* was built by Goss & Sawyer at Bath, Maine, and was launched Aug. 31, 1875. She was well built and a first class vessel in every way, 210 feet, by 40, by 24 feet; 1525 tons register. Her figurehead was an image of her namesake, a member of the old established firm of A. S. Simpson & Brother, shipwrights and operators of the floating dry dock on the Delaware River, at the foot of Christian street, Philadelphia. The Simpson firm owned an eighth interest in the ship and following the death of Adam M. Simpson, in July, 1878, this was sold at auction for $4775. The remaining shares in the vessel had all along been held by her builders and their friends.

The first two voyages of the *Simpson* were rounds between Philadelphia, San Francisco and the United Kingdom under command of Capt. George Sumner. Early in his career Captain Sumner had been master of the ship *Tamerlane*, of Philadelphia, and following her loss in 1870, was appointed to command the steamship *Indiana* of the American Line, plying between Philadelphia and Liverpool. The captain died while the *Simpson* was at Philadelphia, in April, 1879, and Capt. Alban Call was appointed master in his stead.

Under command of Captain Call, the *Simpson* made a voyage from Cardiff to Hong Kong, with coal and then one with railroad iron from New York to the Columbia River, returning with wheat to the United Kingdom. Following this she took case oil from Philadelphia to Yokohama; crossed to British Columbia to load coal for San Francisco, and from the latter port took wheat to Liverpool, arriving out Dec. 21, 1882. All her passages had been made in fair average time and had been free from mishaps or unusual incidents.

In 1883 the *Simpson* took case oil from New York to Hong Kong, later proceeding to Iloilo where a cargo of sugar was laden for New York. In December of that year, when only a few days at sea on the latter passage, she struck a reef in the Palawan Passage and became a total loss. Captain Call and the ship's crew left in the boats to try and obtain assistance and on their return found that the natives had looted the vessel of everything they could take away, besides destroying the cabin furniture, fixtures, etc., with their spears and knives. Captain Call was subsequently in command of the ship *City of Philadelphia*.

AGENOR

THE ship *Agenor* was built at East Boston, by Curtis, Smith & Co., and was launched in April, 1870. She was 202 feet, by 39:9, by 24:2 feet and registered 1414 tons. She was built to the order of E. Williams & Co., prominent merchants of Boston. For some years prior to 1905 her managing owner was given as B. B. Williams, her hailing port still being Boston. The name "Agenor" is said to refer to residents of a district in France, near Bordeaux.

Early in her career the *Agenor* made several transatlantic voyages and also took coal to the West Coast of South America, thence proceeding to San Francisco to load grain for Europe. Thereafter she was operated between Atlantic ports and those of the North Pacific Coast or the Far East. Her sailing record is very good and includes a number of fast passages among which was one of 30 days from Callao to San Francisco. This run was made in 1874 with Capt. Allen H. Knowles in command and is but one day longer than the record which is held by the bark *Martha*, originally the clipper ship *Rattler*, built in Rockland, Maine, in 1852. In 1879, and again in 1881, the *Agenor* crossed from Kobe to San Francisco in 29 and 27 days respectively, being in the latter instance only 22 days from clearing the Japanese coast to destination. In 1904 she made the run from Guayaquil to San Francisco in the record time of 43 days, this run and also that from Panama being practically always a very long and tedious one for sailing vessels due to the prevalence of light and variable winds making it particularly difficult to get clear of the coast and into the belt of trade winds.

The *Agenor's* fastest passage around Cape Horn to the westward was in 1876 in 120 days from New York to San Francisco, and her fastest eastward was 113 days from San Francisco to Antwerp, in 1882.

The *Agenor* enjoys the distinction of having obtained the highest rate of freight from San Francisco to Liverpool ever paid a wooden ship of the old-time grain fleet — £5.12.0. per ton. This was in October, 1872, when, following two years of excessive drought, California was favored with a copious rainfall during the winter of 1871-1872 and an unparalleled wheat harvest resulted. As soon as it was apparent that a large crop was in sight the matter of transportation became of great importance and strenuous efforts were made by shipowners to get their vessels to San Francisco. In March and April, 1872, £3 was offered for vessels to arrive during the summer months and when loading actually commenced the rates had advanced to £4 and then to £5 and upwards, and high figures continued until January, 1875. Shipowners made excellent profits but it is noted as an offset, in the case of the *Agenor*, that after she arrived at San Francisco, in October, 1891, she lay in port until July, 1893, for lack of remunerative business. Her stay exceeded that of the next oldest maritime resident, the British bark *Auchencairn*, by five months.

The last long distance voyage of the *Agenor* was in 1898, leaving New York in August and arriving at San Francisco, Jan. 3, 1899, after a passage of 132 days. Thereafter she was operated in the export lumber trade out of Puget Sound until 1905 when she was sold to parties in San Francisco who sent her to Alaska. In October of that year she sailed from Saginaw Bay, Alaska, with 1500 tons of salt salmon for Yokohama and had the very long passage of 96 days, being fully two months overdue when she made port and having been about given up as lost. After being discharged, she was sold to Sale & Frazar, American citizens residing in Yokohama, who had her loaded with 1000 tons of wheat for Kobe. On the passage around, the ship, while in a dead calm and being carried by the current towards a nest of pinnacle rocks in a channel some sixty miles from her destination, was brought up with two anchors. The chain of one of these parted and the other anchor was unable to hold the ship against the strong current so she was soon carried on the rocks. Large holes were knocked in her bottom and she soon filled with water. Before long her hull had been broken up into matchwood.

The first master of the *Agenor* was Capt. Allen H. Knowles who was in command four years and left her at San Francisco to go East and take the new Williams & Co. ship *Conqueror*. Captain Knowles's career as a shipmaster is given in account of that ship appearing in "American Merchant Ships," Series I. Capt. Nathaniel Gould then made a voyage in the *Agenor*, after which he also took the *Conqueror* and was in her five years, later purchasing a small steamer for operation on San Francisco bay. Capt. Edgar Nichols, of Brewster, Mass., succeeded Captain Gould but made only one voyage in the *Agenor*, he then taking the *Pocahontas* and later the *Charmer*. Captain Nichols had previously been in command of the ships *T. B. Wales, Gold Hunter* and *Hercules*, all belonging to Boston. He retired from sea life in 1886 to become Port Warden at Boston and passed away in February, 1897, at the age of sixty-eight years while still holding that position.

Capt. John H. Frost, who also had commanded the *Conqueror*, made several voyages in the *Agenor*, as also did Capt. Chas. H. Colby of Newburyport. In 1900 Captain Colby retired from sea life and became superintendent of the rooms of the Marine Society of Newburyport. He had commenced seafaring life in the ship *North Atlantic* and later had been chief mate of the famous ships *Nightingale*, *Grace Darling*, and *Prima Donna*, and subsequently master of the bark *Obed Baxter*. Capt. Henry Mowat of Baltimore, was in command of the *Agenor* when she was lost.

AKBAR

THE ship *Akbar*, named after a celebrated emperor of India who lived during the last half of the sixteenth century, was built by Paul Curtis at East Boston and was launched towards the end of 1863. She measured 159:7 feet, by 32:8, by 21:9 feet, and registered 906 tons. She was a good type of the small American merchantman of that period with no pretension of being a fast sailer, though a good, serviceable vessel, making good returns to her owners, William Perkins & Co. of Boston.

The maiden voyage of the *Akbar* was from Boston to San Francisco, she returning home by way of Honolulu, Hong Kong, Penang and Calcutta. In 1868 she made another voyage from Boston to San Francisco, again going home by way of the Orient. The remainder of her career was spent between Atlantic ports and those of China, the East Indies or Australia, although on several occasions she crossed the Pacific to load at San Francisco for New York or the United Kingdom. Her last completed voyage to Melbourne, Sydney, Newcastle, Sourabaya and New York was quite eventful, she being obliged to put back to Sydney from Newcastle, leaky and partially dismasted. On the following voyage, which was in 1877-1878, she was abandoned in latitude 35° south, longitude 27° east, while homeward bound from Batavia with sugar.

The first master of the *Akbar* was Capt. Benj. F. Chase of Cape Cod, and the second, Capt. Elijah Crocker of Barnstable, who later was in command of the ship *Conqueror*. Capt. C. W. Lamson took the *Akbar* in 1870 and continued in command until she was lost. During the Civil War Captain Lamson was Acting Master of the *Pampero*, known as one of the fastest of the old clipper fleet but then an armed cruiser of the United States Navy.

ALASKA

THE ship *Alaska* was built by Capt. N. L. Titcomb, at Kennebunk, Maine, and was launched in December, 1867. She measured 188 feet, by 39, by 23:8 feet and registered 1316 tons. She was a well built vessel and one of the first American ships to be fitted with wire standing rigging. During the first six years she was owned by Thayer & Lincoln of Boston and was employed in the general carrying trade, making transatlantic, East Indian and Californian voyages. While in port at New York, in June, 1874, she was purchased by C. L. Taylor & Co., shipping merchants of San Francisco, who, in addition to their other business, ran a line of sailing vessels between that port and Boston. The *Alaska* then continued in the Cape Horn trade until April, 1878, when she was sold to Samuel Blair of San Francisco, owner of a number of vessels employed in the Pacific, and the *Alaska* became one of that fleet making an occasional transpacific voyage with lumber but principally carrying coal coastwise.

In April, 1893, while bound from Bellingham Bay, Washington, to San Francisco, coal laden, she was discovered to be leaking when not long at sea. The leak increased steadily in spite of the steam pumps being kept continuously going. At 7 P.M. on April 22d the port pump broke down and the ship, then having eight feet of water in the well, was abandoned, the crew taking to the boats. She soon after went down. Fortunately the barkentine *Melancthon* soon hove in sight and after being only about an hour in their boats, the crew was rescued. The first voyage made by the *Alaska*, under the Taylor & Co. ownership, was from Philadelphia to Acapulco. Off Cape Horn the cargo was discovered to be on fire and Captain Anderson decided on attempting a novel scheme in an effort to save his ship. He steered for Orange Bay where in smooth water and on a good bottom he scuttled his ship and extinguished the fire. Then with the assistance of the captain and crew of a trading schooner she was pumped out and floated, no material damage having been sustained. The schooner captain was paid $1,000 for the assistance rendered. Captain Anderson completed his passage to Acapulco and the ship later proceeded to Puget Sound to load coal for San Francisco and took grain thence to Liverpool.

The first master of the *Alaska* was Capt. James M. Small, who, in 1871, left her to take command of the new Thayer & Lincoln ship *Hamilton*. Capt. M. A. Humphrey then made a round voyage in the *Alaska* after the completion of which Captain Anderson took charge for her new owners. Captain Anderson completed two round voyages, his last passage being from San Francisco to Antwerp. Capt. Geo. N. Armstrong then took the ship from Hull to San Francisco and she being resold after arrival he left her to take the ship *Templar*. An account of a momentous passage made by the Captain in that ship appears in "American Merchant Ships," Series I.

While owned by Samuel Blair, the *Alaska* had a number of different masters. Capt. J. H. Brennan was in command when she was lost. Capt. Brennan was a native of New Haven, Conn., and born in 1848. As a boy he sailed in coasters on Long Island and in 1866 went to San Francisco on the ship *Rival*. He stayed on the Pacific Coast and in 1875 obtained his first command, the brig *Tanner*. Thereafter he was master of different vessels prior to taking the *Alaska*. Following her loss he commanded the schooner *C. H. Merchant*, a number of years, when he retired from sea life and is said to have spent the remainder of his life in Sailor's Snug Harbor.

ALEX. GIBSON

THE ship *Alex. Gibson* was built by Edward O'Brien, at Thomaston, Maine, and was launched Oct. 24, 1877. A three-decker, she was 247:3, by 42:6, by 29:6 feet and registered 2121 tons. In common with other O'Brien ships she was conspicuous through having several strakes of her planking in the natural wood, varnished, and was heavily sparred although not lofty, as none of her companions in the fleet crossed any yards above royals. During the early '90's her immense wooden lower masts and yards were replaced by iron spars. The man after whom she was named, was the largest shipper of deals from St. John, N. B., with whom Mr. O'Brien and other Maine shipowners had extensive dealings.

The maiden voyage of the *Gibson* was from Norfolk to Liverpool with cotton, she arriving out Jan. 27, 1878, after a passage of 20 days. She then took coal to Callao and guano thence to Antwerp. Then followed a voyage from Liverpool to San Francisco with coal and she continued in trade with California principally until 1901, making to San Francisco seven passages from Liverpool and five from New York. At intervals she made three voyages to the Far East with case oil. Of homeward bound passages, she appears in the California grain fleet on seven occasions and in that of Tacoma once. She took two general cargoes from San Francisco to New York and two lumber cargoes from Puget Sound to Great Britain.

On the last westward passage around Cape Horn, the *Gibson* left New York, July 1, 1900, at which time there was no other ship on the berth for San Francisco, an unprecedented state of affairs, and her departure from port marked practically the end of sailing ships on this route, due to the overpowering competition of the steamers of the new American-Hawaiian line. Shortly before this she had been purchased by John Rosenfeld's Sons of San Francisco, they, the following year, selling her to the California Shipping Company. Following her arrival at San Francisco, on the passage just referred to, she was employed principally in the export lumber trade out of Puget Sound, making voyages to South Africa, Australia and the West Coast of

South America. For some two years prior to May, 1910, she was laid up at San Francisco, then loading lumber at Tacoma for New York. Arrived out in January, 1911, after a long and hard passage; had put into Valparaiso with ship leaking, pumps broken, upper works carried away and a considerable portion of her deck load jettisoned. At New York she was sold to the Luckenbachs for conversion into a coal barge and was towed up and down the Atlantic Coast until Dec. 28, 1915, when she stranded and became a total loss on McCreigh Shoal, coast of New Jersey. Her crew of five men was saved.

The *Gibson*, as all other O'Brien ships, was modeled to carry large cargoes, but her sailing record is very fair. The average of her passages from Atlantic ports to San Francisco is 138 days, the shortest being 123 days from Liverpool. The average of the return passages is 122 days, with 108 days to Liverpool as the shortest. On her first passage to San Francisco she left Liverpool in company with the O'Brien ship *Alex. McCallum* of the same model but a trifle smaller. Both arrived at Callao the same day. They left there practically in company, passed through the Golden Gate the same day, were chartered at the same time and left San Francisco in company but the *Gibson* beat her companion a month on the run to Liverpool.

Aside from the last voyage made by the *Gibson* as a sailing ship, which has been referred to, she met with no serious mishaps. On one occasion she was struck by lightning when off the Falkland Islands, but fortunately only slight damage to the mainmast resulted. An incident rather out of the ordinary occurred during the passage from Liverpool to San Francisco in 1892 when, one very dark night, one of the ship's boys fell overboard. A life buoy was immediately thrown overboard while Captain Speed flashed a dark lantern on it and saw the boy gain it. A boat was lowered but after a long absence returned to the ship without having found the missing lad. The ship was then wore around and when she came to again the boy was seen close aboard and was hauled on deck.

In August, 1906, while off the Mexican Coast, the *Gibson* experienced a very heavy earthquake shock which shook the ship from stem to stern as though she was bumping over a ledge of rocks. Tools were shaken out of the racks in the carpenter shop; galley and pantry utensils were thrown down from hooks and all chimneys shaken off lamps. The crew came running aft, not knowing what was the matter, and Captain Wayland thought the yards were coming down. The first shock was soon followed by a second but much lighter one, and within a few hours two more shocks were felt. Captain Wayland had experienced an earthquake at sea on a previous occasion but the present one far eclipsed it in force and duration. The sea at the time was perfectly smooth and the ship under full sail in a light wind with fine, clear weather.

Among the slow passages made by the *Gibson* was one made in 1901 in 134 days from Puget Sound to Cape Town on which occasion she had been about given up as lost nearly a month before she made port.

The first master of the *Alex. Gibson* was Capt. James R. Speed of Thomaston, who had previously been in the O'Brien ship *Andrew Johnson*. Captain Speed commanded the *Gibson* some twelve years, being drowned while the ship was at Puget Sound in May, 1889. Capt. Isaac N. Hibberd, who had previously been in the ship *Cyrus Wakefield*, succeeded in the *Gibson* and after about three years retired from sea life to engage in business in San Francisco. Capt. David J. Hodgman then had the *Gibson* some five years, retiring from her to pass his remaining years at his home in Thomaston. Captain Hodgman had sailed in many ships belonging to that port, among them being the *Loretto Fish*, *Cyrus Wakefield*, *J. B. Walker* and *Belle O'Brien*. He was highly respected, a first-class navigator and was called a true blue Yankee sailor.

Capt. Jos. W. Holmes, formerly in the ship *Charmer*, commanded the *Gibson* two years prior to January, 1901, when he retired from sea life. The Captain was one of the best known of American merchant shipmasters and was long in the ship *Seminole*, in account of which ship, appearing in "American Merchant Ships," Series I, his career is more particularly given. Following him in the *Gibson* were a number of different masters, among them being Capt. J. A. Wayland, who at one time had been an officer in the British Army in

South Africa. Later on Captain Wayland made his home in Berkeley, Cal., but traded his place for a farm in the San Joaquin Valley. During the World War he took a vessel from San Francisco to Australia.

ALEX. McCALLUM

THE ship *Alex. McCallum*, built and owned by Edward O'Brien, was launched at Thomaston, Maine, in May, 1870, and although somewhat smaller, was practically a sister ship to the later products of the O'Brien yard, the *Alex. Gibson, Edward O'Brien, J. B. Walker*, and others. The *McCallum* was 220 feet, by 42, by 29 feet, and registered 1951 tons. She was named after a successful shipbuilder of Warren, Maine, who subsequently located in Thomaston.

The *McCallum* was employed during her career, in trade with San Francisco and the West Coast of South America, making an equal number of voyages to each section of country. On the outward passages she carried coal and, returning, took guano from South America and wheat or lumber from the North Pacific. While none of the O'Brien ships were built to sail fast, the sister ships of the *McCallum* have better records in that respect than she. The average of the eight passages made by the *McCallum* to San Francisco is 162 days, and those from the Pacific 137 days, nor does her work in the South American trade show to advantage. However, she carried large cargoes and met with but one serious mishap. On one occasion she was employed in the coastwise coal trade on the Pacific and at another time she was laid up at San Francisco, over a year, in company with many other ships waiting for remunerative business.

On Aug. 12, 1892, the *McCallum* sailed from San Francisco, for London, with a cargo of selected lumber, principally redwood of best quality, and two weeks later encountered a hurricane which lasted the greater part of two days. She lost sails, bulwarks, boats, and everything movable from decks; had the forward house stove in and in addition started to leak. With eight feet of water in the hold and the ship having a bad list, Captain O'Brien put back to San Francisco. Repairs were made and the ship arrived at London, in March, 1893. Sailing from London, in May, for New York, when near the American coast she was in collision with the steamship *Servia* and foundered. All but two of the crew were saved by boats from the steamer which landed them at Queenstown.

While sailing deep water the *McCallum* was commanded by Captains John W. Moody, Geo. W. K. Masters, William Tattersall, and William T. O'Brien. During the year or so she was sailing on the Pacific Coast, Capt. Geo. E. Wallace was her master. Captain Masters, a native of Thomaston, had the ship for the longest period, some nine years, after which he was three years in the *Baring Brothers*. Subsequently he commanded vessels running coastwise on the Pacific and on retiring from the sea, made his home in Alameda, Cal., and died there in April, 1898. Captain Moody, who had been master of the bark *Ocean Favorite*, prior to her sale at Buenos Ayres, in 1869, had the *McCallum* six years, and Captain O'Brien the last three years of her career. He is more particularly referred to in account of the "Big" *Edward O'Brien*. Captain Tattersall was a native of England who came to this country on one of Mr. O'Brien's ships but was not long in the employ of the latter. He made but one voyage in the *McCallum* and subsequently one in the *J. B. Walker*.

ALICE BUCK

THE ship *Alice Buck* was built at Belfast, Maine, in 1870, by Capt. Henry McGilvery, Columbus Carter being the master carpenter. She measured 198:6 feet, by 38:2, by 24 feet and registered 1425 tons. She was owned by Captain McGilvery, J. P. White, and others, of Belfast, and R. P. Buck & Co. of New York. She was named after a daughter of William Buck of Bucksport, Me., and Bucksville, S. C.

Early in her career the *Buck* made a few voyages in the transatlantic cotton trade but most of her operations during the ten years of her career were to the Far East or San Francisco and while she has no fast voyages to her credit, she made good passages and was called a successful ship. She was built to be commanded by Capt. Phineas Pendleton, 2nd, of Searsport, but he soon turned her over to his son-in-law, Capt. Wm. H. Blanchard. Captain Pendleton later had the ship *Phineas Pendleton* and his seafaring life is contained in account of that ship. Capt. Wm. H. Blanchard was also in the *Buck* but a short time. He is mentioned in account of the ship *Gov. Robie,* appearing in "American Merchant Ships," Series I. Capt. James R. Herriman of Stockton, Me., was master of the *Alice Buck* some five years but had remained at home the passage during which the ship was lost, she then being in charge of her former mate. Captain Herriman had commanded various barks and brigs and, in addition to the *Buck,* the full-rigged ships *Wm. Woodbury* and *America.* After retiring from sea life he bought a fine ranch in California and was also for a time engaged as a marine surveyor in San Francisco. He came from an old seafaring family and was a brother of Captains Ezekiel Horace, Ferdinand de Soto, Albert Louis, Hezekiah, and Horatio Nelson Herriman. Capt. James R. was a resident of Alameda, Cal., when he passed away.

Capt. Henry McGilvery, builder of the *Alice Buck,* was a native of Stockton, Me., and started sea life as a boy. Rising through the various grades from seaman to master he for many years commanded the clipper ship *Resolute* and other vessels in the China trade and is said to have been master of the first American ship to enter the harbor of Singapore. In 1865 the captain retired from sea life to embark in the business of shipbuilding in Belfast. Among the vessels he constructed were the ships *Nancy Pendleton* and *Frank Pendleton.* He was a man of high character and of remarkable ability both as a shipmaster and business man. He died at an advanced age while visiting a daughter in Brooklyn, N. Y., but for some ten years previously had made his home in Hallowell, Me. A brother, Capt. William McGilvery of Searsport, also engaged in business as a shipbuilder after retiring from sea life and was one of the most prominent citizens of his State.

The following is an account of the loss of the *Alice Buck* on the Pacific Coast, some twenty miles south of the Golden Gate, in September, 1881, while bound from New York to Portland, Ore., with a cargo of railroad iron.

On August 28th the ship encountered a hurricane in latitude 16° N., Pacific, and sprung a leak in the bows. The following day a second gale was met with resulting in double the quantity of water entering the hold. It was then decided to steer for San Francisco for repairs, the leak gaining in spite of the pumps being worked night and day. At 4 P.M., September 26th, the ship was figured to be fifty-five miles S.W. of the Golden Gate and the course was set N.E. On making the coast a dead calm was encountered and the ship commenced to drift towards the shore, finally striking a reef, bows on, at midnight. She bumped five or six times and at last hit hard and held on forward but soon broke in two. The men were exhausted and the master had been on deck steadily for three days and nights. A dingey was launched but almost immediately upset, two of the men in her being washed ashore and one drowned. The whale boat containing the two mates, steward and two sailors was launched but was stove while being lowered and only the two sailors were able to get aboard the wreck again. One by one the men jumped overboard and by 2 A.M. the captain and seven men were the only ones remaining on board. The captain, with two life buoys on, jumped overboard but could not make headway on account of floating wreckage and drifted about until eight o'clock when he was assisted ashore. Those lost were the two mates, four seamen, one boy, the steward and the cook, the two latter being Chinese.

ANDREW JACKSON

THE ship *Andrew Jackson*, launched in May, 1864, was built and owned by D. D. Kelley, a shipwright, dry dock operator and shipowner of Boston. She was 183 feet, by 36, by 23 feet and registered 1095 tons. She had a round stern, no figurehead and crossed nothing above royal yards. In model she was what was known as a

"ABNER COBURN," 1878 TONS, BUILT IN 1882, AT BATH, MAINE

"AGENOR," 1414 TONS, BUILT IN 1870, AT EAST BOSTON

"ARYAN," 1939 TONS, BUILT IN 1893, AT PHIPPSBURG, MAINE

"BELLE O'BRIEN," 1903 TONS, BUILT IN 1875, AT THOMASTON, MAINE

From an oil painting by W. H. York, 1894. Photograph by George E. Noyes, Newburyport

kettle-bottomed ship, having considerable tumble-home in her sides due to the lower deck being much wider than the upper. She was a good sea boat but a dull sailer. About the year 1888 she was sold for conversion into a barge and was eventually lost on Romer's Shoal, New York.

The first two voyages of the *Andrew Jackson* were from New York to San Francisco but most of her life was spent in the transatlantic or guano trades. In 1872, while under command of Capt. Jos. C. Field, she sailed from Boston for Chatham, N. B., thence going to Liverpool, Valparaiso, Iquique, Guanape, Valencia in Spain, Tybee and St. John. This itinerary occupied nearly two years, all the various passages being made in quite slow time, particularly the run from Guanape, Ecuador, with guano to Gibraltar. Capt. Frank P. Whittier, who was then first mate of the ship, recalls very vividly the voyage and gives the following details:

"Soon after crossing the line in the Atlantic we got up our last barrel of flour, this having been nearly two years in the alleyway abreast the after house. We figured this would last us 25 days but it requires none too keen an imagination to describe our looks and feelings when we found that rats had gnawed a hole in the barrelhead and consumed all but about ten pounds of the contents. For 18 days we had no meat at all except a ham which we obtained from a passing Boston bark. When we got close to Gibraltar the wind came out dead ahead and the ship was hove to under Cape Spartel, we hoping to obtain some much needed provisions from a passing vessel. However the only one we saw was a French bark, 130 days out of Mauritius with sugar, her crew being on an allowance of food due to her long run. The only meat they had was part of a pig and of that I got about a pound to make soup for Captain Field's wife who was nursing an infant child born while the ship was at Iquique. I also got a small supply of dried vegetables, a bag of rice and some sugar. The easterly wind continued for a week, with rice as our diet throughout. During the evening of the seventh day the thick fog which had been enveloping the ship cleared off and from an Italian brig bound from Africa to England with barley, we got two bags of ship biscuit and on this our nearly starved crew crunched all night. The next day we were able to make Gibraltar and took on stores sufficient for three months. Mrs. Field, who was a sister of Capt. Phineas Pendleton, 3rd, the first master of the ship *Henry B. Hyde*, never ate rice the remainder of her life."

Capt. Jos. C. Field left the *Andrew Jackson* after the termination of the voyage described to take the bark *Henry Buck* to Java and Sydney. While aboard a local steamer at the latter port he fell overboard and was drowned. The mate, Edward L. Colson, took the bark to San Francisco where she was sold. Captain Field was a native of Searsport and but 34 years of age when he lost his life. Prior to taking command of the *Andrew Jackson* he had been in the bark *Volunteer*, an account of the abandonment of which and the sufferings of the crew is contained in "American Merchant Ships," Series I.

Chief officer Frank P. Whittier of Searsport had also been mate of the *Volunteer* and in later years was master of different barks, brigs and schooners. He was an elder brother of the late Capt. Albert T. Whittier of the ships *Aryan* and *Paul Revere* and although now at an advanced age is still living and in good health at his home in Maine.

A medium clipper ship named *Andrew Jackson*, built at Mystic, Conn., in 1855, had an excellent record as a fast sailing ship, one of her runs being 90 days, 12 hours from New York to San Francisco, the third fastest made over that course, beaten only by the two runs of the *Flying Cloud*. This *Andrew Jackson* was sold to go under the British flag in 1863 and was lost in Gaspar Straits in 1868.

ANNIE H. SMITH

THE ship *Annie H. Smith* was built for F. H. and William H. Smith, brothers, composing the firm of F. H. Smith & Co., New York, and was launched from the yard of Nickerson & Rideout, Calais, Maine, in December, 1876. She was named after the daughter of F. H. Smith who later became Mrs. Mel. Bartlett. Mr. Bartlett was the son of Capt. J. F. Bartlett and was subsequently a partner in

ARYAN

THE *Aryan*, the last wooden, full-rigged ship to be built in this country, was launched July 14, 1893, from the yard of C. V. Minott, Phippsburg, Maine, and measured 248:6 feet, by 42:3, by 26 feet, registering 1939 tons net. Her principal owners were Mr. Minott, Capt. Wylie R. Dickinson, who was her first commander, and the firm of J. W. Elwell & Co. of New York. Among other parties who had minor interests in the ship was Eugene P. Carver, recognized as one of the most prominent marine lawyers of his time and who maintained offices in New York and Boston. Mr. Carver, who was the only child of Capt. Nathan P. Carver, a leading old-time shipmaster of Searsport, had, from boyhood, a very strong sentimental interest in sailing ships and this continued unabated throughout his whole life. In 1901 he purchased all shares in the *Aryan* then owned by other parties, thus becoming sole owner of the ship. She was the only vessel Mr. Carver owned outright although he had interests in other ships. In 1917 the *Aryan* was purchased by L. A. Pedersen of San Francisco and he owned her during her subsequent short career. On taking her over Mr. Pedersen had her rerigged as a bark.

With her three skysails crossed the *Aryan* was a remarkably fine looking vessel, especially when, with her hull painted white, she was at anchor, fully laden and ready for sea. On making port at San Francisco, in October, 1901, Captain Pendleton sailed her up the harbor to an anchorage off the city front without the assistance of a tug and all who witnessed the scene were enthusiastic over the unusual and beautiful spectacle presented.

Aside from a voyage from New York to Yokohama, in 1897, and one from Norfolk to Honolulu, in 1899, the *Aryan* was employed in the Cape Horn trade with San Francisco or other North Pacific Coast ports until 1914, being for about the final ten years the only wooden, full-rigged American sailing ship in commission. Her being kept running was due to Mr. Carver's somewhat romantic ideas which it was said were not to his financial advantage. The outward passages of the ship during this period were invariably from New York or Baltimore,

the Smith firm. In 1883, Smith & Co. had the ship *William H. Smith* built at Bath, but their principal interests were in schooners and barkentines. Subsequently they operated steamers in the coastwise trade on the Atlantic but were not successful and in 1892 were forced to liquidate. The following year the *Annie H. Smith* was sold to Lewis Luckenbach who had her converted into a coal barge and as such she was operated until May 6, 1917, when she foundered off Fire Island. The three men aboard were saved.

The maiden passage of the *Annie H. Smith* was from New York to Melbourne, her charter being for £3350 sterling. She took out general cargo and some 360 passengers, mostly natives of the British Isles. The run out to Melbourne was made in the very good time of 74 days and after the last of her cargo had been discharged at Sydney, she took coal from Newcastle to San Francisco, in 62 days, and then wheat to Liverpool in 118 days. Later she crossed to New York and thus completed a very successful round-the-world voyage.

Thereafter the *Annie H. Smith* was operated in trade mainly with ports in the Far East, although at intervals she made passages from the Atlantic to Puget Sound or San Francisco and at times crossed the Pacific from the Orient to load California wheat for Europe. Her passages averaged well and in 1883, Capt. Rowland B. Brown had the good time of 97 days from Cardiff to Hong Kong. Her last eastward run around Cape Horn was 119 days from Port Blakely to New York with lumber.

On her first departure from San Francisco, leaving port January 21, 1878, the *Smith* ran into a fresh southeast gale just outside the Heads. This increased in violence with very high seas which smashed boats, skylights, pilot-house, etc., filled the cabins with water and in addition considerable damage was done aloft. While the upper foretopsail was being furled, a seaman was thrown from the yard but fell into the hauled-up foresail and clung there until rescued. The ship was kept standing off and on outside the bar until the gale blew out four days later and an opportunity was presented to transfer the pilot to an inward-bound ship. The ship *Alfred D. Snow* had a similar hard experience in getting to sea in the same gale, her pilot being on board

13 days before he could be transferred to an inbound vessel. Later, on this same passage, the *Smith* experienced a heavy pampero off the River Plate, having bulwarks stove, decks swept, sails lost, etc. It was necessary to run the ship before the wind for some time but in spite of all obstacles the passage from San Francisco Heads to Liverpool was accomplished in 118 days.

The *Annie H. Smith* had a trying experience in the great blizzard that swept the Atlantic Coast, in March, 1888, which is not forgotten to this day as many vessels suffered total wreck and others extensive damage. The *Smith* had been towed from New York and had just dropped anchor in the Chesapeake, preparatory to loading coal for San Francisco when the storm broke. She parted both anchor chains but miraculously was brought up with a manila hawser attached to a spare anchor to which she successfully rode until the gale blew out three days later.

On her last westward, Cape Horn passage, the *Annie H. Smith* left New York, April 30, 1892, and had the long run of 210 days to Seattle. She had a hard time off Cape Horn, being severely damaged in sails, spars and rigging and also having the rudder-head twisted off. The ship *San Joaquin* and bark *Adolph Obrig*, both also bound for the Pacific Coast, were caught in the same storm and all three vessels were forced to put into Port Stanley for repairs, causing a detention of over a month.

The first master of the *Annie H. Smith* was Capt. J. F. Bartlett who, some six years later, was transferred to the new ship *William H. Smith*. Capt. Rowland B. Brown succeeded to the command of the *Annie H.* in which he had purchased an interest. Captain Brown, a native of Castine, Maine, born in 1840, first went to sea in a Grand Banks fisherman when twelve years of age. Several years later he started sailing offshore and at the outbreak of the Civil War was second mate of the bark *Albion Lincoln*. Then, after studying navigation ashore for a time, he enlisted in the United States Navy being appointed an ensign. Later, he was Acting Master of the U.S.S. *Shamrock* when she became Commodore McComb's flagship in the North Atlantic Squadron. At the close of the War, in 1865, he was

transferred to the West India Squadron as Executive Officer U.S.S. *Florida* and two years later resigned from the Navy enter the merchant marine. Entering the employ of John W. D of Castine, he was master, successively, of the brigs *Bagaduc Silas M. Martin*, and the barkentine *J. W. Dresser*, making vo to the Mediterranean, the River Plate, Demerara, and to Java. *Martin* was a finely modeled vessel and Captain Brown made very fast passages in her to South America. Retiring from sea after being ten years in command of the *William H. Smith*, the tain spent his remaining years at his home in Castine and passed a there July 4, 1920.

Captain Brown was married in 1864 and from 1867 until was accompanied on practically all of his voyages by his wife family, their five children being taken to sea when very young. youngest of these, Walter C. Brown, started sea life at the age of months on the ship *Annie H. Smith* and was third mate of *William H. Smith* when she was sold. Young Brown then stay ashore, becoming a marine draftsman and consulting engineer un the United States entered the World War when he joined the Ame ican-Hawaiian Steamship Company as a third mate. In 1922 he w appointed master of that company's steamer *Nebraskan*, later havir others of their steamers. Since 1926 he has been in command of tl *Texan*.

The third and last master of the *Annie H. Smith*, while she wa being operated as a sailing ship, was Capt. Charles S. Kendall wh had been appointed to command the very fine Boston ship the *Sara toga*, when she was launched in 1874. Captain Kendall's last ship wa the *I. F. Chapman* after which, his health being poor, he is said t have made his home in one of the Southern States where he passec away years ago.

the Smith firm. In 1883, Smith & Co. had the ship *William H. Smith* built at Bath, but their principal interests were in schooners and barkentines. Subsequently they operated steamers in the coastwise trade on the Atlantic but were not successful and in 1892 were forced to liquidate. The following year the *Annie H. Smith* was sold to Lewis Luckenbach who had her converted into a coal barge and as such she was operated until May 6, 1917, when she foundered off Fire Island. The three men aboard were saved.

The maiden passage of the *Annie H. Smith* was from New York to Melbourne, her charter being for £3350 sterling. She took out general cargo and some 360 passengers, mostly natives of the British Isles. The run out to Melbourne was made in the very good time of 74 days and after the last of her cargo had been discharged at Sydney, she took coal from Newcastle to San Francisco, in 62 days, and then wheat to Liverpool in 118 days. Later she crossed to New York and thus completed a very successful round-the-world voyage.

Thereafter the *Annie H. Smith* was operated in trade mainly with ports in the Far East, although at intervals she made passages from the Atlantic to Puget Sound or San Francisco and at times crossed the Pacific from the Orient to load California wheat for Europe. Her passages averaged well and in 1883, Capt. Rowland B. Brown had the good time of 97 days from Cardiff to Hong Kong. Her last eastward run around Cape Horn was 119 days from Port Blakely to New York with lumber.

On her first departure from San Francisco, leaving port January 21, 1878, the *Smith* ran into a fresh southeast gale just outside the Heads. This increased in violence with very high seas which smashed boats, skylights, pilot-house, etc., filled the cabins with water and in addition considerable damage was done aloft. While the upper foretopsail was being furled, a seaman was thrown from the yard but fell into the hauled-up foresail and clung there until rescued. The ship was kept standing off and on outside the bar until the gale blew out four days later and an opportunity was presented to transfer the pilot to an inward-bound ship. The ship *Alfred D. Snow* had a similar hard experience in getting to sea in the same gale, her pilot being on board

13 days before he could be transferred to an inbound vessel. Later, on this same passage, the *Smith* experienced a heavy pampero off the River Plate, having bulwarks stove, decks swept, sails lost, etc. It was necessary to run the ship before the wind for some time but in spite of all obstacles the passage from San Francisco Heads to Liverpool was accomplished in 118 days.

The *Annie H. Smith* had a trying experience in the great blizzard that swept the Atlantic Coast, in March, 1888, which is not forgotten to this day as many vessels suffered total wreck and others extensive damage. The *Smith* had been towed from New York and had just dropped anchor in the Chesapeake, preparatory to loading coal for San Francisco when the storm broke. She parted both anchor chains but miraculously was brought up with a manila hawser attached to a spare anchor to which she successfully rode until the gale blew out three days later.

On her last westward, Cape Horn passage, the *Annie H. Smith* left New York, April 30, 1892, and had the long run of 210 days to Seattle. She had a hard time off Cape Horn, being severely damaged in sails, spars and rigging and also having the rudder-head twisted off. The ship *San Joaquin* and bark *Adolph Obrig*, both also bound for the Pacific Coast, were caught in the same storm and all three vessels were forced to put into Port Stanley for repairs, causing a detention of over a month.

The first master of the *Annie H. Smith* was Capt. J. F. Bartlett who, some six years later, was transferred to the new ship *William H. Smith*. Capt. Rowland B. Brown succeeded to the command of the *Annie H.* in which he had purchased an interest. Captain Brown, a native of Castine, Maine, born in 1840, first went to sea in a Grand Banks fisherman when twelve years of age. Several years later he started sailing offshore and at the outbreak of the Civil War was second mate of the bark *Albion Lincoln*. Then, after studying navigation ashore for a time, he enlisted in the United States Navy being appointed an ensign. Later, he was Acting Master of the U.S.S. *Shamrock* when she became Commodore McComb's flagship in the North Atlantic Squadron. At the close of the War, in 1865, he was transferred to the West India Squadron as Executive Officer of the U.S.S. *Florida* and two years later resigned from the Navy to re-enter the merchant marine. Entering the employ of John W. Dresser of Castine, he was master, successively, of the brigs *Bagaduce* and *Silas M. Martin,* and the barkentine *J. W. Dresser,* making voyages to the Mediterranean, the River Plate, Demerara, and to Java. The *Martin* was a finely modeled vessel and Captain Brown made many very fast passages in her to South America. Retiring from sea life, after being ten years in command of the *William H. Smith,* the captain spent his remaining years at his home in Castine and passed away there July 4, 1920.

Captain Brown was married in 1864 and from 1867 until 1900 was accompanied on practically all of his voyages by his wife and family, their five children being taken to sea when very young. The youngest of these, Walter C. Brown, started sea life at the age of six months on the ship *Annie H. Smith* and was third mate of the *William H. Smith* when she was sold. Young Brown then stayed ashore, becoming a marine draftsman and consulting engineer until the United States entered the World War when he joined the American-Hawaiian Steamship Company as a third mate. In 1922 he was appointed master of that company's steamer *Nebraskan,* later having others of their steamers. Since 1926 he has been in command of the *Texan.*

The third and last master of the *Annie H. Smith,* while she was being operated as a sailing ship, was Capt. Charles S. Kendall who had been appointed to command the very fine Boston ship the *Saratoga,* when she was launched in 1874. Captain Kendall's last ship was the *I. F. Chapman* after which, his health being poor, he is said to have made his home in one of the Southern States where he passed away years ago.

ARYAN

THE *Aryan*, the last wooden, full-rigged ship to be built in this country, was launched July 14, 1893, from the yard of C. V. Minott, Phippsburg, Maine, and measured 248:6 feet, by 42:3, by 26 feet, registering 1939 tons net. Her principal owners were Mr. Minott, Capt. Wylie R. Dickinson, who was her first commander, and the firm of J. W. Elwell & Co. of New York. Among other parties who had minor interests in the ship was Eugene P. Carver, recognized as one of the most prominent marine lawyers of his time and who maintained offices in New York and Boston. Mr. Carver, who was the only child of Capt. Nathan P. Carver, a leading old-time shipmaster of Searsport, had, from boyhood, a very strong sentimental interest in sailing ships and this continued unabated throughout his whole life. In 1901 he purchased all shares in the *Aryan* then owned by other parties, thus becoming sole owner of the ship. She was the only vessel Mr. Carver owned outright although he had interests in other ships. In 1917 the *Aryan* was purchased by L. A. Pedersen of San Francisco and he owned her during her subsequent short career. On taking her over Mr. Pedersen had her rerigged as a bark.

With her three skysails crossed the *Aryan* was a remarkably fine looking vessel, especially when, with her hull painted white, she was at anchor, fully laden and ready for sea. On making port at San Francisco, in October, 1901, Captain Pendleton sailed her up the harbor to an anchorage off the city front without the assistance of a tug and all who witnessed the scene were enthusiastic over the unusual and beautiful spectacle presented.

Aside from a voyage from New York to Yokohama, in 1897, and one from Norfolk to Honolulu, in 1899, the *Aryan* was employed in the Cape Horn trade with San Francisco or other North Pacific Coast ports until 1914, being for about the final ten years the only wooden, full-rigged American sailing ship in commission. Her being kept running was due to Mr. Carver's somewhat romantic ideas which it was said were not to his financial advantage. The outward passages of the ship during this period were invariably from New York or Baltimore, while those homeward originated at either San Francisco or Honolulu, with the exception of two instances when she took lumber and spars from Puget Sound to Boston. Considering the fact that she was a large carrier and loaded over 3000 tons of coal on passages to the westward around Cape Horn, her sailing record is good. In 1901, Captain Pendleton was 116 days from Baltimore to San Francisco, and in 1894, Captain Dickinson took her from San Francisco to New York in 106 days. In 1897 she made the run from Yokohama to Honolulu in 17½ days, averaging nine knots per hour throughout. In 1914 she took lumber from Vancouver to South Africa in 106 days, notwithstanding the fact that much heavy weather was met with off Cape Horn; the deck load shifted, preventing the pumps being worked and for a time it was feared that the ship would not pull through.

From 1914 until her loss, the *Aryan* remained in the Pacific. In July, 1918, she took general cargo from San Francisco to Wellington, N. Z., and on December 15th left that port laden with flax, tallow, etc., bound for San Francisco. The following account of her loss by fire was given by her chief officer Patrick Ryan who is now a master mariner on the Great Lakes.

"When eight days out and approximately 800 miles from Wellington, fire in the cargo was discovered at one o'clock in the morning, it being apparently in the between decks at the break of the poop. We bored holes in the deck, pumped water below and tried to break out cargo but all efforts to extinguish or control the fire were futile. The boats were put over the side and we stayed on the ship until the decks became too hot to remain longer. At 11 A.M., the day before Christmas, all hands abandoned the ship, Captain Larsen taking the number one boat with nine men; I taking the number two with five men; and the second officer the number three boat with eight men. The latter, being a larger and better boat, relieved me of one man. The smoke and flames had prevented access to the store room so we had been unable to properly provision any of the boats. Each, however, had a supply of ship biscuits but ours were soaked to a pulp and were useless as food besides being likely to cause a craving for water.

"The ship was abandoned in latitude 45° S., one of the most stormy regions in the Southern Hemisphere, a district known as the 'Roaring Forties.' At the time there was a heavy sea running although the wind was no more than fresh. We were 500 miles to leeward of the nearest land. Ten minutes after we left the *Aryan* her mizzenmast went over the side and flames shot up from various places although the fire seemed to be principally aft. We set our course for the Chatham Islands, some 800 miles to the eastward of New Zealand. Capt. Larsen's boat outsailed that of Mr. Graham and his in turn was getting ahead of my boat. These conditions soon changed, however, when I was able to set an improvised sail and at dusk Mr. Graham's boat was five miles astern of the other two. This was the last ever seen or heard of that boat and her complement of ten men.

"That night there materialized a heavy gale and by midnight the wind and a cross sea had so increased as to cause us to worry over the safety of our boat. We sailed beyond the bounds of prudence as we had a long distance to sail before any land could be made. At 3 o'clock Christmas morning we shipped a sea that filled the boat awash. We headed into the seas and bailing was all that saved us. For nine hours all hands were occupied in handling the boat, one steering, two handling the sheet and two bailing. The precautionary measure would have been to heave to but success justified our decision to take chances.

"We sighted number one boat that morning and again on the morning preceding our night landing. The day before we landed heavy weather was encountered and around 10 o'clock in the forenoon squalls developed. Between squalls we sighted the other boat far ahead and later we were close together but then separated and at dusk lost sight of one another. Early in the afternoon we had sighted land and as we neared it, a high surf signified disaster. About 10 o'clock that night we sighted a light in the hands of natives who had seen us earlier in the evening. They directing our passage between rocks and surf, we reached land, the natives wading out waist deep assisting us to make shore. We were unable to use our legs from the constant exposure to boarding seas.

"Our first act was to have a fire started on the highest hill to guide our missing shipmates. That night the wind came out of the west and we would have been unable to make headway in the face of accompanying high seas. There was but one white man on the island. By means of a wireless station on a neighboring island we communicated with New Zealand and in 14 days a Government lighthouse tender appeared and conveyed us to Wellington. Our stay on the island had been made comfortable by the hospitable natives. As for the New Zealand people, they are the kindest I have ever met with. Among the *Aryan's* survivors were the cook and his wife."

The occupants of Captain Larsen's boat were also able to make land but Mr. Ryan's account does not mention any details.

Capt. Wylie R. Dickinson commanded the *Aryan* for the first three voyages she made, then staying ashore a year but again resuming command for another voyage or two. The captain's career as a shipmaster is given in account of the ship *Rappahannock*, "American Merchant Ships," Series I. Capt. Albert T. Whittier succeeded Captain Dickinson in the *Aryan* and was also in her on two different occasions, making in all four round voyages. He left her for good in 1911, and then retired from sea life. The captain was a native of Searsport and had previously been master of the bark *Evie J. Reed*, running to New Zealand, and also of the ship *Paul Revere* which was engaged in the East India trade. He died at Norfolk, in 1918, at the age of sixty-eight years. An elder brother, Capt. Frank P. Whittier, is still living.

Capt. Andrew S. Pendleton of Searsport took command of the *Aryan* when his uncle, Eugene P. Carver, became her sole owner, and completed three round voyages in the ship, then retiring from the sea. His last prior command had been the ship *Emily F. Whitney* and before taking that ship he had been master of a number of barks including the *Thomas Fletcher*, *Trovatore* and *Emma T. Crowell*, being in the latter several years. Later masters of the *Aryan* included Capt. H. O. Sorenson, who made two voyages, and Capt. James Mc-Lachlan, who made four voyages.

BARING BROTHERS

THE ship *Baring Brothers* was launched from the yard of Edward O'Brien at Thomaston, Maine, on June 14, 1877, and in her construction master builder Hermon Bonner had done his best work up to that time. She was named in honor of the prominent London firm of bankers, merchants, and shipowners with whom Mr. O'Brien had large business dealings for many years. She was 243:7 feet, by 42:2, by 29:5 feet, and registered 2090 tons. A typical O'Brien ship, she was built to carry large bulk cargoes and while in the Pacific Coast coal trade loaded 3500 tons on a draft of 27 feet. On one occasion she struck the bar on entering San Francisco harbor and had to be towed on the Mission Bay mud flats after arrival.

The first two voyages of the *Baring Brothers* were from Norfolk to Liverpool, with cotton, the last passage being made in 15 days which was several hours shorter than the run of the fine ship *Florence* made at the same time. On making port on this occasion and while in tow of two tugs, the *Baring Brothers* was struck by the Spanish steamer *Ponce*, the vessels being then off the Crossley Light Ship. The steamer foundered while the ship had her bows stove in and made water so rapidly that she was beached to prevent her sinking. Extra pumps were installed, she was docked and discharged and after being repaired, loaded coal for San Francisco. Thereafter she continued in trade with that port, making thereto seven passages from Liverpool, two from New York, and one from Philadelphia. In 1890-1891 she took case oil to Japan, thence crossing to Tacoma to load wheat for Havre. While on the Pacific Coast she was, on two occasions, employed in carrying coal from Puget Sound to San Francisco and once was laid up at the latter port for about a year.

The average of the passages made by the *Baring Brothers* to San Francisco is 141 days, 121 days being the shortest and 184 days the longest, on which latter occasion she had nothing but light weather in the Atlantic and was 48 days rounding Cape Horn. The average of her eight passages from San Francisco to Liverpool is 127 days, 117 days being the shortest and 138 days the longest.

In September, 1892, the *Baring Brothers*, under command of Capt. Timothy Murphy, who had previously been in the ship *John Bryce*, left Philadelphia for San Francisco, but was aground for a short time near Wilmington, Del. She was floated without having sustained damage and left the Breakwater on October 1st. Some three weeks later she put into Barbados leaking. A portion of her cargo was discharged into a schooner for forwarding to New York while the ship had temporary repairs made and then proceeded to that port for a thorough overhauling. Some three months later the voyage was resumed with Capt. J. F. Eldridge in command of the ship and he took her out to San Francisco, making port Sept. 23, 1893, 358 days from Philadelphia, and 141 days from New York. Captain Murphy resumed command and then had the long passage of 185 days to Liverpool with a cargo of choice, selected redwood lumber. The ship had a hard experience in the North Atlantic, meeting with gales of hurricane force in latitude 47° when the decks were filled with water for 13 consecutive days, but she got through with but nominal damage. She had been 50 days in the South Pacific and 57 days from the Line in the Atlantic to destination.

The last round voyage completed by the *Baring Brothers* was from New York to San Francisco, Mollendo, Puget Sound, and Plymouth, Eng., with Capt. Thos. G. Libby, formerly in the *General Knox*, as commander. The ship then crossed to New York and in December, 1897, sailed with case oil for Yokohama. The crew was unruly and semi-mutinous almost from the start and on arrival of the ship at Japan, in June, 1898, a number of seamen were put under arrest. The ship discharged at Yokohama and then proceeded to Kobe where, by August 12th, she had taken on a large part of her cargo of silk, matting, etc., for New York. On that date those members of her crew who had been ashore under arrest were carried aboard as they refused to walk and they then also refused to do duty. That night the ship was found to be on fire and was scuttled. Later she was floated but was so badly damaged that she was condemned and sold. About half of the cargo aboard was burned or ruined by scorching or salt water. There was no questioning the fact that the ship had been delib-

erately set on fire by some of her disaffected crew, several of whom
had declared that they would resort to anything rather than make the
passage to New York in the vessel. An official inquiry, however, failed
to attach responsibility to anyone.

The *Baring Brothers* was built to be commanded by Capt. Eben A.
Thorndike of Rockland, Me., whose ancestors had settled there in
1650, the family becoming one of the best known and most highly
respected in that vicinity. Captain Eben was born in 1826 and started
seafaring at an early age. One of his first commands was the ship
Empire, built at East Thomaston, in 1851. He later was master of
many other Thomaston ships and always ranked as a high-grade man.
He retired from the sea after making two voyages in the *Baring
Brothers*. The second commander of the ship was Capt. H. O. Giles,
of St. George, Me., who had previously been master of the bark
Sarah Newman. He had the *Baring Brothers* four years when Capt.
Chas. A. Pascal of Rockport made one voyage and then Capt. Geo.
W. K. Masters, formerly in the ship *Alex. McCallum*, was master
three years. Thereafter the *Baring Brothers* had several different
commanders for short periods, these including Capt. Thos. G. Libby,
who is mentioned in account of the ship *Gen. Knox*, and Capt. Timothy G. Murphy. The latter gave up sea life in 1895 and subsequently engaged in the milk business in Thomaston, where he died
about five years ago.

BELLE O'BRIEN

THE ship *Belle O'Brien* was built at Thomaston, Maine, by Edward O'Brien and was named after his niece. She was 237:5
feet, by 42, by 26:2 feet and registered 1903 tons. She was similar in
model and general appearance to the other large O'Brien ships, a
good carrier, well adapted to loading heavy bulk cargoes.

Early in her career the *Belle* was operated in the cotton and deal
trades across the Atlantic but later made many voyages with coal to
ports on the east and west coasts of South America, returning to the
Atlantic with guano. She made one or two voyages with case oil to

the Far East and four Cape Horn passages to San Francisco, these latter being at intervals between 1884 and 1895. On the first she had the long run of 175 days from Baltimore, accomplished in the face of great difficulties. She was 45 days from port to the line and when 76 days out, encountered a pampero in latitude 45° S., during which the sling of the foreyard parted and the spar came down on deck. All the other yards on the foremast were carried away and the main and lower maintopsail yards were sprung. The decks of the ship were continually filled with water so it was ten days before Captain Pascal was able to get his yards aloft again. When 40 days from the Line, the ship crossed 50° S., but was driven back and recrossed that parallel seven days later. A week thereafter Cape Horn was sighted but the ship was again driven back and it took 16 days for her to regain that position. During all this time very cold weather was experienced, the decks were filled with snow and ice and all hands suffered severely from frost bite. Finally, however, these stormy latitudes were cleared and then followed a slow but pleasant passage of 60 days up the Pacific to San Francisco. After arrival the ship was laid up for nearly two years, then taking grain to Havre. On entering that port she was damaged by collision with the British ship *Royal George* and started to leak so badly that she was not allowed to enter the dock.

On June 19, 1895, the *Belle O'Brien* sailed from San Francisco with 2685 tons of wheat, bound to Queenstown for orders, and on November 18th was about sixty miles from destination when very heavy weather was encountered and Captain Colley stood to the westward for sea room. The ship soon became disabled in the heavy seas, the covering boards were washed away and almost at once there was nine feet of water in the hold, with the vessel settling rapidly. The crew took to the boats at 10 P.M. and the ship is supposed to have foundered soon after. One boat was able to make the coast and one was picked up by a tug sent to the rescue, but the second mate of the ship and four men were lost.

The first, or one of the earliest masters of the *Belle O'Brien*, was Capt. Sanders Curling, a native of Liverpool, who came to this country at an early age and settled at Thomaston. He soon took up seafaring and became prominent as a shipmaster and ship owner. He was given command of many ships as they were launched by Edward O'Brien and generally took them to New Orleans or some other Southern port to load cotton for Liverpool and at times sold them after arrival. Among the ships Captain Curling commanded were the *S. Curling, Eagle, Andrew Johnson, Mary A. Campbell, Wm. A. Campbell* and *Belle O'Brien.* In the latter ship he is said to have made the passage from Norfolk to Liverpool, with cotton, in 13½ days, the record for sailing ships. The captain died at Thomaston, about 1895, aged seventy-eight years. A son, Capt. Frank F. Curling, was an unsuccessful shipmaster and did not sustain the reputation his father had for first-class ability and high and noble character.

Among other masters of the *Belle O'Brien* were Capt. William T. O'Brien, a nephew of her builder; Capt. Chas. A. Pascal, and Capt. David J. Hodgman, who is referred to in account of the ship *Alex. Gibson.* Capt. Edward S. Colley was in command of the *Belle* when she met her fate and had been her master for several years. He is more particularly referred to in the account of the ship *Isaac Reed.*

BELLE OF BATH

THE ship *Belle of Bath* was built by Goss & Sawyer, at Bath, Maine, and was launched May 26, 1877. She is described as being a handsome vessel in all respects and was admired at every port she visited. She was 204 feet, by 39, by 24 feet and registered 1418 tons. She was built for Parker M. Whitmore and others, who, in August, 1883, sold her to Capt. Jonathan C. Nickels of Searsport, for $47,500. She was built to be commanded by Capt. William Whitmore of Bath, but was soon taken over by Capt. William H. Starkey. Later Capt. Chas. J. Carter made one voyage and following her sale her commanders were all Searsport shipmasters, Captains David Nickels, Wm. Green Nichols, Henry G. Curtis and Clifton Curtis.

The *Belle of Bath* was but little in evidence in the Cape Horn trade, making but one such passage to San Francisco and three to the

Columbia River. On several occasions she crossed the Pacific from the Orient, to load on the Coast for Atlantic ports, but her principal employment was in trade with the Far East. Her passages averaged well and Capt. Clifton Curtis had so much faith in her sailing ability that when about to leave the Columbia River, in November, 1893, for Queenstown, he wagered $500 that his ship would arrive out ahead of two fine British iron ships that were sailing at the same time, the *Irby* and the *Poseidon*. Unfortunately for Captain Curtis, however, the *Belle* was third in the race, being beaten two and three days, respectively, by her rivals.

On June 2, 1897, the *Belle* left New York with a cargo of case oil for Hong Kong. When about two weeks at sea she was discovered to be on fire and as it could not be controlled, the ship was abandoned and blew up not long after the crew had left her. The crew was able to make Barbados in the ship's boats. Prior to this, the ship had been very fortunate in escaping mishaps. In 1880 she grounded in the Columbia River and remained fast for some time, but a portion of her cargo of railroad iron was lightered and she was floated without having sustained material damage. In 1891, while bound to Havre from Tacoma, she picked up the crew of the ship *Charles Dennis*, abandoned in a sinking condition off Cape Horn, and landed them at Rio de Janeiro.

Capt. William H. Starkey, who made two voyages in the *Belle of Bath*, was born in Woolwich, Me., in 1834, and died in Bath in May, 1913. His first voyage was made in the ship *Geneva*, Capt. John R. Kelley, in 1849, and eight years later he was given his first command, the ship *Rhine*. Later on he was master of the bark *C. O. Whitmore* and the ships *Jennie Eastman, B. P. Cheney, Thomas M. Reed, Iroquois* and *Shenandoah*. He made but one passage in the last named ship, from New York to San Francisco, in 1898, and then retired. The captain was proud of his record of never having lost a man nor a ship during his forty years as master.

Capt. David Nickels was the oldest of six sons of Capt. David Nickels, Sr., of Searsport. All of these took up seafaring and five became prominent as masters of deep water sailing ships, David, Jr.,

Albert V., John Fred, E. D. P., and Jonathan C. Nickels. These are mentioned in "American Merchant Ships," Series I. The sixth son was Capt. Amos Nickels who, at the age of twenty-one years, died at Havana, of yellow fever, while in command of the bark *David Nickels*. Aside from the *Belle of Bath*, in which Capt. David Nickels served some four years, he was master of the bark *Lucy A. Nickels*, and also of the ship of the same name, the bark *Clara* and the ship *E. Sherman*. He retired from sea life on relinquishing command of the *Belle of Bath*, in 1886, and died in Searsport two years later.

Capt. William Green Nichols was in command of the *Belle of Bath* the three years between 1886 and 1888; he then going back to his former ship, the *Frank Pendleton*. Details of his seafaring life will be found in account of that ship. Capt. Henry G. Curtis succeeded Captain Nichols in the *Belle*, taking her from New York to San Francisco, where, on account of ill health, he turned her over to his brother, Capt. Clifton Curtis, and the latter continued in the ship until she was burned. He subsequently located on the Pacific Coast and commanded steamers belonging to the Pacific Mail Steamship Co., and the Union Oil Co. Later he was sent East to take out to the Pacific Coast the steamship *President Arthur*, which was later renamed *City of Honolulu* and operated between Los Angeles, Cal., and the Hawaiian Islands. Captain Curtis went on that run, his last command being the steamship *Diamond Head*. After three years he was forced to retire on account of ill health and not long thereafter passed away at Los Angeles.

BELVEDERE

THE ship *Belvedere* was built by Paul Curtis, at East Boston, and was launched in January, 1857. She was 192 feet, by 36:7, by 24 feet and registered 1320 tons. She was a fine looking vessel with an elliptical stern and an eagle did duty as a figurehead. While her model was called medium clipper her passages did not average as fast as many later-day cargo carriers. Until April, 1875, she was owned by William F. Weld & Co. of Boston. That firm was then disposing of their sailing fleet and while the *Belvedere* was on a passage from Calcutta to Boston, they sold her to Vernon H. Brown & Co. and Capt. N. Kirby for $40,000. In January, 1877, she arrived at San Francisco from Valparaiso and was purchased by Goodall, Nelson & Perkins, of the Pacific Coast Steamship Co. For twenty years the *Belvedere* was one of the best known ships sailing out of Boston. During the first ten years of her career she made eight passages from that port, or New York, to San Francisco, generally returning home by way of the East Indies. Thereafter, until sold to San Francisco parties, she made a couple of transatlantic voyages, a further one to San Francisco, and the remainder to ports in the Far East. She was employed in the coastwise coal trade by her San Francisco owners until she was lost.

On Nov. 29, 1886, the *Belvedere*, while bound from San Pedro, Cal., to British Columbia, in ballast, went ashore in a dense fog and a very heavy swell, on Bonilla Point, opposite Cape Flattery. She was pulled off by a tug and proceeded towards Port Townsend but soon filled with water and sank in thirty fathoms.

The first commander of the *Belvedere* was Capt. Isaac N. Jackson, a native of Winthrop, Me., whose first command was the new bark *Marmion*, built by Chapman & Flint, at Thomaston, in 1847. In 1855 he was master of the celebrated clipper ship *Spitfire*, leaving her to take the *Belvedere*, and was in command of that ship ten years. There is a story to the effect that the *Belvedere* was chased by the Confederate privateer, *Alabama*, in the Java Sea, while she was homeward bound from Manila in December, 1863. It was said that she sailed away from her pursuer, but that Captain Semmes, being for some reason particularly anxious to effect her capture, then lay for some time in wait at the outlet of the Straits of Sunda for her appearance. Captain Jackson, however, taking advantage of a dark night, slipped out to sea and got safely away. The log of the *Alabama* does not mention this or any other instance wherein Captain Semmes was unsuccessful in overtaking a vessel he was pursuing.

After leaving the *Belvedere*, Captain Jackson took the ship *Anahuac*, another of the Weld fleet, from Boston to San Francisco, on her maiden passage, then going East to assume command of the famous ship *Great Admiral* which had just been built for Weld & Co. In that ship he made three round-the-world voyages, some sections of which were covered in remarkably short time. In 1874, Captain Jackson purchased an interest in the new ship *Spartan* and in her he completed three voyages between New York, San Francisco and Liverpool, all in fast time. In March, 1878, the *Spartan* was driven ashore on Long Island and was sold. The Captain then retired from sea life to make his home in Milford, Mass., and died there in 1898.

Captain Jackson stood in the front rank of masters in the old-time American mercantile marine. He possessed great courage and resource and was a strict disciplinarian, of quick action, although of a kindly disposition. A dignified and polished gentleman he was known as the "Dandy Captain," from the great care he took of his personal appearance.

Prior to buying into and taking command of the *Belvedere*, Capt. N. Kirby is said to have been master of the ship *Ne Plus Ultra*. When the *Belvedere* was sold to San Francisco parties, the Captain bought a controlling interest in the ship *Jeremiah Thompson* and ran her some four years, on long distance voyages, when she, also, was sold in San Francisco to be operated in the Pacific. Captain Kirby then made a voyage in the ship *Continental* after which he gave up seafaring on account of ill health. In September, 1886, after living at his home on Cape Cod about a year, he passed away.

Capt. James S. Gibson was in command of the *Belvedere* when she was lost, having been appointed her master a year previously. Early in life the Captain had sailed on the Atlantic, in 1873 being third mate of the ship *City of Brooklyn*. He subsequently located on the Pacific Coast and following the loss of the *Belvedere* commanded the ship *America* some three years. In 1894 he went East to become chief officer of a steamer running between New York and New Orleans, later returning to the Pacific Coast on the whale-back *City of Everett*, in a similar capacity. After retiring from the sea he located in Seattle and became prominent in shipping matters there. He is said to have gone to Manila a number of years ago and to have died there.

BERLIN

THE ship *Berlin* was launched from the yard of C. V. Minott at Phippsburg, Maine, in October, 1882, and was 222 feet, by 40, by 24:6 feet and 1553 tons register. She was strongly built, and well sparred, having nothing above royals, but with double topgallant yards on fore and mainmasts. She was built to be commanded by Capt. F. D. Whitmore who continued as her master some nine years and who had previously been in the ship *Alice M. Minott* seven years.

The *Berlin* was owned by her builder and friends until she was sold to George E. Plummer of San Francisco, in June, 1890, following her arrival at that port from the Orient via Puget Sound. Thereafter, for about seven years, she was operated on the Pacific Coast, principally in the coal trade, also making seasonal voyages as a "salmon packer" under charter. During the last fifteen years of her career she was owned by the Alaska Portland Packers Association and hailed from Portland, Ore. On Feb. 17, 1922, when making port at Chignik Bay, Alaska, she stranded on the Ugaguk Flats and became a total loss. She had a cargo of cannery supplies and a large number of workmen, but all the people on board, 225 in number, were saved.

During her first ten years the *Berlin* took general cargo or coal from domestic Atlantic ports to San Francisco and grain thence to Liverpool or the Continent. Thereafter, for seven years, she was in the case oil trade with the Orient. Her passages were made in fair time, the shortest to San Francisco being 117 days from Philadelphia and the shortest to the eastward, 107 days to Liverpool. On Jan. 16, 1887, she sailed from Philadelphia with general cargo for San Francisco and all went well until she reached Cape Horn. There she lost a number of spars and sails and the cargo shifted so badly that Captain Whitmore bore up for Port Stanley. There a large portion of the cargo was discharged for restowing and after repairs were made, the voyage was resumed. The crew had refused to proceed in the ship and the captain had to go to Valparaiso for new men, the whole affair causing a detention to the ship some two months. Soon after leaving port the ship was knocked down in a terrific squall and some sails had to be cut away before she righted. Heavy weather continued until the ship was well into the South Pacific and the passage from Port Stanley to San Francisco took 101 days. On the passage of the ship from Philadelphia, in 1889, the lookout one evening reported a light ahead and the order was immediately given to luff. A large British iron ship, whose identity was not learned, then passed so close under the stern of the *Berlin* that a person could have jumped from one ship to the other. The crew of the Britisher gave a yell, thinking they were going to strike the *Berlin* aft, and Captain Whitmore said that he had never had so close a call in being dashed into eternity.

In January, 1897, Capt. Chas. H. Reed left New York in the *Berlin* with some 57,000 cases of oil for Amoy and Swatow. When three days out the ship encountered a hurricane which was followed by very stormy weather for a long period. Captain Reed doubted the correctness of his chronometer and, sailing by dead reckoning, wished to sight St. Paul's Rocks to check his instruments. This he did, but getting in too close, the ship touched bottom, being set in by currents in a dead calm. A portion of the cargo was jettisoned, when a breeze springing up, the ship cleared herself from the reef, uninjured.

BIG BONANZA

THE ship *Big Bonanza* was launched at Newburyport, in July, 1875, from the yard of J. Currier, Jr., and he and friends were owners until September, 1891, when she was sold to James Madison and others of San Francisco. Subsequently she appears to have been the property of the Golden Gate Shipping Co., who, in 1909, resold her and she was towed to Seattle and converted into a barge. For a number of years she was towed between Puget Sound and Alaska and later to and from San Francisco from northern ports, being then owned by the Charles Nelson Co. In 1920 she completed her last trip, a tow from San Francisco to the Hawaiian Islands and return and was then laid up having outlived her usefulness. She finally disintegrated from old age after a service of forty-five years.

The *Big Bonanza* was a fine ship, 210 feet, by 40, by 24 feet and registered 1399 tons. Early in her career she made four passages from Atlantic ports to San Francisco but the remainder of her operations, while under her original ownership, were between New York or Liverpool and the Far East, mainly to Calcutta. She was a good carrier and her voyages were made in fair, average time.

After being purchased by Pacific Coast interests, while she was at New York in September, 1891, she took a cargo of coal from Baltimore to San Francisco and then, until October, 1893, was operated in the coastwise trade, after which she loaded lumber at Puget Sound for Cardiff. Then followed a round voyage to St. John, N. B., after which she took coal from Cardiff to Cape Town, then going to New York. On March 23, 1895, she left Baltimore for San Francisco, but on May 7th put into Hampton Roads in distress. Captain Bergman's experiences in connection with this occurrence are graphically described in a letter he wrote friends, as follows:

"We struck a hurricane in latitude 37°, longitude 60°, which robbed us of our principal spars and broke our new iron foremast below the deck. We pumped by steam with both pumps from 8 P.M. March 28th till 11 A.M. of the 29th before the first sign showed that we were gaining on the water in the hold. The hurricane occurred four days after the tug let us go off Cape Henry but we had to make a long detour in order to meet favorable winds to get back there. The gale lasted a little over two days while the cyclonic disturbance of the centre, which dismasted us, only lasted three or four hours and, added to the unpleasantness of the whole affair, it was often so dark that I could not recognize a person standing alongside of me except by the voice. Looking up at the masts that were left, though not able to make out the spars on account of darkness, we could see the St. Elmo fires on the extremities. When our bowsprit and foremast were carried away I was standing on top of the after house, alongside the forward skylight, and though the terrible crash was heard and it was evident that something uncommon had happened, just what it was could not be seen until a big flash of lightning revealed a sickening spectacle.

There was the iron mast lying across the lee rail, the rigging still holding it, having smashed both lifeboats on top of the forward house as it fell across them. The water was pouring into the hole left by the mast, for it broke underneath the deck, and heavy seas were sweeping over the whole ship without interruption. The broken end of the foremast, working up and down just above the hole it had left, made it dangerous for anyone to attempt to work underneath it; therefore before we could think of closing up the hole we had to get rid of the mast which was no easy matter. But when the gale moderated the ship leaked but very little. We pumped only 20 minutes in the 24 hours. We lost bowsprit and jibboom; the entire foremast from truck to keelson; the maintopgallant and the mizzen topgallant masts and the monkey gaff, with all the yards and sails attached thereto."

The cargo of coal was later discharged and the ship went to East Boston where she received an extensive overhauling at the Atlantic Works and, on being rerigged, was fitted out as a bark. She then took case oil to Japan, thence going to San Francisco by way of British Columbia. Thereafter her voyages were mainly from Puget Sound to Australia, with occasional seasonal trips to Alaska. The last of her offshore voyages was a round between San Francisco and Australia, in 1907-1908.

The first commander of the *Big Bonanza* was Capt. Jas. H. Stanley, a native of Newburyport, born in 1833. At the age of twenty-three years he started sea life as carpenter on the new ship *Crown Point*. While on a voyage from New York to San Francisco, in 1863, this ship was captured by the Confederate privateer *Florida* and was burned. Stanley then engaged as carpenter on the Newburyport ship *Volant* and continued in her until joining the ship *Winona*, as third officer, although he had never been before the mast. Rising through the grades of second and first mate to become her master he was such until the *Big Bonanza* was built. Except for two voyages when he stayed at home, he was in the last named ship until Nov. 29, 1884, when, on a passage from Calcutta to New York, he was washed overboard and drowned.

Capt. Oliver C. Jones relieved Captain Stanley in the *Big Bonanza*, at Liverpool, towards the close of 1881. The ship loaded railroad iron at Hull for San Francisco; then took wheat to Liverpool and from there, salt to Calcutta and Indian produce thence to New York. Captain Jones then bought a half interest in the ship *Samar* in which he made several East Indian voyages, after which he retired from sea life to pass the remainder of his days at his home in Newburyport where he was a prominent citizen and highly respected. For a number of years he was treasurer of the Marine Society of that place. The captain's first voyage was as boy on the brig *James Caskie*, of which his father was master, the vessel leaving Boston in November, 1849, for San Francisco. She had a cargo of house frames, lumber, coal and bricks and lay at anchor in the harbor, peddling these out several months, in a dull market. One night when there was aboard only the captain, his wife and son and a young man, robbers invaded the cabin from a boat and after nearly killing the captain, barricaded its inmates and escaped with a box of silver containing about $900. Captain Jones recovered from his wounds and before the brig left port for the Chincha Islands had the satisfaction of seeing four of the robbers convicted of the crime and hanged. Young Jones continued a seafaring life, sailing in various vessels as boy, seaman and officer, until in 1877 he was given command of the ship *Ellen Munroe* and made a voyage to San Francisco and Liverpool. He then made two round voyages in the ship *Sarah Hignett*, following which he took the *Big Bonanza*.

The mate of the *Big Bonanza*, Collin I. Andrews, completed the voyage on which Captain Stanley was lost and was then given command of the ship. Her first commander, after her purchase by San Francisco parties, was Capt. Adolph Bergman, a native of Prussia, who first went to sea at the age of seventeen years and arrived on the Pacific Coast in 1872. He sailed in the brig *Curlew* and later in the barkentine *C. L. Taylor*, of which he was second mate. He was master of the bark *Lizzie Marshall* when she went on the rocks of Vancouver Island in a blinding snow storm, in 1884, and became a total loss. Then for several years he ran a hotel in San Francisco until in

1891 he went East to take the *Big Bonanza*. After five years in command of that ship he retired from the sea to engage in the sail making business in San Francisco and so continued until his death in 1917 at the age of sixty-six years.

BOHEMIA

THE ship *Bohemia* was built by Houghton Brothers, at Bath, Maine, and was launched in September, 1875. She measured 221:7 feet, by 40, by 25:5 feet and registered 1663 tons. In 1897 she was sold by Houghton Brothers to the Alaska Packers Association of San Francisco, who operated her in connection with their salmon canneries in Alaska, until 1925, when she was sold to ship breakers. She did not meet that fate, however, soon being purchased by the C. B. de Mille interests for moving picture purposes. She was renamed *Yankee Clipper* and appeared in a picture produced under that name.

Prior to her sale in 1897, the *Bohemia* made twelve passages from Atlantic ports to San Francisco; one from Antwerp to Yokohama, Kobe and San Francisco; one from Cardiff to Rio de Janeiro, British Columbia and San Francisco; and one from New York to Rio, Newcastle, Australia, Manila and Philadelphia. Her sailing record is very good for a cargo carrier. The average of her twelve passages to San Francisco is 132 days, one of 118 days from Liverpool being the shortest. In 1895, on her passage from Philadelphia, she was forced to put into Rio de Janeiro and was 77 days thence to San Francisco, her actual sailing time of the whole run being equivalent to 120 days. The average of eleven of her passages from San Francisco to Atlantic ports, all but one being to Europe with grain, is 119 days, the fastest being 108, 109, 110 and 110 days. On her 77-day run from Rio she was only 31 days from 56° S., 59° W. to 8° N. 116° W. and on two occasions she was only nineteen days from latitude 50° S. in the Pacific to the equator. Her passage from Antwerp to Yokohama in 1880 was accomplished in 117 days and her voyage from New York to Rio, Australia, Manila and Philadelphia was performed in record fast time. The figures of 30 days, 29 days and 35 days for the first three sections are not fully confirmed but are closely approximate. From Manila to the Delaware Breakwater her time was 88 days which is but four days longer than the record passage from the Philippines to any American Atlantic port made by the extreme clipper ship *Wizard* in 1861, to New York. Captain Hogan was in command of the *Bohemia* on the voyage referred to (1894-1895), and the ship arrived at Philadelphia several days ahead of her papers which had been forwarded by steamer. Captain Hogan was also in command on the last voyage the ship made prior to her sale in San Francisco, a round between that port and Sydney, she going down in the fast time of 48 days and returning in 64 days.

The *Bohemia* met with several mishaps during the course of her voyages. When crossing in ballast from Japan to San Francisco, in 1880, she encountered a typhoon the day after leaving port, the full strength of which lasted five hours. The maintopmast head and all three topgallant masts were carried away besides which almost a complete set of sails were lost, including those furled on the yards. Strong gales and high seas continued for 14 days but Captain Trask pulled his ship through and was given much credit for not having put into Yokohama for repairs. In January, 1891, the *Bohemia* left Liverpool for San Francisco and when two days out took a heavy gale during which the cargo shifted, bulwarks were carried away and a number of sails were lost. The next day the ship put into Waterford; the crew refused to proceed in her and a new crew had to be signed on. The occasion for the ship putting into Rio de Janeiro, in 1895, was her being struck by a hurricane when in latitude 33° S., and having the foretopmast and jibboom carried away.

The *Bohemia* was built to be commanded by Capt. John P. Delano, but he made only one voyage in her, then returning to his prior ship *Austria* which had also been built for him by Houghton Brothers. Captain Delano died in December, 1893, at the age of 67 years. He ranked very high as to ability as a shipmaster as well as in all personal respects. Capt. G. G. Trask, the second master of the *Bohemia*, was in her from 1877 until 1890, making in all nine round voyages. In later life he was prominent in San Francisco shipping affairs.

The third and last master of the *Bohemia*, under the Houghton ownership, was Capt. William J. Hogan who, as a boy of fourteen, left his home in Bath to become cook on a coasting schooner. Later, on going deep water, he passed through the various grades of seaman and officer until in 1886 he was appointed master of the ship *Columbia*. Four years later he took the *Bohemia* and continued in her until she was sold. He then was for a short time in the *Wachusett*, leaving her to buy into the old South Sea Islands trading bark *Helen W. Almy*, then being fitted out at San Francisco to take gold seekers to Alaska. Leaving port in her under orders from her principal owners but contrary to his best judgment, as heavy weather was prophesied, he and all on board the vessel met their fate the night they sailed. The bark was found bottom up the following day and no bodies were ever recovered. Captain Hogan was only forty-one years of age at the time but was considered one of the best shipmasters ever coming from the state of Maine.

BONANZA

THE ship *Bonanza* was launched from the yard of William Rogers at Bath, Maine, May 6, 1875, and was immediately purchased by Pope & Talbot, lumber merchants of San Francisco, who had large mills on Puget Sound and exported in cargo lots. They paid $90,000 for the *Bonanza* ready for sea but not then coppered. She was a fine three-royal-yard ship with wire rigging and measured 207:8 feet, by 39, by 24 feet and registered 1356 tons. In 1887 she was rerigged into a bark.

With the exception of a passage from Liverpool to Manila, in 1877-1878, the *Bonanza* was employed in trade between Atlantic ports and San Francisco, prior to November, 1882, when, after going to the Pacific Coast from Havre in ballast, she was laid up at San Francisco until July, 1885. Thereafter she did a little coastwise work but most of her voyages were from Puget Sound to South Africa or Australia. On Aug. 30, 1894, she sailed from Port Gamble and on December 22d was wrecked at the entrance to East London. Part of her cargo had been discharged when bad weather coming on she was forced to proceed to sea. On attempting to return to port she got ashore in shoal water and eventually broke up.

The voyages of the *Bonanza* were always made in fair time. The fastest was a round just prior to the one on which she was lost, when she was 90 days from Puget Sound to Algoa Bay, thence 35 days to Newcastle, N.S.W., and 63 days from that port to San Francisco. Much publicity was given to a report that she had made a passage from San Francisco to Queenstown in 82 days but there is no foundation for this story, her fastest time from the Golden Gate to any port in the United Kingdom being 120 days, she having two such runs to Liverpool to her credit.

The *Bonanza* was twice in collision with other vessels, once in her only run to Queenstown when, on arriving out, she lost bowsprit and had her bows badly damaged. The other instance was in the Straits of Juan de Fuca when she was also damaged in the bows. On one occasion she lost three of her principal yards off Cape Horn and in another she lost everything above the foremast head and the jibboom and put into San Francisco before completing the passage from Sydney to Puget Sound.

In March, 1894, the *Bonanza* sailed into the harbor of Newcastle without the assistance of a tug and on completing her lading left the port also under her own canvas, which feat was the subject of considerable favorable comment at the time.

The first master of the *Bonanza* was Capt. Michael J. Daly who previously, for about a year, had been in the new bark *Fresno*, belonging to the same owners. In 1878 Captain Daly bought into the ship *Hamilton*, managed by Thayer & Lincoln of Boston, who were also the principal owners of the ships *Valiant* and *Wm. H. Lincoln*. The *Hamilton* went from San Francisco to Baker's Island to load guano for Hamburg. On the latter passage she struck an iceberg off Cape Horn, losing her bowsprit and billethead. After her arrival out she was sold on German account and Captain Daly took command of the *Valiant*. In 1882 this ship was burned at Calcutta and the Captain then took the *Wm. H. Lincoln* and continued in her until she was burned at Sydney, in December, 1891. Captain Daly died while in command of the steamship *Finance* which ran between New York and the Isthmus of Panama.

Capt. Geo. W. Leach succeeded Captain Daly as master of the *Bonanza* and continued in her until May, 1887, when he retired from active sea life to become port captain for Pope & Talbot. The Captain was an old experienced shipmaster and for several years commanded the clipper ship *Euterpe*. He was in that ship when, in 1871, while bound from Callao to Falmouth, she was abandoned in a sinking condition. Captain Leach and sixteen men reached the Brazilian coast but the mate and eight men, in another boat, were never heard from.

Capt. Isaac W. Keller, whose actual name was Kalloch, and who was related to a one-time mayor of San Francisco, was born in Rockland, Me., in 1834, and in early life sailed in small vessels in the West India trade. He arrived in San Francisco in 1853 and remained on the Pacific Coast, commanding a number of vessels, among which were the barks *Gold Hunter, Roswell Sprague, King Philip, Fresno, Arkwright* and *James Cheston,* and the ships *Eliz. Kimball, Bonanza* and *Palmyra.* He lost the *King Philip* while outward bound in ballast, in 1878, through her drifting ashore on the ocean beach at San Francisco during a calm. He had been in command of the *Eliz. Kimball* for several years prior to her leaving Puget Sound in March, 1873, for Iquique. A month later, when the ship was about 600 miles from Easter Island, she sprung aleak and her deck load of lumber was jettisoned. Every effort was made to free her of water but unsuccessfully and Captain Keller determined to beach her on Easter Island and when she was run ashore there she was full of water. The ship's provisions and some of her sails and rigging were saved and Captain Keller built a 10-ton schooner out of material from the wreck. On July 29th the Captain, his wife and eight of the crew left for Tahiti, 2550 miles distant and made the trip in 24 days. The rest of the crew remained on Easter Island with plenty of provisions until taken off by a steamer sent for them.

Captain Keller took command of the *Palmyra* in 1891 and after about ten years service in her, he retired from the sea and was for a time port captain for Pope & Talbot. He had never married.

The last master of the *Bonanza* was Capt. Wilder F. Stetson whose sea career is contained in account of the ship *Carondelet*.

C. C. CHAPMAN

THE ship *C. C. Chapman* was built by William Rogers, at Bath, Maine, and was launched in February, 1877. She was 222 feet, by 40, by 25 feet and registered 1587 tons. She was of the same model as the *Bonanza* built by Mr. Rogers two years previously, and when launched was described as being one of the best ships belonging to Bath at that time. She was owned by J. S. Winslow & Co. of Portland, Me., and is said to have been named in honor of a prominent resident of that city. In 1895 she was sold on the East Coast for conversion into a barge but does not appear to have had a long career as such for in a few years her name was dropped from shipping registers.

The maiden voyage of the *Chapman* was from Boston to Calcutta and Madras, with ice, and she continued in trade with India some four years. Thereafter her voyages were mainly between Atlantic ports and those of the North Pacific Coast. On one occasion she took coal from Cardiff to Callao, thence going to Puget Sound to load lumber and spars for Boston. Two of her voyages were to the Orient with case oil. Her last as a sailing ship was from Philadelphia to Marseilles with crude petroleum in barrels.

On several occasions the *Chapman* was laid up in port for lack of remunerative freights and she also made many long passages, being at times five or six months to or from the North Pacific, grave fears being felt for her safety on more than one occasion. On her passage from Dublin to San Francisco, with steel rails, in 1882, she encountered high cross seas in the South Atlantic and her lower hold cargo not being properly stowed, she rolled and labored heavily. Capt. Samuel Pote, who had taken command of the ship when she was launched, suffered a stroke of apoplexy and chief officer Welch squared away for the Cape of Good Hope, completing the voyage by going around New Zealand and then through the Eastern passages. The ship was 182 days from Dublin to San Francisco. On the following passage to San Francisco, which was from Antwerp, the ship had been on fire for a month before making port. The fire was extinguished by the use of great quantities of water but both ship and cargo were badly damaged.

Capt. Geo. H. Pierce took command of the *Chapman*, in September, 1882, after her arrival from Dublin and continued in her as master some five years. He then remained on the Pacific Coast and commanded a number of sailing vessels among which were the *Carrollton* and *Sea King*. During the Spanish American War he was running between San Francisco and Manila as master of an army transport and later was ashore for a time as a port captain and a marine superintendent in different employs at San Francisco. Later, still, he resumed seafaring, returning to the army transport service, and while so employed died suddenly at Manila in August, 1913, his body being shipped to the Coast for interment. Captain Pierce was an excellent navigator, a thorough gentleman, modest and unassuming. At the time of his death he was fifty-eight years of age. Born in Yarmouth, Me., he was adopted when two years old by Capt. David Pierce of that town, a master of coasting vessels. Young Pierce went to sea at an early age and when nineteen became chief mate of the new ship *C. F. Sargent*. After serving as such five years he was given command of the Yarmouth ship *El Dorado* and three years later took the *Chapman*.

Capt. Adelbert Hichborn of Stockton, Me., succeeded Captain Pierce in the *Chapman* but retired from sea life after a few years. The *Chapman* is said to have been the only large vessel Captain Hichborn commanded.

C. F. SARGENT

THE ship *C. F. Sargent*, named after Cyrus F. Sargent, a ship-builder of Yarmouth, Maine, was built at that place, in 1874, by Blanchard Brothers, Joseph A. Seabury being the master carpenter. She was 220 feet, by 41, by 26 feet and registered 1704 tons. The oak, birch, maple, etc., used in her frame was cut in Canada; the hackmatack for her top frames came from Nova Scotia while the yellow pine was shipped by schooner from a Southern port. The winter of that year was very severe and the river froze over before the schooner arrived, so a part of her cargo was discharged on the ice and hauled to the yard by ox teams. Later on, tugs were employed to break the ice in the channel and the schooner was able to discharge the rest of her material on the wharf.

The *Sargent* was owned by her builders and her namesake until January, 1877, when she was purchased by John Rosenfeld of San Francisco who, a year or so later, sold her to George E. Plummer and associates of the same place. In 1906 she took a cargo of lumber from the Columbia River to New York, being sold after arrival to the Luckenbachs for conversion into a coal barge. In October, 1917, she was purchased by the United States Government.

Under her original ownership the *Sargent* was operated as a general carrier, being in the transatlantic cotton, California grain and South American guano trades, besides taking coal or case oil to China and other ports in the Far East and Australia. After her purchase by San Francisco parties she took one cargo of wheat from San Francisco to Europe and following her return passage from New York, was operated in the Pacific, at times coasting but principally in the export coal and lumber business out of Puget Sound. She is described as being a pretty ship, with quite a long run and a neat stern with a rather high transom. She was a dry, comfortable boat and would run well in heavy weather. Some authorities said that she was too lightly sparred and called her a slow sailer but her passages appear to have been made in fair average time and some were fast. Captain Atherton was much elated over her performances on a voyage from Cardiff to Hong

Kong, San Francisco and Liverpool, the gross time on the whole round being but 12 months, 21 days and this notwithstanding the fact that the run from China to San Francisco was made with bad weather throughout and occupied 74 days. On the run to Liverpool she crossed the Line in 17 days from San Francisco and her passage of 111 days was three days shorter than that of the *Ennerdale*, a British iron ship with a good reputation for fast sailing ability. On a prior passage Captain Atherton had made Falmouth in 108 days from the Golden Gate. Her cargo of wheat had been laden at Port Costa and the *Sargent* had the distinction of being the first ship to load at a place that later became well known to shipowners and masters the world over. In 1887, while bound from New York to San Francisco, under command of Captain Baker, she was only six days, eight hours between the two parallels of 50° S., a run which has seldom been equalled and probably never surpassed. In 1889 she ran from Port Townsend to San Francisco in four days, the fastest time that had been made in many years.

The *Sargent* met with many mishaps. When Captain Swett was in command, she was loading guano at Huanillos when the tidal wave of May, 1877, swept the coast. The ship was light with only some 250 tons of cargo aboard and was spun around by the seas like a top. She lost her rudder stock and anchors and chains, besides having the main transom started and had to go to Callao for repairs. The damage, however, was slight in comparison to that had by other vessels at the time. In 1885, while on a voyage from Cardiff to Hong Kong, she was set by a strong current, on a bold, rocky shore in the Straits of Timor and when the tide fell, she listed off shore with the rail under water. Captain Atherton put his two daughters and their piano into a boat and sent them to a ship further out in the Straits, while the crew, believing the ship would prove to be a total loss, left her with what few effects they could gather in a hurry. While this was going on some of the natives entertained them by shooting at them with arrows. At the next flood tide, however, the ship righted and finally floated off, when all hands returned to her. She did not leak and the voyage was resumed. After being docked at Hong Kong it was found that the port

"BIG BONANZA," 1399 TONS, BUILT IN 1875, AT NEWBURYPORT
Courtesy of Edward S. Clark

"BOHEMIA," 1663 TONS, BUILT IN 1875, AT BATH, MAINE

Courtesy of Firemen's Fund Insurance Co., San Francisco

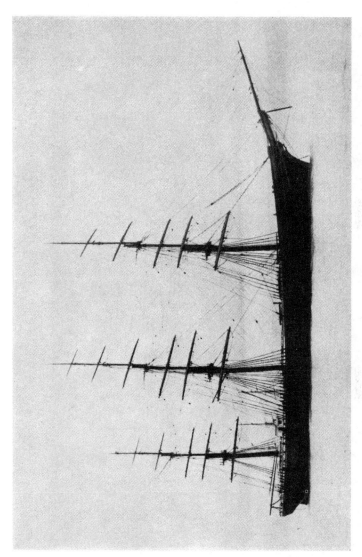

"CARL FREDERICK," EX "RED CLOUD," 2208 TONS, BUILT IN 1877, AT QUINCY, MASS.
Courtesy of Edward S. Clark

"CARRIE REED," 1352 TONS, BUILT IN 1870, AT KENNEBUNKPORT, MAINE
From an oil painting by C. J. Waldron. Photograph by George E. Noyes, Newburyport

bilge was somewhat damaged but otherwise the hull was in good condition.

In 1889, while bound to San Francisco from Liverpool, the *Sargent* was putting into Montevideo when she grounded and had the rudder damaged. The cargo was discharged and sold, the voyage abandoned and the ship ordered to New York for repairs. In 1891, while bound from Sydney to San Francisco, she was partially dismasted and had to put back to port for repairs. In 1895 she lost the foremasthead and everything above; the maintopgallant mast and the jibboom, while on a passage from Seattle to San Francisco. In December, 1901, while lying in the stream off Folsom Street, San Francisco, her coal cargo was found to be on fire and she narrowly escaped total destruction. Fire boats and crews from Government vessels in the vicinity succeeded in getting streams of water on the coal and the ship was finally towed on the Mission mud flats with fifteen feet of water in the hold.

Capt. Walter K. Swett of Falmouth, Me., was the first commander of the *Sargent* and was in her four years, leaving her at Cardiff on account of ill health. Capt. D. H. Atherton was master for the seven years prior to her sale when he is said to have retired from sea life to make his home in California. Capt. James G. Baker was the first master of the *Sargent* after the change in ownership and following him was Capt. Chas. C. Morse and many other shipmasters best known on the Pacific Coast. Captain Baker had previously commanded the ship *Sterling* and is more particularly referred to in the account of that ship appearing in "American Merchant Ships," Series I. Captain Morse is referred to in account of the ship *George F. Manson.*

CALIFORNIA

THE ship *California* was built at East Boston, in 1864, by Samuel Hall, for W. F. Weld & Co. of Boston, and was 194 feet, by 38, by 24 feet and 1413 tons register. She was of good model, well constructed and presented a handsome appearance. In 1875 she was sold at Antwerp for £6150 to parties in Amsterdam who had her re-named *Westerschelde*. A few years later she was resold and became the German ship *Hermann*, thereafter, for some ten years being operated in the transatlantic barrel oil trade.

The *California* was operated in trade with San Francisco prior to 1873 after which she made a voyage to the Orient. Her passages were much slower than had been expected, the average of the six made from Atlantic ports to San Francisco being 166 days. On three of the return trips she went to the West Coast of Mexico to load dye woods; two were to the United Kingdom direct, with wheat, and the other was by way of Manila, all of these being longer than average. Her voyages appear, however, to have been without unusual incident and her name does not appear in any lists of mishaps or disasters.

The first master of the *California* was Capt. Henry Barber who had previously been in command of Weld & Co.'s clipper ship *Galatea*. He was succeeded in 1868, in the *California*, by Capt. Robert C. Adams, another Weld & Co. shipmaster whose former commands had been the ship *Golden Fleece* and the bark *Rocket*, both clippers. Thereafter, the *California* had several different masters, most of whom made but a single passage in the ship.

CARONDELET

THE ship *Carondelet* was built for Abner Stetson of Damaris-cotta, Maine, by Edwin Flye & Co. and was launched from their yard at Newcastle, Me., in December, 1872. She was 202:5 feet, by 40:3, by 24 feet and registered 1376 tons. Abner Stetson had himself been a shipbuilder but was then living retired, being one of the wealthiest citizens of his community. When the *Carondelet* was launched he presented interests in her to his sons, Captains Jos. A. and Wilder Francis Stetson, and both of them were subsequently in command of the ship. In 1887 she was sold to Pope & Talbot of San Francisco, lumber merchants, who had large mills on Puget Sound. In January, 1909, they sold her to parties in Seattle, who converted her into a barge and she was employed in carrying cement until Dec. 1, 1911, when she foundered off Prince Rupert, B. C.

Prior to 1888 the *Carondelet* was operated principally in trade across the Atlantic or with ports in the Far East, she making but two passages to the North Pacific by way of Cape Horn. The last of these was from Liverpool to Tacoma, she being the first vessel to have a cargo from Europe to any American port on Puget Sound. Sailing from Liverpool on Oct. 1, 1886, she had a hard time in getting started, being obliged to put into Holyhead, the second day out, through inability of her tug to make headway against the strong wind that was blowing. The following day she made another start but the wind and sea increasing, the towing hawser parted and sail had to be made on the ship. While this was being done the vessel rolled so heavily in the trough of the sea that it was feared the masts would go over the side at any moment. Finally, however, she was able to work back to Holyhead and after the cessation of the gale the voyage was resumed and on November 6th the ship was cast off by the tug near Tuskar Light. Then, for four days, very heavy weather was met with; the main hatch was stove in, bulwarks were carried away, the cabins filled with water and other damage received. The ship was kept before the wind until the hatch could be covered with lumber and spare sails when a course was steered for Madeira and four days were spent there in making necessary repairs. However, the remainder of the passage was made without incident and the ship arrived at Puget Sound, March 13, 1887, in 124 sailing days from Liverpool.

In 1881 the *Carondelet* took coal from Cardiff to Yokohama, thence crossing to San Francisco in ballast in 22 days which is the record fast passage over that course. She left Yokohama at midnight October 8th, thirty inches down by the head and arrived at San Francisco early in the morning of the 30th, sailing into the harbor without tug or pilot. She had been favored with strong winds from the westward all the way while the ship *Frank Pendleton*, leaving Yokohama 13 days before her, met with nothing but light easterly winds and was 35 days on the run to the Golden Gate.

While the *Carondelet* was owned by Pope & Talbot she made some coasting voyages but she was principally employed in carrying lumber from Puget Sound to Australia. In 1890 she made the run from Sydney to the Sound in 43 days, a record fast passage and in 1902 she was 20 days from San Francisco to Prince William Sound, Alaska, which was four days shorter than the best previous run.

Capt. Jos. A. Stetson, the first master of the *Carondelet*, was born in Damariscotta, in 1848, and took up seafaring in early life. For a time he was master of the ship *J. H. Stetson* engaged in the transatlantic cotton trade. After being some five years in the *Carondelet*, he relinquished command to his younger brother Wilder F. Stetson and settled on Puget Sound. For a number of years he was engaged in the stevedoring and ship brokerage business at Port Townsend and died in Tacoma about 1898. Capt. Wilder F. Stetson was born in 1850 and he also sailed in the ship *J. H. Stetson* under his brother. When the *Carondelet* was built he became her first mate and later her master, so continuing for many years. For a time he was in the bark *Bonanza* and was her commander when she was lost at East London, South Africa. The Captain retired from sea life about 1907 and died at Yakima, Wash., in March, 1925.

CARRIE CLARK

THE ship *Carrie Clark* was built at Waldoboro, Maine, by Clark & Sons, and was launched in November, 1874. She was 185 feet, by 38, by 24 feet and registered 1327 tons. She hailed from Boston and was owned by her builders and others. In 1883, after arriving at Dunkirk from San Francisco, via Valparaiso, where she had put in to have repairs made to the rudder, she was sold to go under the German flag, being renamed *Anna*. She was operated in transatlantic trade nearly twenty years when she was purchased by Lewis Luckenbach of New York, and converted into a barge. Her original name was restored and she carried coal along the Atlantic Coast until Nov. 28, 1921, when, being in the same tow with the barge *Gov. Robie*, both vessels foundered off Highland Light, N. J., taking down with them their crews of three men each.

While under the American flag the *Carrie Clark* was employed as a general trader. In 1878 she crossed from Shanghai to Puget Sound and thereafter, for a time, carried coal from British Columbia to San Francisco. Her subsequent operations, prior to her sale, were between Great Britain and San Francisco, coal on the outward and grain on the return passages. Her voyages were, as a rule, rather longer than average, but she was regarded as a good ship and had no major mishaps.

Capt. Ira A. Storer of Waldoboro was in command of the *Carrie Clark* during all of her career as an American ship. He is more particularly referred to in account of the ship *John McDonald*.

CARRIE REED

THE ship *Carrie Reed* was built by David Clark, at Kennebunkport, Maine, for J. S. Winslow & Co. of Portland, Me., and was launched in April, 1870. She was 200 feet, by 39:3, by 24:6 feet and of 1352 tons register.

After a voyage or two in the transatlantic cotton trade, the *Carrie Reed* was operated between Atlantic ports and San Francisco, making good average passages, the fastest being a run from Liverpool in 119 days, in 1871. Following her arrival at Liverpool, in January, 1876, with grain from San Francisco, she was sold to go under the German flag, being renamed *Gustav & Oscar*. When old and about worn out she was resold and became the Chilian ship *Adela*. As such she carried lumber from Puget Sound to Valparaiso, being so employed as late as 1907 and possibly later.

Capt. Elkanah Crowell, Jr., took command of the *Carrie Reed*, in 1871, and continued in her until she was sold. He then bought into the new bark *Gerard C. Tobey* and his career as a shipmaster is mentioned in account of that vessel.

CASSANDRA ADAMS

THE *Cassandra Adams* was one of the few large, square-rigged vessels built on the Pacific Coast and she upheld the fine record established by the ships *Western Shore* and *Wildwood*, which had previously been built in that section of the country. She was owned by W. J. Adams, a lumber merchant of San Francisco, who had extensive mills at Seabeck, Wash., and was launched at that place in November, 1876. Her plans were drawn by George Middlemas of San Francisco and the master builder in charge of construction was Hiram Doncaster. Her dimensions were 196:5 feet, by 40:3, by 22:2 feet, and tonnage, 1083. She had two decks. While being able to load large cargoes, as much as 1750 long tons of wheat, she was modeled on the lines of a half clipper and was heavily sparred for a vessel of her tonnage. The mainmast was 82 feet long; topmast 50, and topgallant and royal masts 56 feet. The masts and yards on the foremast were of the same dimensions as those of the main, except that the foremast was but 78 feet in length. She had double-topgallant sails and her yards were in length, 90, 80, 72, 63, 56, and 45 feet. The mizzenmast was 87 feet long and the topmast 65 feet. The spanker boom was 54 feet, and gaff 35 feet; bowsprit 40, and jibboom 50 feet. She was named after the wife of Mr. Adams and a life-sized image of the lady served as the vessel's figurehead.

The first four years of the *Adams'* career were spent in the trade for which she had been built, coastwise lumber. In October, 1880, Mr. Adams replaced her with his new and much larger ship *Olympus* and sold her to the proprietors of the Departure Bay coal mines. Six months later she was resold to John Rosenfeld of San Francisco, for $55,000, her new owner putting her in the Cape Horn trade. For the following five years she was so employed and always gave a good account of herself as will be seen by the following record of her voyages.

1881	San Francisco to Liverpool, 114 days;			Liverpool to San Francisco, 110 days
1882	do	do	105 "	do	do	115 "
1883	do	New York	94 "	New York	do	107 "
1883-84	do	do	104 "	do	do	127 "
1884-85	do	do	148 "	do	do	119 "

On her first passage from Liverpool she crossed the Line 32 days out, was off the pitch of the Cape on the 61st day, crossed the equator 92 days out, and made the Farallons 17 days later but was unable to get into port until the next day. Off Cape Horn she was in company with the fast British iron ship *Golden Gate* and led the latter six days into port. On the following passage she was 16 days covering the final 1000 miles of the run, yet her whole run was eight days shorter than that of the British ship *Ennerdale* and six days shorter than that of the ship *South American*, both also from Liverpool and well known as smart sailers. Her long passage to New York in 1884 was accounted for by her encountering much light and calm weather and then, on nearing destination, getting ashore on Rockaway Shoals. In this, however, she received no material damage.

Following the return of the *Adams* to San Francisco, in July, 1885, she made one voyage to Australia but otherwise was employed in coastwise trade. In December, 1887, she was purchased by Charles Hanson of the Tacoma Mills and in August of the following year sailed from San Francisco with a small quantity of supplies for the mills. Capt. F. F. Knacke had just been appointed to command her and lost her on the passage as per his report which follows:

"I know every mile of the coast from San Francisco to Seattle. After I left San Francisco on this unfortunate passage, I had very thick weather all the way up the coast and many times it was so bad that I could not see the men on deck. I ran by dead reckoning and supposing I was to windward of Cape Flattery I headed her south so as to sail into the Straits of Juan de Fuca. We were going along at good speed on the evening of August 15th, when all at once I saw the tops of trees on shore. I supposed at first it was the coast of Vancouver Island. There must be a fearful current on that shore or I never could have got to where I found myself. I wore ship but before the vessel rounded she struck on a reef off what afterwards proved to be Destruction Island. When I found she was on hard and fast I gave orders to clew up the small sails and lower the boats. Within three hours we had all left in small boats and landed under the lee of the island."

Capt. William F. Edwards was master of the *Adams* during the time she was owned by William J. Adams. The Captain was a native of Maine, born in 1847, and started a seafaring life on the Atlantic in the Government Coast Survey service. In 1866 he went to the Pacific Coast, before the mast, in the ship *Live Oak* and remained there, sailing in a number of different vessels. He was in the employ of Mr. Adams as master for seventeen years and commanded his ships *Dublin* and *Olympus* and bark *Oregon*, besides others. In later years he was master of coastwise steamers, being quite a long time in the *Humboldt*. Subsequently he was a pilot on the Alaskan coast and is said to have died in the Far North many years ago.

Capt. Fred T. Henry, whose seafaring career is given in account of the ship *Cyrus Wakefield*, "American Merchant Ships," Series I, was in command of the *Adams* while she was engaged in the Cape Horn trade. On the return of the vessel to the Pacific for future operations thereon, Capt. C. B. Weldon was appointed master and he served as such until ownership passed to Mr. Hanson, who gave the command to Capt. Frank W. Gatter. The latter had been sailing on the coast for many years but in old vessels which were dull sailers, and he regarded his appointment to the captaincy of the *Adams* as a distinct promotion. On his first voyage in her, while bound from Puget Sound to San Pedro, Cal., with coal, he saw thirty-six miles registered by the log in two hours. When sixty hours out from Cape Flattery the *Adams* was abreast of Point Reyes and on the sixth day was off Point Conception. Captain Gatter called the *Adams* a perfect witch, steering like a pilot boat and, during the time he was in her, never meeting her match as to sailing qualities. He was very proud of her, kept her in perfect condition and when her owner suggested economy, resigned his charge to take the old bark *Emerald*, one of his prior commands. The *Adams* was then given over to Capt. F. F. Knacke, with disastrous results, and Mr. Hanson was greatly distressed over the whole affair.

Captain Gatter was born in New York, in 1843, and as a boy sailed in New York-Liverpool packet ships. When eighteen years of age he was third mate of the ship *Good Hope*, making a voyage from New

York to San Francisco, Callao, Calcutta and Savannah, the ship arriving at the latter port about the time Fort Sumter was surrendered to the Confederates. The ship was ordered to leave port at once under penalty of confiscation so she proceeded to New York. Young Gatter was urged to join the Rebel naval forces but refused, and on arriving at New York enlisted in the United States Navy, being assigned for duty on the frigate *Roanoke*. Two years later he was discharged on account of sickness and, on recovering, re-entered the mercantile marine. In 1866 he went to the Pacific Coast and remained there. In 1869 he was given his first command, the old bark *Brontes* and later he had the *Atalanta, Emerald, Guardian* and other vessels. When the Northern Pacific Steamship Co. was organized, about 1890, Captain Gatter was appointed Puget Sound pilot for their vessels and he so continued until shortly before his death, which occurred in 1903 while he was in a hospital at Victoria.

CELESTIAL EMPIRE

THE ship *Celestial Empire* was built by Jotham Stetson, at South Boston, in 1852, and was 193 feet, by 37:7, by 29 feet and registered 1630 tons. For many years she was owned by Charles H. Parsons & Co. of New York. Her later years were spent under the management of Snow & Burgess and they were reported as her owners when she was lost.

At widely separated intervals the *Celestial Empire* made five voyages between Atlantic ports and San Francisco, the first being in 1852 and the last in 1875. She was of full model, narrow and deep and most of her career was spent in transatlantic trade, for which she had been built. Her passages on the long distance voyages she made were all slow, the average of those to San Francisco being 164 days, one of 144 days being the shortest.

Among the numerous commanders of the *Celestial Empire* were Captains John Siler Taylor and James H. Stewart, and they appear to have been the only shipmasters who had her for any extended period. Captain Taylor had previously been master of the ships *Tona-wanda* and *Hemisphere* and after serving nine years in the *Celestial Empire* he had the *Fleetford* from 1873 until early in 1879 when she was sold to go under a foreign flag. The Captain died in Mobile the same year.

Capt. James H. Stewart had been in command of the ship *Robert C. Winthrop* a number of years, before taking the *Celestial Empire* in 1872. After her loss he bought the ship *John Harvey*, of Newburyport, and sailed her in transatlantic trade many years, being so engaged in 1891 and possibly later.

CENTENNIAL

THE ship *Centennial* was built by Smith & Townsend, at East Boston, and was launched in July, 1875. Her keel had been laid in August of the previous year, her timbers had been extra well seasoned and she was slowly and carefully built. Her length over all was 206 feet, beam 38 feet, and depth of hold 24½ feet; registered tonnage, 1223. The spars on the fore- and mainmasts were of the same size, the lower masts, single sticks, being 93 feet in length; topmasts 55½ feet and topgallant and royal masts 51 feet, including a nine foot pole. The lower yards were 77 feet long and those above, in order, 68, 63, 50 and 38 feet. Smith & Townsend owned a controlling interest in her and acted as managers. In 1896 she was sold at San Francisco, to the Alaska Packers Association. In December, 1904, while lying up in Oakland Creek, she caught on fire, it is believed through rats gnawing at matches in the fishermen's quarters. The main and mizzenmasts were burned as also some deck beams and altogether damage to the extent of about $10,000 was done. On being rebuilt she was rerigged as a four-masted barkentine and for many years continued her operations as a "salmon packer." In March, 1927, she was sold to Capt. Frank Weidemann who, after making a voyage to Australia, sold her on returning to the Coast, to moving picture operators of Southern California.

The first voyage of the *Centennial* was from New York to San Francisco and thence to Liverpool. Thereafter she made three other passages from Atlantic ports to the Golden Gate, the last of which was 1896, following which she was sold. Her other operations had been with ports in Australia, the East Indies and China. She was credited with being a good sailer; made one passage from San Francisco to Liverpool in 102 days; one of 107 days from Astoria to Queenstown and one of 84 days from New York to Sydney. As a rule she was quite fortunate in making her voyages without receiving damage, an exception being her last long-distance passage, New York to San Francisco. On this occasion she was forced to put back to the Falkland Islands to repair damages received off Cape Horn and was on her way back there a second time, with the cargo shifted, but on nearing Port Stanley a storm came on and Captain Colcord decided it was dangerous to attempt to enter port so he put the ship about for Montevideo. The remainder of the passage was without incident and San Francisco was reached Oct. 2, 1896, 199 days after the ship had left New York.

Except for two voyages when he was relieved by other masters, Capt. Isaac M. Bearse of West Harwich, Mass., was in continuous command of the *Centennial* from the time she was launched until September, 1888, when he sold his interest in the ship to Capt. Benjamin F. Colcord and retired from sea life. He was appointed port warden of Boston but died within a year. Prior to taking the *Centennial*, Captain Bearse had commanded the fine bark *Edwin H. Kingman*, built at Bath, in 1874, by Goss & Sawyer, and owned by that firm, Hinkley Bros. of Boston, Captain Bearse and D. E. Mayo of Chelsea. The *Kingman* went out to San Francisco from Baltimore and then loaded guano at Howland's Island for Liverpool. Leaving the Island, Dec. 25, 1874, all went well until Feb. 12, 1875, when at 3:30 P.M. the vessel was struck, without any warning, by a whirlwind. The jibboom, fore- and mainmasts and mizzen topmast were carried away and the ship's boats crushed and the pumps broken by the falling wreckage. This was finally cleared away but the vessel was unmanageable and rolled heavily in the trough of the sea. At 9 P.M.

there was twenty-two inches of water in the well and no means of freeing the vessel. During the next four days strong gales were encountered, the weather was very cold and the vessel labored heavily with decks frequently flooded. The water in the hold gained steadily and the ship was settling fast when early in the morning of the 16th, a ship was sighted running under short sail in the heavy gale that was blowing. The *Kingman's* distress signals were seen and the stranger bore down and hove to. Captain Bearse consulted with his officers and crew and it was decided to abandon the wreck which was then near the ice region. At 7 A.M. a boat from the other vessel took off the *Kingman's* people who were unable to save anything except the clothing they wore. Soon after the distressed vessel was abandoned she was seen to be on fire near the after house. The rescuing ship proved to be the *Carisbrook Castle* of London, Capt. J. Freebody, bound from San Francisco to Queenstown, and the shipwrecked crew was landed at that port.

Capt. Benjamin F. Colcord, who is still living, commanded several ships after leaving the *Centennial* when she was sold, his last being the *William H. Connor* and his career as a shipmaster is contained in account of that ship in "American Merchant Ships," Series I.

Capt. Frank Weidemann, who purchased the *Centennial* from the Alaska Packers Association, had previously been a master in the employ of that company. He had an idea that the days of sailing ships were not over and that properly handled they could compete as cargo carriers with steamers or motor ships. He secured a lumber charter for Australia and was confident of ability to obtain a remunerative return cargo. Later on he even anticipated placing the *Centennial* on the Cape Horn run between Atlantic and Pacific ports, but the outcome of the Australian voyage convinced him that he had been laboring under a delusion. The *Centennial* had a long passage down and he was then unable to get a cargo for the Coast although he went to the Fiji Islands looking for copra. Finally he sailed in ballast and after an exceptionally long passage arrived at San Francisco, in February, 1928, Captain Weidemann soon thereafter selling his vessel as previously stated.

CHARLES E. MOODY

THE ship *Charles E. Moody* was launched Nov. 9, 1882, from the yard of Goss & Sawyer at Bath, Maine. Dimensions: 233:9 feet, by 43:4, by 26:1 feet, 1915 tons register. Her owners were Charles Davenport, Capt. John R. Kelley, John R. Patten, all of Bath, Charles E. Moody of Boston and Capt. Henry R. Otis, she having been built for the latter to command. While the ship was in port at San Francisco, in September, 1898, her owners offered her for sale, asking $50,000, but such a figure did not appeal to prospective purchasers, so the *Moody* was chartered for a voyage to New York. Negotiations for her sale continued, however, and before the passage had been completed she changed hands, Lewis, Anderson & Co. of San Francisco paying $40,000. Some years later they resold her to Henry Nelson, also of San Francisco, and he, after being owner about ten years, resold her to the Northwestern Fisheries Company. The last long distance voyage made by the ship was in 1899 when she ran out to Honolulu from Norfolk, following the first change in ownership. Thereafter she was operated in the Pacific, her later life being spent as a "salmon packer." On June 28, 1920, she caught fire while at Bristol Bay, Alaska, and burned to the water's edge.

Aside from one voyage to the Orient all the passages made by the *Moody* from Atlantic ports, prior to 1899, were to San Francisco or Puget Sound, they numbering eleven and two respectively. Of these, four were from Liverpool, seven from New York and one each from Baltimore and Philadelphia. All were made in good time as is shown by the average of the eleven to San Francisco — 125 days. The shortest was 115 days, and longest, 135 days. The average of the passages made from San Francisco to Liverpool is 114 days, 102 and 121 days being the shortest and longest. Six runs were made from the Golden Gate to New York, one of which was made in the fast time of 100 days while the slowest was 121 days; the average of the six is 114 days. The *Moody* was a lucky ship and the memoranda of her various voyages make no mention of any damage to hull, spars or rigging being received.

Capt. Henry R. Otis, the first master of the *Moody*, died from injuries received from a fall on deck while the ship was bound from San Francisco to Liverpool, on her second voyage. The mate had the vessel put into Valparaiso whence the Captain's body was sent home for interment. On arrival of the ship at Liverpool, Capt. Robert L. Leonard was appointed commander and he continued in the ship until she was sold, a period of fourteen years. Captain Leonard's record as a shipmaster is given in account of the *Florence*, "American Merchant Ships," Series I.

Capt. M. A. Woodside, who for many years previously had been master of the ship *Sintram*, took command of the *Moody* for her new owners, at New York, in February, 1899, and then had a tedious passage of 191 days from Norfolk to Honolulu. His crew was made up of eight white sailors and fifteen Japanese. The Captain was much disappointed with the work of the latter, saying that it took three of them to do the work of one real sailorman. On one occasion three Japs and one white sailor were furling the jib when the ship took a plunge and the white man was washed into the sea. The Japs were about half an hour finishing the job and it was not until then that they notified the mate of the loss of their companion. The ship was 53 days from Norfolk to Cape Horn and Captain Woodside then deeming discretion better than valor, altered the course of his ship and completed the passage by way of the Cape of Good Hope. On arrival at Honolulu the log showed that 30,000 miles had been covered since the vessel had left Norfolk.

CHARMER

THE ship *Charmer*, the fifty-ninth vessel built by William Rogers, was launched from his yard at Bath, Maine, Sept. 22, 1881, after having been some eight months in course of construction. She was 221:7 feet, by 42:4, by 26:3 feet and registered 1881 tons. In model she was an enlarged *Highland Light* and in general appearance was a typical three-skysailyard Down East cargo carrier. She was built for Nickerson & Co. of Boston to replace a former ship of the same name which they had just sold to Germany.

The new *Charmer* was built for the California trade and aside from two voyages to the Orient and one to the West Coast of South America, all her passages from Atlantic ports prior to 1900 were to San Francisco. In 1887 she was sold to John Rosenfeld of San Francisco and twelve years later she again changed hands, being purchased by the California Shipping Company. Thereafter, under bark rig, she was operated in the Pacific, mainly in the export lumber trade. During this period she was manned by seventeen hands while, when built, her complement was twenty-eight, all told. In 1909-1910 she made a voyage from Puget Sound to South Africa, thence going to New York where she was sold to Scully Bros. and converted into a barge. On Jan. 3, 1912, she stranded on the Middle Grounds, Chesapeake Bay, and became a total loss but all on board were saved.

The *Charmer* was one of the best known ships engaged in the Cape Horn trade and always attracted attention by the fine manner in which she was kept up. She made to San Francisco nine passages from New York and one each from Liverpool and Philadelphia. Eastbound from the Pacific Coast she took grain to Europe on four occasions, general cargo to New York on six, and sugar from Honolulu on one. Her passages averaged well for a ship of her model, being 132½ days to the Pacific and 121 days returning to the Atlantic. Three of her runs to San Francisco, from New York, were made in 114, 117 and 118 days, and four, in the opposite direction, in 103, 106, 107 and 107 days. On her shortest to the westward, Captain Holmes received a bonus of $160, being $10 per day for every day under 130. On one occasion the ship was inside the Farallon Islands in 15 days from the equator and on the passage during which she put into Callao for provisions she was only 25 days from the Peruvian port to latitude 26° N., 740 miles distant from San Francisco. That run was from Liverpool and she had crossed the Line in the Atlantic in 19 days from Cape Clear.

On May 13, 1887, the *Charmer*, Captain Holmes, and the *Seminole*, Capt. A. J. Hatch, sailed together from New York and on the same day the ship *George Curtis,* Capt. T. F. Sproul, took her departure from Philadelphia, all bound to San Francisco. Captain Holmes had commanded the *Seminole* for over twenty years and had just been transferred to the *Charmer.* Captain Hatch had succeeded in the *Seminole,* of which ship he had previously been chief officer. Great interest was taken in the proposed test of speed between the three ships, shipping men playing the *Seminole* to win, with the *Curtis* as a close second, she being regarded as a smart ship. Judging from the time made, however, the affair could hardly be called a race, but at any rate the *Charmer's* run to the Golden Gate of 145 days was ten days shorter than that of the *Seminole* and 15 days shorter than that of the *Curtis.*

While engaged on long distance voyages the *Charmer's* only mishap of consequence was in 1892 when, in continuation of her voyage from New York to Hong Kong, she was crossing the Pacific to San Francisco. When just to the eastward of the Loo Choo Islands she encountered a typhoon and had several sails carried away. A few days later she ran into a second typhoon and the ship's rudderhead was twisted off so she put back to Hong Kong. On again proceeding she was caught in another typhoon of three days duration. During one spell of twenty hours she was driven under bare poles, 230 miles to north and east, but this time she got clear without receiving any material damage.

Capt. J. S. Lucas was in command of the *Charmer* on her first voyage, he then retiring from sea life. Captain Lucas had also commanded Nickerson & Co.'s former *Charmer* during all her career as an American ship. This ship had been built by T. L. Townsend, at Boston, in 1869, and was largely employed in the California trade until 1880 when she was sold, going under the German flag as the *Marie.* Later she was the Norwegian ship *Sverre* and in 1916 was still afloat as the Swedish ship *Svea.* Prior to taking command of the *Charmer,* just referred to, Captain Lucas had also been master of a still earlier ship of the same name during the ten years she had been sailing under the American flag. That *Charmer* was of medium clipper model, built at Newburyport in 1854 for Bush & Wildes of Boston and was en-

"CHARLES E. MOODY," 1915 TONS, BUILT IN 1882, AT BATH, MAINE

From an oil painting by J. E. Carvill, 1923

"CENTENNIAL," 1223 TONS, BUILT IN 1875, AT EAST BOSTON
From an oil painting showing her at Hong Kong. Photograph by George E. Noyes, Newburyport

"COMMODORE," 1781 TONS, BUILT IN 1879, AT YARMOUTH, MAINE
Courtesy of William H. Rowe

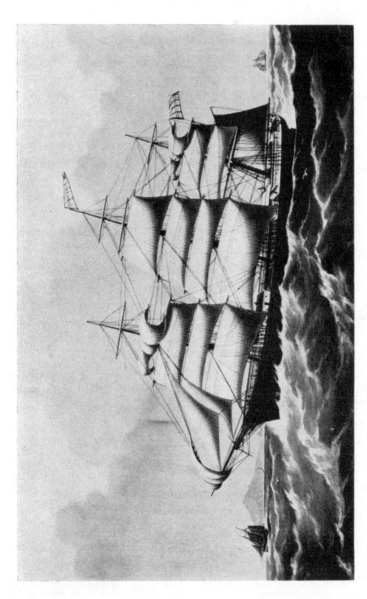

"DAUNTLESS," 995 TONS, BUILT IN 1869, AT MYSTIC, CONN.

From an oil painting by J. Hughes, Liverpool

gaged in the California and East India trade until she was sold during the Civil War to go under the British flag without change of name.

After Captain Lucas relinquished command of *Charmer* No. 3, in 1883, different masters made a passage or a round voyage in the ship until Capt. Jos. Warren Holmes took her over and continued in her the twelve years prior to her purchase by the California Shipping Co. Captain Holmes is more particularly referred to in account of the ship *Seminole*, in "American Merchant Ships," Series I.

During the ten years the *Charmer* was being operated in the Pacific she had several different masters, but Capt. John Slater was in command for most of that period. Captain Slater commenced sailing on the Pacific Coast in 1873 and was master of a number of vessels among which were the ship *Oriental* and the barks *Wilna* and *Aureola*. On the Charmer going East the Captain retired from the sea and passed the remainder of his life at his home in Berkeley.

CHESEBROUGH

THE following, to supplement the history of the ship *Chesebrough*, which appears in "American Merchant Ships," Series I, is the account of her loss given by one of her four survivors, Mr. Richard Beck of Philadelphia, who was making a voyage before the mast for the benefit of his health. It was published in the "Japan Mail" newspaper.

"The *Chesebrough* came to Kobe from Philadelphia, with 65,000 cases of oil and after discharging most of it, proceeded with some 5,000 cases and sand ballast, to Hakodate. There the ship was loaded with 2230 tons of sulphur for New York and sailed Oct. 28, 1889, having in going out taken the ground at the entrance to the harbor but had been successful in kedging off. Capt. Erickson decided instead of going to the eastward into the Pacific, to pass through the straits to the westward. At starting in the morning of the 28th we had a fair wind but it headed us in the course of a few hours and we anchored for the night. The wind freshened to a gale and in the morning we had to up anchor and stand out to get clear of the land.

"The gale blew very hard all day from the northwest, the vessel shipping a great deal of water and at six o'clock that evening we were close over to the northern side of the straits. We tacked and stood across the straits and during the night lost our maintopgallant and had the head sails blown away. By half past five the following morning we found ourselves close under the southern shore. We attempted to tack but being partially disabled and having besides a great quantity of sulphur in the lower hold which made the ship as lifeless as a log, she would not come around. We then tried to wear her and did actually get the yards all but braced around, when the powerful current running along the land swung the ship back and she drifted stern first on the shore. We struck about a mile off the beach and the huge seas which swept over the vessel at once drove her around until she lay broadside to the waves. Just before she struck orders had been given to let go both anchors and this was done but it proved of no avail.

"As soon as we took the ground attempts were made to lower the starboard lifeboat and a longboat which lay on top of the forward house but they were immediately smashed. We had lost the port lifeboat while running down our easting on the voyage out. Some now went into the fore rigging and others, of whom I was one, took refuge at first in the cabin but quickly left that shelter and 14 of us at length found ourselves in the mizzen rigging. The mizzen course, being set, presented a large surface to the wind and seas. The ship soon began breaking up, the sulphur covering the water all around to leeward and in a couple of hours after she struck, the mizzenmast went by the board. Those who were not crushed by the fall of the spars and rigging now found themselves in the water. The boatswain I saw jammed against the lee rail as the mast fell and I believe his back was then broken. The Captain was on the mast when it fell and I saw him afterwards in the water battling, as did several others, to get back to the ship, but what with the sulphur getting into their eyes and the dreadful struggle to fight their way through the rigging, which with

hands got ashore safely in the ship's boats and at that time the cargo had been dissolved and melted away.

The island was found to be inhabited by the employes of an Australian company engaged in gathering the phosphatic guano. It was a low atoll, with no vegetation and no water supply. There were a few whites and nearly a hundred South Sea Island laborers who gathered the guano powder into piles for grading, after which it was sacked and taken off by boat to small vessels into whose holds it was dumped. At this time there were two of these vessels lying off the reef loading, one of which was a Danish iron bark, the *Norwester*, Captain Nielsen. Captain Davidson recovered considerable provisions from the wreck of his ship so that there was plenty of food on the island but the water supply was meagre, being gathered into cisterns from the roofs of the few buildings during the rainy season. Fish were plentiful inside the reef and the kanakas embarked nightly in a canoe and by using flaming torches were able to scoop up large catches from the schools attracted by the light. The islanders then built fires and roasted their catch on hot stones, feasting until late at night. In fact this seemed to be their principal means of subsistence, although they were furnished food by the guano company, most of this was non-perishable and was hoarded up pending their being returned to their homes in the South Seas after the close of the season.

When the smaller guano vessel was loaded the second mate of the *Commodore* and his watch proceeded in her to Melbourne. After being three weeks on the island, Captain Davidson, his wife and the rest of the crew went to Dunedin in the *Norwester*. This vessel belonged to the Danish island of Fanoe, her captain and all his crew being natives thereof. They were a happy family, apparently all equals, for it was customary for all hands to assemble in the cabin to witness Captain Nielsen work out his daily position and post his chart. In the Nielsen family, besides the captain and his wife, were six daughters and one son, most of whom had been born at sea and named after their respective birthplaces, such as India, Atlanta, etc.

On arrival at Dunedin, after a very pleasant passage, Captain Davidson sold to the guano company, for $200, the wreck of the *Commo-*

dore as he had left her, then upright but with one side considerably stove in. The company sent another vessel to the island to wind up the season's work but on arrival it developed that the ship had broken up in a blow and practically all wreckage had drifted out to sea. When lost the *Commodore* was valued at $50,000, covered by insurance of $25,000. The cargo was insured for $217,000. Middlemas & Boole, Capt. James Davidson, and others of San Francisco, were owners of the ship at the time.

Capt. David W. Blanchard retired from sea life after the sale of the *Commodore* in 1885. He is more particularly referred to in account of the ship *Admiral*, appearing in "American Merchant Ships," Series I. Capt. F. W. Jordan, who was the first master of the *Commodore*, under her Pacific Coast ownership, was born in Newton, Mass., in 1848, and went to sea as a boy in coasters out of Boston. He then served in an East Indiaman and came to the Pacific Coast as chief officer of the ship *Cultivator* in 1873. Leaving her to take command of the coasting bark *Marmion*, he was in that vessel until she was abandoned at sea in November, 1879, the crew being picked up. Later he was master of the ship *Belvedere*, some two years, and then in the *Commodore* an equal length of time. His next command was the steam collier *Wellington* and in 1890 he was appointed a San Francisco bar pilot.

Following Captain Jordan in the *Commodore* was Capt. James G. Baker, and after him his son Capt. Rufus K. Baker. The latter had been mate of the ship *Henry Villard* and then master of the *Mount Washington*. He was not long in the *Commodore*, leaving her to become chief officer of the steamship *Advance*. In January, 1892, yellow fever broke out on board the steamer and Captain Baker was so suddenly stricken that he had to be carried from his post of duty to his room. Two days later he passed away and was buried at Bahia, Brazil. The Captain was very highly respected, a thorough navigator and acknowledged to be the most promising officer in the employ of the United States & Brazil Steamship Co. He was a native of West Harwich, Mass., and only thirty years of age when he died. The career of Capt. James Davidson, who is still living at the age of eighty years, is given in the account of the ship *Undaunted*, "American Merchant Ships," Series I.

CREMORNE

THE ship *Cremorne* was built by Maxson, Fish & Co. at Mystic, Conn., in 1862, and measured 161:6 feet, by 38:9, by 23:6 feet, with a registered tonnage of 1091. At first her managing owners were Lawrence Giles & Co., and later on that firm retiring from business, Pray & Dickens looked after the business of the ship. Capt. Charles H. Gates was in command of the vessel during the whole of her sea life.

The *Cremorne* completed six voyages from New York to San Francisco, returning direct to New York in five instances and in the other to Liverpool. The seventh voyage was from New York to San Francisco, also after which she loaded wheat and passed through the Golden Gate, June 1, 1870, bound for Liverpool. She was never thereafter heard from nor was a trace of any of the twenty-three persons on board ever learned. She had made no other voyages than those referred to.

The sailing record of the *Cremorne* is good. Her last passage to San Francisco was made in 115 days and she has to her credit runs of 102, 106, 111 and 113 days from the Pacific Coast port to New York. On the 106-day passage she crossed the equator when only fourteen days out from San Francisco and eleven days later stopped off Pitcairn Island. She then fell in with calms, head winds and heavy gales and was not up with the Cape until 34 days later. From there she made excellent time, being but 23 days from the Cape to the Line and 24 days thence to port.

The *Cremorne's* only mishap of importance, prior to her loss, was in the passage to San Francisco in 1869, when she was partially dismasted off the River Plate and finished the run under jury rig. In spite of this, however, her time on the whole passage was only 134 days. Repairs made at San Francisco cost $5,000.

Capt. Charles H. Gates was a native of Mystic, and his son was

mate with him on the ill-fated voyage of the *Cremorne*. Captain
Gates was one of four brothers, all deep-water shipmasters. One of
these, Capt. Gurdon Gates, was in command of the first *Twilight*,
built at Mystic in 1857. Capt. Geo. W. Gates was master of the
Twilight, built in 1867, and Capt. Isaac D. Gates had the ships *Elizabeth F. Willets* and *Racer*, all these being Mystic ships. In later
years Capt. Isaac D. was in command of steamers. He died in Mystic
by being poisoned through the error of a physician when he was aged
forty-five years.

DAKOTA

THE ship *Dakota*, built and owned by William Rogers, was
launched from his yard at Bath, Maine, in February, 1881, and
measured 195:9 feet, by 38, by 23:5 feet. She had an elliptic stern
and was modeled to carry cargoes weighing fifty per cent more than
her registered tonnage, which was 1203. She cost about $60,000.

The first voyage of the *Dakota* was from New York to New Tacoma with steel rails and railroad equipment and supplies. From
Tacoma she took wheat to Havre and then, after crossing to New
York, went out to San Francisco and from there to Liverpool. She
was then sold to Germany and under her original name was operated
for some years in the barrel oil trade across the Atlantic.

The *Dakota* is chiefly remembered as having opened up the export
grain trade from Puget Sound. On arriving at Tacoma in September,
1881, her commander, Capt. Isaac F. Gilkey of Searsport, conceived
the idea of having a cargo of wheat shipped there by rail from Portland rather than take his ship up the Columbia River to load, or accept a coal charter for San Francisco. He found the Portland merchants
unwilling to accept his plans, they considering such movement detri-
mental to the interests of their port. Captain Gilkey persisted in his
efforts, however, and was finally able to secure a cargo by accepting
delivery at Portland and then having it sent by rail to Tacoma on his
own account. This arrangement worked out very satisfactory and the
ship was saved over $5,000 through not having to go to Portland.

"DON QUIXOTE," 1174 TONS, BUILT IN 1868, AT MEDFORD, MASS.

From a copy of a daguerreotype showing her on the stocks

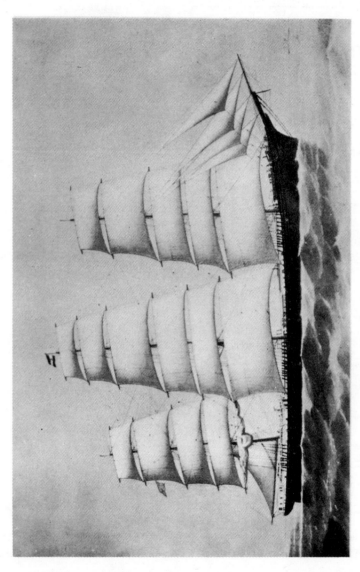

"E. B. SUTTON," 1758 TONS, BUILT IN 1881, AT BATH, MAINE
From an oil painting. Photographed by George E. Noyes, Newburyport

"ECLIPSE," 1536 TONS, BUILT IN 1878, AT BATH, MAINE

Courtesy of Edward S. Clark

"EDWARD O'BRIEN," 2157 TONS, BUILT IN 1882, AT THOMASTON, MAINE
Courtesy of Edward S. Clark

Tacoma merchants were much elated over the success of the venture
and Captain Gilkey was given an elaborate banquet during the course
of which he was presented with a valuable watch and chain. Other
vessels soon followed the lead of the *Dakota* and Tacoma became a
very large grain-shipping port.

Capt. Isaac F. Gilkey was born in Searsport in 1838 and died at
Portland, Me., in 1904. He commanded many ships among which
was the celebrated clipper *Messenger*. He was master of the *Continental* when she was lost in 1888 and he then retired from the sea.

Another ship named *Dakota*, of 1370 tons register, was launched
from the shipyard of Goss & Sawyer, Bath, in November, 1876. She
cost about $75,000 and was built for John W. Marr and her first
commander, Capt. Edwin O. Day. She took a cargo of ice from the
Kennebec River to New Orleans and then loaded cotton for Liverpool. On Jan. 7, 1877, when about 400 miles distant from the Azores
Islands, she encountered a severe storm with thunder and lightning.
The ship was struck and set on fire and almost immediately was a
mass of flames. Captain Day, his wife and two young children, with
the ship's crew, left in two boats. After three days of suffering, the
weather being very cold and stormy, all hands were picked up by a
passing vessel and taken to Fayal.

DANIEL BARNES

THE ship *Daniel Barnes* was built by William Rogers at Bath,
Maine, and was launched in August, 1877. She was 210 feet, by
39:9, by 24 feet, with a registered tonnage of 1435. Her managers
and principal owners were R. P. Buck & Co. of New York, of which
firm Daniel Barnes was a member. After Mr. Buck's death, Mr.
Barnes carried on the business under the former style until sailing-
ship days were about over when he retired to become cashier of the
Seaman's Savings Bank and subsequently its president. Mr. Barnes
never married, yet he maintained a fine home in Brooklyn until his
death some six years ago, at the age of eighty-eight years.

The ship *Daniel Barnes* was operated in the general carrying trade, making voyages to all parts of the world. Her career appears to have been uneventful and her voyages were made without mishaps of any consequence. In December, 1897, she sailed from New York with case oil for Hong Kong and was burned in the Straits of Malacca.

Capt. Joseph G. Stover, a native of Maine, took command of the *Daniel Barnes* when she was launched and continued in her until his death in April, 1892, when the ship was at Puget Sound. The Captain was then quite an old man and had sailed for R. P. Buck & Co. for many years, taking their ship *Free Trade* on her being built in 1854 and continuing in her over ten years. Later on he was master of the *Bennington* and other ships. He was a successful shipmaster and stood high in his profession. For many years Mrs. Stover and daughter made their home on board the *Daniel Barnes* and the family enjoyed a happy life.

Capt. J. Arpe was appointed master of the *Barnes* after the death of Captain Stover and continued in her until she was burned.

DAUNTLESS

THE ship *Dauntless* was built by Maxson, Fish & Co. at Mystic, Conn., and was launched in December, 1869. She registered 995 tons and was 181 feet, by 35, by 22:9 feet. She crossed a skysail yard on the mainmast, was of handsome model in common with all other products of Mystic yards, and was frequently described as closely resembling a yacht in general appearance.

Prior to 1879 the *Dauntless* was engaged in trade with San Francisco, making in all seven passages to that port from New York. In 1871-1872 she made two round voyages between San Francisco and Australia. After 1879 she was operated between Atlantic ports and the East Indies with the exception that in 1882 she made a passage from New York to the Columbia River, thence going to Manila and Boston. Her passages averaged well as to length and include one from

New York to San Francisco in 118 days and one, her last, from Manila to Boston in 96 days.

In August, 1879, the *Dauntless*, after having discharged a cargo of guano from the Peruvian coast, was proceeding from Dunkirk to New York, when she got ashore on the English coast. At first it appeared as though she would prove a total loss but fortunately she was floated without material damage being sustained. Aside from this she escaped mishaps of consequence during the course of her voyages. Her end came during the autumn of 1883 when she was driven ashore by a squall while on the African coast, having been at the time anchored some three miles off. Captain Chester being ashore at the time, chief officer Robert McDonald attempted to make sail and work out to sea but could not gain an offing. The ship went to pieces a few hours after she struck but all hands were saved in the boats.

The first master of the *Dauntless* was Capt. Robert P. Wilbur who left her early in 1875 to take the new ship *M. P. Grace* and he is more particularly referred to in account of that ship. On his last passage in the *Dauntless* Captain Wilbur picked up the crew of the British ship *Cornwallis*, from San Francisco for Liverpool, which had been wrecked on Pitcairn Island. They were landed at New York and for this act the ship was awarded some £200 sterling by the British Government.

Captain Wilbur was succeeded in the *Dauntless* by Capt. Daniel W. Chester, a native of Noank, near Mystic. Captain Chester had previously been master of the three-masted schooner *William C. Bee* of Noank and was succeeded therein by his brother, Capt. Chas. I. Chester.

DON QUIXOTE

THE ship *Don Quixote* was built at Medford, Mass., by John T. Foster for William Hammond and others of Boston and was launched in October, 1868; 176 feet, by 37:5, by 23:7 feet and 1174 tons register.

On her maiden voyage the *Don Quixote* sailed from Boston, Dec.

9, 1868, under command of Capt. W. H. Nelson, bound for San Francisco. Soon after getting clear of the land she encountered heavy gales which became of hurricane force and during the course of which the ship was dismasted and had her hull badly damaged. On putting about for New York she was picked up and towed there, arriving Jan. 5, 1869. After being repaired and refitted she sailed February 4th and arrived at San Francisco after a passage of 149 days. This disaster appears to have been the only one she met with.

The *Don Quixote* made one other passage from New York to San Francisco, being 156 days on the way. The two returns were to Liverpool in 139 and 146 days respectively. The rest of her career while an American ship was spent in trade with the East Indies and China, and although she was a fine ship, of good model, her passages were made in from fair to slow time.

Following the arrival of the *Don Quixote* at New York, in June, 1879, from Manila, she was sold for $30,000 to L. F. Kalkman of Bremen, and went under the German flag without change of name. Some ten years later she was resold to parties in Christiania, Norway, and registers of 1896 list her as still operating under her original name rigged as a bark.

The shipmasters who were in command of the *Don Quixote* for the longest periods were Capt. W. H. Nelson, who is mentioned in account of the ship *Northern Light*, and Capt. Chas. T. King, who had her the six years preceding her sale.

A fine medium-clipper ship named *Don Quixote* was also a product of a Medford shipyard, being built by Samuel Lapham in 1853. She was employed in trade with San Francisco and the East Indies and had a good sailing record. In 1864 she was sold to go under the French flag, becoming the *St. Aubin* of Havre.

E. B. SUTTON

THE ship *E. B. Sutton* was built and owned by Isaac F. Chapman of New York and was launched from the Chapman yard at Bath, Maine, in August, 1881, Samuel P. Hitchcock being the master builder. She was 228 feet, by 48, by 25 feet and of 1758 tons, net, register. Originally she crossed but one skysail yard, that on the mainmast, but shortly thereafter she became a three skysail-yard ship and is best known under that rig. For many years she was one of the most prominent American merchant ships afloat and was always spoken of as a handsome vessel in all respects, alow and aloft.

After Mr. Chapman's death in January, 1895, his business was carried on by his son-in-law Albert G. Ropes, who was a partner in the Chapman firm, although he had no financial interest in its vessel property. Following the business depression of 1907-1908, the affairs of the firm were taken charge of by an attorney who wound up the business. The *Sutton* was sold to the Scully Towing & Transportation Co. and converted into a barge for operation along the Atlantic coast. During the World War she was fitted out and rigged as a bark but after making one passage or so her spars were again removed and she resumed her career as a coal carrier at the end of a tow rope. A year ago she was still listed as being in service as a barge owned by the Neptune Line of New York.

The *Sutton* was named after the senior member of the firm Sutton & Co., who for many years loaded ships out of New York and Philadelphia for San Francisco and Portland, Ore., on a commission basis, later on chartering for a lump sum. Mr. Sutton died in May, 1891, at an advanced age, leaving six sons engaged in the shipping business. When they were forced to liquidate, the business was taken over by Flint & Co. and Dearborn & Co., who took the firm name of Flint, Dearborn & Co., and subsequently with others, organized the American-Hawaiian Steamship Co. The formation of this company closed to sailing ships what is now known as the Intercostal Trade.

Between 1882 and 1901 the *Sutton* made from Atlantic ports to the Orient two voyages and to San Francisco fourteen. The average

of the latter is 134 days; two from New York were made in 115 and
116 days. The average of the returns to New York or Liverpool is
116 days. From 1901 until she was sold she was operated in trade
with the Far East, her passages therein being also made in very good
average time. In 1902, when in command of Captain Butman, she
passed St. Helena when 64 days out from Hiogo bound for New
York and on the following voyage was at Manila in 108 days from
New York. She made several runs from Honolulu to Philadelphia
with sugar and these always compared favorably in point of time with
those of other first-class ships going over the course at about the same
period.

The first commander of the *E. B. Sutton* was Capt. C. O. Carter
who is said to have been master of the ship *Monte Rosa* for the five
years prior to her sale foreign. Aside from one voyage when he was
relieved by his brother E. L. Carter, Capt. C. O. Carter continued in
the *Sutton* until 1897 when he retired from the sea. The Captain, who
was a native of Woolwich, Me., was a first-class navigator and highly
respected by all with whom he came into contact. On one occasion he
fell into the hold of his ship and received severe injuries to his head.
Later, at times, he was rather excitable but always had his affairs well
in command and continued a thoroughly competent shipmaster.

Capt. Andrew L. Carver, who had previously been master of the
ship *Iceberg*, succeeded Captain Carter in the *Sutton*, making two
voyages, when Capt. James P. Butman of Searsport took command
and continued in the ship until she was sold. On the last passage of
the *Sutton*, Hong Kong to New York, he made the run from the Cape
of Good Hope to destination in 42 days. Later he was for a time in
command of a four-masted schooner in which he had an interest and
after giving her up, retired from sea life. The first command of Captain Butman was the Searsport ship *John Bunyan* and after her he had
the ship *Marcia C. Day*, in which he made the run from Callao to
New York in 80 days, a very good passage for a vessel of the model
of the *Day*. Later he was master of the ships *Louis Walsh, Abner
Coburn, William H. Connor, Governor Robie, Elizabeth* and *Henry
B. Hyde*, making in the latter a run from New York to San Francisco

in 108 days. The Captain ranked in the highest class of American shipmasters, being an excellent navigator and a good, energetic manager and business man who always made money for his owners. He died at his home in Searsport in January, 1920, aged seventy-two years.

While Captain Butman was in command of the *William H. Connor* he had as chief mate a young man who afterwards became prominent as a steamship master, Mr. James B. Parke. Parke had previously been chief officer of the bark *Edward Cushing* which in 1893 became waterlogged in the North Atlantic, the crew being 16 days on the wreck before being taken off by a passing schooner. Mate Parke made a number of voyages on the *Connor* under Captain Butman and his successor, Capt. John G. Pendleton, and then left sailing ships to go into steam. For a time he was with the New York & Porto Rico Steamship Co., who thought so well of him that they gave him command of their new steamer *Pathfinder*. Later on Captain Parke went into the service of the American-Hawaiian Steamship Co. as master, and commanded a number of their steamers, his last being the *Dakotan*, in 1915. During the World War he was with the Shipping Board and thereafter was a pilot commissioner and marine surveyor at New York until ill health compelled his complete retirement in June, 1927. He died at his home in Searsport in February, 1928, at the age of sixty years, a sincere and modest man who stood very high in his profession.

E. F. SAWYER

THE ship *E. F. Sawyer* was built at Bath, Maine, by Goss & Sawyer, and was launched in May, 1883. She was 230:4 feet, by 43:4, by 27 feet and of 1897 tons register. Her owners were Capt. John R. Kelley, John O. and F. H. Patten and A. B. Haggett of Bath, Charles E. Moody of Boston, and others, including Capt. Fred B. Dinsmore, who was in command of the ship all her sea life. Elijah F. Sawyer, in whose honor the ship was named, joined Capt. Guy C. Goss in establishing the firm of Goss & Sawyer, in 1866, and when the business was taken over in 1884 by the New England Shipbuilding Co. he was yard superintendent of that concern until November, 1886, when he resigned.

The first voyage of the *E. F. Sawyer* was from New York to San Francisco and Havre. The second from Cardiff to San Francisco and Liverpool. The third from Cardiff to San Francisco and Antwerp, and the fourth and last from Antwerp to San Francisco and Falmouth. After arriving at Falmouth in November, 1887, she was ordered to Hull for discharge. On November 22d, when off Folkstone, she was run down by the British steamer *Palinurus*, from China for London, and was beached but became a total loss. Suit was entered against the steamer but was decided against the ship because, although she had a fixed light astern, no flare was used.

The *Sawyer's* four voyages were made in fair average time and without mishap.

Capt. Fred B. Dinsmore, who belonged to Richmond, Me., had commanded the ship *Undaunted* for ten years and the *Chesebrough* for five years, before taking the *Sawyer*. Later he was for a short time in the *Eureka* and also in the brig *Galilee*, a South Sea Island trader. His last commands were schooners. For some years prior to his death he made his home in Alameda, Cal.

ECLIPSE

THE *Eclipse* was a three skysail-yard ship built by Goss & Sawyer at Bath, Maine, and launched in July, 1878. She was 221:7 feet, by 40:3, by 24:4 feet and registered 1536 tons. She was built for J. H. Kimball, a prominent shipowner of Bath, and his associates. In 1891 she was purchased by Lewis, Anderson & Co. of San Francisco, and they, in 1896, sold her to Eschen & Minor of the same port, who were her owners during the remainder of her sea life.

Prior to 1892 the voyages of the *Eclipse*, from Atlantic ports, were to San Francisco or the Far East, being about equally divided. Her first passage was from Wiscasset, Me., to Madras with ice, and took

104 days. She met with but minor mishaps and her voyages were made in good average time, the shortest to San Francisco being 128 days from New York, and from San Francisco, 113 days to Liverpool. After 1892, except for a passage from Puget Sound to Greenock, she was operated in the Pacific. In 1897 she crossed in ballast from Kobe to San Francisco in 27 days, and two years later ran from Puget Sound to Algoa Bay in 90 days.

On Oct. 16, 1907, the *Eclipse* sailed from Newcastle, N. S. W., for San Francisco and all went well until December 4th when heavy gales were encountered and two days later the foretopmast and main topgallant mast were carried away, and the ship started to leak. However, the pumps kept the leak under until Jan. 6, 1908, when, in another gale, the ship commenced to fill and it became evident that she was doomed. Capt. C. B. Larsen ordered the boats provisioned and he with eight men left the ship in the lifeboat. Mate Cameron and six men took the ship's boat but she was immediately capsized, her people being picked up by the captain's boat. Their position was 950 miles from Honolulu; the boat was overloaded and due to the loss of provisions that had been in the mate's boat, there was insufficient food and water. All hands suffered severely, being exposed to a tropical sun, blistered by day, and nearly frozen nights. Contrary to Captain Larsen's orders three of the men insisted on smoking and thereby becoming very thirsty, they drank sea water and ultimately became insane and died. The ship *Fort George*, bound for Honolulu from San Francisco, passed within two miles of the boat but it was not seen and the ship went on to the utter dismay of the *Eclipse* crew who were even then too weak to shout or otherwise signal for assistance. However, they continued at the oars to the extent of their strength and after being 13 days in the boat they were gladdened by sighting land, one of the Hawaiian Islands. The boat was, however, then carried off by strong currents and all hands were ready to give up when in three days land again appeared and they were able to effect a landing at Hana. All were in a pitiable condition, some temporarily insane, but on being subsequently taken to an hospital in Honolulu, they recovered and were sent to San Francisco by steamer.

The *Eclipse* was built to be commanded by Capt. Dennis McCobb Humphreys of Brunswick, Me., who, as a young man, helped on the books in the shipyard of his father, Maj.-Gen. John C. Humphreys. At the age of nineteen "Denny," as he was known by his friends all his life, shipped on the *Annie Kimball*, engaged in transatlantic trade, and when twenty-five he became her master. In 1867 he had the bark *C. O. Whitmore* built and commanded her until 1872 when he supervised the building of the ship *John H. Kimball*. Leaving Japan in 1876 with a cargo of rice for Amsterdam he made the passage to Niew Dieppe, whence the cargo was lightered sixty miles through an old canal to its destination. Later the ship sailed for Cardiff to load coal for Hong Kong but while the pilot was in charge, she stranded on the island of Terschelling and although Captain Humphreys and his crew stood by for two months trying to get her off, their efforts were unsuccessful, so she was sold for about $1500 and eventually was broken up. The *Eclipse* was the Captain's next ship and he continued in her until 1883 when he sold his interest to remain ashore and engage in the insurance business but soon gave that up to become an inspector for Lloyds.

During his career as shipmaster Captain Humphreys doubled Cape Horn twelve times and the Cape of Good Hope eight times, besides making many transatlantic voyages. In 1865, while on a passage from New Orleans to Liverpool, in the *Annie Kimball*, he fell in with the ship *Harry of the West*, on a similar voyage, the latter vessel being a mass of flames. Captain Humphreys was successful in rescuing the crew of twenty men and the following day the master of the burned ship was able to render valuable assistance in repairing the *Kimball's* rudder which had been disabled. On that same passage Captain Humphreys launched his boats and picked up the crew of a Dutch brig, waterlogged, near the entrance to St. George Channel. For some ten years the Captain was accompanied on his voyages by his wife and some of his children were born at sea.

Capt. Joseph R. Shillaber purchased Captain Humphrey's interest in the *Eclipse* and was in command until she was sold to San Francisco parties. The Captain's prior commands had been the ships *Cal-*

cutta and *Grandee* and the bark *C. O. Shillaber*. Captain Shillaber narrowly escaped death by drowning while the *Eclipse* was at Kobe in May, 1890. When going ashore with two men in the dingey, an oar was lost and in an attempt to regain it, the boat was overturned. Fortunately, however, a couple of sampans were near enough to rescue the three men.

EDWARD O'BRIEN (SECOND)

THE ship *Edward O'Brien*, built and owned by the party after whom she was named, was launched at Thomaston, Maine, in November, 1863, and measured 200 feet, by 40:5, by 28 feet, registering 1803 tons. She was the second ship bearing the name, the original *Edward O'Brien*, of 797 tons, having been built by Mr. O'Brien at Warren, Me., in 1848, and sold at the outset of the Civil War to go under the British flag as the *Arthur*. In 1882 Mr. O'Brien built a larger *Edward O'Brien* which became known as the "Big Edward," to distinguish her from the ship built in 1863, which was called the "Little Edward." In October, 1883, both ships were in port at San Francisco, and in May, 1887, the same tug that towed the "Little Edward" to sea from Puget Sound, then picked up the "Big Edward" off Cape Flattery and took her through the Straits of Juan de Fuca into the Sound.

The maiden passage of the "Little Edward" was from New York to San Francisco and in 1867 she made a similar run, these being her only direct trips from the Atlantic to the Golden Gate, although she made several by way of South American West Coast ports, the last of which was in 1883. During the interim she had been employed in the transatlantic deal and cotton or the South American coal and guano trades. For the nine years subsequent to 1883 she was operated on the Pacific Ocean, trading coastwise to a small extent but mainly carrying lumber from Puget Sound to South America or Australia, generally returning to the Coast with coal from Newcastle. In 1893 she took lumber and spars from Vancouver to London, having the very long passage of seven months. Then after crossing the Atlantic she loaded coal at Newport News for Panama and after arrival out was converted into a barge. As a rule her passages were of more than average length.

While on a passage from Liverpool in 1879 the *O'Brien* rescued the crew of the British bark *Clarence* which had been abandoned at sea in a sinking condition. A year or so previously she had picked up the crew of the British ship *J. P. Wheeler*, for which service Capt. Geo. E. Wallace had been awarded a handsome silver mug by the English Government.

Among the mishaps met with by the *O'Brien* was one in 1867 when, while bound to San Francisco, the rudder was twisted off near Cape Horn and the ship was entirely unmanageable for fourteen hours. Much water got below and damaged the cargo to a considerable extent. The voyage was completed with a jury rudder. In December, 1872, she arrived at Falmouth from Callao in such a leaky condition that Captain Oliver refused to obey orders to proceed to Hamburg until repairs had been made. The ship went on graving dock at Liverpool and was not ready for another voyage until six months later. In 1891 the hull of the ship was practically rebuilt while afloat alongside the wharf at San Francisco, the job taking one hundred men two months to complete and costing about $30,000. The keelsons were replaced and as the ship's fore- and mainmasts were of iron, the work of jacking them up was difficult. However, everything was completed in such a satisfactory manner that the inspectors restored the former classification of the ship which had expired.

The Hon. Edward O'Brien was of Scotch-Irish descent and was born in Warren, Me., in July, 1793. As a boy he spent several years sailing on coasting vessels but soon took up the shipbuilding trade and in 1823 began building on his own account in Warren. Later he moved his yard to Thomaston and is said to have built in all over 100 vessels. He frequently owned the cargoes carried by his ships and for years was his own insurer. After 1858 it was his custom to own entirely the vessels he built and it is said his only departure from this rule was the presentation of a 1/16th interest in a ship to his friend Dr. J. B. Walker. His ships were strong and staunch, a peculiarity in the larger ones being their rather light spars and a broad strake destitute of paint running from stem to stern along the sides.

Mr. O'Brien was of large frame, over six feet in height. For more than half a century he was one of the most famous American shipbuilders and owners. A man of great enterprise, he built large steam sawmills in Thomaston; established lime kilns and a bank and was the first shipbuilder to procure white oak timber from the South, cut from his own lands. He held many public offices and represented his native town in the Legislature for several terms. He was always esteemed for his integrity and philanthropy. He died at Thomaston, May 6, 1882, retaining almost to the last his full faculties, conducting his own correspondence and directing the movements of his large fleet of ships, in itself an undertaking of great magnitude. His monument is a life-size figure representing him standing beside an anchor on which his hand rests. At the time of his death he owned upwards of 20,000 tons of shipping and had on the stocks the frame of a large ship which, on being completed, was named in his honor by his son and successor, Edward E. O'Brien.

The *Edward O'Brien* was built to be commanded by Capt. Geo. W. Gilchrest, a prominent shipmaster and father-in-law of William R. Grace. The Captain was a native of St. George, Me., and his first occupation was that of school teacher. He later went to sea in small vessels, some of which he commanded. Subsequently he sailed in ships engaged in foreign trade and had been master of the *Rochambeau*, *Chimborazo* and *S. Curling*, all belonging to Thomaston, before taking the *O'Brien*. In that ship he made only a few voyages, then retiring to engage in the ship chandlery business in New York as Gilchrest, White & Co., and was so occupied until his death in June, 1883, at the age of seventy-one years.

Capt. David P. Oliver, who later was master of the "Big" *Edward O'Brien*, succeeded Captain Gilchrest, and then in turn came Capt. Geo. E. Wallace, who was later well known in connection with his command, the *J. B. Walker*; Capt. Joseph Henry and Capt. Thos. G. Libby, both of whom were subsequently in the *General Knox*; and Capt. Charles Taylor.

EDWARD O'BRIEN (THIRD)

THE ship *Edward O'Brien*, which was under construction when Mr. O'Brien died, was completed by his son Edward E. O'Brien and was launched in November, 1882. She was 259 feet, by 42, by 28:6 feet and registered 2157 tons. She was the last ship built in the O'Brien yards and was generally known as the "Big Edward," to distinguish her from a previous ship of the same name built in 1863, which, although of 1800 tons register, was called the "Little Edward," to prevent confusion, as both vessels were being operated during the thirteen years prior to 1895.

On her maiden voyage the "Big Edward" took cotton to Liverpool, coal thence to San Francisco and wheat back to Liverpool. Thereafter except for three or four voyages in the Pacific Coast coal trade, one round between the Golden Gate City and Sydney, and one voyage with case oil to Japan and return to Boston from the Philippines, she was continuously employed in trade between San Francisco and Liverpool or New York. For a vessel modeled to carry large cargoes her sailing record is good. The average of nine out of her ten Cape Horn passages to San Francisco is 132 days, one of 113 days from Liverpool being the shortest, and of those to the Atlantic 126 days and 110 days respectively. In 1883 she was 17 days, 18 hours, from 50° S., to the Line in the Pacific and in 1884 made the run around Cape Horn to the westward in nine days. Her passage to San Francisco in 1885 was very long and tedious, 182 days, she being 42 days to the Line from Liverpool, 32 days covering 12 degrees of latitude in the South Atlantic and not sighting Cape Horn until 103 days out. On one of her passages she lost some sails and spars in a circular storm in the North Atlantic, also having the cargo shifted and this appears to have been the only mishap she had prior to her loss.

The *O'Brien* sailed from Nanaimo, B. C., in February, 1899, with coal for Honolulu, and arrived off the entrance to the harbor February 27th, coming to an anchor. Her cables parted and she went on the reef, becoming a total loss. Prospects for salvage appeared to be so small that when vessel and cargo were sold at auction, only $1,225 was realized.

The first commander of the *O'Brien* was Capt. Wm. T. O'Brien, a nephew of Edward O'Brien. On the passage from San Francisco to Liverpool, in 1886, the wife of Captain O'Brien and the chief mate of the ship were washed overboard and lost and the Captain then retired for a time. Later he took the ship *Alex. McCallum* and was in her the four years prior to her loss in 1893. He was succeeded in the *O'Brien* by Capt. David P. Oliver who continued in the ship until his death at sea in February, 1898. The vessel had left Cebu, in October, 1897, bound to Boston, the Captain being ill when leaving port. His condition did not improve and his son, who was mate, put into St. Helena for medical assistance, the ship then being 123 days out from the Philippines. After a three days stay the voyage was resumed but Captain Oliver passed away the evening the ship sailed. The mate, Edwin P. Oliver, had his father's remains placed in a sealed box and they were subsequently interred at Thomaston.

Captain Oliver was born in Warren, Me., in November, 1830, and commenced a seafaring career at the age of twelve. He was master in his early twenties and commanded the ships *Ironside, Aquila,* "Little" *Edward O'Brien, Eric the Red, Joseph S. Spinney* and *Alex Gibson,* before taking the "Big" *Edward O'Brien.* He was a man above the average size, jovial, big-hearted and whole-souled in proportion and was in every way a fine type of the high class gentleman shipmaster.

On completion of the voyage from Cebu to Boston, in 1898, the *Edward O'Brien* was purchased by Flint & Co. of New York, who sent her to San Francisco from Baltimore with coal, under command of Capt. Richard Banfield. Capt. Ansel D. Lothrop took her after her arrival on the Pacific Coast but she was lost during the course of his first voyage in her. Captain Lothrop's career as a shipmaster is contained in account of the ship *Conqueror* and that of Captain Banfield in that of the bark *St. James,* both being in "American Merchant Ships," Series I.

ELCANO

THE ship *Elcano* was built by John Currier, Jr., at Newburyport, Mass., in 1864, and was 196 feet, by 38, by 24 feet; 1228 tons per register. She was built for John N. and William Cushing of Newburyport, who, in 1882, sold her to go under the German flag. Her subsequent career appears to have been short as she is not listed in registers of 1887.

The *Elcano* was built for the East India trade and the greater number of her voyages were with Calcutta and Bombay, they originating or terminating at Liverpool, London, or European continental ports. She was never engaged in the Cape Horn trade. Capt. Lawrence W. Brown, who was in command during fourteen out of the eighteen years spent by the *Elcano* under the American flag, said she was a successful ship, made several remarkably quick passages and turned her cargo out in first-class condition. For these reasons she stood well with exporters of valuable merchandise and commanded the highest going freight rates.

In July, 1879, the *Elcano* was run down while off the African coast, bound from Bombay to Havre with cotton, by H.B.M. troop ship *Euphrates*, and escaped being cut in two by a very narrow margin. She was towed the 170 miles to Simonstown and repaired in the government dockyards. After discharging her cotton at Havre she left for New York in ballast and made the passage in 16½ days. Having encountered strong gales from the eastward at starting she had been unable to discharge the pilot, so carried him to New York. He was returned by steamer and was home 24 days after he had left there.

Capt. James K. Pritchard of Newburyport was the first commander of the *Elcano* but was washed overboard and drowned before the ship reached Calcutta on her maiden passage from Boston. When the ship returned home Capt. Albert Cheever was appointed master and completed two voyages. On the third, while the *Elcano* was bound from Calcutta to London, he was stabbed by the Malay cook who, one night, ran amuck. The maniac had slipped up behind the second mate, the officer on watch, and slashed him so badly that he was left as dead.

CAPT. ISAAC N. JACKSON
Ship *Belvedere*

CAPT. GEO. W. K. MASTERS
Ship *Alex. McCallum*

CAPT. ALEX. H. NICHOLS
Ship *St. Mark*

CAPT. DANIEL C. NICHOLS
Ship *Wandering Jew*

CAPT. JAMES P. BUTMAN
Ship *E. B. Sutton*

CAPT. CLIFTON CURTIS
Ship *Belle of Bath*

CAPT. DAVID GILMORE
Ship *Servia*

CAPT. DAVID J. HODGMAN
Ship *Belle O'Brien*

Then slipping into the cabin he surprised Captain Cheever and chief mate Fred A. Kezar and after wounding them, killed the steward. Mr. Kezar, however, was not seriously injured and overpowering the assassin had him put in irons. Six days later the ship put into Port Louis for medical aid but surgeons said that Captain Cheever could not live and the same opinion was expressed by doctors from the U.S.S. *Hartford* which was subsequently met at St. Helena. The ship had a long spell of bad weather off the Cape and the passage from Mauritius to London took nearly four months. Prior to arrival the only American member of the ship's crew died and the Malay assassin also died. Captain Cheever was apparently convalescing when the ship made London and subsequently fully recovered his health. Mate Kezar was fairly used up by the time the passage ended, having been the only officer on duty for four months. Capt. Lawrence W. Brown was sent to London to assume command of the ship and continued in her as master until she was sold. The seafaring career of Captain Brown is given in the account of the ship *Mary L. Cushing*.

Captain Cheever was a native of Castine, Me., but made his home in Newburyport many years and the ships he commanded were owned at that place. After regaining his strength he bought into the ship *Calumet* and made a few voyages in her but she was lost on Bermuda, in 1873, and the Captain then retired from sea life. He was president of the Marine Society of Newburyport three years and vice-president the previous eight years. He passed away in January, 1898, aged eighty years. Captain Kezar's career as a shipmaster is given in account of the ship *Charles Dennis*, appearing in "American Merchant Ships," Series I.

EMILY F. WHITNEY

THE ship *Emily F. Whitney* was built by Abiel Gove at East Boston and was launched in October, 1880. She was 193 feet, by 37:7, by 23:1 feet, 1207 tons register. She was owned by J. H. Flitner of Boston, Leonard Whitney of Watertown, Mass., L. A. Roby of Nashua, N. H., and her first commander, Capt. Henry B.

Rollins, their respective interests being 17, 16, 8 and 14 sixty-fourths. Parties in Boston owned the few remaining shares. She was managed by J. H. Flitner & Co. of Boston for the first seventeen years of her career. In 1898 she was reported as being wrecked at Shanghai during a typhoon but this was not correct although she appears to have been driven ashore and subsequently was sold as shipping registers of 1899 list her as the British ship *Emily F. Whitney* of Shanghai with T. R. Twentyman as her managing owner.

In 1900, following her arrival at Honolulu, after a five months passage from New York, the *Whitney* was sold to Alexander & Baldwin who employed her in the Island sugar and export lumber trades on the Pacific, when they resold her to the Alaska Salmon Co., and she was operated as a "salmon packer" until 1924, when she was laid up at San Francisco. In December, 1928, she was purchased by Earle Derby, an official of the Standard Oil Co., who had her reconditioned and refitted to be preserved as a souvenir of the days when "wooden ships and iron men" upheld the prestige of the American flag on the high seas. Now at anchor at Sausalito, across the bay from San Francisco, fully rigged as a bark, as she had been during the last years of her life as a sailing vessel, she attracts much attention by her trim and shipshape appearance.

On her maiden voyage the *Whitney* sailed from Boston Dec. 30, 1880, and was 126 days to San Francisco; thence 115 days to Liverpool. She then returned to San Francisco in 140 days, and went back to the United Kingdom in 141 days. Her third voyage was from Boston to Melbourne with general cargo; thence to San Francisco in ballast; after which she made a round voyage to British Columbia and on return to San Francisco went to Antwerp in 123 days. She was then diverted from the Cape Horn to the Cape of Good Hope run, making voyages to Melbourne, Hong Kong and Shanghai. The Australian voyages were generally completed by the ship taking coal from Newcastle to Manila and sugar and hemp thence to New York or Boston. On one occasion she sailed in ballast from Boston to Barbados to load back with sugar and was the first vessel to make such a voyage. After her purchase by Alexander & Baldwin she took sugar from Honolulu to San Francisco, her appearance at the latter port, in June, 1900, being the first for sixteen years. At that time she was in excellent condition and had recently been assigned the highest rating in Bureau Veritas.

The voyages of the *Whitney* were made in fair average time and during her long career she was exceptionally fortunate in escaping damage from the elements. Her stranding at Shanghai appears to have been her nearest approach to disaster but she could not then have been materially injured as following her return to New York it was only necessary to have a portion of the shoe replaced.

The *Emily F. Whitney* was built to be commanded by Capt. Henry B. Rollins of Cape Cod, who had been master for many years of the bark *Nettie Merryman*, of which Dearborn Brothers of New York were managing owners. Captain Rollins served a long time in the *Whitney*, and on leaving her, retired from the sea. He passed away during the summer of 1928 at the age of sixty-five years.

Among other commanders of the *Whitney*, while she was engaged on long distance voyages, were Capt. Andrew S. Pendleton of Searsport and Capt. Geo. A. Dearborn. The former is further referred to in the account of his later ship the *Aryan*. Captain Dearborn took command of the *Whitney* in 1890 and had a good passage of 85 days from New York to Melbourne, thence from Newcastle to Acapuco and home by way of the West Coast of South America. The Captain subsequently made two other Australian voyages in the ship after which he stayed ashore and for twelve years was connected with the New York Dock Department. He was a native of Pittston, Me., and originally had been many years in command of transatlantic packets among which were the *Yorkshire* and *Switzerland*. Later he went into steam on the Atlantic Coast, but subsequently returned to sail, taking the *Whitney*. He died in November, 1915, aged nearly ninety-three years. A brother, David B. Dearborn, formerly of the firm of Dearborn Brothers, and for many years one of the most prominent shipping men in New York, died in February, 1930, at the age of ninety-eight years.

EMILY REED

THE ship *Emily Reed* was built by A. R. Reed at Waldoboro, Maine, and was launched in November, 1880. She was 215 feet, by 40:6, by 24 feet and of 1565 tons register. Yates & Porterfield of New York were her managing owners. In April, 1880, after her arrival in Puget Sound from Hong Kong, she was purchased by Hind, Rolph & Co. of San Francisco, at a figure reported to be $40,000 and that firm owned her the remainder of her career. Her first commander was Capt. O. D. Sheldon of Bowdoinham, Me.

Prior to 1900 the *Reed* was operated in trade mainly between Atlantic ports and those of Australia, China or Japan. She made only four passages to San Francisco by way of Cape Horn but on several occasions crossed the Pacific from the Orient to load grain for Europe. After her purchase by San Francisco parties she was operated in the Pacific Ocean, generally taking lumber to South Africa or Australia and returning to the coast or to Honolulu with coal from Newcastle. She was called a good ship and made fair passages.

The *Emily Reed* met with a number of mishaps during the course of her voyages. On her passage from New York to San Francisco in 1885 she fell in with heavy weather off Cape Horn during which the cargo shifted, a number of spars were sprung and most of her fresh water supply was lost, so Capt. Sheldon bore up for Montevideo to effect necessary repairs. In 1888, when bound from San Francisco to Hull, she sprung aleak when some ten days at sea but as it was believed that this could be controlled by the pumps, the voyage was continued. Later on, however, when near the Line, a particularly severe storm was encountered and the leak increased to such an extent that the crew became exhausted from pumping and Captain Sheldon was forced to put into Valparaiso. Following the completion of this passage the ship went out to Japan, then crossed to San Francisco and left that port in July, 1890, with wheat for Rio de Janeiro. On this passage fair weather was met with until the neighborhood of the Horn was reached when heavy gales and tremendous seas kept the ship practically submerged for four successive days. The forecastle was stove in and washed overboard with all the cooking utensils, the same sea taking also six of the crew, who were lost. The next morning two more men were swept overboard without any chance of being rescued. The ship was tossed about like a feather and was absolutely uncontrollable despite all that Captain Sheldon and his crew could do. After the gale subsided an old pot was found in a forward locker, after much rummaging, and this was put to use on a small stove in the cabin to cook the meagre meals for the greatly depleted crew. Much suffering from cold and lack of food was felt until the ship finally reached Rio. Additional men were shipped and the vessel went to New York in ballast, then loading back for San Francisco. Her troubles, however, were not at an end. When 66 days out on the passage, the ship being then well down in the South Atlantic, the rudderhead was sprung in a gale and the ship was put about for Rio de Janeiro where a new rudder had to be made. The passage of 95 days thence to San Francisco was uneventful but his repeated disastrous experiences in the ship appear to have been sufficient for Captain Sheldon for he then relinquished command. Prior to 1877 the Captain had been master of the Damariscotta-built ship *Criterion* and in that year he bought into the new ship *Mabel Clark*, 1661 tons, at that time the largest ship ever built at Waldoboro. Her career, however, was very short. Having crossed the Atlantic to Liverpool, she left that port in March, 1878, and during the following May went ashore to become a total loss on the island of Tristan d'Acunha.

Capt. Elbridge W. Simmons was sent to San Francisco to relieve Captain Sheldon in the *Emily Reed* and he, in November, 1895, was succeeded by Capt. Daniel C. Nichols of Searsport, who continued in her until she was sold. Captain Nichols' long career as a shipmaster is given in the account of ship *Wandering Jew* in "American Merchant Ships," Series I.

The first master of the *Emily Reed*, under her San Francisco owners, was Capt. G. A. Baker of Nova Scotia, who had been chief officer of the Pacific Mail steamship *China*. Captain Baker made a couple of voyages without incident but then began a series which resulted disastrously to the ship's owners. In 1902 she took lumber from Puget

Sound to Cape Town, thence proceeding to Hobart to load back with ironbark for Government work at the Cape. This cargo was duly laden and the ship sailed, but some time afterwards news was received that the ship was at Christchurch with Captain Baker sick. After an extended delay the passage was resumed and the vessel arrived at Simonstown and was discharged. Quite a while later word was received at San Francisco that Captain Baker was living ashore and the ship was practically deserted with no one in charge. Capt. James Davidson was immediately dispatched to look after the owners' interests but had to proceed by way of England. He found the *Reed* in poor condition, she having been extensively looted. After considerable difficulty Captain Baker was located and paid off, he then taking passage on a steamer to Australia where his wife was living.

At considerable expense the *Emily Reed* was again made ready for sea and proceeded to Newcastle, N. S. W., where she loaded coal for San Francisco, reaching that port nearly two years after having left Puget Sound. The ship then made several coastwise voyages and a further one to Australia. When about ready to sail from San Francisco, in July, 1907, for Newcastle, in ballast, to load back with coal for Portland, Ore., the command was turned over to Captain Kessel, who had been some four years master of the bark *Alden Besse*. Leaving Newcastle in November the ship encountered heavy weather and made slow progress. At 2 A.M. on Feb. 14, 1908, when 103 days out, she went ashore on the rocky coast of Oregon near the mouth of the Nehalem River. Captain Kessel's account of the disaster follows.

"When the ship struck, the mainmast jumped out of her and she broke in two just abaft the mainmast. Myself, wife and four men were on the after end while the mate and the rest of the crew were forward. The mate was getting a boat off the forward house when a particularly big sea swept everything and everybody forward overboard. The mate and four men managed to hang on to the boat but nine men were drowned. The boat was nearly swamped and in an effort to bail her out, the freshwater breakers were lost. After some days of suffering and hardship the boat's occupants made land, but one man, the cook, had died from drinking sea water.

"In the meantime the Captain and his companions were holding on to the after end of the ship. The mizzen rigging was cut so as to allow the mast to go over the side. After a time the after house broke loose from the hull and drifted closer inshore. A sailor named Sullivan, after being swept back by the breakers several times, managed to get a line ashore and attached to a tree. By means of the line the rest of the Captain's party were able to make a landing, after much buffeting by the breakers. The party then tramped some twelve miles before reaching an habitation.

"The ship was lost through an error in the chronometers, they showing her position to be sixty miles offshore when she struck. The weather was very foggy at the time."

Prior to taking command of the *Emily Reed*, Captain Kessel had been in the ship *Occidental* and after the loss of the *Reed* he was in the *Henry Villard*. After a seafaring life of some fifty years the Captain and his wife are now living on a small plot of ground on a small island near Seattle.

ENOCH TRAIN

THE ship *Enoch Train* was built in 1854 by Paul Curtis at East Boston for Isaac Rich & Co. and measured 209 feet, by 45:6, by 26 feet, registered tonnage, 1787. Early in her career she was purchased by William F. Weld & Co. of Boston, who were her owners until 1873 when they sold her to Henderson Bros. of Liverpool, and she went under the British flag. On Jan. 21, 1883, she sailed from New York for Bremen, at that time leaking to a slight extent, but her cargo being oil in barrels, this was not thought of moment. However, when not long out of port she met with heavy gales and the leak increased. On February 8th she had twelve feet of water in the hold, the pumping gear had given out and all her boats had been smashed. The brig *Lilly* then being sighted, it was decided to abandon the *Train* and the brig took off the crew in their boats and proceeded on her voyage to Plymouth. The *Train*, which had all along been sailing under her original name, then hailed from Nassau, N. P., and though a British ship, was said to be owned by Boston parties of whom James W. Edgett was the principal.

The *Train* was named in honor of Boston's then most prominent shipping merchant who, in addition to other activities, operated a line of large ships between that port and Liverpool, carrying passengers and cargo on a regular schedule. In 1852, Donald McKay had built a fine large clipper ship to the order of George Francis Train, a nephew of Enoch and connected with his firm, and according to young Train this ship was to have been named the *Enoch Train*. The senior member of the firm, however, not evidencing much appreciation for the honor about to be bestowed on him, young Train became piqued and on the ship being completed, had her called *Sovereign of the Seas*.

Prior to her sale in 1873 the *Train* was employed in the general carrying trade and had an eventful career. In 1863, on a passage from Liverpool to San Francisco, she sprung aleak and had to put into Rio de Janeiro for repairs. Four years later, when bound to the Pacific Coast from Philadelphia, she put into Norfolk, leaking and disabled. All hands except the ship's officers deserted. The subsequent passage to San Francisco took 167 days and the ship then had the long run of 143 days to Liverpool. After crossing to New York she loaded for San Francisco and after a momentous voyage reached that port 476 days out. On first making Cape Horn she was badly damaged by heavy gales and sprung aleak. She put about and arrived at Rio de Janeiro nearly four months after leaving New York. She was repaired and sailed, but again met with disaster and put back to Rio a second time, being on this occasion four months in port repairing. Underwriters suffered a loss of over $80,000 in connection with this voyage.

In October, 1872, when bound from Liverpool for Hong Kong with coal the *Train* was dismasted in a typhoon off the China Coast. In addition, the cargo shifted, bulwarks and boats were stove, the cabins flooded and stores spoiled. For two weeks the crew was steadily employed in cutting away wreckage, trimming cargo, etc., the ship rolling heavily and taking aboard much water. A passing steamer was signalled but went on without stopping and Captain Thompson had about despaired of ever being able to work out of his difficult position when the ship finally drifted near enough to a small island off the China Coast to be brought to an anchor. There she was seen by a passing Chinese gunboat which made an attempt to take her in tow but was unable to make headway against the strong currents. However, she took letters to Hong Kong which resulted in a steamer being sent to rescue the ship. In the interim another typhoon came on but fortunately the ship held to her anchors although she rolled rails under in the trough of the sea. The *Train* was three months at Hong Kong repairing, then going to Manila to load for New York. This voyage was the last made by the *Train* as an American ship.

Henderson Bros. are said to have bought the *Train* for the small sum of $10,000, but they were not her owners long, she being purchased by parties in Glasgow prior to 1878. While under the British flag she was employed in transatlantic trade, principally carrying oil.

Capt. Benjamin Thompson, who was master of the *Enoch Train* on the Hong Kong voyage in 1872, was later in command of the *Great Admiral* and is mentioned in the account of that ship.

EUREKA

THE ship *Eureka* was built by T. J. Southard & Son at Richmond, Maine, and was launched in June, 1876. She was 230:9 feet, by 42, by 26:5 feet and registered 1996 tons. She cost $110,000 and was a first-class ship in every way, having all the latest improvements known at that time, including an engine and condenser. Her builders owned a three-quarter interest, the other quarter being held equally by J. W. Elwell & Co. and Capt. James O. Woodworth, the ship having been built for him to command.

The first voyage of the *Eureka* was disastrous. She took deals to Liverpool and then loaded 400 tons of ballast and an equal amount of salt for Key West. During the evening of Nov. 8, 1876, she was struck by a hurricane and almost entirely dismasted, the hull also being damaged by floating wreckage. On December 6th she limped into Tybee, under jury rig, and was towed from there to New York.

After being repaired the *Eureka* loaded for San Francisco and for the following fifteen years was employed in trade with that port. During this period she made eleven passages around Cape Horn to the westward, seven of which were from New York; two from Baltimore and one each from Liverpool and Hull. All the return passages were with wheat, two being to Rio de Janeiro and the remainder to the United Kingdom or the Continent. Her shortest outward run was 124 days from New York and that homeward, 119 days to Havre and 20 days thence to New York. The passages to Rio de Janeiro occupied 69 and 91 days respectively.

Following the last arrival of the *Eureka* at San Francisco, which was in November, 1891, from Baltimore, she was laid up for a year and then went to the West Coast of South America to load nitrate for New York. On the latter passage she sprung aleak off Cape Horn, during a succession of heavy gales, and Captain Woodworth put back to Valparaiso for repairs. After the completion of the voyage the ship loaded for Melbourne and had a hard run out of 119 days. The ship lost a number of sails, the cargo shifted and the ship went over on beam ends. Oil was used on the seas with advantage and after much labor the ship was righted. Captain Woodworth's health, however, apparently suffered as a result of his experiences on his last two voyages, as he was reported very ill on arrival of the ship at Melbourne and shortly thereafter he committed suicide by shooting himself. Capt. Geo. T. Getchell was sent out to complete the voyage, which was to Hull with wheat.

The *Eureka* then made a couple of voyages to the Orient with case oil, in 1897, crossing the Pacific to load lumber for Yokohama. In March, 1899, she was sold to F. W. Munn of Philadelphia who had her converted into a coal barge, but her subsequent career appears to have been short for her name is not shown in lists after 1902.

In addition to the mishaps already mentioned, the *Eureka* met with a serious one on her passage to San Francisco in 1888, when Capt. F. E. Southard was relieving officer. When well down in the South Atlantic the ship encountered very heavy gales and leaked in the topsides to such an extent that she was put about for Rio de Janeiro. A portion of the cargo had to be discharged and the ship was in port three months repairing. The passage thence to San Francisco took 99 days with, contrary to the usual conditions, light winds and fine weather prevailing off Cape Horn.

Capt. James O. Woodworth, a native of Richmond, Me., was a very close friend of the Southard family and off and on commanded the *Eureka* for eighteen years. He had previously been master of the Southard ship *Moses Day*, which was also owned in part by Sewall, Day & Co. of Boston, and had been built in 1868. This ship was wrecked in December, 1873, on the coast of Mindanao, but all hands were able to reach Manila in her boats. Captain Woodworth was an experienced navigator though he is said to have not always been attentive to his duties, being of a convivial disposition, but his relations with his owners held him in good stead.

Capt. Fred B. Dinsmore, who is referred to in account of the ship *E. F. Sawyer*, was in command of the *Eureka* for five years. Her last master was Capt. W. B. Darrah.

EXPORTER

THE ship *Exporter* was built by G. W. Jackman at Newburyport, Mass., and was launched in January, 1874. She was 199 feet, by 38:2, by 24 feet and registered 1312 tons. Her bow was flaring, rather sharp, and she had a fairly long run aft, being described as approximating a medium clipper in model although her passages do not bear out this view. She, however, was a good looking ship, well built and cost $96,000. A ship of similar model, though a trifle smaller and named *Reporter*, was built by Mr. Jackman later in 1874 for the owners of the *Exporter*, Sumner, Swasey & Currier of Newburyport.

While designed for the general carrying trade the *Exporter*, prior to 1890, ran almost exclusively between Atlantic ports and the East Indies, most of her voyages being to Calcutta or Bombay. In April, 1890, she left New York for Sydney, thence going to various ports in the Pacific and then to Boston, the whole voyage occupying two years. She then took lumber from Portland, Maine, to Buenos Ayres where she was laid up for a spell on account of lack of business and then went to New York in ballast. Another lay up then ensued and no offer of purchase was received when the ship was advertised for sale. Finally she was chartered for general cargo to Sydney and had the fair run out of 93 days. On arrival a financial panic was found to prevail and the ship was again laid up. After three months Captain Kezar undertook the experiment of laying the *Exporter* on the berth for London and to the astonishment of everyone, tallow, hides and wool came forward in such quantities that in twenty days a full cargo was engaged.

After arrival at London in 1894, no business for the ship offering, all hands were paid off, a ship keeper put in charge and the ship offered for sale. People came from all parts of the Continent to look at her but made no offers. At last she was sold to Norwegians for the small sum of £1600 sterling. At that time she was the last full-rigged ship owned in Newburyport. In ship registers of 1908 she appears as the Italian bark *Fantasie* of Genoa, but the next year her name was dropped.

The voyage of the *Exporter*, which originated at New York in 1890 and terminated at Boston two years later, was replete with unusual incidents. On arrival at Sydney a strike of longshoremen was found to be in effect and when the ship was able to proceed to Newcastle to load for Honolulu, a similar state of affairs was found to be existing there. These conditions caused a detention to the ship of five months and when loaded and ready for sea, she suffered a further delay through being run down by a steamer and having the bowsprit and head gear carried away. She had a long run from Newcastle to Honolulu and was a year out from New York on arrival at Puget Sound from the Hawaiian port. In June, 1891, she left Vancouver for Melbourne and when near the Australian coast encountered a heavy gale during which the bowsprit was carried away and the deck load had to be jettisoned to save the ship. Captain Kezar's son was killed and his body washed overboard. The ship limped into Sydney and was there a month repairing. However, she finally got to Melbourne and after discharging, loaded one of the largest cargoes ever dispatched to Boston. That passage was made without incident and the ship was later put on dry dock for a thorough overhauling.

The first commander of the *Exporter* was Capt. John H. Brooks, who previously had been master of the ship *Edward Hymen* of New Orleans. In December, 1879, Captain Brooks sold his interest in the *Exporter* to Capt. Fred A. Kezar and except for two Calcutta voyages made by Capt. John T. Howard in 1888-1889 as relieving officer, Captain Kezar commanded the *Exporter* until she was sold in 1894. The seafaring career of the Captain is more particularly detailed in the account of the ship *Charles Dennis*, appearing in "American Merchant Ships," Series I.

After leaving the *Exporter*, Captain Howard served three years as master of the bark *Benj. F. Hunt, Jr.*, then retired from the sea to live at his home in Newburyport.

FANNIE TUCKER

THE ship *Fannie Tucker* was built by Hodgkins & Brown at Wiscasset, Maine, and was launched in November, 1875. She was 211 feet, by 40, by 24 feet, and of 1527 tons register. She was named after the daughter of Capt. Joseph Tucker, one of the principal owners of the ship although she was managed by William P. Lennox for some years and later by her commander, Capt. Silas N. Greenleaf, who held a number of shares. Capt. Joseph Tucker was the son of Capt. Richard H. Tucker and both had commanded and owned ships for many years. Following the death of Captain Joseph, the *Fannie Tucker* was sold in April, 1889, for $35,000 to A. F. Stafford, a sailmaker of New York, an American citizen who was said to really represent the firm of Troop & Son, shipowners, of St. John, N. B.

The *Fannie Tucker* made a couple of voyages to India, the outward cargoes being ice, and then for a time was operated in the California grain trade, making three round voyages. For three years she then remained in the Pacific making two voyages to Australia but being mostly employed in carrying coal from Seattle to San Francisco.

Later she took lumber from Puget Sound to the West Coast of South America and nitrate thence to New York where she was sold.

The career of the *Fannie Tucker* seems to have been beset with misfortunes. On her first voyage freight rates were so low on her arrival at Calcutta that she was laid up for a year and dried up to such an extent that she had to be overhauled and refitted at considerable expense. On her first passage from San Francisco to the United Kingdom, which was in 1880, she was discovered to be leaking badly when in latitude 38° S., and Captain Roberts bore up for Callao. On arriving off that port it was found to be blockaded by the Chilian war fleet so the ship proceeded south to Coquimbo. There a portion of the cargo had to be discharged and expenses for repairs, etc., amounted to some $10,000. After the arrival of the ship at San Francisco in October, 1884, from Cardiff, after a five months passage, she was laid up until November, 1885, when she went to British Columbia to load coal.

Under the Troop ownership the *Fannie Tucker* made a voyage to the Orient with case oil and on its completion loaded at New York for Tacoma. Sailing on July 5, 1891, she put into Bahia, in August, leaking badly. A portion of her cargo had been discharged, to facilitate repairs, when the ship was found to be on fire and she became a total loss. Charges of foul play were made but they were proved to be without foundation.

Capt. J. M. Roberts of Massachusetts commanded the *Fannie Tucker* the first six years. On arriving at Boston in March, 1877, in completion of the first voyage made by the ship, Captain Roberts reported having rescued the crew of the British ship *Kate Gregory*, which was on fire. Later on the British crew, headed by their captain and mate, attempted mutiny and were only kept down by show of force. Something over a month later they were landed at the Cape of Good Hope and when Captain Roberts was ashore, the Britishers carried off their boats which were being held for salvage. These were afterwards recovered, and on Captain Roberts continuing his voyage, they were left in charge of the United States Consul.

Capt. Silas N. Greenleaf purchased Captain Roberts' interest in the *Fannie Tucker*, taking command and continuing in her until she was sold. The Captain, who was born in Maine in 1837, had gone to the Pacific Coast in 1858 and remained there as mate and master of different vessels some fifteen years. For eight years prior to taking the *Fannie Tucker*, he commanded the ship *Union*, of Damariscotta, employed in the transatlantic cotton trade. On retiring from the *Tucker* he settled at Seattle and spent his remaining days there.

Capt. J. N. Frost, a native of Massachusetts, purchased Captain Greenleaf's interest in the *Fannie Tucker* and continued in her until her end. The Captain had previously been master of the ship *McNear* and following the loss of the *Tucker* he invested in a big four-masted steel bark named *Ancyra*. On a passage in her from Manila to Boston the ship struck a northwester off Nantucket Light which iced her up and caused the loss of nearly a suit of sails. Captain Frost then squared away for warmer weather to thaw out and was finally able to make St. Thomas. He sent to New York for new sails, and his first wife having died at Manila, he got married again and eventually reached Boston nearly a year out of Manila.

FARRAGUT

THE *Farragut* was the ninety-second vessel built by John Currier, Jr., of Newburyport, Mass., and was the finest ship built at that place up to the time she was launched in September, 1876. Mr. Currier's next ship was of similar model and on completion was immediately purchased by the Howes brothers and named *Jabez Howes*. The *Farragut* was 212:7 feet, by 40, by 25:2 feet and of 1549 tons register. A full-sized image of the Admiral after whom she was named was mounted as a figurehead. Thayer & Lincoln were managers and the principal owners of the ship.

The maiden voyage of the *Farragut* was from New York to San Francisco in 124 days; thence, 46 days to Manila, and 114 days from there to Boston. On the following two voyages she took ice from Boston to ports in India, on the first going out to Madras in 106 days, which was claimed to be a very good run. The return passages were from Manila and Calcutta respectively. The fourth voyage was from New York to San Francisco in 135 days; thence to Queenstown in 114 days. In 1884 she made a round between Hong Kong and San Francisco, that being her final appearance at the latter port. Her later operations were all in the Far East trade, principally with Calcutta. Her passages were made in good average time and she was said to be a successful, money-making ship.

On Jan. 20, 1888, the *Farragut* left Calcutta for New York, under command of Captain Hardwick, and nothing was ever heard of her or the twenty-five persons aboard, among whom were Mrs. Hardwick and daughter. A ship which sailed some three weeks after her reported seeing a wreck in the Indian Ocean, 1200 miles from Calcutta, which was thought to be the *Farragut*.

A peculiar incident happened to the *Farragut* when she was being towed up the East River, New York, in December, 1878. The fore royal mast struck a buggy in which were two men painting the cables of the bridge then under construction. The men saw the approaching danger and had climbed to a safe place on the cables. The paint pots and tools of the men were thrown into the river and about thirty feet of the ship's mast was broken off. The vessel was backed and then started ahead a second time. The tide was running strong and it was difficult to keep the vessel on her course. Her main royal mast grazed the upstream storm cable and carried away the ball above the truck. The vessel had no cargo aboard and struck the cable at first at a point 155 feet above high water mark. A similar accident befell the ship *Undaunted* in September, 1882, when she fouled the bridge and had both fore and main topgallant masts carried away. It was stated at the time that the ship's owners were to start suit to recover the $1500 damages received.

Capt. John P. Wilbur was in command of the *Farragut* from the time she was built until his death from cholera at Calcutta in May, 1878. The Captain had been a master twenty-two years and among his prior commands were the bark *Sappho* and ship *Thomas Dana*, to both of which vessels he had been appointed master before they were launched. He was a native of Mystic, Conn., a brother of Capt.

Robt. P. Wilbur, long in command of the ship *M. P. Grace*. Capt.
James M. Small was the second master of the *Farragut* and after being in her four years took the *Thomas Dana*. He had sailed for
Thayer & Lincoln many years, two of his earlier ships being the
Alaska and *Hamilton*, he taking the latter when new in 1871. Capt.
Charles S. Kendall succeeded Captain Small and was in the *Farragut*
until the voyage prior to her loss. In 1874 the Captain had been appointed to command the new ship *Saratoga* and continued in her until
she was sold in 1880. Other ships of which he was later master were
the *Gardner Colby, Hercules, Annie H. Smith, L. Schepp* and *I. F.
Chapman*.

FAVORITA

THE *Favorita* was a small, fine looking ship, built by George
Greenman & Co. at Mystic, Conn., in 1862, for John A. Mc-
Gaw of New York, and measured 188 feet, by 37, by 24 feet, registering 1194 tons. During her later years as an American ship she was
managed by Capt. John S. Pray of Portsmouth, N. H., who, before
retiring from active sea life, had been master of the well-known ship
Prima Donna.

The *Favorita* was engaged principally in trade between New York,
San Francisco and the United Kingdom, making in all nine such round
voyages. Her average passages to the westward figure out 130 days
with one of 114 days as the shortest and 148 days as the longest. Of
her runs to the eastward the average is 113 days, 103 days to New
York and 111 days to Liverpool, being the two shortest, and one of
122 days to Queenstown the longest. Her last completed voyage as
an American ship was in 1876, Boston to Melbourne, San Francisco,
Manila and home. She was then sold to go under the German flag
without change of name and was employed in transatlantic trade until
1891 when she was purchased by the German East African Government. She took a cargo of coal from Bremerhaven to Dar-es-Salaam,
the colony in Africa, and after her arrival there was dismantled and
used as a hulk.

Capt. Samuel W. Pike took the *Favorita* from New York to San Francisco on her maiden passage. The ship had a hard buffeting off Cape Horn and lost her figurehead. Captain Pike was later stricken with paralysis and was forced to relinquish command of the ship at the termination of the voyage. The Captain belonged to Newburyport and had previously been in command of a number of vessels including the clipper ships *Sea Serpent, Meteor* and *Mameluke*. In March, 1861, he was presented by the marine underwriters of New York and Boston with a handsome chronometer in appreciation of his "skill, perseverance and energy in bringing his ship *Mameluke* into port from Baker's Island, she being in a very leaky condition." Captain Pike died in January, 1885, at the age of sixty-five years.

Capt. John C. Bush was the second master of the *Favorita* and continued in her until Mr. McGaw had the ship *Frolic* built at Mystic, in 1869, when he was transferred to her. Capt. William Greenman was master of the *Favorita* from 1869 until 1875 when he took over the Mystic-owned bark *Galveston*. This vessel was considered a very fast sailer and had just been rebuilt, at considerable expense, but her subsequent career was very short. In October, 1876, she was driven ashore on Duck Key, some sixty miles from Key West, and finally became a total loss. Captain Greenman stayed by the vessel some six months in an effort to float her but his exertions were unavailing. Prior to taking command of the *Favorita* the Captain had been master of the bark *I. M. Hicks* and he was in command of the New York steamer *Constitution* when she was lost on Cape Lookout, during the last week of 1866, twenty persons being drowned, including some of her passengers. A brother of the Captain, who was first officer, was among those who perished. Captain Greenman was the son of Silas Greenman, shipbuilder, of Westerly, R. I., and a nephew of George Greenman who built many ships at Mystic.

Capt. Edward A. Gerrish, a brother-in-law of Capt. John Pray, was master of the *Favorita* on her last voyage. He had previously been nine years in the ship *Semiramis* which was also managed by Captain Pray. Following the sale of the *Favorita* he was given com-

mand of the new ship *Paul Jones*, but a few years later he retired from
sea life and eventually died at an advanced age in the Marine Hospital at Chelsea, Mass.

FLEETFORD

THE ship *Fleetford* was built by Paul Curtis at East Boston and
was launched in August, 1864. Her dimensions were 178 feet,
by 36, by 23:4 feet, and tonnage per register 1104. She hailed from
Portsmouth, N. H., and at first was managed by E. F. Sise & Co.
Later her managing owners were Pray & Dickens and in May, 1875,
they offered her for sale but there were no bidders. She was finally
sold in 1878 to Norwegians who renamed her *Aarvak* and employed
her in transatlantic trade some twenty odd years.

On two occasions, for about a year each time, the *Fleetford* was in
the cotton and oil trade with Europe. All the rest of her voyages were
between Atlantic ports and San Francisco, these totalling eight and
all were made in slow time. The shortest to San Francisco was 147
days and from that port, 134 days, both having originated and terminated at New York. She took three cargoes of wheat to Great
Britain at an average of 153 days per passage.

The first passage of the *Fleetford* was made by Capt. Charles S.
Salter who became sick shortly after the ship left New York and she
was put into Rio de Janeiro for medical assistance. Part of the crew
had been mutinous and they were sent home in irons. On arrival of
the ship at San Francisco, Captain Salter relinquished command to go
home and Capt. N. G. Weeks took her to New York with guano from
the Chincha Islands. Captain Salter's seafaring career is given in the
account of the ship *Coldstream*.

Capt. Josiah A. Stover took command of the *Fleetford*, at New
York, early in 1866, and continued in her until arriving at Liverpool
in February, 1873. He had been very ill on the passage from San
Francisco and the ship had put into Pernambuco for medical aid. The
prior passage from New York to San Francisco had been a hard one,

taking 209 days, the ship being 54 days in rounding Cape Horn. Captain Stover put into Callao for fresh water and provisions and to land four seamen who were suffering from scurvy.

Capt. John Siler Taylor, who is mentioned in the account of the ship *Celestial Empire,* took the *Fleetford* at Liverpool in February, 1873, and remained her master until she was sold. On her last passage she left San Francisco in November, 1876, to load guano at Jarvis Island for Hamburg. She struck on the reef at the Island and had to go to Honolulu for repairs. These being completed she returned to the Island and finally reached Hamburg in February, 1878.

FRANCIS

THE three skysail-yarder *Francis* was the second full-rigged ship built by the New England Shipbuilding Co., successors to Goss, Sawyer & Packard, and was launched at Bath, Maine, in October, 1885. She was 231 feet, by 43:4, by 26:6 feet, and of 1974 tons register. She was built to the order of Francis and Horatio Hathaway, William J. Rotch, William W. Crapo and Capt. William H. Besse, all of New Bedford, and John M. Forbes of Boston and to be commanded by Capt. Francis H. Stone, a cousin of Horatio Hathaway. The hailing port of the ship was New Bedford and Captain Besse managed her affairs.

On her first voyage the *Francis* took case oil from Philadelphia to Hiogo in 145 days; crossed to British Columbia and loaded coal for San Francisco; took wheat thence to Havre in 141 days; and then crossed to Philadelphia in 24 days. She then went again to Hiogo in a long run of 180 days; thence to Manila, to load sugar for San Francisco; went back to Manila for a second sugar cargo and then took wheat from San Francisco to Liverpool in 119 days. The third voyage was also out to Hiogo, 138 days passage, and after her oil cargo had been discharged she loaded 2123 tons of tea, proceeded to Yokohama where 1578 additional tons were laden, all for Tacoma. This passage was made in 33 days. Her freight list was $38,480, which

was some $10,000 more than that of the wheat cargo she later took
from Tacoma to Liverpool. The latter run was made in 122 days.

The *Francis* was then diverted to the Cape Horn run and completed four round voyages between Atlantic ports and San Francisco.
The shortest passage to the westward was 129 days but to the eastward she made one run to New York in 102 days and one to Liverpool in 111 days. Then followed another voyage to Japan, Java and
Philadelphia. On the latter passage the ship lost fore and main topmasts and mizzen topgallant mast in a hurricane in the Indian Ocean,
completing the run under jury rig. She then went out from Philadelphia to San Francisco and after loading an assorted cargo, of which
the principal item was 4000 barrels of wine, she passed through the
Golden Gate, Jan. 17, 1897, bound for New York. When near her
destination, May 8th, the cargo under the cabin on the port side was
discovered to be on fire. Pumping on of water had no effect nor were
the efforts of the tugs, which soon appeared on the scene, of any avail.
The vessel was then beached on the bar at the entrance to Little Egg
Harbor, near Beach Haven, N. J., where she burned to the water's
edge. The crew had been taken off by tugs without having been able
to save any effects. It was believed that the fire was caused by spontaneous combustion as the cargo included 200 bales of rags and 500
barrels of whale and fish oil, some of which may have leaked out.

Aside from a couple of voyages made by relieving masters, the
Francis was commanded by Captains Francis H. Stone and Alfred
H. Doane during her sea life. Captain Stone, however, made but one
round voyage, the first, but in 1892 he took the ship from New York
to San Francisco after which he retired from the sea. The Captain,
who is still living, first went to sea as ordinary seaman on the bark
Jonathan Bourne, under Captain Doane. In her he worked up to
master and continued in her until she was lost in June, 1884.

The long career of Captain Doane is given in account of the ship
Cleopatra, "American Merchant Ships," Series I.

FRANCONIA

THE *Franconia* was built by W. V. Moses & Son, at Bath, Maine, and was launched in September, 1874. She was 205:8 feet, by 40:4, by 24 feet, and registered 1313 tons. Her builders were the principal owners as also the ship's managers. Capt. William Strickland of the ship *Invincible*, and Capt. William H. Otis, her commander throughout her sea life, owned each a number of shares, that of the latter being 16/64ths.

For the first six years of her career the *Franconia* was employed as a general trader, making voyages to South America, India and other ports of the Far East. Early in 1881 she loaded her first cargo for San Francisco, this being of assorted merchandise totaling $250,-000 in value. She never made port, being wrecked on the Farallon Islands during the night of June 23d. The following account of the disaster was given by her chief officer, Mr. Williams:

"The ship was going along before a strong westerly breeze in a dense fog supposedly being in the vicinity of Point Reyes, when, without a moment's warning, she fetched up all standing on Middle Rock about two miles northwest from the South Rocks. She immediately slid off and as we were wearing around for the purpose of hauling offshore, land was discovered first on the port bow and soon after on the starboard bow and then all around. About fifteen minutes after she first struck she went hard and fast on a sandy beach on South Farallon. The long boat was cut from its lashings but on being launched it was stove and sunk. The Captain's gig was then launched from the davits and with a few hands pulled around in search of a landing place. A third boat was also gotten over the side safely and by 5 o'clock A.M., three hours after the ship first struck, all hands were ashore in a partially sheltered cove, though one boat had been capsized in the surf. Chief mate Williams and two men clambered over the steep rocks and rough summit of the bleak island of rock and after much difficulty came to the lighthouse station. Immediate assistance was sent to those shivering on the beach and they were later taken to the station.

"It appeared from an observation taken at noon, June 23d, that the ship was then 160 miles to the westward of the Farallons. A dense fog then set in. At 11 o'clock the patent log indicated the distance run since noon had been 140 miles and Captain Otis, desiring to have plenty of sea room, wore ship and stood offshore under topsails in a stiff breeze. When she first struck the pumps showed no water in the hold."

The ship *Alfred D. Snow*, arriving at San Francisco, June 24th, reported seeing a ship ashore on the South Farallon, apparently lying easily, and three tugs were at once sent to the scene but only the *Wizard*, Captain Randall, completed the trip through the heavy sea that was running. With difficulty the tug's skiff was launched and the *Franconia's* party of twenty-one persons, including Mrs. Otis, were taken off and brought to San Francisco.

Two days after stranding, the *Franconia* started to break up and within a week the island was covered with wreckage in such broken condition as not to be worth transportation. Considerable gear and most of the ship's rigging had been salved and subsequently a small amount of cargo was recovered.

Capt. William H. Otis, an elder brother of the well-known Captains Henry R. and Albert C. Otis, was a native of Brunswick, Me., and a master in the employ of W. V. Moses for many years. His first command was the bark *Georgia*, built in 1842, and in 1850 he had the ship *Rome*, from New York to San Francisco. His next ship was the *American Union*, built in 1852, and in 1865 he took command of the new bark *Rome*. He had not visited San Francisco from 1850 until the *Franconia's* loss and this was the first serious mishap he had. His $12,000 interest in the last named ship was but partly covered by insurance and being then an old man his loss was very inopportune. He then gave up seafaring and spent his last days at his home in Maine.

Another ship named *Franconia* was built at Newburyport in 1872, but she did not operate long under the American flag, being sold in June, 1877, to go under the British flag as the *Don Erique*.

FRANK N. THAYER

THERE were two ships named in honor of Frank N. Thayer, who, prior to his death in April, 1882, was senior member of the firm of Thayer & Lincoln of Boston, and both had been built for account of that concern. The first was a main skysail-yard ship of 1160 tons, built by David Clark, at Kennebunkport, Maine, and launched in December, 1868. She was engaged principally in the transatlantic and California trades, but in 1874 made a voyage to Hong Kong, thence crossing to the Columbia River to load grain for Liverpool, being one of the first vessels to so engage. In 1869 she had loaded at San Francisco for Liverpool and when not long at sea, shifted cargo and sprung aleak. The pumps choked but were finally cleared and Capt. W. H. Towne proceeded on his way. Some two weeks later the pumps again became choked so the ship bore up for Honolulu where, after three weeks, she arrived with the crew all sick and two men nearly asphyxiated from the foul odors arising from the rotting grain. This had also turned to a blue color all the ship's white paint work. The cargo had to be discharged to allow of repairs being made and the ship was detained in port about a month. Then followed the long passage of 144 days to Liverpool.

In 1876-1877, the *Frank N. Thayer*, No. 1, went home from San Francisco by way of the Philippines and shortly after her arrival was sold to parties in Bremen who changed her name to *Doris*.

Frank N. Thayer, No. 2, was a three skysail-yard ship, built by John Currier, Jr., and launched at Newburyport, Mass., in October, 1878. Her dimensions were 220 feet, by 40, by 26:3 feet, and she registered 1648 tons. Capt. Andrew Mack, formerly in the ship *Yosemite*, was appointed her commander and following his death at San Francisco in March, 1881, Capt. George D. Morrison, previously in the ship *Friedlander*, succeeded. In 1884, Capt. Robert K. Clarke, Jr., generally known as "Sunrise Clarke," took the *Thayer* and continued in command until her end.

The first three years of the *Thayer* were spent in trade between

New York, San Francisco and Liverpool. She then made a couple of voyages to the Far East and met a tragic fate while employed therein. On Nov. 1, 1885, she left Manila for New York, with sixteen men before the mast, two of whom were Manilamen. These soon became disaffected and troublesome and were punished. One night they stabbed to death the two mates and cut Captain Clarke so badly that he was left for dead. The watch on deck attempted to round up the Malays with capstan bars but they were routed after four had been stabbed. The helmsman, carpenter and lookout-man were then murdered and the rest of the crew driven to their quarters and barricaded therein.

During the following two days the crew was so frightened that they made no move but on the third day Captain Clarke was able to force a sailor, who had been hiding in the cabin, to fire around the deck at random and his shots struck one of the Malays who immediately jumped overboard. His mate then ran forward and after setting fire to the hemp cargo, followed his companion over the ship's side. On the crew being released it was found impossible to control the fire so two boats were hurriedly provisioned and launched but one capsized and was lost. Captain Clarke, his wife and their young daughter, with the rest of the ship's company, got into the other boat and abandoned the ship which was then in flames. Their position was some 700 miles from St. Helena and, by use of an improvised sail, the distance was covered in six days. All the wounded men eventually recovered.

Capt. Andrew Mack of Portland, Me., took command of the Portsmouth ship *Yosemite* when she was launched in 1867 and was continuously in her until the *Thayer* was built eleven years later. The Captain had been to sea from boyhood and after his marriage had been accompanied on his voyages by his wife. The couple owned a $20,000 interest in the *Thayer* and she was always kept in the best condition, her cabins being fitted up as nearly like a home ashore as was possible. Captain Mack never met with a disaster and during his twenty-five years as master lost only two men and those through sickness.

The seafaring career of Capt. Robert K. Clarke, Jr., and the reason for his being called "Sunrise Clarke," are given in account of the ship *Sunrise* in "American Merchant Ships," Series I.

FRANK PENDLETON

THE ship *Frank Pendleton* was named after Capt. Benjamin Frank Pendleton of Searsport, who was at one time master of the ships *Nancy Pendleton* and *William H. Connor* and subsequently of the firm of Pendleton, Carver & Nichols, shipowners, of New York. The ship was built by Henry McGilvery for Capt. James G. Pendleton, a brother of Capt. Benjamin Frank, and was launched at Belfast, Maine, in October, 1874. Her dimensions were 200 feet, by 39, by 24 feet and she registered 1351 tons. She was built to be commanded by Capt. William Green Nichols of Searsport and, aside from three years he spent as master of the ship *Belle of Bath*, Captain Nichols was in the *Frank Pendleton* during the whole of her sea life. A brother, Capt. Edward P. Nichols, commanded the *Frank Pendleton* during the three years referred to.

The *Frank Pendleton* was a good and successful ship and made money for her owners. Her first voyage was from Belfast to New Orleans, thence to Revel, Russia, and Gefle, Sweden. She left the latter port in August, 1875, went to Melbourne in 138 days, and thence to London in 94 days. Thereafter she was operated mainly between Atlantic ports and those of South America or the Far East. She made no passages from Atlantic ports to San Francisco but on several occasions reached there from the Orient to load wheat for Europe. Her last voyage was from New York to Calcutta, where she loaded part cargo for San Francisco, finishing at Madras. Off Formosa she was thrown on beam ends in a typhoon and her decks were continuously under water for 36 hours. She was short a full cargo by some 150 tons. Had she been full and deeply laden, Captain Nichols believed that she must have foundered. From San Francisco she went to New York, where, after her arrival in March, 1893, she was sold to Lewis Luckenbach and converted into a barge. On March 8, 1917, she foundered in Ambrose Channel, New York, but the four men aboard were saved.

In May, 1887, an attempt was made to scuttle the *Pendleton* when she was about to start loading coal at Newcastle, N. S. W., for San Diego, Cal. While shifting her berth an augur hole was found some fifteen inches above her copper. It had just been bored and the vessel was saved by the fact that the tool had broken in striking metal in the hull.

While Capt. Edward P. Nichols was in command of the *Pendleton* he had a small printing press on board and at intervals published a breezy little sheet which he called the "Ocean Chronicle." This contained accounts of interesting occurrences on board and was mailed to friends of the Captain from different ports of call. From a copy of one number the following references to a passage from San Francisco to Liverpool is condensed.

The day after the ship passed Cape Horn a heavy gale was encountered during which the decks were full of water. The cargo shifted; the thick work around the mainmast and fife rail was started, as also the pumps, these causing the ship to take considerable water below. The watch was taken into the cabin to sleep or rest. A number of sails were lost; the boats were stove and the ship was well wrecked about decks. The pumps could only be worked by ropes led on to the poop. When the weather moderated the leaks around the pumps were found to be very bad from started fastenings and opened seams but these were finally closed and the ship pumped out. Later, in the South Atlantic, the ship passed through two hurricanes and a very hard gale but fortunately escaped without damage.

On April 30th a German sailor was found to be missing. It was thought that he had jumped overboard as he had told some of the men he would do so, but they thought it was only talk on his part. Referring to this incident Captain Nichols threw out some suggestions to the sensational press when they came to write up the affair, as follows: "Cannot some of our most worthy emblems of peace and quiet, with their vivid imaginations, picture something horrible in this disappearance? We mean the papers which said 'The Captain was not killed but the public would not have many regrets had he been one of the victims.' Let them picture that man fleeing from a brutal captain who is chasing him with a royalyard in his grasp; picture that spar as it breaks over the man's head; show how the captain in a fiendish rage, then grasped a spare topsail yard and hurled it at the man, who, rather than be killed, ran out on the spanker boom, jumped over the bow and was drowned. Sketch the man as the ship passes, catching the end of the jib sheet which is towing over the stern; put in a few wails of agony and cries of 'Help.' Paint the captain calmly walking the deck, eating peanuts, heedless of these cries; then continue on in about that style. It will be just as sensible and only a slight change in form from the usual."

As a sequel to the termination of this passage, it is of interest to learn that the underwriters of the cargo acknowledged by letter, accompanied with a substantial award of money, Captain Nichols' good judgment in having dried out on deck the wheat which had been wet by sea water, thereby greatly minimizing the damage done.

San Francisco shipping papers of November, 1881, published the following, shortly after the arrival of the *Frank Pendleton* from Yokohama:

"As neat a compliment as we have ever heard of was given early the present week when the ship *Frank Pendleton*, Capt. William Green Nichols, docked at Vallejo Street wharf. The entire crew was by the ship and assisted in docking and making her fast, after which everything was straightened up, running gear coiled nicely and nothing left in other than perfect shape. The crew then went over the side and, mustering in a body on the wharf, gave three hearty cheers for the ship; next, three for Captain Nichols and then three more for the officers. Although it was from 'Poor Jack,' the demonstration showed that the Captain is a good humane commander and his ship a good vessel. May she float long under him."

Capt. William Green Nichols was born in Searsport in 1834. Before he was twenty-one he was master of the bark *Lillias*, named after his wife, and a few years later was given command of the bark *Del-*

phine, named for his sister-in-law. On Dec. 29, 1864, the *Delphine,* while bound from London to Akyab, to load rice for the United States, was captured in the Indian Ocean by the Confederate privateer *Shenandoah.* The bark's company was taken on board the privateer and the vessel set on fire and burned. Four weeks later the *Shenandoah* put into Melbourne and landed the party belonging to the *Delphine,* with the exception of six members of her crew who had been persuaded to sign on the raider.

Prior to taking command of the *Frank Pendleton,* Captain Nichols had been in the ship *David Brown.* His term of service in the *Belle of Bath* was from 1886 until 1888. He died on board the *Frank Pendleton* a few days after reaching port at New York from San Francisco, in March, 1893.

After Capt. Edward P. Nichols had turned back to his brother the command of the *Frank Pendleton,* in 1888, he retired from sea life to engage in the hay and grain business in Bucksport, Me., and passed away there, in October, 1899, at the age of fifty-five years. The Captain had previously been master of the Searsport bark *Clara* and was in her when she was lost near Port Elizabeth, during the early '80's. All hands, including his wife and daughter, reached shore safely, but with some difficulty, by breeches buoy.

FRIEDLANDER

THE ship *Friedlander* was built by Capt. N. L. Thompson, at Kennebunk, Maine, for Thayer & Lincoln of Boston, and was launched in September, 1872. She was named after Isaac Friedlander who, for a number of years prior to his death in August, 1878, was the principal charterer of ships and exporter of wheat at San Francisco, being known as the "Wheat King."

The ship *Friedlander* measured 215:8 feet, by 39:4, by 26:4 feet, and registered 1638 tons. She was built for the California trade and was so employed while under the American flag with the exception of one voyage between Liverpool and Calcutta in 1876. On that occasion her outward passage was made in the good time of 96 days and her various runs to and from San Francisco averaged well, the shortest being her maiden passage, 122 days from New York. She had the distinction of being the first ship to discharge a cargo at the Oakland, Cal., wharves.

On Jan. 14, 1875, the *Friedlander* sailed from New York and arrived at San Francisco, November 9th, 84 days from Rio de Janeiro. Soon after leaving New York she met with heavy gales and squalls of hail and snow during which she sprang aleak, taking in seven feet of water. The ship was hove to but rolled yards under which hampered pumping and she was only freed after three days of incessant work. Captain Morrison made for Rio de Janeiro where extensive repairs were required necessitating a stay in port of nearly six months. On the second half of the following voyage, which was from San Francisco to Hamburg via the Peruvian guano deposits, the ship sprung her mainmast off Cape Horn and was forced to put into Valparaiso. Shortly after arriving at her final destination she was sold to parties in Bremen for $48,000, and for some years was employed in the oil trade between New York and that port under her original name. In 1896 she appears as the Dutch ship *Friede*.

Capt. George D. Morrison was in command of the *Friedlander* the four years preceding her sale. He had previously had the ship *General McClellan* and subsequently was in the *Frank N. Thayer* and *Vigilant*, being in the latter when she made port at Manila from Norfolk with the coal cargo on fire and was later condemned. Captain Morrison was then given command of the new steamer *Californian* which established the service of the American-Hawaiian Steamship Co., taking her from San Francisco to Manila and thereafter running her in the intercoastal trade via the Straits of Magellan. In 1902 the Captain was transferred to the company's new steamer *Texan* and was in command of her when he died at Philadelphia, of typhoid fever, the following year. Captain Morrison stood at the head of his profession, was highly regarded in all personal respects and was quite a writer on maritime subjects.

FROLIC

THE *Frolic* was built by George Greenman & Co. at Mystic, Conn., in 1869 and was 192 feet, by 39:9, by 24:6 feet, registering 1348 tons. Her first owner was John A. McGaw; in later years, while still under the American flag, her managing owner was the firm of Pray & Dickens. She was a fine looking vessel, neat and trim. Capt. John C. Bush, previously in command of the Mystic ship *Favorita*, also one of Mr. McGaw's fleet, was in the *Frolic* on her maiden voyage and continued in her as master until she was sold.

The *Frolic* made a number of passages to San Francisco by way of Cape Horn and was for about an equal length of time trading to the West Coast of South America or the East Indies. She is not known to have any fast passages on long distance voyages to her credit; in fact, her runs to San Francisco were slower than average. In March, 1871, she and the ship *Ringleader*, left New York within five minutes of each other, bound for San Francisco, and as both were of about the same model there was much talk about a race being on. The result, however, showed that the "race" was more of a drifting match than a trial of speed, for the *Ringleader's* time was 147 days and the *Frolic's* 165 days. In 1871-1872 the *Frolic* made two passages from San Francisco to Newcastle, N. S. W., in good time, 47 and 42 days, but that season was favorable for runs shorter than average and several ships beat the *Frolic's* time. One of the shortest passages she made in the East India trade was in 1876, 95 days from Batavia to New York. This voyage had originated at Manila but the ship had struck a shoal in the Java Sea necessitating Captain Bush making for Batavia for repairs.

The last voyage of the *Frolic*, as an American ship, was from New York to Bombay and Calcutta, in 1878-1879. On her return home she was sold and went under the German flag, being renamed *Elise*. Later, she was resold to Italians and as the *Elise*, of Genoa, she is listed in shipping registers as late as 1908 but not thereafter.

GARIBALDI

THE ship *Garibaldi* was built by Maxson, Fish & Co. at Mystic, Conn., in 1860, and was 183 feet, by 40:3, by 28 feet, registering 1336 tons. She was a three decker, had a flat floor and sides and very little flare to the bows, being almost a perfect wedge forward from covering board to keel. She was originally owned by Calvin Adams and hailed from New York, but was subsequently purchased by Howes & Crowell of Boston.

The *Garibaldi* was one of the prominent members of the early California grain fleet and, although she made several voyages in the Far East trade, most of her life was spent in trade between San Francisco, New York and Liverpool. In common with other ships built by Maxon, Fish & Co., notably the celebrated ship *Seminole*, her sailing record is good and she has to her credit a round voyage made in quite fast time — 110 days from New York to San Francisco; thence 111 days to Liverpool and from there, 19 days to New York.

On her passage from San Francisco to Liverpool, in 1876, the *Garibaldi* sprung aleak and put into St. Thomas. While in port the leak increased, the ship making about one foot of water an hour. A portion of her cargo was discharged and forwarded by another vessel. Temporary repairs were made to the *Garibaldi* and a steam pump was installed, after which she proceeded and completed the passage. On a prior passage to San Francisco the ship had very heavy weather for 65 days off Cape Horn, the hull being badly strained and a number of sails lost.

In August, 1879, a 1/16th interest in the *Garibaldi* was sold for a small sum, reported as only $1,000, and the following year the whole ship was sold to go under the German flag. She was renamed *Anni* and for some ten years operated in transatlantic trade.

Among the commanders of the *Garibaldi* was Capt. Horace Atwood who had previously been master of the ship *Blandina Dudley* and in later years of the ship *Tennyson*, both of which were employed in the East Indian trade. Capt. Rufus P. Bowdoin, who in later years

"EMILY F. WHITNEY," 1207 TONS, BUILT IN 1880, AT EAST BOSTON

Courtesy of Edward S. Clark

"EUREKA," 1996 TONS, BUILT IN 1876, AT RICHMOND, MAINE
Courtesy of Edward S. Clark

"GRECIAN," 1677 TONS, BUILT IN 1876, AT KENNEBUNK, MAINE

"HENRY FAILING," 1976 TONS, BUILT IN 1882, AT BATH, MAINE

From an oil painting by W. H. York, Liverpool, 1884. Photograph by George E. Noyes, Newburyport

had the ship *Regent,* was in the *Garibaldi* several years and Capt. Samuel H. Thacher had her for the last five years. Captain Thacher was born in Yarmouth, Mass., and died there in 1901. Among other vessels he commanded were the bark *Carleton* and the ship *Valley Forge,* the latter in 1881, after relinquishing which he retired from the sea. An elder brother, Capt. Edwin Thacher, commanded the ships *Audubon, Ringleader,* and others.

GARNET

THE *Garnet* was a small but handy and fine looking ship built by John Taylor, at Chelsea, Mass., for Bramhall & Hall of Boston, and was launched in March, 1858. She measured 178 feet, by 38, by 23 feet, and registered 1119 tons. She was described as having good lines with quite sharp ends and had the reputation of being a good sailer. She was employed in the general carrying trade but most of her career is said to have been spent in the coal and guano business with South America. She made but two voyages to San Francisco, arriving there on the last in November, 1874, after a long passage of 200 days from Baltimore, during the course of which she was damaged by heavy gales off Cape Horn. Following this she made a round voyage to British Columbia for coal and then took guano from Jarvis Island to Antwerp.

In March, 1876, the *Garnet* left Newcastle-On-Tyne for San Francisco, but soon encountering very heavy weather she was forced to come to anchor. The cables parted but assistance was fortunately near at hand and she was taken in tow to Greenock, her salvors receiving £500. The voyage was continued and all went well until the ship reached Cape Horn when in heavy gales the rudder was carried away, the stern post was split and a bad leak developed. For three days the ship lay helpless and was in imminent danger of foundering when the ship *Latona,* of Liverpool, rescued her crew and landed them at Callao a month later.

Capt. Edward St. Clair Oliver was the last commander of the *Garnet* and had been in her some six years. His last previous ship was the *Harry Bluff*, a fine vessel of 1200 tons, built by Jotham Stetson, at Chelsea, in 1855. Captain Oliver had made a couple of fine passages to San Francisco in her, on the last going to Valencia with guano from the Peruvian deposits. The ship later loaded salt, wine and cork at Cadiz, for Boston, and on Feb. 26, 1869, struck on Nantucket South Shoal, soon filling with water to a depth of sixteen feet. Her anchors were dropped in thirteen fathoms and the crew took to the boats, two men being drowned in leaving the ship. The remaining survivors suffered greatly through cold before being picked up by the *Clara Jennings*, two men having been frozen to death. The rest, all more or less frostbitten, were placed in a hospital at Boston.

GATHERER

THE ship *Gatherer* was built at Bath, Maine, by Albert Hathorn and launched in August, 1874. She measured 208 feet, by 40, by 24 feet, and registered 1509 tons. At first she had double topgallant yards on the foremast. Her builder owned 5/12ths and her first commander, Capt. Joseph A. Thomson, owned 1/8th. The remaining shares were held by a number of parties including Capt. George Thomson and Parker M. Whitmore, the last named being managing owner. In April, 1888, when in port at San Francisco, she was purchased by Jacob Jensen who, some seventeen years later, resold her to the Lambert's Point Towboat Co. of New York. She then took a lumber cargo from Puget Sound to New York and was converted into a coal barge. On Nov. 29, 1909, while laden with 2400 tons of coal and in tow of a tug bound from Norfolk to Boston she foundered to the eastward of Assateague Lightship, coast of Virginia, but her crew was saved by the tug.

The first voyage of the *Gatherer* was from Bath to New Orleans with hay. She then took cotton to Liverpool, thence crossing to Philadelphia to load coal for Honolulu on Government account. On the latter passage she fell in with the bark *Jessie Scott*, of Sunderland, in a sinking condition in the South Pacific and succeeded in rescuing her crew. From Honolulu the *Gatherer* proceeded to the Columbia River and loaded wheat for Liverpool. She then made two voyages to Hong Kong with coal, following which she was put on the run between Atlantic and North Pacific Coast ports and continued therein until purchased by San Francisco parties. Thereafter she sailed coastwise and offshore on the Pacific, rigged as a bark.

The *Gatherer* was a first class ship in all respects, turning out cargo in excellent condition and generally making good voyages. The average of her eight passages to San Francisco or other North Pacific ports, from the Atlantic, is 129 days and that of the seven returns, all being with wheat to Europe, is 122 days. The run from Honolulu to the Columbia River, in 1875, was made in 14 days, on three of which she covered 375, 350 and 348 miles. In 1890 she was four days and ten hours from Nanaimo to San Francisco, beating the steamer *Empire* thirty-six hours on the run down.

For practically all of her career, while engaged on long distance voyages, the *Gatherer* was commanded by Captains Joseph A. and George Thomson, and J. S. Lowell, all humane men. She was unfortunate, however, in having as a master, a Capt. John Sparks, on the passage from Antwerp to Wilmington, Cal., in 1881. Captain Sparks acquiesced in chief mate Charles Watts' inhuman treatment of the crew and occurrences on the voyage gave the ship a bad name which has never been allowed to die. Sensational papers and other publications continuously referred to the "Hell Ship" *Gatherer* as though it was she that was at fault and not her brutal officers. The crew was treated horribly, Mate Watts killing one seaman while two others suicided by jumping overboard rather than endure further ill treatment. One boy was beaten so badly about the head and face that he became blind. Immediately on arrival of the ship at Wilmington, Captain Sparks was removed from command, but he escaped punishment, there being no evidence that he in person actually committed any of the atrocities. However, he did not live long thereafter for having been given command of the ship *Red Cross*, at San Francisco, in

1884, he suicided by jumping overboard on the passage to Liverpool. Mate Watts went into hiding when the *Gatherer* made port and a few months later shipped on the *Imperial*, at San Francisco, under an assumed name. The fact became known, however, and on arrival of the ship at Liverpool, he was arrested and returned to San Francisco, where, on being tried, he was convicted and sentenced to serve six years in State Prison.

Among the mishaps met with by the *Gatherer* were her grounding in the Columbia River in September, 1880, after making port from Philadelphia and being obliged to lighter 1000 tons of cargo to get off. She received but little injury but on later proceeding to British Columbia to load coal for San Francisco, she got ashore on Vancouver Island and was badly damaged. She was got off and after going to San Francisco in ballast was repaired there at a cost of about $20,000. In 1886 she had a hard passage from Baltimore to San Francisco. When four days out the fore topgallant mast broke off due to the parting of the martingale backstay. In the South Atlantic she had a gale of hurricane force with a high, cross sea; lost the fore- and maintopmasts and had the heads of the lower masts sprung; a new lower foretopsail was blown out of the bolt ropes and the ship labored heavily for two days with decks full of water. When the gale moderated the masts were secured as well as possible and the passage was completed without further incident.

Capt. Joseph A. Thomson was best known as master of the ship *I. F. Chapman* and his seafaring career is given in account of that ship. Capt. George Thomson had been in command of the ship *Ella S. Thayer*, built in 1865, and owned by the Hathorns. He had the reputation of being a first class seaman and navigator and while a strict disciplinarian, never allowed his crews to be abused. He belonged to Woolwich, Me. Capt. J. S. Lowell was a native of Phippsburg, but later made his home in Bath. One of his early commands was the ship *Mary E. Riggs*, built at Phippsburg, in 1864. Leaving her in 1870, to take the new ship *Merom*, he was master of that vessel until 1881. Just prior to taking the *Gatherer* he was in the *George Stetson* for a short time. The Captain stood high in his profession and

was as kind-hearted a man as ever trod a quarterdeck. He died at
Winchester, Mass., in 1908.

GENERAL KNOX

THE three-deck ship *General Knox*, 252 feet, by 42:4, by 29:4
feet, registering 2141 tons, was built by Edward O'Brien at
Thomaston, Maine, and was launched in December, 1881. She was
named in honor of Henry Knox who was born in Boston in 1750 and
who early took a part in the affairs of the Revolutionary War, being a
volunteer at the battle of Bunker Hill. Later he was commissioned a
major general and in 1785 was appointed secretary of war which position he filled for eleven years. In 1798 he was called upon to take a
command in the army but the peaceful arrangement of affairs between this country and France soon permitted him to return into his
retirement at his home in Thomaston, Me., and he died there in
1806, one of the state's most prominent figures. Fort Knox, built on
the Penobscot River by the government, was recently transferred to
the state.

The *General Knox* was built to be operated in trade between New
York, San Francisco and Liverpool and her whole life as a sailing ship
was spent therein with the exception of about a year's employment in
the coal trade between Seattle and San Francisco. In common with
other O'Brien ships she was a large carrier and her eight round voyages between Atlantic and Pacific ports, via Cape Horn, averaged
fairly well, being 133 days on the outward passages and 130 days for
those homeward. Strange to say several of her eastward runs were
longer than those to the westward. Prior to her being burned she had
no mishaps of consequence.

At 3 A.M. on Aug. 18, 1894, while the *General Knox* was alongside
the wharf at New York, loading general cargo for San Francisco and
had some 1000 tons aboard, she was discovered to be on fire. A quantity of the cargo was discharged undamaged but all efforts to extinguish the fire were unsuccessful and the ship was scuttled, settling
on the bottom. Later on she was floated but was found to be so badly

damaged that she was sold for $7,750 to Lewis Luckenbach who had her converted into a barge. She was evidently cut down as thereafter her tonnage was given as 1587 tons. In October, 1917, she was purchased by the United States Government but does not appear to have been long in service as she had been laid up on the beach for some years prior to August, 1928, when she and the barges *San Joaquin* and *Solitaire* were reported as about to be towed to Eastport, Me., to be burned for their metal. This, however, was not done and the three barges, all former sailing ships, were still on the beach at Hammond Flats, opposite Whitestone, Long Island, in the summer of 1930.

Capt. Joseph Henry of Thomaston, a brother of Capt. Fred T. Henry, took command of the *Knox* when she came off the stocks and left her in December, 1885, at San Francisco, following her arrival from Liverpool. The Captain had originally been mate of the ship *Belle O'Brien* and later made two round voyages in the "little" *Edward O'Brien*. This ship and the *General Knox* are said to be the only ones he commanded. Capt. Thomas G. Libby of Brunswick, Me., followed him in the *Knox* and continued in the ship until her end. Captain Libby had previously been master of the "little" *Edward O'Brien*, some four years, and after the burning of the *Knox* was in the *Baring Brothers* one voyage. He passed away at his home about three years ago.

GENERAL McCLELLAN

THE ship *General McClellan* was built by Samuel Watts, at Thomaston, Maine, and was launched in July, 1862. She was 191 feet, by 39:3, by 28:6 feet; 1518 tons register. She was built for transatlantic trade and modeled for carrying, with short and quite bluff ends; the stern was elliptic. Early in her career she was purchased by Lawrence Giles & Co., New York, and they owned her until 1881 when she was sold for $35,000 to parties in San Francisco. Some three years later she was sold at New York to parties representing Troop & Son of St. John. In 1889 her managing owners appear as J. W. Elwell & Co. The following years she again changed hands, being purchased by Philadelphia parties who converted her into a barge. She was named after General George Briton McClellan, a prominent officer in the Mexican and Civil Wars, who subsequently was a presidential candidate, and from 1878 until 1881 was Governor of New Jersey. The General died in 1885.

For her first five years the McClellan was in the transatlantic trade. In 1867 she started running to San Francisco and during the following sixteen years was continuously employed between New York, San Francisco and Liverpool, making during that period fourteen round voyages. She became one of the best known vessels in the trade and while her passages were slow they were very uniform and never varied much from the average she has, 145 days to San Francisco and 128 days from that port. Her voyages appear to have been uneventful and her name does not once appear in lists of mishaps or disasters during this period.

On being sold at New York, early in 1884, the McClellan was kept in the Atlantic about four years, when she loaded coal at Baltimore for San Francisco. She grounded twice on proceeding to sea but sustained no injury and all went well until she was approaching Cape Horn when she sprung a bad leak. The steam pumps being unable to keep her free, a portion of the cargo was jettisoned. Fortunately fine weather was experienced during the actual passage around the Cape and with pumps working intermittently she reached San Francisco, Oct. 17, 1888, 174 days out from Baltimore. She then loaded lumber at Puget Sound and sailed Feb. 25, 1889, for Buenos Ayres. By some authorities she was not considered seaworthy on leaving port and no surprise was expressed when, a week later, she returned in tow, half full of water and on her beam ends. Over 300,000 feet of her lumber cargo was discharged, she was repaired and finally completed the voyage. She then proceeded to New York, having a very long passage due to a series of calms and being obliged to put into Barbados for provisions. Following her arrival at New York she was sold and converted into a barge as previously stated.

The first commander of the General McClellan was Capt. Alfred Watts, a brother of Samuel Watts, and later superintendent of the

Watts shipyards. While in trade with San Francisco Capt. William S. Williams was her master for three voyages; Capt. George D. Morrison for three and Capt. Charles A. Wheeler for eight voyages. Captain Wheeler had been at sea as master nineteen years, without a break, prior to relinquishing command of the *McClellan* on her being sold in 1884 and during this time his only employers were Lawrence Giles & Co. and John Rosenfeld.

GEORGE F. MANSON

THE ship *George F. Manson* was built for Edwin Reed and others, by A. Hathorn, and was launched at Bath, Maine, in October, 1875. She measured 206:1 feet, by 39:2, by 23:9 feet, and registered 1418 tons. She is said to have been named after a prominent ship broker of New York. Mr. Reed was her manager.

For the first ten years the *Manson* was operated about equally between Atlantic ports and San Francisco or the Far East and made fair passages. Early in her career she took coal from Liverpool to Bombay and made the run in 96 days, which was considered fast time, as she was in the Indian Ocean during the season of northeast monsoons. In 1877 she made the passage from Norfolk, Va., to Liverpool, in 14 days, maintaining an average speed of nine and one-half knots throughout. In 1881 she was 107 days from San Francisco to Liverpool.

Following the discharge of her cargo at Bombay, in 1876, she sailed for Calcutta and at 4 o'clock in the morning of the second day at sea, was in collision with the steamer *Ambassador* of Liverpool, which went down within twelve minutes, but her crew were all saved by the *Manson's* boats. The ship had her bows stove in but the ballast was shifted aft to raise her head and after the broken planks had been patched with tarpaulins, she put back to Bombay. At the subsequent inquiry it was proven that the *Ambassador* had attempted to cross the bows of the *Manson* and Captain Humphrey, of the latter, was absolved from all blame for the disaster.

In 1886 the *Manson* was sold at San Francisco and thereafter Albert Rowe appeared as managing owner. For a few years she was operated in the coastwise coal trade subsequently being employed in carrying lumber from Puget Sound to Australia. Her last voyage was from Port Blakely to Sydney in 1898, following which she sailed from the latter port in May, with coal for San Francisco, and was never thereafter heard of.

Capt. Calvin R. Humphrey of Yarmouth, Me., was the first commander of the *Manson* and served in her six years. He had previously been master of the ship *Bertha*, owned by members of the Humphrey family. He left the *Manson* at Liverpool, in July, 1881, to go home to Yarmouth, and died there, quite suddenly, the following May.

Capt. Charles C. Morse of Bath took command of the *Manson* at San Francisco, early in 1886, and served as her master some four years. One of the early commands of the Captain's was the ship *Moravia* of Bath, which he took in 1872. In January, 1875, she left Cardiff with railroad iron for Mollendo and when not long at sea encountered heavy gales during which the rudder was carried away and the cargo shifted. The ship was thrown on beam ends and was about to founder when a Swedish brig hove in sight and succeeded in rescuing Captain Morse, his crew of twenty-one men, and the three passengers. A few days later they were landed at Queenstown. Captain Morse then had the *Ellen Goodspeed* five years, engaged in trade with San Francisco and China, and on taking command of the *Manson* made his home in San Francisco and sailed in ships belonging to that port, the *C. F. Sargent, Occidental* and *Fort George*. In 1901 he made a short voyage in the *Lord Templetown* and then retired from sea life. He died at San Francisco in July, 1905, at the age of sixty-one years.

Capt. Peter Crack was in command of the *Manson* on her ill-fated voyage.

GEORGE STETSON

THE ship *George Stetson* was built by A. Hathorn, at Bath, Maine, for Parker M. Whitmore and others and was launched in July, 1880. She measured 232 feet, by 41:3, by 26:3 feet, and registered 1780 tons. She had three decks, was a fine vessel in all respects and considered a good sailer for a ship of her class.

Practically the whole sea life of the *George Stetson* was spent in trade between Atlantic ports and San Francisco, the only exceptions being one voyage to the Orient and one to the Columbia River on the outward runs, and two from the Hawaiian Islands on those homeward. She was successful and profitable. Her first wheat cargo to Liverpool netted $36,500. She made fourteen passages to San Francisco, of which the shortest were 109 and 117 days and the average 143 days, which high figure was due to six passages of 150 days or over caused by particularly unfavorable weather. The average of the other eight is 128 days. Homeward bound the average of her four passages to New York is 112 days, the two shortest being 103 and 104 days. The average of the seven made in the grain trade is 125 days; shortest 114 days to Liverpool and longest 135 days to Havre. The first run from the Hawaiian Islands to New York was 117 days and the second 127 days, but on this she had put into port Stanley for some minor trouble.

An account of a test of speed between the *George Stetson* and the ship *W. F. Babcock*, commanded respectively by the brothers Eben L. and James F. Murphy, on a round voyage from San Francisco, is contained in account of the *Babcock*, in "American Merchant Ships," Series I.

The only serious accident occurring to the *George Stetson*, during the course of her voyages, was during the passage from San Francisco to Liverpool in 1887-1888. In the North Atlantic she was partially dismasted and had her hull damaged. She was put into St. Thomas where in still water she was found to be leaking at the rate of seven inches an hour. Part of the cargo was discharged and she was in port some six weeks undergoing repairs.

The last voyage of the *George Stetson* was from New York to San Francisco, she going thence to the Columbia River to load lumber for Taku. On the latter passage she was found to be on fire, Aug. 27, 1899, and all efforts to save her were futile. She was abandoned about sixty miles north of Formosa and after being forty-eight hours in the boats, Capt. Frank W. Patten, wife and child, and the ship's crew, effected a landing on a small island. From there they were taken to Nagasaki and subsequently to San Francisco.

The first commander of the *George Stetson* was Capt. William S. Higgins of Bangor, Me., for whom the ship had been built and who owned an interest. Captain Higgins was a brother-in-law of Capt. James F. Murphy which explains how the latter's brother, Capt. Eben L. Murphy, was subsequently appointed master of the *Stetson*. Captain Higgins made but two voyages in the *Stetson* after which he retired from sea life to engage in business in Bangor and died there.

Capt. Edward H. Wood of Wiscasset, Me., who had previously been master of the ship *Richard 3d* many years, had the *George Stetson* from 1884 until 1889 when Capt. Eben L. Murphy succeeded. The latter had originally been in command of the ship *Northampton*, engaged in transatlantic trade, owned by Houghton Brothers of Bath, and when that firm became sole owners of the ship *Harry Morse*, Captain Murphy was transferred to her and continued as her master until he took the *Stetson*. Following the arrival of the latter ship at Portland, Ore., from New York, in 1898, Captain Murphy and his chief officer were prosecuted for alleged cruelty to a half-witted sailor, but both were acquitted. The affair, however, resulted in the illness of Captain Murphy and he died in Portland, in January, 1899. Just prior to his death he had been appointed to the command of the big ship *Shenandoah*.

GERARD C. TOBEY

THE *Gerard C. Tobey* was a double-topgallant, main skysail-
yard bark built by Goss, Sawyer & Packard, at Bath, Maine, and
was launched in July, 1878. She measured 208:7 feet, by 39:1, by
23:6 feet, and registered 1390 tons. She was owned by her builders,
Capt. William H. Besse of New Bedford, and others and was managed by Captain Besse. In model and general appearance she closely
resembled the *Guy C. Goss*, built a year later in the same yard and
owned by the same parties, although the *Goss* was larger by nearly
200 tons.

On her maiden voyage the *Tobey* sailed from Wiscasset, Me.,
Aug. 4, 1878, with 1,200,000 feet of lumber and was 20 days to
Cardiff. There she was docked and metaled, loaded 2000 tons of
coal and made the passage to Yokohama in 134 days. After discharging she loaded part cargo for San Francisco and made the run across
the Pacific in 24 days. Then taking on a cargo of wheat and flour she
was 109 days to Liverpool, thence going to New York in 20 days.
The whole round voyage occupied 14 months, 14 days and was very
satisfactory to her owners. Thereafter, until she was sold in 1900, the
Tobey was employed in trade between Atlantic ports and China,
Japan and San Francisco, always making good to fair average passages without meeting with serious mishaps and having the reputation of being a successful vessel. Her nearest approach to disaster
was once, when laden with oil and slate for London and at anchor
near Bedloe's Island, New York, she was run down by the steamer
City of Savannah and damaged so badly that she was towed on the
nearby flats to prevent sinking. The cargo was discharged into lighters
after which the vessel was floated and put on dry dock for repairs.

The *Tobey* was sold in 1900 to Welch & Co. of San Francisco, for
the sugar trade between that port and the Hawaiian Islands and eight
years later was purchased by Capt. William Matson to continue in the
same business. In 1910 she was again sold and converted into a barge
and for a few years was operated by the Ocean Barge and Towboat

Co. of Seattle. In July, 1914, she went ashore in Seymour Narrows, B. C., and became a total loss.

Among the commanders of the *Gerard C. Tobey*, while she was employed on long distance voyages, were Captains Elkanah Crowell, Jr., Benjamin D. Baxter, and S. B. Gibbs. Captain Crowell was a native of Yarmouth, Mass., one of seven sons of Capt. Elkanah Crowell, Sr., who was engaged in the coasting trade many years. All the sons became shipmasters, Capt. Elkanah, Jr., being considered one of the most successful clipper ship commanders. In 1854 he was mate of the celebrated clipper *Spitfire* and subsequently commanded the *Galatea*, *Boston Light*, and *Fair Wind*. He owned an interest in the *Tobey* but made only two voyages in her, after which he retired from the sea to make his home in Hyannis, Mass., where he finally passed away.

Capt. Benjamin D. Baxter was a native of Hyannis and prior to taking command of the *Tobey*, in 1881, had been master of the ship *Nearchus*. Capt. S. B. Gibbs was for many years master of the *Olympic* and is more particularly mentioned in the account of that ship.

GLENDON

THE *Glendon* was a first class ship built by Capt. N. L. Thompson at Kennebunk, Maine, and launched in January, 1880. She measured 225 feet, by 43:7, by 28:4 feet, and registered 1897 tons. Following her arrival at San Francisco on the termination of her first passage, which was from New York, she was purchased by Howes & Crowell for $85,000 and thereafter her hailing port was Boston. On the failure of her owners in 1884 she was sold to parties represented by Edward Lawrence, Jr., who became managing owner. When she was lost, George W. Rice appears as such.

The first two voyages of the *Glendon* were between New York, San Francisco and Liverpool and on the third she took railroad iron from Philadelphia to Tacoma; thence coal to San Francisco, arriving in March, 1883. She was laid up from that date until March, 1886, when she took wheat to Liverpool. She then made three voyages with case oil to the Far East and was lost on the fourth.

The passages of the *Glendon* were made in good average time, the shortest being one of 110 days from San Francisco to Liverpool. On one occasion she met the ship *P. N. Blanchard* in the North Atlantic bound in the same direction and during the course of the following day ran her out of sight astern.

In March, 1890, the *Glendon*, when nearing Yokohama on her passage from New York, got ashore on a rocky coast and had her bottom stove. All hands were saved and after about one-third of her cargo of 66,000 cases of oil had been discharged, she was floated and towed into Yokohama. The hull was found to be badly hogged so she was sold as not worth repairing.

Capt. Edwin Thacher of Yarmouth, Mass., was sent to San Francisco to assume command of the *Glendon*, on her purchase by Howes & Crowell, and he continued in her as master until her loss. The first command of the Captain had been the ship *Audubon* of Boston, which he took in 1864 and in which he was shipwrecked near Manila in June, 1868. He subsequently commanded the *Ringleader* and *Ericsson*. Following the loss of the *Glendon* he retired from sea life and passed away at Yarmouth in June, 1918, at the age of eighty-three years. A brother, Capt. Samuel H. Thacher, was well known in connection with his commands, the ships *Garibaldi* and *Valley Forge*.

GLORY OF THE SEAS

THE ship *Glory of the Seas* was built by Donald McKay, at East Boston, on his own account and was launched in October, 1869. She measured 240:2 feet, by 44:1, by 28 feet; and registered 2009 tons, net. She was constructed of the best materials obtainable and in the strongest manner as is evidenced by her long career in heavy trade. Although she was often called a clipper she was in fact of full model and on Cape Horn voyages generally loaded 3000 tons in dead weight cargoes, although when employed in the coal trade along the

Pacific Coast she once had nearly 4000 tons, but being then evidently overloaded, her later cargoes ran between 3300 and 3600 tons. She was a good looking ship, with an elliptic stern while the bow was ornamented with a beautifully carved image of a classical female with flowing drapery. She had eight and one-half inches dead rise at half floor and seven feet shear. She crossed a skysail yard on the mainmast and is said to have spread 8,000 yards of canvas in a single suit of sails, but as the ship *Great Admiral*, of 500 tons less measurement, set 7,889 yards, the *Glory* would seem not to have been particularly heavily sparred. She was the last ship built by Mr. McKay, famous as the constructor of the *Flying Cloud* and other celebrated clippers.

Of recent years the *Glory of the Seas* has been given much publicity in the press as being a very fast ship, a record breaker and the like, and while she did make good passages yet facts do not justify the extravagant praise bestowed. She does hold the record of passages made from San Francisco to Australia and her run from New York to San Francisco, in 1873-1874, has not since been beaten. It had previously been surpassed only in eight instances and four of those passages were made by ships built by Mr. McKay, but of clipper model. On the fast passages of the *Glory* she did not attain any high speed nor make any great day's runs but her log books show that she generally met with favorable winds and weather allowing her to keep close to her course, besides which, practically no delays were had in the doldrums of the tropics.

The following is a list of the voyages made by the *Glory of the Seas*, prior to 1886:

1870	New York to San Francisco		120 days	San Francisco to Queenstown		112 days
1871-72	Cardiff to	"	120 "	" to Liverpool		112 "
1872-73	Liverpool to	"	120 "	" to	"	128 "
1873-74	New York to	"	96 "	" to	"	118 "
1874	Liverpool to	"	131 "			
1874-75	San Francisco to Sydney		35 "	Sydney to San Francisco		53 "
1875-76				San Francisco to Liverpool		133 "
1876-77	Liverpool to San Francisco		114 "	" to	"	103 "
1877-78	"	"	144 "	" to	"	107 "
1878-79	"	"	153 "	" to Queenstown		111 "
1880	New York to San Francisco		118 "	" to	"	120 "

1881-82	Cardiff to San Francisco	120 days	San Francisco to Havre	131 days
1882	New York to "	120 "		
1883-84	Laid up at "			
1885			" to Liverpool	117 "
1885	Liverpool to San Pedro, Cal.	121 "		

The time quoted on the passage to Havre, in 1881-82, is actual sailing time, the ship being at Valparaiso three months repairing and making the passage thence to Havre in 77 days.

According to the above table the passages made by the *Glory*, from the Atlantic to the Pacific, averaged 123¾ days and the returns, 117 days.

The following details of the fast passages made by the ship are from a copy of her abstract log:

New York to San Francisco

Oct. 13, 1873. At 8 A.M. took tug *C. F. Walcott*, at Pier 18, and went on board with quite a party of friends. At 10 o'clock started for San Francisco. At 12, noon, off Sandy Hook.

First week. Sailed 1208 miles; best day, 252 miles. Started off before a light wind in a smooth sea. Thereafter, moderate to strong winds, mostly from N E to N N E.

Second week. Sailed 1019 miles; best day, 188 miles. Moderate winds from N W to N, shifting to S S W and S S E.

Third week. Sailed 1160 miles; best day, 231 miles. Four days of moderate trades followed by fair to light breezes.

Fourth week. Sailed 903 miles; best day, 214 miles. Light to moderate winds, ending with good trades. Crossed the Line 27 days out. For three days in company with a bark bound in the same direction.

Fifth week. Sailed 1129 miles; best day, 210 miles. Moderate trades to latitude 18° S, when take winds from W to S W and S S W with a heavy head sea.

Sixth week. Sailed 1119 miles; best day, 220 miles. Winds mostly from N E.

Seventh week. Sailed 1233 miles; best day 261 miles. Winds from W N W to N E.

Eighth week. Sailed 590 miles; best day, 194 miles. Winds from W N W to S W. On 50th day out made west end of Staten Island, intending to go through the Straits of Le Maire but wind forced us around Cape St. John.

Ninth week. Sailed 1531 miles; best day, 228 miles. Crossed 50° S. in the Pacific, 60 days out, having made the Cape Horn run in 11 days, sailing 1380 miles at an average of 5¾ knots. Off the Cape passed six vessels bound in the same direction.

Tenth week. Sailed 1271 miles; best day, 228 miles. Moderate S E trades.

Eleventh week. Sailed 1301 miles; best day, 202 miles. Moderate S E trades.

Twelfth week. Sailed 1334 miles; best day, 237 miles. Crossed the Line 78 days out, 18 days from latitude 50°. Carried the S E trades to latitude 6° N. where picked up the N E trades.

Thirteenth week. Sailed 974 miles; best day, 181 miles. Lost the trades in latitude 24°; then moderate to light winds from N E to N N E. On the 93rd day out the wind shifted to S E and developed into a hard blow with thick and rainy weather, the ship making 166 miles and the following day 300 miles, which was the best day's run on the passage. At 6 p.m. Jan. 16, 1874, took in all sails that had not been blown away, except the lower topsails, and hove to. At noon the next day was up to the San Francisco bar, 95 days from New York, but it was breaking heavily and the pilots were all inside. Stood off and on all night and next morning entered port after a passage of 96 days.

Total distance sailed, 15,344 miles; daily average, 161½ miles.

SAN FRANCISCO TO SYDNEY

March 14, 1875. Hove up anchor at 6.30 a.m. and dropped pilot outside the bar at 9.30.

First week. Sailed 1606 miles; best day, 278 miles. Winds from N N W to N N E first four days when picked up the N E trades. Ship very crank so cannot carry as much sail as otherwise would.

Second week. Sailed 1436 miles; best day 236 miles. Dropped the N E and picked up the S E trades the same day.

Third week. Sailed 1231 miles; best day, 238 miles. Moderate to light trades.

Fourth week. Sailed 1801 miles; best day, 284 miles. First five days strong to fresh trades. Then moderate winds from E N E. Crossed the 180th meridian in latitude 23° S. 25 days out, 13 days from the Line which had crossed in longitude 145° 30' W.

Fifth week. Sailed 952 miles; best day, 149 miles. Light winds from E N E to S S E.

Arrived at Sydney, May 19, 1875, 35 days, 5 hours passage, pilot to pilot; 35 days 11 hours, anchor to anchor. Total distance sailed, 7026 miles; distance made good, 6884 miles; average rate of sailing, 8⅛ knots.

SYDNEY TO SAN FRANCISCO

April 4, 1875. Left Sydney Heads at 9.30 A.M.

First week. Sailed 766 miles; best day, 184 miles. Mostly light and baffling, shifting winds. Some heavy swells and high head seas.

Second week. Sailed 1096 miles; best day, 204 miles. Light to strong winds, mostly from the westward with many rain squalls. Passed a ship which left Sydney in company and the next day she was out of sight astern.

Third week. Sailed 1630 miles; best day, 263 miles. Strong winds from N to N W. Picked up the S E trades.

Fourth week. Sailed 1516 miles; best day, 243 miles. Moderate to strong trades.

Fifth week. Sailed 1113 miles; best day, 192 miles. Lost S E trades in latitude 4° N. where picked up the N E trades.

Sixth week. Sailed 1240 miles; best day, 207 miles. Fresh to light trades.

Seventh week. Sailed 876 miles; best day, 192 miles. Light winds from N E, shifting to moderate from S E.

Eighth week (part). Sailed 660 miles; best day, 256 miles. Light winds from W, then strong from N to N E, ending light.

Arrived at San Francisco, July 26, 1875, 53 days from Sydney, the fastest passage that had been made for some time. Total distance sailed, 8897 miles. Distance made good, 8613 miles.

The following are some comparisons between the passages made by the *Glory of the Seas* in the grain trade and those of other ships of her class leaving San Francisco at approximately the same time.

In 1870 the *Glory* made the fastest run of any ship sailing within a month of her and beat the *Charger* two days, and the *Black Hawk* one day.

In 1872 she beat the British ship *La Escocesa* ten days.

In 1873 she was beaten by the British ships *John Duthie*, and *Montgomery Castle* six days each.

In 1874 she was beaten six days by the *Seminole* and 15 days by the *Ericsson*.

In 1876 she beat the *America* 12 days; the *Triumphant* 15 days, besides a number of other American ships by a greater extent and the first-class British ships *City of Perth* five days, and the *Brodick Castle*, *Seaforth*, *City of Nankin*, and others by a month or more. She was, however, beaten by the *Hawkesbury* which made the passage to Havre in 100 days, three days better than the *Glory's* run to Liverpool.

In 1879 she was beaten by the *St. Stephen* 11 days, but beat a number of other American ships, including the *Challenger* and *Josephus*, each 15 days and the *Frank Pendleton* five days.

In 1885 she was beaten by the *Sutherlandshire* 12 days, *Brodick Castle* eight days, *Troop* seven days, and *C. F. Sargent* six days, but beat a number of other British ships and some Americans from 7 to 27 days.

The *Glory of the Seas* and the fast British iron ship *Langdale* left Liverpool in company Aug. 13, 1874, the *Glory* arriving at San Francisco one day in the lead. They met in the Straits of Le Maire on October 8th and two weeks later were close to each other for three days. On arriving at San Francisco, Captain Jenkinson of the *Langdale* took exception to the published memorandum of the *Glory* and

Captain Knowles replied with a card in the newspapers, stating: "If it will satisfy the captain of the *Langdale*, I will say that whenever I raised his ship, she was astern of the *Glory* but came up and passed her. When I got to San Francisco there was no *Langdale*, but as the passages of the ships were 131 and 132 days respectively, I think that is sufficiently long to prevent any discussion as to the great speed of either."

While employed on long distance voyages the *Glory* was quite fortunate in escaping damage from the elements. The most serious accident was on her passage from San Francisco to Havre in 1881. Meeting with very heavy weather when nearing Cape Horn she was badly strained, the decks being twisted and started. Many sacks of wheat in the lower hold burst, choking the pumps and about 2,000 sacks in the upper and lower between decks were wet by salt water. Captain McLaughlin put into Valparaiso where the cargo was discharged into lighters and the damaged portion was sold. The ship was in port three months at an expense of nearly $25,000.

On her passage from Liverpool to San Francisco, in 1874, the *Glory* had a narrow escape from destruction by fire. Her cargo of Lancashire coal became heated and steam could be seen coming from the hatches for a considerable length of time. In handling, the coal was frequently found too hot to be touched and only by the great attention and diligence of Captain Knowles and his crew in pumping on water, digging down and also keeping hatches open for ventilation was the fire finally subdued. The ship herself was but slightly damaged.

Capt. John N. Geit was sailing master of the *Glory of the Seas* on her maiden passage although on her arrival at San Francisco the name of her commander was given as Donald McKay, he having gone out on the trip. Captain William Chatfield took the ship back East, she being then purchased by J. Henry Sears & Co. of Boston and others and Capt. Josiah N. Knowles was appointed master. Captain Knowles continued in command until 1880 when Capt. Daniel McLaughlin succeeded. He made two round voyages from San Francisco, the ship being laid up on the termination of the second in November, 1882. In

1884, Sears & Co. failed and their shipping interests were sold, these including a 1/16th in the *Glory*. In February, 1885, just prior to her resuming operations, Capt. Joshua S. Freeman, a relative of Mr. Sears, bought into the ship and went out to San Francisco to take command. His first voyage was to Liverpool and thence to San Pedro, Cal., and this was the last Cape Horn passage made by the ship, Captain Freeman keeping her in the coastwise coal trade until 1902 when she was sold and he retired from the sea. Thereafter she was owned for some years by the Seattle Shipping Co. and by Barneson & Hibbard. Her last voyage as a sailing vessel was in 1907-1908, from Puget Sound to the West Coast of South America, and on returning she was laid up and later sold to parties in Victoria, B. C. It was stated that she was to be used in connection with a scheme to manufacture hardwood lumber in the New Hebrides but the proposition did not materialize and in 1911 the ship was sold to satisfy creditors. She was purchased by parties who had her converted into a floating salmon cannery, the intention being to have her towed to places where fish were plentiful and have them packed on board. The venture, however, was not a success, due principally to the towing expense and also to the instability of the vessel in the ocean swells. The *Glory* was subsequently fitted with an ice plant and as a floating refrigerator was stocked with fish for cold storage. After some years in such service she was laid up and was finally burned for her metal on the beach near Endolyne, Washington.

The late Walter Francis, a personal friend of the author, then living in Seattle, took a keen interest in old ships and particularly in the *Glory of the Seas*, having sailed in her under Captain Freeman. The following letter, which was accompanied with his sketch of the burning hull of the *Glory*, expresses Mr. Francis' sentiments in the matter. It is dated May 23, 1923.

Dear Mr. Matthews.

Well, old *Glory* has gone at last and by some curious working of the mind, I was inspired, directed or allowed to be present at her finish.

Sunday, May 13, was gloomy and threatening so I stayed home until about 3 P.M., then suddenly determined to take a ride some place. Was just about to board a car for town as a starting place, when "something" directed me to return, get my sketch pad and ride to Endolyne to see if anything had happened to the old ship since I last saw her six weeks before.

Nearing the beach, instead of her topmasts through the trees, I saw a thin cloud of smoke and felt that she might have been smouldering for a week and I would see nothing but her keel.

Down to the beach and found that she had been burning only a few hours but at that nothing was left of her but a fire-punctured shell, a section of which would occasionally fall into the waters of Puget Sound with a dull explosion. Her badly charred fore and main masts were alongside, the mizen hanging over the port quarter, the whole mixed up with bolts, wire and remnants of another burned hull. The picture made one think of the effect of a tidal wave followed by fire. My sketch will let you visualize it.

The only spectacular bit I saw was when, from the weight of the bowsprit, the entire bow from catheads to stempost at the bobstays fell overboard in one huge chunk. I felt glad that the goddess who formerly capped the stem, was saved the humiliation of being smashed to splinters by gravel and shallow water in a junk yard. She was an old friend and I had sketched her more than once.

That the old ship was to be burned that day was not made public so only a few residents, mostly children, saw the end of what was to them merely a lot of wood bolted together and called a "boat." Had it been given publicity, probably thousands would have driven there to see the smoke and to most of them it would have been an entertainment.

Well, what with gloomy sky, silent water and certain fire, I felt rather badly but at the same time superior to the other few spectators in that I knew what it all meant. Also, for consolation that after the death notice, we of the faithful will have some rest from the drivel that has been written about a fine old ship that was rather extravagantly named.

The place is Endolyne, on the Sound, about five miles from Seattle. Nothing is there but a tiny strip of pebble beach and the hull. Her nose was almost under the trees that grow on the high banks. Within a mile passed Blue Funnel, Admiral-Orient liners and other big steamers to and from Tacoma.

Capt. Josiah N. Knowles, who made nine round voyages in the *Glory of the Seas* and was in command on her exceptionally fast passages, a brother of Capt. Allen H. Knowles, well known as master of the *Conqueror*, *Agenor*, and other Boston ships, was a native of Eastham, Mass., and had previously been master of the *Kentuckian*, *Wild Wave* and *Charger*. The *Wild Wave* was a fine ship built at Rich-

mond, Me., in 1854, and was commanded by Captain Knowles during
her life of four years. Details of her loss and the subsequent achievements of her captain and part of his crew read like romance. She left
San Francisco in February, 1858, in ballast, for Valparaiso, Captain
Knowles having $18,000 in gold coin in his care. When 24 days out
she was wrecked on the uninhabited atoll of Oeno, in latitude 24° S.,
longitude 131° W., due to an error in the chart. At midnight breakers
ahead were reported and in tacking the ship missed stays and struck
the reef, almost immediately being bilged. Fortunately she went on in a
comparatively smooth place otherwise all hands would have been lost.
The next morning the crew got ashore in the boats with provisions,
sails, etc., and set up a camp; sea birds, eggs and fish were found in
abundance and water was had by digging. After seven days a lull in
the surf permitted the launching of a boat and Captain Knowles, chief
mate J. H. Bartlett and five men set out to reach Pitcairn Island for
assistance, taking the two boxes of treasure. They reached their destination after three days of heavy seas during which the boat was nearly
swamped. Finding Pitcairn uninhabited, its people having gone to
Norfolk Island according to notices posted in the cabins, the castaways
set about the construction of a small schooner after their boat had been
smashed by the breakers. The only tools they found were some axes
and a hammer. They hewed boards and timber from trees; obtained
a small supply of nails from the cabins and made many wooden pins.
Oakum was picked from some old cordage and rope made on an improvised ropewalk. After six weeks of hard labor the materials for
a schooner 30 by 8 by 4 feet were assembled and the keel of the
vessel was laid. She was launched in shortly more than four months
after the castaways had landed on the island and was provisioned
with fruit, meat, etc., there being many sheep, goats, bullocks, and
chickens that had been left by the former inhabitants. A small pump
was rigged; an old anvil served as an anchor, while a copper kettle
was made to do duty as a stove. An ensign was made from red cloth, a
shirt and a pair of blue overalls, and on July 24th a start was made
for Tahiti, three men who elected to stay on the island being left behind. Contrary winds forced a change of course and on the eleventh

day the party made one of the Marquesas group but the natives look-ing treacherous, their invitation to land was ignored and the schooner continued on to Nukahiva. They were agreeably surprised to find the sloop-of-war *Vandalia* at anchor there and were taken on board, the *Vandalia* sailing the same day for Tahiti where Captain Knowles and his party were landed. The Captain arrived at San Francisco in Sep-tember, by way of Honolulu, and as nothing had been heard of the *Wild Wave* or any of her crew during the previous seven months, she had been given up as lost with all hands. The treasure had been care-fully looked after, being buried while the party was at Pitcairn and then taken in the schooner to Tahiti, the little vessel being sold there for $250.

Captain Knowles retired from sea life on relinquishing command of the *Glory of the Seas* and became one of San Francisco's most prominent and enterprising shipping merchants. He died in June, 1896, at the age of sixty-six years.

Capt. Daniel McLaughlin, who succeeded Captain Knowles, was born close to the shores of the Bay of Fundy, but for many years made his home in Eastport, Me. He was the first master of the ship *Gray Feather*, built at Eastport in 1850, and subsequently command-ed various ships, among them the clippers *Swallow* and *Herald of the Morning*, in which he made some very fast voyages. He engaged in ranching in California, after leaving the *Glory*, and died while on a visit to his birthplace in January, 1896, at the age of seventy-two years.

Captain McLaughlin was a thorough seaman and navigator and his record is a clean one. In 1855 he was appointed master of the new ship *Ætos*, 1400 tons, built at Eastport for Boston parties, and the following copy of a letter written by him to Lieut. M. F. Maury, while the latter was compiling his "Sailing Directions," gives a side light on the way old-time shipmasters planned voyages. The *Ætos* was about leaving Liverpool for Bombay and the letter is dated April 22, 1856.

There is one thing I have to contend with on this passage, that is three British clippers which sailed today for Bombay; the ship *Conflict*, iron, 1320 tons, extreme clipper, noted for her last passage to Bombay in 83 days; the iron clipper *Kunjee Oadunjee*, 1000 tons, very sharp and in good trim, and the *Tiger*, 1000 tons, very long and drawing only seventeen feet. All those ships in better trim than mine and old traders to Bombay. My ship is 1430 tons, American measurement, 1352 tons, English; has 1236 tons dead weight and 532 tons measurement cargo; draft, aft, 21 feet and forward 21:3, the mistake occurring through her being on the ground when finishing loading at the docks.

Now as it is against the principles of a Yankee to get beat, I will try these fellows hard. Wind allowing, I will pass say three degrees east of the Western Islands; then straight for the west cape of the De Verde's; cross the line in 26 to 28 degrees; let her go with a good full sail through the S. E. trades; then get into the west winds as soon as possible. Pass the Cape in latitude 38 and go to 50 E. in 30 S.; then go to the eastward of Madagascar and cross the line in longitude 62 or 64, thence run straight to port. Now I think I can cross the line in 25 days; [did it in 29]; pass the Cape in 50 days [was 52]; make port in 80 days.

The *Ætos* made the passage in 77½ days while her closest competitor, the *Conflict* was 80 days. Lieut. Maury regarded Captain McLaughlin's proposed route as having been very well projected.

Capt. Joshua Freeman, Jr., made his home in Victoria, B. C., after selling the *Glory of the Seas* in 1902, and was engaged in business there several years. He was born in Brewster, Mass., in 1835, the son of Capt. Joshua Freeman who died in 1839 at the early age of thirty-three years. Capt. Joshua, Jr., went to sea at the age of sixteen and shortly after attaining his majority he became master of the ship *Christopher Hall*. Subsequent commands were the *W. B. Dinsmore*, *National Eagle*, and *Gold Hunter*, he being master of the last named many years prior to her loss in 1878.

Mr. J. H. Bartlett, mate of the *Wild Wave* when she was lost, later became Captain Bartlett and lost his life in the ship *Ellen Sears* which went missing on a passage from San Francisco to Liverpool in 1867.

GOLD HUNTER

THE *Gold Hunter* was a fine ship built by J. Clark & Sons at Waldoboro, Maine, and launched in December, 1867. She measured 180 feet, by 38:6, by 24 feet and registered 1256 tons. She was built for J. Henry Sears & Co. of Boston, and they were her managing owners during the thirteen years of her sea life.

The *Gold Hunter* made four voyages between Atlantic ports and San Francisco; spent two years in transatlantic trade and during the rest of her career carried coal or case oil to China. She made fair passages, was generally fortunate in her operations and met with no major mishaps. On one occasion she was run down in San Francisco by the ship *Anahuac*, outward bound in tow, and had her bowsprit carried away. Some years later her rudderhead was twisted off while she was rounding Cape Horn and tackles had to be used the rest of the way to San Francisco. She gained some notoriety in November, 1878, when, while in port at Shanghai, the crew mutinied and engaged in a shooting affray with the ship's officers and police from shore, several men on both sides being wounded.

In February, 1878, the *Gold Hunter* sailed from New York for Shanghai, thence crossing to Puget Sound and then taking lumber to Callao. On returning to the Sound she loaded coal for San Francisco and then wheat for Falmouth. After discharging this at Dunkirk she loaded coal at Cardiff for Hong Kong and was lost on the passage by striking a coral reef in the South China Sea. All hands made shore in the ship's boats, although with great difficulty, and subsequently got to Manila.

Captains Edgar Lincoln, C. Howard Allyn and John F. Baker each made a voyage in the *Gold Hunter*. Aside from these she was commanded by Capt. Joshua S. Freeman, Jr., from the time she was built until she was lost. Captain Freeman's seafaring career is given in the account of the ship *Glory of the Seas*, in which he sailed as master for eighteen years.

GOOD HOPE

THE ship *Good Hope* was built by J. O. Curtis at Medford, Mass., in 1855, and was 187 feet, by 38:6, by 23 feet, registering 1177 tons. At different periods she is listed as owned by Robert L. Taylor, Francis Burritt and E. E. Morgan's Sons, all shipping merchants of New York. Capt. J. F. Miller was her first commander and continued in her as master during most of her career as an American ship.

The maiden passage of the *Good Hope* was from New York to San Francisco and thereafter, at quite widely separated intervals, she made three other such runs. All of these were in quite slow time, their average being 141 days and the shortest 136 days. She went back East from the Pacific Coast only once, to Liverpool in 1873, being 143 days on the way. The greater portion of the remainder of her operations were between Liverpool or London and Calcutta and on that route her passages were somewhat better, averaging about 110 days so that on the whole she cannot be said to have lived up to the reputation she was supposed to have, that of a good sailer. She was, however, a good carrier, having on one of her passages to San Francisco 550 tons of dead weight cargo and 1900 tons of measurement goods.

In 1860 the *Good Hope* went from San Francisco to Callao, but prospects for obtaining a good guano charter proving poor, she immediately proceeded to Calcutta and thence to Savannah. Arriving at the latter port just at the outset of the Civil War she was given twenty-four hours to leave under penalty of confiscation by the Confederates, so immediately continued on to New York.

In April, 1873, the *Good Hope* sailed from Ardrossan bound to San Francisco but having encountered heavy weather south of the Line in the Atlantic, she put into Bahia for repairs. The cargo was discharged and following a survey of the ship she was sold to Frederick Hasselmann who had her repaired and put under the Brazilian flag, renamed after himself. A few years later she again changed hands, becoming the Swedish ship *Solide* and was operated in transatlantic trade. In November, 1881, she was reported ashore and wrecked near Quebec.

GRECIAN

THE ship *Grecian* was built by Titcomb & Thompson at Kennebunkport, Maine, and was launched in June, 1876. She was 215:8 feet, by 40:5, by 26:9 feet and registered 1677 tons. J. Henry Sears & Co. of Boston were managers and principal owners. She was a fine ship in all respects and was always kept in spick and span condition and with her bright spars and white yardarms and blocks presented an attractive appearance.

The life of the *Grecian* was short as she completed only six round voyages from North Atlantic ports, three being to San Francisco, two to Hong Kong and one to Yokohama. She had the reputation of being a fast sailer and her master, Captain Dunbar, was a "driver," but her passages averaged only fairly as to length. The two shortest were from San Francisco to Queenstown, 102 days, and from Cardiff to Hong Kong, 104 days.

In March, 1885, while bound from Iloilo to New York, the *Grecian* stranded on Great Danger Bank, off the island of Balabac, one of the Philippine group, and became a total loss. All hands reached shore safely and were later taken to Manila. On being put up at auction the wreck of the ship, with what remained of her cargo, brought only $660.

During her whole sea life the *Grecian* was commanded by Capt. Albert H. Dunbar, a native of Yarmouth, Mass., born in 1837. The Captain had previously been master of the ships *Josiah Bradlee, Alhambra, Gardner Colby, Thatcher Magoun,* and *Kentuckian.* After the loss of the *Grecian* he settled in San Diego, Cal., and in partnership with Capt. James Connolly, formerly master of the ship *South American,* was engaged in the real estate business until his death in 1892.

GREAT ADMIRAL

THE ship *Great Admiral* was built by Robert E. Jackson at East Boston and was launched April 10, 1869. She was 215:6 feet, by 40:2, by 25:6 feet, and had a tonnage of 1497 net. Her lines approached those of a medium clipper, her ends being quite long and her capacity for dead weight cargo was only one-third in excess of her registered tonnage. She was designed by Constructor W. H. Varney, U. S. Navy, and was built in the strongest manner and of the best materials. In her frame there were 343 tons of hard wood and in her construction were used 105 tons of iron, twenty tons of copper and 253 hogsheads of salt. Not a single iron spike, bolt or nail was used on her outside, all fastenings being of copper from keel to monkey rail and all upper deck and house fastenings were of the same metal. The three anchors weighed 12,301 pounds, the best bower weighing 4,681. The chains weighed 33,950 pounds. She was heavily sparred; had but one skysail, that on the mainmast; and set studding sails as high as royals. The mainmast was 90 feet long; topmast, 48 feet; and topgallant, royal and skysail mast, 55 feet. The mainyard was 91 feet long; lower topsail yard, 79 feet; upper topsail yard, 72 feet; topgallant, 60 feet; royal, 46; and skysail yard, 40 feet. The yards on the foremast were but slightly shorter than those on the main, the foreyard being 86 feet long. The mizzenmast was 86 feet long and the crossjack yard 67 feet. She spread 7,889 yards of canvas exclusive of studding sails. She had hemp rigging until 1883 when wire was substituted. Her crew consisted of three mates, boatswain, carpenter, steward, cook and twenty-eight men and boys.

The *Great Admiral* was built to the order of William F. Weld & Co. of Boston, who at that time had the largest sailing fleet in America. It had been the intention to call the ship *Jason* in remembrance of a ship of that name which during the War of 1812 had been commanded by Capt. William Gordon Weld, father of William Fletcher Weld, who in 1832 established the Weld firm in partnership with Richard Baker, Jr. Another reason for the selection of *Jason*, as a name for the new ship, was that this would be appropriate as she would be run in connection with the owners' clipper *Golden Fleece*. However, about this time Admiral Farragut, called the "Great Admiral," had become very popular, so the ship was named in his honor and a life-sized image of him was carved to do duty as a figurehead. This image is now a feature of interest on the Weld estate near Boston.

From the time the *Great Admiral* was built until the launching of the *South American*, she was conceded to be the finest wooden merchant ship afloat and was the center of admiration in every port she visited. During the twenty-eight years she was owned by Weld & Co. she was kept in perfect order and in spite of having been hard driven and spending much time in Oriental waters, her timbers were found to be in first-class condition when she was opened up for reclassing in 1889. She was sold by Weld & Co. in March, 1897, to Capt. E. R. Sterling for $12,500, and to quote Captain Rowell, "The 'Black Horse' flag was hauled down for the last time from the last survivor of that great fleet which carried it the world over for years."

The *Great Admiral* was remarkably fortunate in escaping damage from the elements, having no mishaps of consequence while owned by Weld & Co. During this period she covered a distance of 726,968 miles in 5,360 sailing days, an average of 135.6 miles daily. The greatest distance sailed in any one day was 305 miles and the greatest in any consecutive ten days, 2,735, of which 304 miles was the best day's work and 240 the poorest. While she broke no records, several of her passages were very close to the fastest time ever made. Her shortest runs were as follows:

New York to San Francisco	111 days	New York to Melbourne	73 days
Philadelphia to Tacoma	111 days	Cardiff to Anjer	77 days
Manila to New York	89 days	Hakodate to San Francisco	25 days
Newcastle, Aus., to Hong Kong	37 days	San Francisco to Hong Kong	37 days
Hong Kong to San Francisco	38 days	Hong Kong to San Francisco	39 days
Hong Kong to New York	95 days	New York to Sydney, Aus.	90 days
Sydney to London	90 days		

The following table, presented through the courtesy of the Weld office, is a complete record of all the voyages made by the *Great Admiral* prior to her sale in 1897.

CAPT. I. N. JACKSON

Year	Passage	Days	Distance	Average
1869	New York to San Francisco	121	15,925	131½
1869	San Francisco to Hong Kong	37	7,097	192
1870	Hong Kong to Manila	4	632	158
1870	Manila to New York	89	12,656	145½
1871	New York to San Francisco	128	15,705	123
1871	San Francisco to Manila	43	7,181	167
1871	Manila to New York	114	13,905	122

CAPT. WILLIAM CHATFIELD

1871	New York to San Francisco	121	15,829	131
1872	San Francisco to Manila	44	7,534	171
1872	Manila to Iloilo	3	300	100
1872	Iloilo to Boston	115	14,172	123

CAPT. I. N. JACKSON

1873	New York to San Francisco	114	15,542	136
1873	San Francisco to Queenstown	114	14,160	124
1873	Queenstown to Havre	3	390	130
1873	Havre to New York	30	3,503	117

CAPT. BENJAMIN THOMPSON

1874	New York to San Francisco	125	16,226	130
1874	San Francisco to Liverpool	113	16,781	148½
1875	Liverpool to San Francisco	115	15,868	138
1875	San Francisco to Iloilo	45	6,824	151½
1875	Iloilo to Cebu	3	300	100
1875	Cebu to New York	111	14,119	127
1876	New York to San Francisco	133	17,486	131½
1876	San Francisco to Liverpool	114	15,608	137
1876	Liverpool to Hong Kong	99	15,455	156
1877			details lacking	
1878	Hong Kong to San Francisco	38	5,969	157
1878	San Francisco to Havre	126	16,083	127½
1879	Havre to New York	31	3,397	109½
1879	New York to San Francisco	111	16,290	147
1879	San Francisco to Queenstown	111	16,182	146
1880	Queenstown to Havre	9	513	57
1880	Havre to Cardiff	3	500	167
1880	Cardiff to Hong Kong	107	15,321	143

1880	Hong Kong to San Francisco	63	8,193	130
1881	San Francisco to Queenstown	112	15,655	140
1881	Queenstown to Dublin	2	240	120
1881	Dublin to Philadelphia	34	4,156	122
1881	Philadelphia to Tacoma	111	16,055	145
1882	Tacoma to San Francisco	8	746	93
1882	San Francisco to Dublin	119	16,506	139
1882	Dublin to Cardiff (in tow)			
1883	Cardiff to Hong Kong	121	15,455	128
1883	Hong Kong to San Francisco	57	6,147	108

CAPT. J. F. ROWELL

1883	San Francisco to Manila	43	7,642	178
1884	Manila to Hong Kong	7	708	101
1884	Hong Kong to New York	95	14,069	148

CAPT. BENJAMIN THOMPSON

1885	New York to Melbourne	87	14,178	163
1885	Melbourne to Newcastle	7	600	86
1885	Newcastle to Hong Kong	37	4,986	135
1886	Hong Kong to Manila	11	703	64
1886	Manila to New York	126	13,551	107½

CAPT. J. F. ROWELL

1887	New York to Melbourne	73	13,745	188
1887	Melbourne to Hong Kong	48	5,446	113½
1887	Hong Kong to San Francisco (via Hakodate)	52	6,295	121
1888	San Francisco to Hong Kong	57	7,661	135
1888	Hong Kong to San Francisco	56	6,444	115
1888	San Francisco to Hong Kong	51	7,266	142½
1888	Hong Kong to San Francisco	39	6,464	166
1889	San Francisco to Hong Kong	49	7,884	161
1889	Hong Kong to San Francisco	41	6,390	156
1889	San Francisco to Hong Kong	51	7,689	151
1890	Hong Kong to New York	104	14,267	137
1890	New York to Melbourne	98	13,916	142½
1890	Melbourne to Newcastle	7	600	86
1891	Newcastle to Hong Kong	51	5,882	115
1891	Hong Kong to Vancouver	51	6,200	121½
1891	Vancouver to Melbourne	72	8,006	111
1892	Melbourne to Boston	94	13,751	146

Capt. Edward P. Nichols
Ship *Frank Pendleton*

Capt. Joshua B. Nichols
Ship *S. P. Hitchcock*

Capt. David Nickels
Ship *Belle of Bath*

Capt. Frank I. Pendleton
Ship *William H. Connor*

CAPT. CHARLES H. REED
Ship *Storm King*

CAPT. DAVID A. SCRIBNER
Ship *St. Frances*

CAPT. EDWIN S. SMALLEY
Ship *Manuel Llaguna*

CAPT. IRA A. STORER
Ship *John McDonald*

1892	Philadelphia to Genoa and Leghorn	40	4,163	104
1892	Leghorn to Trepani	7	450	64
1893	Trepani to Boston	59	5,906	100
1893	New York to Sydney	90	14,255	158½
1894	Sydney to London	92	14,234	155½
1894	London to New York	23	3,107	135
1895	Baltimore to San Francisco	127	15,797	124
1895	San Francisco to Manila	46	7,091	154
1895	Manila to Boston	130	14,826	114
1896	New York to Melbourne	91	13,867	152½
1896	Melbourne to Hobart	5	500	100
1896	Hobart to Gibraltar	90	12,868	143
1896	Gibraltar to Marseilles	8	699	87
1896	Marseilles to New York	48	4,211	83½

Of the commanders of the *Great Admiral*, mentioned in foregoing table, Captain Jackson's seafaring career is given in account of the ship *Belvedere*. Captain Chatfield had previously been master of the *Glory of the Seas* for a short time and on retiring from the *Great Admiral* he took the *Lightning*, also belonging to Weld & Co. Captain Thompson was a native of Winterport, Me., and in 1857 was in command of the ship *Sportsman*, engaged in the East India trade. During the Civil War the *Sportsman* was under charter to the United States Navy as an ordnance ship and Captain Thompson was complimented by Rear Admiral Farragut for the fine manner in which he handled his vessel. On the *Sportsman* being sold in 1864, the Captain took command of the ship *Peruvian* and subsequently the *Enoch Train*, both being owned by Weld & Co. On relinquishing command of the *Great Admiral*, he was employed in the Weld office in Boston some twelve years, after which he lived in the old Thompson homestead at Winterport until his death in October, 1905, at the age of seventy-one years.

Capt. James F. Rowell was born at Frankfort, Me., in March, 1842. At the age of sixteen he shipped in coasting vessels and before he was nineteen was second mate of the ship *John H. Jarvis*, engaged in transatlantic trade. In 1861 this ship was captured by a Confederate steamer when nearing New Orleans, and the crew was imprisoned for a month when they were turned loose to either starve or enlist in the Rebel army. Young Rowell was fortunate in being allowed to work his way to Bordeaux and St. John in the Bangor ship *Charles Cooper*, then under the British flag. He then enlisted in the Maine Infantry and was in service until August, 1863, when he was mustered out. He then joined his old ship *John H. Jarvis* as second mate and in 1873 got his first command, the ship *Rainbow*. He retired from sea life when the *Great Admiral* was sold and was employed by the Weld office until his death at Malden, Mass., in February, 1903. The Captain stood high in his profession, was intelligent and cultured and was noted for his kindly disposition. A paragraph from one of his articles published in 1898 reads: "The writer may with propriety claim to be a typical American seaman. Typical, in that he started to sea at the age of sixteen with a fair common school education and passing through every grade, has commanded in the past twenty-five years the ships *Rainbow, Zouave, Lightning, Thomas Dana* and *Great Admiral*. American, in that his ancestors settled in New England 268 years ago. A seaman, in that he was taught the business when the American ship was the pride of every seaman's heart and when their sails whitened every sea."

Capt. E. R. Sterling, the new owner of the *Great Admiral*, had previously been master and owner of the ship *Patrician*, which was lost in 1896. He sailed his new command in the coal and lumber trade on the Pacific for nine years, during which time she had hard usage and met with a number of mishaps. Her end came in December, 1906, as per the following details from the ship's log book:

"Port Townsend, Dec. 2, 1906. At 4 A.M. tug *Wanderer* came alongside; made fast hawser, hove up anchor and proceeded to sea. At 4 P.M. passed Tatoosh Island with light easterly breeze. At 7 P.M. set topsails and fore and aft sails. At 8 P.M. let go tug's hawser, made all sail and stood away to the S. S. W. bound to San Pedro, Cal., with lumber. Fine weather and moderate sea from N. W.

"Dec. 3. Fresh to moderate breeze from south'ard; misty, with clear weather at times. 6 P.M., strong breeze; in all light sails. Middle and latter part, wind freshening and ends the same.

"Dec. 4. Begins with strong breeze from south'ard and high sea.

At 8 P.M. wind hauled to westward. Wore ship to the south'ard and reduced sail. Ends with fresh gale, hard squalls and sleet.

"Dec. 5. First part, fresh breeze from N. W. and moderating at times. Made all plain sail; sea moderating. Middle and latter part, wind and sea increasing. Barometer falling and weather looking threatening. Shortened sail. Wind veering to south'ard and increasing. Ship under small canvas. Midnight, wore ship to the westward. Wind and sea increasing and ends the same, with falling barometer.

"Dec. 6. Position by account, 46:43 N. 127:58 W. This day comes in with wind and sea increasing and hard passing squalls from S. S. W. and rapidly falling barometer, which now is 29:10. Took in and furled fore and mizzen lower topsails. Ship now under main lower topsail, laboring very heavily and shipping much water. Barometer still falling and wind increasing with terrific squalls and a mountainous sea running. 4 P.M., wind blowing with hurricane force and a terrific high, confused sea. Wind hauling more to the south'ard and westward. Ship falling off, laboring very heavily and lying with the starboard side under water most of the time. Wind still increasing and blowing the sails out of the gaskets and some of them to ribbons. Examined the pumps and wells and found the ship making no water. 6 P.M., wind and sea still increasing. Barometer now 28:80 and falling. Sea now continually breaking over the vessel. 6:30 P.M. Found ship settling in the water and upon examination of the pumps saw that she was rapidly filling, the water being up to within twenty-four inches of the between decks. Put the helm up to get the ship before the wind but she would not pay off, owing to the severity of the gale. Immediately ordered fire to be made in the donkey boiler and start main and steam pumps but the engine room was partly under water and the boiler submerged, making it impossible to start a fire. In ten minutes found the ship had made seventeen inches of water and was settling very rapidly with the sea now continually going over her, washing away part of the forward house and deck load. Vessel rolling very heavily, dipping the yard arms at times and in imminent danger of rolling over on beam ends. In order to try and save the vessel, cargo and crew, if possible, cut away the main and mizzen masts with all attached. Ship now all under water and sea breaking furiously over her, with top of after house just awash, onto which all the crew, including the mate's wife, had taken refuge, it now being about 7:30 P.M. With the wreckage of the main and mizzen masts hanging alongside, the ship came round on the other tack, carried away the jibboom with all attached which caused the foremast to fall over the side. Ship now a complete wreck, with top works and deck load washing away. The vessel was struck by a tremendous sea which washed away the top of the after house upon which the crew were still clinging, taking it to leeward, clear of the wreck. Wind and sea now something terrific, picking up the floating lumber and wreckage and dashing it against the top of the after house which broke into two parts. Upon a part of each, the crew still clung. Passed the night in this manner, with terrific hail squalls and the sea continually washing over the wreckage, the people partly benumbed by the terrible exposure. At daybreak the cook and the cabin boy died from exposure. Finding that the piece of wreckage was scarcely able to float those now upon it, it being at times two feet under water, the bodies were put overboard in order to lessen the weight upon it. It had now drifted away from the other wreckage.

"Next day. Still blowing a gale with a tremendous sea continually washing over the piece of the house, greatly exhausting the crew. About 2 P.M. again sighted the other wreckage and, being to windward, was carried by the wind and sea towards it, finding one seaman still clinging to it. He had become separated from the rest of the crew during the night and had been carried into a mass of broken lumber and spars which afforded some protection from a very heavy sea. The night was again passed under terrible exposure, it being intensely cold with passing squalls of hail and sleet. People very much exhausted and scarcely able to hold on to the wreckage, having had no food, water or shelter since being washed away from the wreck and having continually to hold on to keep from being washed into the sea. At daybreak a sail was seen heading for the wreckage. After coming to a safe distance and getting the ship into position, which required much skill owing to the strong gale and high seas, soon found they were lowering a boat which, after great exertion on the part of its crew, reached the wreckage. After many attempts, all the crew that were still alive were picked up and transferred to the ship which was found to be the *Barcore* of Liverpool, Capt. J. C. MacKenzie, bound from Vancouver to Adelaide, who, with his wife, received us with the greatest kindness and solicitude, administered to our many wants and liberally supplied us with dry clothing and everything required for our comfort."

The following is the story of the rescue as given by Captain Mac-Kenzie. "In latitude 47:5 N. longitude 128:10, by account, during a strong gale accompanied by a high, confused sea, sighted at daybreak a mass of wreckage of lumber and broken spars and on closer observation found there were people clinging to the wreckage and in a very perilous condition, the sea apparently breaking right over them. The ship at the time being under storm sails, viz: three lower topsails, the helm was immediately put down and the ship's way stopped by backing the crossjack yards, it being then too dark for us to locate the extent and direction of the floating wreckage. On daylight breaking sufficiently for us to see, we got the ship as close as possible to the wreckage and with great difficulty got a boat into the davits and called for volunteers to man it. Chief mate Franert, boatswain Graham and three A. B.'s responded and with the aid of large quantities of oil, the boat was safely launched. After great exertion, the boat's crew succeeded in reaching the wreckage and after various attempts reached the greatly exhausted people who were on two separate portions of the wreckage and assisted by the boat's crew, they were all picked up. After rescuing all the people on the first portion of the wreckage the boat, with great difficulty, picked its way to the remainder of the survivors. On getting all on board found they were sixteen in number, including master, mate, mate's wife and twelve seamen, two having died from exposure the previous night while clinging to the wreckage. After various unsuccessful attempts we at last, with the use of oil freely, managed to get the boat alongside and the shipwrecked people on board. They were all in an exhausted and pitiable condition, some of them being on the verge of insanity from exposure. After getting them on board gave them restoratives, dry clothing and such things as were needed for their general comfort. In our opinion had it not.been for the wreckage acting as a breakwater to the crew on top of the housetop, they must all have perished. On inquiry found the party to be the crew of the American ship *Great Admiral*.

"Dec. 24, 1906. 34:59 N., 129:24 W. At 8 A.M. sighted a sail to westward and upon approaching found it to be the American bark *Andrew Welch*, Capt. E. Kelly, from Honolulu bound to San Francisco. Set signals asking if shipwrecked crew could be taken by her. This was answered in the affirmative, whereupon preparations were made to get a boat over, Captain Kelly in the meantime shortening sail and placing his ship in position by running to leeward, making it as easy as possible for our boat to get alongside. At 10:45 A.M. all the people were safely landed on board the *Andrew Welch*."

GUY C. GOSS

THE bark *Guy C. Goss* was launched at Bath, Maine, Nov. 27, 1879, from the yard of Goss & Sawyer, being the thirteenth vessel they had put afloat since the previous January and the one hundredth they had built. She measured 213:8 feet, by 39:8, by 24 feet and registered 1524 tons. She was owned by her builders, Capt. William H. Besse and others and Captain Besse managed her business affairs.

The *Goss* was the largest bark-rigged vessel built in this country and that she was first-class in all respects is evidenced by the fact that she had a seagoing career of forty-seven years, most of which was spent in hard service. She outlived her sister ship, the *Gerard C. Tobey*, eleven years. Her first voyage was from Philadelphia to Yokohama in 153 days; thence to San Francisco in 25 days, and from that port to Antwerp in 117 days. Thereafter until 1892 all her passages from Atlantic ports were to China or Japan and all those homeward, except two made direct, were by way of San Francisco, the Columbia River or Puget Sound. From 1892 until 1901 she was employed in trade between Atlantic ports and San Francisco, Port Los Angeles or Tacoma, making in all seven outward passages. In 1900, while she was at Philadelphia, bound for San Francisco, she was sold to Bennett & Goodall of the latter port, but during the course of the passage out that firm resold her to the Pacific Steam Whaling Co., who, as part of their operations, had salmon canneries in Alaska. A few years later she was purchased by the Pacific Packing & Navigation Co. of Seattle, but they shortly thereafter sold her to the Northwestern Fisheries Co., who operated her as a "salmon packer" between Seattle and Alaska for twenty years. Her last voyage as such was in 1925, she being sold after its completion to Seattle parties who sent her to Auckland, N. Z., with a cargo of lumber from Vancouver. Following her arrival she was libeled for debt, the claims of her crew aggregating some $5,000. In August, 1926, she was sold at Auckland, under order of court, and was bid in for the small sum of £308.

The sailing record of the *Goss* is good. She made three passages in the Pacific Coast grain trade, two being from San Francisco in 117 and 115 days, and one from the Columbia River in 127 days. In 1897 she made her only voyage with general cargo to the Atlantic, being 108 days from San Francisco to New York. The shortest passage she made from an Atlantic port to the Pacific Coast was 132 days to Tacoma and the longest 164 days to the same port.

In 1877 Captain Goss visited the Pacific Coast and while at Puget Sound was so impressed with the excellence of its timber that he had an experimental cargo forwarded East in the bark *William H. Besse* for shipbuilding purposes. The result bearing out the Captain's judgment, many similar cargoes were sent forward to New York, Philadelphia, Boston and Bath. The *Goss* took her first one in 1886 and subsequently loaded six others. On one of these she had 230 pieces suitable for masts and spars, some being thirty-six inches in diameter and 112 feet long, without a knot or blemish and valued at $900 each. Some of the timbers were thirty-six inches square. These passages were made in much better time than those of any other vessels engaged in the trade, the average length of the seven being 137 days, one of 119 days being the shortest and one of 147 days the longest.

The *Goss* was remarkably fortunate in escaping damage during the course of her voyages, her most serious mishap being in 1888, while bound from Hiogo to Boston. When a week out of port the wind, which had been light, suddenly increased and within an hour the barometer dropped to 28:28. The sails were immediately taken in but before they could be furled they were blown to pieces. For six hours the vessel felt the full force of a typhoon and was thrown on beam ends, necessitating the rigging being cut away to right her. The main and mizzen topmasts and fore-topgallant mast went over the side which relieved the ship and on the wind moderating the following day, Captain Mallett rigged up jury spars and made for San Francisco where he arrived November 3rd, 47 days from Hiogo. Seven weeks were taken in refitting the ship after which the run to Boston was made in 113 days.

Capt. Guy C. Goss was born in Sangerville, Me., in October, 1822, and after receiving a good education, taught school at Georgetown, near Bath. Not liking that occupation, however, he took up a seafaring life and at the age of thirty years was master of the brig *Florence Nightingale* of Boston. Two years later he was given command of a full-rigged ship belonging to Trufant & Drummond of Bath and sailed for them as master for eight years, his last ship being the *Ella*. In 1865 he associated himself with B. L. White in the shipbuilding business and in February, 1866, they launched their first vessel, the 200-ton schooner *John Cooper*. That year he and Elijah F. Sawyer formed a partnership and began building vessels in the old Johnson Rideout shipyard. In 1873 Benjamin F. Packard became associated with them in part, the new firm of Goss, Sawyer and Packard building vessels in the southern half of the yard, while Goss & Sawyer built in the northern half. The last ship built by Goss & Sawyer was the *John R. Kelley* in 1883, and their last vessel, the auxiliary, three-masted schooner *Lorenzo D. Baker*. The last ship constructed by Goss, Sawyer and Packard was the *Benjamin F. Packard* in 1883, and the last vessel, the steamer *Alki*, in 1884. Altogether the two firms had built 185 vessels up to 1884, several of the latest having auxiliary power, the first of which was the bark *George S. Homer* in 1882. It was thought that this type of vessel would have a tendency to revive the American shipping industry and their builders invested considerable capital in them. However, they did not prove successful and this was the cause of the financial embarrassment of their builders, who in 1884 were forced to ask an extension from their creditors. A new concern, the New England Shipbuilding Co., was then organized to take over the business of the allied firms, Messrs. Sawyer and Packard becoming connected therewith. Captain Goss retired and made his home on Staten Island, N. Y., passing away there May 18, 1890.

Capt. Abel B. Reynolds, formerly master of the bark *Xenia*, built and owned in part by Goss & Sawyer, commanded the *Goss* on the first voyage. He was succeeded by Capt. John Freeman, Jr., a native of Brewster, Mass., who had originally commanded coasting schooners and later the bark *National Eagle*. Captain Freeman made two voyages in the *Goss*, then taking the bark *Pilgrim*. On retiring from her he engaged in the ship chandlery business in Boston and died there in 1900, at the age of sixty-five years. Capt. Alfred Doane, whose career as a shipmaster is given in account of the ship *Cleopatra* in "American Merchant Ships," Series I, made two voyages in the *Goss*, after which Capt. W. W. Mallett took over the command and continued in her some thirteen years until 1900. He was succeeded by Capt. W. W. Hardy who took the *Goss* to San Francisco in 1901, but having his arm broken and being otherwise injured on the passage, he relinquished the command on arriving at his destination. Captain Hardy had been master of the bark *William W. Crapo* during her whole sea life of fourteen years except for one voyage made by Captain Hallett.

H. S. GREGORY

THE ship *H. S. Gregory* was built by Samuel Watts at Thomaston, Maine, and was launched in October, 1875. She measured 228:9 feet, by 41:9, by 29:1 feet and registered 2020 tons. She was owned by Mr. Watts and was built to be commanded by Capt. Rasmus B. Anderson. The party in whose honor she was named was a prominent stevedore of St. John, N. B., and a friend of her builder.

During the whole of her short career the *Gregory* was engaged in trade between Atlantic ports and those of the North Pacific. Her first five voyages were to San Francisco, thence to Liverpool, the average of the outward passages being 130 days and of those homeward, 128 days. Her first voyage was the shortest, 119 days outward and 118 days homeward.

The sixth voyage of the *Gregory* was from Philadelphia to Tacoma and she left the latter port in September, 1882, with 2782 tons of wheat for Queenstown. On Feb. 16, 1883, when 650 miles west of Fastnet Light, she was abandoned in a sinking condition. Her crew was rescued by the steamer *Glenbervie* and landed at Dublin. The ship had been leaking badly for some time and the foul gas generated by the decaying wheat had caused the death of one man and nearly resulted in the blindness of the rest of the ship's company.

Capt. Rasmus B. Anderson, who was master of the *Gregory* on her first two voyages, was the son of Capt. Rasmus Anderson, who went to Thomaston, when a boy, in a vessel from Arendal, Norway. Taking up a seafaring life he rose to be a master, one of his commands being the brig *Helen A. Hyler*, named after his wife. Young Anderson was brought up in ships belonging to Samuel Watts and in 1872 was appointed master of the ship *Henry L. Richardson*. Three years later he was transferred to the *Gregory* and from her to Mr. Watts's new ship *Snow & Burgess*. After serving as master of the last named ship some thirteen years, Captain Anderson retired from the sea and engaged in the grocery business in Kansas City. Some years later his mind gave way and he is said to have taken his own life.

The second master of the *Gregory* was Capt. John S. Turner, a native of Watling, Eng., who went to St. George, Me., at an early age and was raised in the family of Capt. Charles H. Shaw. He went to sea when quite young, sailing in ships belonging to Samuel Watts and later commanded a number of them, the *Jane Fish, Joseph Fish,* and *Kendrick Fish*. He made two voyages in the *Gregory*, then retiring to pass the remainder of his days at Thomaston and died there in 1900.

The third and last commander of the *H. S. Gregory* was Capt. Edward A. Watts, who subsequently was master of different ships belonging to Bath, his last being the *Susquehanna* which foundered in 1905. In speaking of his seafaring life, some years ago, the Captain said that his experience had always been hard, he seldom making a long voyage when his ship did not suffer damage.

HARRY MORSE

THE ship *Harry Morse* was built by J. Parker Morse at Bath, Maine, and was launched in July, 1871. She was 198 feet, by 37, by 23:8 feet and of 1313 tons register. Mr. Morse died the year after the ship was built and his three-eighths interest in her was sold to Henry L. Houghton of Houghton Brothers for $29,000. Eventually Houghton Brothers purchased the remaining five-eighths of the ship, becoming sole owners. This ship is said to have been the only one ever owned by Houghton Brothers that had not been built by themselves.

In March, 1887, the *Morse* was sold to John Rosenfeld of San Francisco and six months later was resold to George E. Plummer of the same place for a consideration reported as $25,000. The vessel was then rerigged as a bark. In January, 1906, Mr. Plummer sold her to parties in the East and she took a cargo of lumber from the Columbia River to Boston. She had a very long passage and fears had been entertained for her safety when she put into Pernambuco to replenish her stock of provisions after being 160 days at sea. Following her arrival at Boston she was converted into a barge and was operated by the Texas Company of Port Arthur, until July 5, 1916, when she foundered in Mobile Bay after being in collision with the schooner *Emma Lord*. The eight men on the *Morse* went down with the ship.

Prior to 1887 the *Morse* was employed in transatlantic trade or with ports in South America or on the North Pacific Coast. Thereafter she carried lumber or coal in the Pacific, coastwise and offshore. Her voyages were generally without particular incident. Her worst mishap was in 1894 when, on a passage from Hakodate to San Francisco, under command of Captain Herriman, she was badly damaged in a gale which lasted three days. The cargo shifted, bulwarks were carried away with everything movable from decks, cabins were flooded allowing much water to get below, stores and provisions were ruined and a whole suit of sails were blown out of the bolt ropes, while the ship, being out of control, labored heavily. Later on during the passage the vessel shipped a high sea over the stern, damaging the wheel and severely injuring the two men who were steering.

Prior to 1883 the *Morse* had a number of commanders, each for short periods. On Houghton Brothers then becoming sole owners they transferred Capt. Eben L. Murphy from their ship *Northampton* to the *Morse*, both vessels then being in port at New Orleans. Captain Murphy continued in the *Morse* until January, 1889, when he took command of the ship *George Stetson* and he is more particularly referred to in the account of that ship. The chief officer of the *Morse*, J. Hughes, succeeded Captain Murphy and four years later exchanged commands with Capt. Fred Louis Herriman who had the *Highland Light*. A year or so later Captain Herriman went north and for many years was a pilot through the inland passages between Puget Sound and Alaska. He died on board the steamer *Deer Lodge* in 1924. The Captain was a son of Capt. Albert Louis Herriman for many years master of the ship *Ivanhoe*, and later of Herriman & Mills, stevedores, San Francisco. The first command of Capt. Fred L. Herriman was the bark *Don Nicolas* of San Francisco, originally the ship *Eddystone*.

HECLA

THE ship *Hecla* was built by Goss & Sawyer at Bath, Maine, and was launched in September, 1877. She measured 210:3 feet, by 40:2, by 24:3 feet and registered 1476 tons. She was built for John W. Marr of Bath, and on his disposing of her in December, 1897, the Marr house flag that had floated for many years over a fleet of first class sailing ships, disappeared from the high seas.

From Atlantic ports the *Hecla* made eight passages to San Francisco, five to the Orient and one each to Tacoma and Acapulco, all in fair time and without unusual incident. Her last voyage under the Marr ownership was from Philadelphia to San Francisco, thence with railroad ties to Taku, she being the first square-rigged vessel under the American flag to enter that port. She then crossed in ballast to Puget Sound and was sold to A. Anderson and Capt. Henry Nelson of San Francisco. Rigged as a bark she was operated by her new owners in the coal and lumber trade on the Pacific until 1913, when, following her arrival at San Francisco from Newcastle, N. S. W., she was laid up three years and then sold to the Red Salmon Canning Co., who used her as a "salmon packer" until 1925 when she was laid up in fresh water at Antioch, Cal. In 1928 she was sold to ship breakers.

The *Hecla* was built to be commanded by Capt. Edwin O. Day of Woolwich, Me., a well-known shipmaster in the employ of Mr. Marr. His last prior vessel was the ship *Dakota* which was burned at sea on her first voyage. Captain Day served in the *Hecla* fourteen years, after which he made a couple of voyages in the ship *Parthia*, and then retired from the sea. A year or so ago the Captain was living at the age of ninety years, spending his summers at home in Woolwich and the winters with a son-in-law at Flushing, N. Y.

The second commander of the *Hecla* was Capt. Edward A. Cotton, whose life as a shipmaster is given in the account of the ship *John W. Marr*. On his death at Antwerp in 1896, Capt. Charles J. Carter, who had also served as master of the *John W. Marr*, took command of the *Hecla* and continued in her until she was sold. Thereafter and until she became a "salmon packer" the ship was commanded by Capt. Henry Nelson or his brother Capt. Edward Nelson.

HENRY FAILING

THE ship *Henry Failing* was built for Capt. William H. Besse, Henry Failing, Capt. Jacob Merriman and others and was managed by Captain Besse. She was launched from the yard of Goss & Sawyer at Bath, Maine, May 5, 1882, and measured 230:6 feet, by 43:1, by 26:3 feet, registering 1976 tons. On arrival at Philadelphia, to load on her first voyage, she was the largest ship that had ever been at that port. In 1898 she was purchased by the California Shipping Co. of San Francisco, who in June, 1909, while the ship was in that port, sold her to Scully's Towing & Transportation Line, New York, for $20,000, delivery to be made in the East. The ship took a cargo of lumber from Tacoma and on arrival at New York was converted into a barge. As such she was operated until Feb. 26, 1918, when she sprung aleak and foundered off Block Island. The four men on board were saved.

The maiden voyage of the *Failing* was from Philadelphia to Tacoma, with railroad iron, after which she spent a year in the coastwise coal trade, then taking wheat from San Francisco to Liverpool. Thereafter, prior to 1898, she completed four round voyages between Atlantic ports and San Francisco and four to China or Japan. In 1888 she made a round between San Francisco and Sydney. In 1898 she took coal from Philadelphia to Port Los Angeles, returning East by way of Puget Sound and Hong Kong. The following voyage, the last passage made by the ship around Cape Horn to the westward, was from Philadelphia to the Hawaiian Islands and occupied nearly a year. When something over three months at sea, she put into Port Stanley with most of her crew sick and unfit for duty and was detained in port there over three months.

During the time the *Failing* was owned in the East she was commanded by Capt. Jacob Merriman and maintained a good sailing record. The average of her passages from the Atlantic to San Francisco is 125 days, the shortest being 114 days from Liverpool, and longest 130 days from New York. Returning to the United Kingdom with wheat, the shortest run was 115 days; longest 122 days and the average 120 days for the five passages made. So far as can be ascertained the ship met with no mishaps of consequence during this period.

While owned in San Francisco the *Failing* was operated in the lumber trade between Puget Sound and Australia and had several different commanders, the last being Capt. N. H. Anderson who had previously been her chief officer.

HIGHLAND LIGHT

THE *Highland Light* was launched from the shipyard of William Rogers at Bath, Maine, October, 1874, and was built to the order of Nickerson & Co. of Boston, they being well pleased with the performances of their ship *Hercules*, also a product of Mr. Rogers. The *Hercules* was a good carrier as well as a fast sailer and the *Highland Light* was of the same model, both having fairly sharp bows, slightly concave below the waterline and rather long, finely shaped runs. A later ship, the *Oregon*, was also built on the same lines and proved to be successful, both as a carrier and sailer, but the *Highland Light* did not realize the expectations of either her builder or owners.

The *Highland Light* was 194:9 feet, by 38:1, by 24:3 feet and registered 1315 tons. She was owned by Nickerson & Co. until early in 1887 when, after her arrival at San Diego, Cal., from Australia and her crew had refused further duty on the ground that the ship was not seaworthy, she was sold to George E. Plummer and others of San Francisco and they were her owners until she was lost.

Prior to 1887 the *Highland Light* made voyages to South America, the North Pacific Coast, Australia and the Orient. On different occasions she was laid up, once being idle at Portland, Ore., for over sixteen months. Her passages were made in quite slow time, the average of those from Atlantic ports to San Francisco being 141 days and of those from the North Pacific, in the grain trade, 140 days.

Following the purchase of the *Highland Light* by San Francisco parties she was rerigged as a bark and made a few offshore voyages but her principal employment was in coastwise work. In November, 1899, she loaded lumber at Port Blakely but two weeks later put back in a damaged condition, with the loss of the deck load. A second start was made and again she had to put back damaged. The third attempt was equally disastrous, she being towed into San Francisco dismasted and nearly full of water in March, 1900. In December of that year she left Puget Sound for Honolulu, but three weeks later put back with mizzenmast gone, bulwarks and boats smashed and the hull in a very leaky condition. Thereafter for nearly a year she escaped mishaps. On Nov. 16, 1901, when eight days out of Tacoma, bound to Honolulu, she foundered some eighty miles off the coast of Vancouver Island. A schooner happened to be in the vicinity and took off her crew.

The first master of the *Highland Light* was Capt. James Collier, who four years later left her to take the ship *Pharos*. Captain Reynolds succeeded Captain Collier and he in turn was succeeded by Capt. James W. Norcross who continued in the ship until she was sold by Nickerson & Co. Thereafter the *Highland Light* had many different commanders, among whom were Captains Fred L. Herriman and J. Hughes, both of whom were later in the *Harry Morse*, and Capt. Edward Lewis who had long commanded the *Carrollton*.

HIGHLANDER

THE ship *Highlander* was built by Samuel Hall at East Boston and was launched in December, 1868. She measured 190:3 feet, by 38:8, by 24 feet and registered 1352 tons. She was built for Sturgis, Clearman & Co. and others of Boston, but within a year was purchased by B. W. Stone & Bro. of Salem for $100,000. In 1880 a half interest in her was reported to have changed hands for $36,000, but the Stone Brothers appear as managing owners until December, 1893, when she was sold to parties in Amsterdam for the trifling figure of $8,500. Then, under her original name, she was operated in trade on the Atlantic some six years, after which she was purchased by parties in New York who had her converted into a barge. Her name disappears from lists of vessels afloat in 1904.

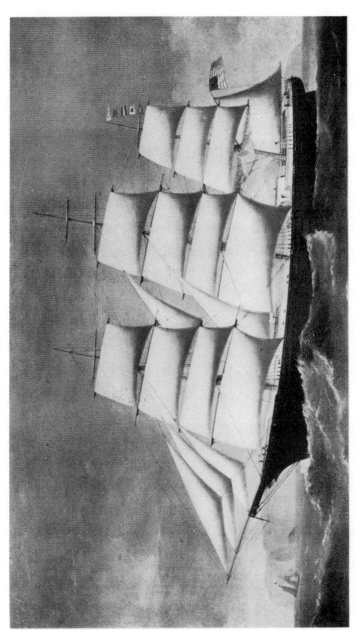

"HIGHLANDER," 1352 TONS, BUILT IN 1868, AT EAST BOSTON

From the oil painting in the Peabody Museum, Salem

"HOTSPUR," 1210 TONS, BUILT IN 1885, AT BATH

"JEREMIAH THOMPSON," 1904 TONS, BUILT IN 1854, AT GREENPOINT, N. Y.

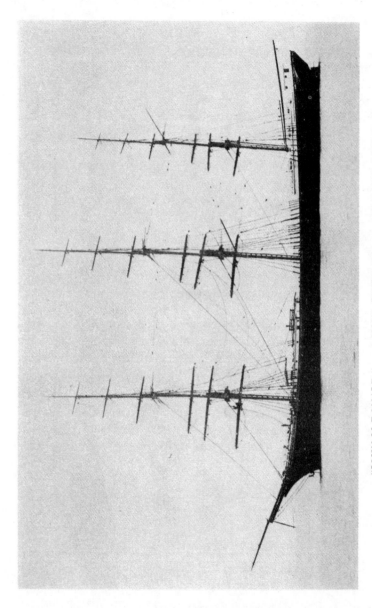

"JOHN McDONALD," 2172 TONS, BUILT IN 1882, AT BATH, MAINE
Courtesy of Edward S. Clark

The *Highlander* made three passages from Atlantic ports to San Francisco and occasionally made that port from China, but most of her operations were with the East Indies. She was a first class ship in all respects and made fair passages but was always a conspicuous vessel through making long stays at different ports she visited. Her owners were wealthy and would not move her unless they got freights in excess of what other managers considered remunerative. On one occasion she is said to have been idle at Hong Kong for two years and following her arrival at San Francisco in October, 1881, from Hong Kong, she was laid up until January, 1885. When she made port, grain freights were as high as £4 per ton, but the *Highlander's* owners did not consider this worth accepting. On leaving San Francisco for Hong Kong in January, 1885, she started leaking in the topsides as soon as she got to sea and a week later was forced to return to port. It would appear that on the whole the ship had been an unfortunate investment for her owners.

The *Highlander* had many different masters, all of whom had been in other ships belonging to Salem. None of these were in the ship for any lengthy period, but those who had her longest were Captains William J. Willcomb, Daniel H. Hutchinson and Nathan A. Batchelder. Capt. Geo. W. Edgett, who was master of the *Charles Dennis* when she was abandoned in 1891, had the *Highlander* on her last voyage, New York to San Francisco, Puget Sound and Dunkirk, where, after arrival, she was sold.

HOTSPUR

THE *Hotspur* was the first full-rigged ship built by the New England Ship Building Co., successors to Goss & Sawyer, Bath, Maine, and was launched Aug. 27, 1885. She measured 191 feet, by 38:8, by 22:8 feet and registered 1210 tons. Her owners were Francis and Horatio Hathaway and Capt. William H. Besse of New Bedford, and various parties in Boston and Bath, including her builders and Capt. William C. Warland.

The *Hotspur* was a handsome, three skysail-yard ship and her spread of 7,000 yards of canvas was said to be greater than that of any other American ship of her size at that time. Her first voyage was from Boston to Melbourne, in 82 days, following which she took coal from Newcastle to Manila and sugar home from Iloilo. She then started on a second voyage but was lost when homeward bound by striking a coral reef on July 25, 1887.

Capt. William C. Warland, who commanded the *Hotspur* during her brief career, belonged in Brooklyn, N. Y., and started sea life in 1854. On retiring in 1909, to make his home in Santa Cruz, Cal., he had been a shipmaster over forty years. He commanded the clipper ship *Endeavor* eight years prior to her sale in 1876 and subsequently had the ships *Annie M. Smull* and *Twilight*. His last command was the bark *Amy Turner*, which he had many years, and in which he made a passage of 88 days from Hong Kong to Baltimore in 1895. Captain Warland was a thorough gentleman in all respects and ranked with the best of the old school of merchant navigators who gave prestige to American sailing ships.

The Messrs. Hathaway had previously owned a medium clipper ship named *Hotspur*, built in New York in 1857 for the East India trade. This ship had a fine record for making fast passages, having on certain occasions beaten the time of accredited "flyers" going over the same course with her and which she had spoken and passed on the way. This *Hotspur* was lost on the Paracels Bank, China Sea, in February, 1863, while bound from Foo Chow to New York.

I. F. CHAPMAN

THE ship *I. F. Chapman*, built and owned by the man after whom she was named, was launched at Bath, Maine, in October, 1882. A prior ship of the same name had been built at Thomaston in 1855 by Mr. Chapman and his brother Benjamin Flint, and under command of Capt. James F. Chapman, a half brother of Isaac F., and of Capt. Galen O. Norton, had operated mainly in transatlantic trade until 1872 when her name disappeared from shipping registers.

The second *I. F. Chapman* originally had double topgallant yards but one of these yards was soon dispensed with and practically throughout her whole life as a sailing ship she was a single topgallant, three skysail-yard ship. She was 237:5 feet, by 42:7, by 27:5 feet and registered 2038 tons. She was built for the California trade and prior to 1896 all her voyages were between San Francisco and New York or Liverpool. During this period she completed eleven rounds, after which she made two voyages in the case oil trade to the Orient. Then followed two additional passages from New York to San Francisco after which she was operated between Atlantic ports and China or the Hawaiian Islands. When the affairs of her owners were wound up in 1908 she was sold at New York for conversion into a barge. During the World War she was rerigged as a bark and loaded coal for Rio de Janeiro but did not complete the voyage being forced to put into Barbados in a leaking condition. There her cargo was discharged and after a long stay in port she returned to New York, had her spars removed and resumed duty as a barge. A year or so ago she was still in commission, being often seen in the James River at the end of a tow line. That she had been built of the best materials and in a most thorough manner is further evidenced by the fact that on being surveyed at New York in 1906 by the Bureau Veritas she was given their highest rating for a further period of six years.

The voyages of the *I. F. Chapman* were made in fair time, the average of her thirteen passages from New York to San Francisco being 139 days and of the eleven made from the Pacific Coast to Liverpool or New York 124 days. The shortest to the westward was 119 days and to the eastward, one to New York in 110 days, and one to Liverpool in 111 days. In 1899 she was one of three participants in a race from the Hawaiian Islands to the Delaware Breakwater, her rivals being the ship *W. F. Babcock* and the bark *St. Katherine*. All three vessels made port the same day, the stakes of $1,000 going to the bark, which made the run in 121 days, which was three days shorter than that of the *Chapman* and nine days shorter than that of the *Babcock*.

During the whole of her career as a sailing ship the *Chapman* was remarkably fortunate in escaping damage from the elements, never having been stranded and only once, when she lost a topgallant mast, having had masts, spars or rigging carried away. Her nearest approach to disaster was in September, 1906, when she dragged down on the ship *S. P. Hitchcock* during a typhoon. The *Hitchcock* was torn adrift, went on the breakwater and became a total loss, but the *Chapman's* anchors fouled those of her unfortunate sister and she was brought up all standing. An incident occurring during one of her passages from Liverpool to New York was the rescue by Captain Thomson of the ten persons aboard the schooner *Lizzie C. Hickman* of Milford, Del., which was in a sinking condition when sighted. Included in the schooner's company were the wife and child of the captain.

The *Chapman* was built to be commanded by Capt. Joseph Albert Thomson and he served in her as master for seventeen years continuously. The Captain was a native of Woolwich, Me., and in early life sailed in small fishing vessels. On one occasion three of the crew of the schooner he was in were washed overboard and drowned during a gale, one of them being Thomson's brother. Thomson, although then only seventeen years of age, was the only survivor with sufficient knowledge to navigate the vessel and he successfully took her into port, following which the owners placed him in command. Subsequently the Thomson family moved to Bath, Me., and young Thomson stayed ashore for a time to learn the trade of rigger. Later on he resumed sea life and in 1869 took command of the ship *J. A. Thomson*, named in his honor and built for him. After a number of years in that ship he took the *L. Schepp* and was her master until the *Chapman* was built. On leaving the latter in 1899 he retired from active life and twenty years later passed away on his eighty-eighth birthday. The Captain was a thorough seaman and a competent navigator. He had a very strong temper and at times when things went wrong was apt to lose control of himself, causing some people to regard him as a hard man and a tough customer, but this was not his general character.

Subsequent commanders of the *Chapman*, while she was a sailing ship, were Captains Omar E. Chapman, Charles S. Kendall and Richard Banfield. Captain Banfield was her last master and on the ship being sold for barging, he retired from sea life.

Isaac F. Chapman, after whom the ship was named, was born at Damariscotta, Me., in April, 1812, and early in life started to learn the trade of caulker under his father, Robert Chapman. Having saved a little money he started a general store in a small way and prospering in this he took in as partner a younger brother, Benjamin Flint Chapman. Their mother had died years before and Benjamin was brought up by an uncle named Flint. On attaining his majority he dropped the Chapman from his name and was thereafter known as Benjamin Flint, the business of the brothers being conducted under the firm name of Chapman & Flint. In 1840 they commenced building small vessels at Damariscotta and in that year launched the bark *Alabama* of 280 tons. In 1842 they moved to Thomaston, where they had a store and shipyard and built ten full-rigged ships and three barks. In 1867 the opening of the Knox & Lincoln Railroad forced them to move to Bath and there, with John McDonald as their master builder, they built nine ships of which the *St. Lucie* was the first and the *Santa Clara* the last. Many of their ships were named "Saints," but not in honor of those of the calendar, as was the general belief but mainly after the given name of a relative or close friend. Thus the ship *St. James*, built in 1856, was named for her first master, Capt. James Colley, and the ship *St. Lucie* for the wife of J. W. Elwell of New York. Originally J. W. Elwell & Co. had been the New York agents for the Chapman & Flint ships but when Charles R. Flint, son of Benjamin Flint, became a partner in W. R. Grace & Co., that firm succeeded to the agency.

In 1877 the ship *St. David* was built in the Chapman & Flint yard but for the individual account of Benjamin Flint and to be commanded by Capt. David A. Scribner whose sister was the second Mrs. Flint. A number of other captains employed by the firm were related by marriage to Mr. Flint, while Mr. Chapman had none such, and the building of the *St. David* was the beginning of the breach in the friendly relations of the partners which led to the dissolution of the firm in 1880. An arrangement was made whereby each partner took certain ships, and Mr. Chapman, as I. F. Chapman & Co., opened an office in New York, with his son-in-law A. G. Ropes as bookkeeper at first and later on as a partner, although the latter had no financial interest in the ships. Benjamin Flint also opened an office in New York, as Flint & Co., his sons Charles R. and Wallace B. Flint being taken in as partners.

Mr. Chapman employed his brother-in-law, Samuel P. Hitchcock, as master builder in his Bath shipyard and in 1881 his first ship, the *E. B. Sutton,* was launched. During the three successive years the *I. F. Chapman, S. P. Hitchcock* and *A. G. Ropes* were built, the last named being the largest, 2342 tons. Mr. Chapman said at the time, "The *Ropes* is, in my opinion, the limit of size for wooden ships and the last one I will build, for the day of wooden ships will have passed before she is twenty-five years old, if she remains afloat that long. The days for sail will also have passed to steam by that time, if not before." This prophesy was fulfilled.

Isaac F. Chapman died at his home in Brooklyn, N. Y., Jan. 30, 1895, aged eighty-two years, nine months. His heirs were his two daughters, one of whom was married to Albert G. Ropes and the latter conducted the business until the financial depression of 1907-1908 forced the winding up of all its affairs. Mr. Chapman was an upright, conscientious, Christian gentleman, fair, just and liberal in all his dealings and without being ostentatious, was very charitable. It was said at the time of his passing that his life might profitably be studied by the rising generation.

IMPORTER

THE ship *Importer* was built by John Currier, Jr., at Newburyport, Mass., and was launched in May, 1870. She measured 196:6 feet, by 36:2, by 23:9 feet and was 1216 tons register. Her owners were Sumner, Swasey & Currier of Newburyport until 1874 when she was sold to Howes & Crowell of Boston. On the failure of that firm in 1883 she was purchased by New York parties who altered her rig to that of a bark and operated her until 1889 when she was sold to go under the German flag, being renamed *F. E. Hagenmeyer*.

The *Importer* was built for the East India trade and made only one Cape Horn passage, that in 1875, when she was 119 days from New York to San Francisco. However, on several occasions she crossed the Pacific from the Orient to load wheat for Europe and all of these passages were made in slightly better than average time. She was a "lean" ship with the reputation of being a good sailer, and one of her captains writes that she always seemed to be going nine knots even in light winds. Her first master, Capt. George T. Avery, was not a "driver," in fact was very careful and cautious, always snugging down nights, yet during the four years he commanded her, the *Importer* was successful and is said to have paid for herself during that period. The Captain had previously commanded the ships *Castine* and *J. P. Whitney*, and after the *Importer* had been purchased by Boston parties, he had the ship *Daniel I. Tenney* six or seven years. He belonged to Newburyport, was very much of a gentleman and was highly respected even by his officers and crews.

Capt. B. F. Sherburne was appointed master of the *Importer* by Howes & Crowell and continued in her about seven years. He had previously been in command of the celebrated clipper ship *Game Cock* and was her master when she made a passage from New York to Melbourne in 75 days. On retiring from the *Importer* he engaged with a relative in the sheep raising business in Humboldt County, Cal., and made his home at Arcata where he passed away not many years ago. The Captain invented what he called a "log watch" designed to supercede the old-time hand glass previously used in heaving the log. The machine resembled an ordinary watch and by pressing the upper case, a spring released a gong which rang exactly fourteen seconds, the same time a sand glass had taken to run out.

Capt. C. Howard Allyn of Hyannis, Mass., succeeded Captain Sherburne and continued in the *Importer* until the failure of her owners caused the loss of practically all his means. He then foreswore

the sea but later was prevailed upon by J. Henry Sears to invest what
money he had left in the ship *Titan* and take over her command. He
sailed in her until her loss in 1894 and having no insurance on his interest he lost about all he had and thereafter has made a living by
running a transfer business in Hyannis and was so engaged at a recent
date, being then eighty-four years of age. Captain Allyn had been
chief mate of the *Glory of the Seas*, under Capt. Josiah N. Knowles,
and later, master of the ships *Expounder* and *Gold Hunter*.

INVINCIBLE

THE ship *Invincible* was built by W. V. Moses & Son at Bath,
Maine, and was launched in September, 1873. She measured
202:4 feet, by 40:3, by 24 feet and registered 1394 tons. She was
owned by her builders, her commander, Capt. William Strickland,
and various parties in Bath. Following her arrival at San Francisco in
October, 1887, she was purchased by Renton, Holmes & Co., proprietors of the Port Blakely Mills on Puget Sound, who operated her
on the Pacific, coastwise and offshore, about six years, after which she
was laid up over a year. In 1903 she was towed from San Francisco to
Puget Sound and the following year was converted into a four-masted
schooner. Under that rig she made a few voyages but was not continually employed and after four years she was sold to Hind, Rolph &
Co., they, in 1914, having her made into a barge. The preceding six
years had been mostly spent at anchor in San Francisco Bay. In January, 1927, being unfit for further service in any way, she was burned
for the copper and iron that had been used in her construction.

Prior to her sale in 1887 the *Invincible* was engaged almost entirely in the coal and guano trades with China and South America. The
only passage she made direct from an Atlantic port to the North Pacific was the one from New York to San Francisco in 1887 when she
was 180 days on the way and established the record of slow runs from
the equator crossing in the Pacific to port, 69 days. Her other voyages

appear to have been usually quite long and her career does not seem
to have been eventful, aside from one occasion when she put into Batavia partly dismasted, as her name is not in lists of important disasters occurring to Pacific shipping.

Capt. William Strickland of Bath was in command of the *Invincible* from the time she was launched until she was sold, except for a
voyage made by Capt. James F. Skewes in 1881-1882. Captain Strickland had previously been master of the ship *Genevieve Strickland*,
built by Moses & Sons in 1869, and retired from sea life when the *Invincible* was sold. Following this, a number of different masters had
the ship, among whom were Capt. J. E. Howland and his son-in-law
Capt. A. E. Chipperfield. The latter is mentioned in the account of a
later command, the ship *M. P. Grace*. Captain Howland had been
master of the clipper ship *Gov. Morton* from 1868 until 1876, and
later had the *Red Cross* and *Kate Davenport*. He retired from sea on
turning the *Invincible* over to Captain Chipperfield in 1896.

An extreme clipper ship named *Invincible* was built at New York
by William H. Webb in 1851 and was conceded to be one of the fastest sailing ships afloat. On her maiden voyage, which was from New
York to San Francisco, she covered 400 miles in one day's run which
was never exceeded on that course except by the *Flying Cloud*, and
Great Republic, and then only by a few miles. That *Invincible* was
burned at New York in September, 1867, while loading for San
Francisco.

ISAAC REED

THE ship *Isaac Reed* was built by A. R. Reed & Co. at Waldoboro, Maine, and was launched Sept. 30, 1875. She measured
212 feet, by 40, by 24:2 feet and registered 1489 tons. She was named
in honor of a prominent citizen of Maine who had served in the State
Senate and who in 1853 and again in 1855 was the nominee for Governor on the Whig ticket, although he was not elected. The ship
Isaac Reed was owned by her builders and others, among whom were

Capt. William S. Colley and his son Lewis S. Colley. She was built to be commanded by the former and was managed by Yates & Porterfield of New York.

The *Isaac Reed* made only four Cape Horn passages to the North Pacific Coast, the remainder of her career, prior to 1900, being spent in the Far East trade. Her voyages were made in fair average time and she appears to have an uneventful career, so far as can be ascertained.

In 1900 the *Isaac Reed* crossed the Pacific from China and was sold to J. Jensen of San Francisco, he reselling her in 1914 to Hind, Rolph & Co. For some years she was operated coastwise and offshore on the Pacific then being converted into a barge. In July, 1924, she foundered off the California coast.

Capt. William S. Colley, whose prior commands are mentioned in the account of the Chapman & Flint ship *St. Charles*, was master of the *Reed* the first five years, he then turning her over to his son Capt. Edward S. Colley. The latter had started seafaring before the mast under his father, rising to become chief officer. In 1876 he was given command of the new Edward O'Brien ship *Alida*, and in that ship made a voyage to Antwerp and from there to the Peruvian guano deposits. The *Alida* was wrecked at Pabellon de Pica by the tidal wave that followed the great earthquake of May, 1877, and young Colley then went mate of the *Isaac Reed*, under his father, subsequently becoming her master and being in her until 1888. He subsequently took command of the ship *Belle O'Brien* and was her master when she was lost in November, 1895. On finally retiring from sea life the Captain passed the remainder of his life at his home in Thomaston. He was a brother of Capt. Lewis S. Colley, part owner of the *Isaac Reed*, master of the ship *Indiana* a number of years, who lost his life in the ship *Bangalore*.

Capt. Frederick D. Waldo was the third and last commander of the *Isaac Reed* prior to her sale on the Pacific Coast.

J. B. WALKER

THE ship *J. B. Walker*, built and owned by Edward O'Brien, was launched at Thomaston, Maine, in September, 1879, and was 247 feet, by 42:2, by 29:8 feet and registered 2106 tons, the largest ship built at Thomaston up to that time. She was named in honor of Dr. J. B. Walker of Thomaston, a prominent citizen and close personal friend of Mr. O'Brien. Dr. Walker was the father-in-law of Capt. Geo. E. Wallace and the ship was built for the latter to command.

The first two voyages of the *Walker* were between St. John and Liverpool after which she was put into trade with San Francisco, and except for a voyage with case oil to Japan in 1891, she was continuously on the run between the Pacific Coast port and Liverpool or Baltimore until 1896. Thereafter she took coal or case oil to ports in the Far East until 1903, when she was purchased by Lewis Luckenbach for conversion into a barge and continued as such until she foundered Oct. 27, 1917. In January, 1900, she had been sold by David B. Dearborn, agent, to James C. Mulligan for $30,000, she then being on a passage from Manila via Hiogo to New York, and rigged as a bark.

On her first voyage around Cape Horn the *Walker* was 75 days from Liverpool to Valparaiso and 68 days from St. George Channel; was in port at Valparaiso eight days, thence 38 days to San Francisco, arriving off the bar on the 34th day, a record fast run. Her sailing days from Liverpool to San Francisco were 113, thence back to Liverpool in 119 days and then to San Francisco, direct, in 109 days. This last round voyage occupied eight months and thirteen days and during it she had carried upwards of 6000 tons of cargo. In 1889, on the passage from Liverpool to San Francisco, under command of relieving Capt. William Tattersall, she had nothing but light winds excepting 36 days off Cape Horn, and was 167 days on the run. In 1894 she had a very stormy passage of 170 days from Baltimore and these two runs make the average of the nine to San Francisco, 135 days, that of the other seven being 125 days, a very good record for a ship modeled for carrying heavy cargoes.

Eastbound from San Francisco, the *Walker* took grain to Liverpool on eight occasions and to Havre once, the shortest passage being 115 days, and longest 150 days, the latter running the average of the whole to 127 days. On several occasions, after arriving at San Francisco from the Atlantic, the *Walker* carried coal along the Pacific Coast and Capt. George E. Wallace claims to have arrived at Tacoma in November, 1889, in three days from San Francisco harbor.

In March, 1894, the *Walker*, while proceeding to sea from Baltimore, bound to San Francisco, Capt. John W. Wallace making his first voyage as master of the ship, she stranded on the Middle Ground and was damaged to such an extent that her cargo had to be discharged. Three months later the voyage was resumed and heavy weather was encountered for practically the whole 170 days of the run. Two men were lost overboard through falls from aloft and the ship had the main deck and some bow planks stove while off Cape Horn. On the return passage to Liverpool the foretopmast was carried away in a heavy squall just south of the Line in the Pacific. These two constitute the major accidents met with by the *Walker* during the course of her voyages.

The *Walker* was at Cebu in December, 1896, when a regatta was being held and Captain Wallace entered one of his boats in a race with three from other ships and a native boat. The *Walker's* crew came out victors and Captain Wallace was presented with a silver cup and tray as a souvenir of the occasion. On the following voyage of the ship, when homeward bound from Hiogo, Captain Wallace decided to proceed by way of Cape Horn and put into Honolulu to learn of the progress of the Spanish-American War. The passage thence to New York was made in 129 days, without incident, but a close lookout was kept for enemy war vessels. The last voyage of the *Walker*, as a sailing ship, was to Manila, Hong Kong and Hiogo, she proceeding home in ballast, putting into Valparaiso for provisions.

Capt. George Edward Wallace was born in Thomaston in March, 1846, one of several brothers, all master mariners. His first voyages were in vessels commanded by his brothers and engaged in transatlantic trade. His first command was the ship *Billow*, after which he had the *J. R. Bodwell* and the second *Edward O'Brien*, leaving the the latter to take the *Walker*. During the time Captain Tattersall was relieving him in the *Walker*, Captain Wallace made several voyages along the Pacific Coast in the ship *Alex. McCallum*. In 1894 he relinquished command of the *Walker* in favor of his son John W. Wallace, who had been a number of years in the ship, rising to become chief officer. Capt. George E. was then appointed a San Francisco Bar pilot and was subsequently a Pilot Commissioner four years. On the completion of his term he retired from active service and died in 1928.

On his last passage in the *Edward O'Brien*, from Liverpool to St. John, early in 1879, Captain Wallace rescued the crew of the British bark *Clarence*, which had been abandoned in a sinking condition. On a prior voyage the Captain had been presented with a silver jug by the British Government for having rescued the crew of the ship *J. P. Wheeler* of St. John, waterlogged and a wreck in the North Atlantic.

Capt. John W. Wallace, son of Capt. George E., was born in San Francisco in 1872, and died there in July, 1929. He first went to sea before the mast in the *J. B. Walker*, and on taking command, was just over his majority, the youngest master of an American full-rigged ship. On retiring from the *Walker* he shipped as chief mate on a steamer and on getting his master's ticket in steam, was appointed a San Francisco pilot. At the time of his death he was Port Admiral of the Bar pilots.

In 1897, while the *Walker* was bound from New York to Yokohama, Captain Wallace passed close to Inaccessible Island, a lonely spot in the South Atlantic Ocean, and sighted a ship ashore there. Launching a boat the vessel was found to be the British ship *Helenslea*. Captain Wallace's offer to take her crew to Japan was declined by her master who announced his intention to stand by his ship until assistance should arrive, but requested that his distress be reported.

Both Captains, George E. and John W. Wallace, were thorough seamen and navigators, men of sterling character and fine personality and had legions of friends.

JAMES BAILEY

THE *James Bailey* was a first class ship built for J. S. Winslow & Co. of Portland, Maine, by William Rogers at Bath, and was launched in March, 1878. Capt. J. P. Tenney was in command during her brief career.

The first voyage of the *Bailey* was to the East Indies, her outward cargo being ice, from Boston to Batavia. The second was from Boston to San Francisco in 146 days, thence to Queenstown in 115 days. She then took coal from Cardiff to Hong Kong in 113 days, and leaving the latter port, Oct. 14, 1880, in ballast, for San Francisco, was lost when three days out as per the following report made by Capt. Tenney:

"The tug dropped the ship at the Nine Pins shortly before noon, the wind being from the northeast and freshening and at 4 P.M. we furled the topgallants. At 6 P.M., Leman Island bearing W. by N. twenty miles distant and it now blowing hard, snugged down to three lower topsails. The barometer was falling being at 8 P.M. 29:70, and the fore and mizen lower topsails were furled. At midnight furled the maintopsail, the wind being from E. N. E. At 8 A.M. 15th, barometer at 29:53 and at noon, 29:10, with the wind blowing furiously from the east. At midnight the barometer was down to 28:50; wore ship on the starboard tack. At 3 A.M., 16th, the sails were blowing to pieces from the yards the wind having increased to hurricane force. At 4 A.M. the fore topgallant and main royal masts broke off, most of the braces were carried away and yards were swinging in all directions. At 11 A.M. three men were washed overboard, two miraculously being enabled to regain the ship. The other man disappeared almost instantly and from the state of the weather and the high sea raging, no efforts could have been put forth to save him with any hope of success. At this time the main topgallantmast was carried away.

"Noon; weather cleared a little and a vessel, apparently in ballast, was seen in the distance with nothing standing but the foremast. During the next twenty-four hours the wind traversed around the compass no less than four times. At 3 P.M. 17th, the main stays and starboard swifters carried away and the yards were all adrift. Cut away the mainmast which took the mizenmast by the board in its fall. At 6 P.M. the ship struck on what was supposed to be the Hainan Sands. Let go both anchors to keep her from going over into deep water; wind still blowing furiously. After striking, found ten feet of water in the hold. At 10 P.M. the wind moderated and land was discerned about half a cable length off. At 2 A.M. 18th the crew landed and at daylight returned on board for clothing and provisions. At this time the natives began to assemble on the beach and commenced stealing whatever they could lay their hands upon. At 4 P.M. they had become so numerous that the crew were unable to offer any resistance and they openly boarded the wreck plundering and destroying everything on board.

"On the 19th, found from one of the natives that the ship was on Hainan Island, nearly abreast of Taya Island and we tried to induce him to show the way overland to Hoilow but without success. The next day we succeeded in procuring a man from another district who agreed to act as guide, the other natives threatening him in the meantime, some of them going so far as to follow us five or six miles and at one time it seemed as if they were about to proceed to active violence. No one was left in charge of the wreck as it was wholly unsafe to remain. Our party arrived at Hoilow at 10 P.M., 21st, and received every kindness and attention from H.B.M. Acting Consul there, Mr. J. Scott."

JEREMIAH THOMPSON

THE ship *Jeremiah Thompson* was built in 1854 at Greenpoint, Long Island, by Perine, Patterson & Stack, for Samuel Thompson's Nephews, a prominent New York shipping firm operating vessels in transatlantic trade. She was 216 feet, by 42, by 28 feet and registered 1904 tons. Samuel Thompson was a nephew of Jeremiah Thompson in whose honor the ship was named. Jeremiah Thompson was born in England and with an elder brother, Francis, came to this country at an early age, later becoming one of New York's most prominent and enterprising merchants. At one time he was the largest shipper of cotton in the country and individually he owned several ships which he loaded with his own cargo for nearly all ports on the globe. In addition, he was one of the organizers of the famous "Black Ball Line" of Liverpool packets, owning a quarter interest in the vessels so operated. He was a Quaker and stood very high in that religious sect, holding a position therein equal to that of an archbishop in other religions. In 1827 he lost his fortune in the great financial crash and did not live long thereafter.

The ship *Jeremiah Thompson* was employed carrying passengers and cargo between New York and Liverpool and was a favorite vessel until 1868 when steamers forced the "packets" out of the trade. Many of them were diverted to the general carrying trade and in that year the *Thompson* was put on the Cape Horn run, subsequently making a number of voyages to San Francisco and the West Coast of South America and later on, a few to the Orient. Considering the model of the ship, which was that of a carrier, she made quite good passages, the average of those to San Francisco from Atlantic ports being 125 days, one from New York in 113 days and one from Liverpool in 109 days being the shortest. East bound she has to her credit a fine run of 104 days to New York.

In September, 1878, the *Thompson* was sold to Capt. N. Kirby, formerly owner and master of the ship *Belvedere* for $30,000. Captain Kirby sailed in her on long distance voyages four years when he sold her for $26,000 to Charles Knudsen of San Francisco, the ship being in good condition at the time. Thereafter she was operated in the coal and lumber trade on the Pacific, the Moore & Smith Lumber Co. being owners after 1886. In May, 1892, having outlived her usefulness, she was broken up at San Francisco.

The *Thompson* was at Huanillos, partly loaded with guano, in May, 1877, when the great earthquake and following tidal wave occurred. Through colliding with other vessels she was seriously damaged but was able to get to Callao for repairs. This appears to have been the only serious mishap she met with during her last twenty-five years.

JOHN BRYCE

THE ship *John Bryce*, built and owned by Edward O'Brien, was launched from his yard at Thomaston, Maine, in October, 1869. She measured 220 feet, by 48, by 30 feet and registered 1968 tons. She was named after a partner in the firm of Bryce, Grace & Co. of Callao.

The *Bryce* made three passages from Atlantic ports to San Francisco, prior to 1886, and for short periods was operated in transatlantic trade, but the bulk of her operations were with ports on the West Coast of South America. In 1887 she made a voyage between Puget Sound and Australia and a couple in the coastwise coal trade. Her passages as a rule were very long and on several she had been practically given up as lost before she made port. In 1876 she was 130 days from Lobos to New York and had on board the bodies of a son of Captain Morse and two others who had been drowned at Lobos while fishing. They had been embalmed in guano and boxed up tightly, so were in a good state of preservation on arrival.

The *John Bryce* was one of the vessels damaged by the tidal wave at Pabellon de Pica in May, 1877, losing her jibboom and foretopmast besides having bulwarks smashed and other injuries done. In December, 1872, while at Penarth, loading for Callao, she was carried from her moorings in a heavy gale and did damage to the extent of $15,000 to four steamers and three foreign barks besides being herself injured to quite an extent.

In October, 1888, the *Bryce* sailed from Puget Sound with 1,462,-000 feet of lumber for Hobson's Bay. Early in December she encountered a hurricane 800 miles west of the Samoan Islands and being waterlogged and a complete wreck, was abandoned by her crew. One man was lost but Captain Murphy and the rest of the ship's company were able to make Apia after being seven days in boats and enduring great hardships.

The commanders of the *John Bryce* were Captains Francis Mehan, O. F. Morse and Timothy Murphy. Captain Mehan was one of Edward O'Brien's foremost masters and had previously been in the *Andrew Johnson*, and other ships. When Mr. O'Brien launched a fine ship in 1876, he named her *Alida* in honor of Captain Mehan's daughter. Captain Morse took command of the *Bryce* in 1872 and died on board in 1879, while on a passage from Liverpool to Callao and San Francisco. Capt. Timothy Murphy took the ship at Callao and continued in her until she was lost. He later had the ship *Baring Brothers*.

JOHN CURRIER

THE ship *John Currier*, one of the finest vessels ever constructed in Newburyport, Mass., was built by the party after whom she was named and was launched in October, 1882. She measured 235:8 feet, by 42, by 26:8 feet and registered 1848 tons. Her owners were Thayer & Lincoln of Boston, Mr. Currier, Capt. John C. Blethen and others. In May, 1900, she was purchased by the California Shipping Co. of San Francisco and they were her owners until she was lost.

The first two voyages of the *John Currier* were between Atlantic ports and San Francisco. Thereafter until she was sold she was engaged in trade with China and Japan, her outward cargoes being principally case oil. While owned in San Francisco she was operated in the Pacific mainly in the export lumber trade but during seasons she went to Alaska as a chartered "salmon packer." On Aug. 9, 1907, while at Nelson's Lagoon, Alaska, about ready to sail for Astoria with the clean-up of the pack of the Alaska Fisherman's Packing Co. and 250 cannery employees, she was driven ashore in a gale and became a total loss, but all the people on board were saved.

The *Currier* was a good carrier and made fair passages. One of her voyages was particularly fast. In 1902 she made the run from Puget Sound to Cape Town in 76 days; was 30 days thence to Newcastle, N. S. W., and 35 days from there to Honolulu, being within sight of the island of Oahu the last three days.

In 1883 the owners of the *Currier* refused 44 shillings for a grain charter to Liverpool, which rate other American ships were glad to get. The *Currier* was idle in port until the following December when an offer of 32½ shillings was accepted for the voyage.

The *Currier* met with a number of mishaps, on some of which her escape from total destruction was almost miraculous. On her second voyage she loaded coal at Liverpool for Wilmington, Cal., and sailed in May, 1884. All went well until the ship was approaching the Line in the Pacific when the cargo was found to be on fire. About 250 tons of coal was jettisoned and although water was pumped on the burning coal and every other effort used to extinguish the fire, it continued to burn. Three days later the British ship *Cressington*, Captain Bromley, Liverpool for San Francisco, hove in sight and stood by the *Currier*. Captain Blethen's family was transferred to her and on Captain Bromley agreeing to keep in company with the *Currier*, the latter was put on the course for San Francisco and both ships made port a month later. In acknowledgment of the assistance Captain Bromley rendered, he was presented with a handsome gold watch suitably inscribed, by San Francisco underwriters.

In February, 1885, the *Currier* left San Francisco for Liverpool, being towed out while the bar was breaking badly. On being cast off by the tug she was unable to get offshore and remained on the bar in the breakers all night, anchored in thirty-six feet of water. Heavy seas swept her fore and aft continuously and all hands, including the captain and pilot, were compelled to get into the rigging for safety. Towards morning the cables parted and the ship drifted towards the beach south of the Golden Gate but was finally brought up by an anchor with seventy-five fathoms of chain out. During the afternoon a favoring breeze sprung up and carried her off to proceed on her voyage. It was found later that the ship's stem and fore foot had been considerably cut up by chafing of the chain during the night.

While the *Currier* was at Kobe, in June, 1890, partially discharged, she had another experience with fire which was nearly fatal. A quantity of dunnage saturated with kerosene had been piled in the fore hold and set on fire by burning oakum thrown from the deck by members of the crew. It got a good start and was only subdued after several hours of hard work by the crew and assistance received from other vessels in port. A number of stanchions and the keelson were badly burned. A quantity of rosin in barrels was stowed near the point where the fire was set and within thirty feet were 10,000 cases of kerosene. Three members of the crew were accused of the crime and on being tried and convicted were sentenced to five years imprisonment.

In October, 1893, the *Currier* loaded part cargo at Shanghai and then proceeded to Hong Kong to complete her lading for New York. She had anchored at the Green Island passage, some three miles from Hong Kong harbor, when a typhoon came on that night and the ship commenced to drag towards the shore although she had both anchors and all the chain out, as well as a stream anchor bent to a hawser. The foretopmast was then cut away, the wreckage in its fall taking also the foremast head. The ship thus relieved held to her anchors although she was very close to the beach. She was rerigged at Hong Kong, the job being as well done as it could have been in New York or Liverpool although it took longer.

Capt. John C. Blethen shipped as mate on the ship *Peru*, when she was built in 1867, and later made one voyage in her as master. Subsequently he commanded the *Columbus* five years, the *America* three years, and was in the *John Currier* from 1882 until 1888 when he retired from sea life. Capt. Reuben I. Lawrence succeeded in the *Currier* and continued in her until she was sold. He had previously been master of the ship *Triumphant* and is more particularly referred to in account of that ship, "American Merchant Ships," Series I.

JOHN DE COSTA

THE ship *John De Costa* was built by Briggs & Cushing at Freeport, Maine, and was launched in August, 1876. She measured 217:2 feet, by 41:6, by 25:4 feet and registered 1753 tons. Her hailing port was Portland, Me., and she was managed by her builders.

She was named after a prominent Liverpool shipping agent who did a large business with American ships and owned interests in a number of them.

The *John De Costa* first made a transatlantic voyage and then one from Philadelphia to San Francisco and Liverpool. The third was from Cardiff to Rio de Janeiro, San Francisco and the United Kingdom and the fourth from Liverpool to Rangoon and Calcutta. Then followed one to Valparaiso, San Francisco and Liverpool after which she loaded 2300 tons of steel rails at Cardiff for Port Moody, B. C., and made the passage in 208 days. She had been turned about from Cape Horn and proceeded by way of the Cape of Good Hope and Bass Straits, covering on the whole passage some 24,000 miles. She then took lumber from Puget Sound to Valparaiso and on returning to the Sound, loaded a similar cargo for Melbourne. At that port she took on a cargo of horses for Calcutta and was wrecked off Cookstown July 18, 1885. All hands were saved but advices made no mention as to what happened to the horses.

The *John De Costa* was a good carrier and made passages in fair average time. On her passage from Philadelphia to San Francisco in 1877, she had her jibboom carried away and twice shifted her cargo. In 1882, when bound to Queenstown, she lost the main and mizzen topmasts and the fore topgallant mast in heavy gales to the westward of Cape Horn. On her passage from Rio de Janeiro to San Francisco in 1879, she sighted the ship *Frank F. Curling* on beam ends and in a sinking condition off Cape Horn. The *De Costa* bore down and, under very difficult conditions, lowered a boat and rescued the people from the distressed ship, though one seaman was drowned while attempting to swim to the boat.

For the greater part of her career the *De Costa* was commanded by Capt. C. F. Museires, who had previously been master of the *Jairus B. Lincoln*, and by Capt. Albert E. Oakes. The latter was a native of Yarmouth, a brother of Capt. Frank L. Oakes of the ship *McLaurin*, and of Capt. Charles C. Oakes of the *Gov. Goodwin*. Albert E. first went to sea on coasting vessels and so continued until becoming a mate. In 1873 he shipped as chief mate on the new bark

S. R. Bearse, under Capt. Levi Marston, whom he subsequently succeeded. Later he commanded the *Detroit* and on retiring from the
merchant service he was master of several seagoing yachts. He died
in New York in 1914, aged sixty-four years.

JOHN McDONALD

THE ship *John McDonald* was built by Benjamin Flint of Flint &
Co., New York, in his shipyard at Bath, Maine, and was launched
Dec. 23, 1882. She was 249 feet, by 43, by 28 feet and registered
2172 tons. In October, 1899, Flint & Co. sold their fleet of ships to
the California Shipping Co. of San Francisco, the *McDonald*, then
on a passage from New York to Hong Kong, being included in the
sale. Following the return of the ship to New York in August, 1900,
she loaded coal at Baltimore and sailed September 17th for San Francisco. On Jan. 16, 1901, she was spoken by the British bark *Adderly*,
in latitude 36° N., longitude 134° W., then signalling that she was
on fire. At the time she was bowling along before a good breeze,
seemed to be all right, and did not ask for assistance. This was the last
seen or heard of the *McDonald* and no floating wreckage was found
to indicate just how she met her fate. The presumption is that gas
from the burning coal had accumulated in large quantities and finally
exploded, the ship then going down with all hands.

John McDonald, in whose honor the ship was named, was born in
Halifax, N. S., in 1825, and at the age of fifteen came to the United
States to learn the trade of shipbuilder. For some years he worked in
the yard of Donald McKay, later moving to Thomaston, where he
was employed by Chapman & Flint. When that firm moved to Bath,
McDonald was made a foreman and subsequently master builder.
His first finished product was the ship *St. Lucie* in 1868. When the
firm of Chapman & Flint dissolved partnership, the former members
each continuing on their own account, McDonald went with Benjamin Flint, while Isaac F. Chapman employed Samuel P. Hitchcock
as his master builder. The only vessel John McDonald ever built on

his own account was the schooner *Myra B. Weaver*, 498 tons, in 1889. He died at Bath in January, 1897.

Prior to 1897 the *John McDonald* made eight passages from New York to San Francisco and one from Liverpool. The average of these is 138 days, the shortest being the first passage, 113 days from New York, in the course of which she ran from latitude 50° S. in the Pacific to the Line in 18½ days. The longest passage was 166 days when more unfavorable weather was experienced than Captain Storer had met with on one voyage during his twenty-three years as master. On her passage from New York to San Francisco in 1895-1896, she crossed the parallel of 50° S. in longitude 62°:40' W. on December 2d and on December 9th crossed the same parallel in 77° W., thus making the Cape Horn run in the phenomenally short time of six and one-half days.

The average of the passages made by the *McDonald*, from San Francisco to North Atlantic ports, is 118 days, her first run being the shortest, 103 days to Liverpool. The last two voyages she made were from the Atlantic to the Orient, that in 1899-1900 being 159 days from New York to Hong Kong, thence 39 days to the Hawaiian Islands, and from there, 114 days to the Delaware breakwater.

Prior to her ill-fated voyage, the *McDonald* was remarkably fortunate and met with no mishaps worthy of notice.

The first commander of the ship was Capt. William Tobey, Jr., he taking her at Bath in January, 1883, and being relieved by Capt. Ira A. Storer at San Francisco in October, 1884. A short biography of Captain Tobey is given in account of the ship *Pactolus* in "American Merchant Ships," Series I. Former commands of Captain Storer had been the ships *Alex. McNeil* and *Carrie Clark*. Except for one voyage when he stayed ashore, the Captain was in the *McDonald* until 1896 when he retired from the sea. He was a native of Waldoboro, Me., but on giving up sea life he made his home in Great Kills, Staten Island, and passed much of his time sailing a small boat for pleasure.

Capt. Theodore P. Colcord, who had commanded the ship *A. J. Fuller* over ten years, made one or two voyages in the *McDonald* towards the end of her career. He is more particularly referred to in account of the *Fuller*. When the *McDonald* was lost, Capt. Seymour Watts was master and J. Wilder Murphy, who had a short and rather sensational career as commander of the ship *Shenandoah*, was chief officer. Captain Watts was the son of Capt. Edward Watts of St. George, Me., and had been brought up in the ship *L. B. Gillchrest* of which his father was master. Capt. Seymour Watts succeeded in the command of the *Gillchrest* in 1874, and continued in her as master some ten years or more. In 1891 he was appointed commander of the new bark *Pactolus* and was in her until taking the *McDonald* shortly before she was lost.

JOHN W. MARR

THE ship *John W. Marr* was built by D. O. Blaisdell at Bath, Maine, and was launched in November, 1875. She measured 186:2 feet, by 39:6, by 24 feet and registered 1296 tons. She was named after her owner who was a prominent shipowner of Bath. Early in 1895, following her arrival at London from San Francisco, with redwood lumber, she was sold to go under the Norwegian flag, being renamed *Atlas*.

Prior to 1888 most of the voyages of the *Marr* were to China or India. Thereafter, until she was sold, she traded between Atlantic ports and San Francisco or the Columbia River, making in all, six such voyages. She was a good ship, was fortunate in her operations and made fair, average passages without any unusual incidents attendant.

The first commander of the *John W. Marr* was Capt. George W. Morse who, seven years later, was succeeded by Capt. Edward A. Cotton, who was in command eight years, after which Capt. Charles J. Carter was master until she was sold. Captain Cotton belonged to Bath, and had been chief mate of the ship *Itaska* under Capt. Henry C. Rush. Captain Rush died aboard the ship, while on a passage from San Francisco to Queenstown in 1874, and Captain Cotton was appointed master on completing the voyage. He continued in that ship until she was sold to Germany and then served in the *Marr* eight years. His next command was the ship *Hecla*, also belonging to Mr. Marr, and he died on board her at Antwerp in April, 1896.

Capt. Charles J. Carter was a native of Bath and for several years was chief mate of the ship *B. P. Cheney*, after which he was appointed to command Mr. Marr's ship *Alexander*. Later he made a voyage in the *Belle of Bath* and one in the *Storm King*. He was master of the *John W. Marr* for the five years prior to her sale and then took the *Parthia*, but she was burned on the first passage he made in her. His next and last square-rigged ship was the *Hecla* which Mr. Marr sold a year later, thereby ceasing to be a shipowner. Captain Carter then bought into coasting vessels plying on the Atlantic and intended to retire from sea life when his command, the four-masted barkentine *May V. Neville*, was sold at the outbreak of the World War. Soon thereafter, however, he was persuaded to take the schooner *Fanny Bowen*, lumber laden at Pensacola, bound for Genoa. The vessel was weak and badly stowed and when about two-thirds of the way across the Atlantic, the deck load got adrift in heavy weather and the vessel was thrown on beam ends. Captain Carter and the mate were washed overboard and drowned Oct. 13, 1916, and several of the crew were injured by flying lumber. The rest were taken off by a passing vessel and carried into Norfolk.

JONATHAN BOURNE

THE *Jonathan Bourne* was a fine bark built by Goss & Sawyer at Bath, Maine, and was launched in November, 1877. She was 203 feet, by 39:8, by 24 feet and registered 1472 tons. She was named after a prominent resident of New Bedford who had interests in other vessels and he with Capt. William H. Besse and her builders were the principal owners. Her hailing port was New Bedford and she was managed by Captain Besse. She had double topgallant yards and a skysail yard on the mainmast. In general appearance she closely resembled the *Gerard C. Tobey* and *Guy C. Goss*, and all three might be called sister ships.

During her short career the *Bourne* was employed principally in trade between Atlantic ports and those of Australia or the Far East. She made one Cape Horn passage to San Francisco but on several occasions crossed the Pacific from the Orient. On one of these passages she had 650 Chinese passengers from Hong Kong to Victoria, B. C., and made the run in the good time of 38 days although she had passed through a typhoon which took away practically an entire suit of sails. This voyage was completed by her going from Tacoma to Sydney, Hong Kong and home. All her passages were made in better than average time.

In 1884 the *Bourne* went out to Australia from New York and then loaded a cargo of coal for Manila. During the course of the latter passage she struck an uncharted reef and was abandoned in a sinking condition. She had several passengers on board and they, with the crew, made a safe landing in the ship's boats on the island of Apo, one of the Philippine group.

The *Bourne* had but two commanders, Capt. Alfred Doane and Capt. Francis H. Stone. Both were later in the ship *Francis*, and Captain Stone is more particularly referred to in the account of that ship. Captain Doane's career as a shipmaster is contained in account of the ship *Cleopatra*, "American Merchant Ships," Series I.

JOSEPH FISH

THE second ship named *Joseph Fish* was built at Thomaston, Maine, by Samuel Watts and was launched in December, 1866. She measured 188 feet, by 39, by 24 feet and registered 1262 tons. Contemporary registers describe her as being extra well built, of the ten year class. The party after whom she was named belonged to Waldoboro, Me., and had a store at Port Clyde, nearby. He built some vessels himself, owned interests in others and was also for a time a school teacher. In addition to the present ship, he owned in and had named for himself a schooner, a bark and another ship, the latter having been built at Thomaston in 1858. In 1861 she was seriously damaged in a collision with the British ship *Juanita*, which foundered with the loss of thirteen of her crew. Mr. Fish married Jane Young of St. George, Me., and the ship *Jane Fish* was named in her honor, while the ships *Kendrick Fish* and *Loretto Fish* were named after a son and a daughter.

The *Joseph Fish* was employed mainly in the transatlantic cotton and South American coal and guano trades and so far as can be learned she had an uneventful career. Under date of Dec. 7, 1877, Mr. C. Jalder, a ship broker of Bremerhaven, wrote friends in England: "I have bought the *Joseph Fish* from Samuel Watts, for $42,000, the ship then being in New York. She yet sails under the American flag and left New York. A few days later she sprung aleak and returned to port. She had to be discharged to allow of repairs being made, which being accomplished, she reloaded and sailed. In future I hope to be more lucky and make money out of her." The passage to Bremen was safely made this time and after her arrival out she was renamed *Atlantic* and put under the German flag for operation in the transatlantic oil trade.

Aside from a voyage or so when Captains George L. Carney and John S. Turner acted as relieving officers, the *Joseph Fish* was commanded, during her life as an American ship, by Capt. Frederick W. Stackpole. After her sale Captain Stackpole was for a time master of the ships *St. Nicholas* and *Manuel Llaguna*. On retiring from the sea he engaged in the banking business in Kansas with Capt. William Tobey, Jr. The firm was successful for a few years but a couple of seasons of drought caused them to discontinue business and Captain Tobey returned to his home in Thomaston. Captain Stackpole was preparing to leave for the same place but died the day before his anticipated departure.

JOSEPH S. SPINNEY

T HE ship *Joseph S. Spinney*, named after a New York merchant who owned a one-sixteenth interest in the vessel, was built at Thomaston, Maine, by Harvey Mills and associates, the principal one of whom was Capt. James A. Creighton, who at one time had been in command of the ship *William Stetson* and other Maine-built ships. The Spinney was launched in October, 1874, and was in every way a fine vessel, measuring 230:9 feet, by 42:6, by 27:5 feet, with a registered tonnage of 1895.

The first two voyages of the *Spinney* were to the West Coast of South America for guano. On her maiden voyage she was to have taken out a cargo of sugar mill machinery but some of the pieces were too large for her hatches so the consignment was forwarded by the ship *Abner I. Benyon* and the *Spinney* went out in ballast. Following the completion of these voyages the *Spinney* entered the San Francisco trade and except for two passages she made to Japan with case oil, and one from Liverpool to Seattle with railroad iron, the remainder of her career was spent on the run between New York, Great Britain and San Francisco. On several occasions while on the Pacific Coast she made side voyages in the coal trade between Puget Sound and San Francisco. Her passages averaged well, being 128 days from Atlantic ports to San Francisco, with one of 117 days from New York as the shortest. Her shortest eastward runs were 99 days from San Francisco to Queenstown, 106 days to Liverpool and 113 days to New York. Capt. Samuel C. Jordan was in command on both the shortest eastward and shortest westward passages.

During the first few years the *Spinney* was operated she was successful and paid good dividends to her owners. From 1882 on, however, she was unfortunate. In that year she went out to San Francisco from Havre in ballast, making the run in 124 days. On arriving off the Golden Gate she was forced to anchor near the bar, and on again getting under weigh, lost an anchor and later, on coming to in the harbor, lost another. Shortly after arrival it was reported that her crew had attempted to scuttle her and it was found that augur holes had been bored through the skin and outer planking, the mischief not being discovered until there was considerable water in the hold. The crew protested innocence and the perpetrators of the outrage were never discovered. On the following passage, from San Francisco to Liverpool, she was spoken off Cape Horn, Captain Curling signalling that his ship was leaking, with pumps choked and that he was making for the Falkland Islands for repairs. It appears, however, that he did not stop but proceeded on his voyage and when the ship reached Liverpool, 148 days out from San Francisco, she was still leaking. The passage of the ship from Liverpool to Seattle in 1887 was long and disastrous. When she was 120 days out, Captain Curling put into Callao to have a leak stopped and the cargo was discharged. The ship was in port nearly four months and the expense incurred was very heavy, reported as some $60,000.

On Dec. 2, 1888, the *Spinney* sailed from Tacoma for Queenstown and soon after getting to sea encountered a succession of heavy gales from the southward, during the course of which the rudderhead was twisted off. When three weeks at sea she put into San Francisco where repairs were effected and the voyage thence to destination made without incident in 122 days. On her passage from New York to San Francisco in 1891 she was damaged about decks and later while alongside the wharf at San Francisco, was run into by the steamer *State of California* and had head gear damaged.

On June 9, 1892, the *Spinney* left New York for San Francisco, and all went well until October 25th when she was abandoned off the California coast some sixty miles north of the Golden Gate. The crew reached San Francisco in the ship's boats. Captain Curling's act of abandonment was very severely criticized as the ship drifted about a full day or so until finally bringing up on the rocky coast where she became a total loss. It developed that assistance could readily have been obtained before the ship was left to her fate had such been necessary. Captain Curling's interest in the vessel was the only portion that was covered by insurance and he had a very unpleasant time trying to explain matters to the agents of the ship and the underwriters of her cargo who accused him of being either a knave or a fool. The wreck was sold for $420 but all that her purchasers were able to recover were some sails and gear.

Capt. Samuel C. Jordan of Thomaston commanded the *Spinney* the first five years. When seventeen years of age, young Jordan and five other Thomaston boys, including Capt. James F. Chapman, later a prominent shipmaster and shipping merchant of San Francisco, left New York on the ship *Ionian*, Capt. Charles E. Ranlett, and arrived at San Francisco, March 31, 1851. Young Jordan continued in the ship to the Sandwich Islands, London and New York and was then promoted to the captaincy of the ship *Cavalier*. Subsequently he commanded the ships *Holyrood* and *Sunbeam* and then bought and operated the ship *National Eagle* until the *Spinney* was built when he purchased an interest in her. He left her with the intention of assuming command of the ship *St. Francis*, which had been built for him, but ill health overtook him before the vessel was completed and he was compelled to abandon sea life. He finally passed away June 12, 1889, aged fifty-six, in Santa Barbara, Cal., where he had been living several years. Captain Jordan was a navigator of high ability, a man of many fine traits of character and had the faculty of gaining warm friends wherever he went.

Capt. David P. Oliver, later master of the ship *Edward O'Brien*, made one voyage in the *Spinney* as successor to Captain Jordan. The third and last master of the *Spinney* was Capt. Frank F. Curling who took her over in 1881. His dramatic record as a shipmaster is contained in account of the ship bearing his name, appearing in "American Merchant Ships," Series I.

JOSEPHUS

THE ship *Josephus* was built by E. Haggett at Newcastle, Maine, and was launched in October, 1876. She measured 213 feet, by 39:2, by 24:4 feet and registered 1470 tons. Her hailing port was Damariscotta and her managing owner was A. Austin until 1893 when she was sold to Pendleton, Carver & Nichols of New York. Seven years later she was purchased by parties who had her converted into a coal barge and at different periods she was owned by the Tice Towing & Transport Co., the Merritt & Chapman Co., and the U. S. Navy. In April, 1924, she and the barge *Sea King*, also converted from a sailing ship, were destroyed by fire at Scotland, Va.

At quite widely separated intervals the *Josephus* made a few Cape Horn voyages but most of her life was spent in trade with ports in the Far East. She was a good carrier, made passages in rather better than average time and was, in general, a fortunate ship. On July 7, 1885, she sailed from Cardiff with 2000 tons of coal for Acapulco and made the passage in 127 days; discharged, ballasted, and sailed for Newcastle, N. S. W., November 30th; arrived Jan. 7, 1886, after a record passage of 38 days. The best day's run was 305 miles and the daily average 205 miles. Total distance sailed, 7,800 miles, some 500 miles greater than would be made on a run from San Francisco to Newcastle. On her arrival at the latter port the *Josephus* was exactly six months out from Cardiff.

Capt. William A. Rogers, the first commander of the *Josephus*, belonged to Frankfort, Me., but having married a Searsport lady he afterwards made his home in that town. He owned an interest in the *Josephus* and was in her as master six years, leaving to take command of the new ship *Tillie E. Starbuck*. In her he made two voyages and then bought a small ranch in California.

Capt. Thomas N. Rogers succeeded his brother William A. as master of the *Josephus*, and served in her some ten years. He had previously been in command of the bark *Daniel Draper* and both he and his brother were smart, capable shipmasters.

Capt. Philip R. Gilkey bought into the *Josephus* in January, 1894, and except for one voyage was in command until she was sold for barging. The *Josephus* was the only square-rigged vessel he was in, his prior commands being schooners. The Captain lived but a short time after being in the *Josephus*, passing away at his home in Searsport in January, 1901, at the early age of thirty-eight years.

Capt. Joseph H. Park of Searsport was relieving master of the *Josephus* for one voyage and he also made one voyage in the ship *State of Maine*. Other than these the vessels he commanded were brigs or barks. On May 8, 1901, he sailed from Portland, Me., for Rosario in the bark *Thomas Goddard*, but died the same day. The mate put back to port and the remains of Captain Park were sent to Searsport for interment.

KENDRICK FISH

THE ship *Kendrick Fish* was launched from the yard of Samuel Watts at Thomaston, Maine, on Oct. 13, 1867, and measured 185:3 feet, by 38:7, by 23:9 feet, registering 1326 tons. Her owners were Samuel and Alfred Watts, Joseph Fish and others, among whom was Capt. Edward Brown Watts, her first commander. She was named after a son of Joseph Fish.

The *Kendrick Fish* made a few guano voyages and in 1873 took coal from Liverpool to Singapore, returning from India with rice, but practically all her career was spent in transatlantic trade. She made fair average passages and was a good carrier. On one occasion Capt. John B. Henry received a premium of £100 for being the first to arrive at Liverpool out of a fleet which had left New Orleans in company.

In August, 1880, Capt. John B. Emerson, who had purchased the 3/16th interest the estate of Capt. John B. Henry held in the *Kendrick Fish* for $4,687, took the ship to Bremen and sold her to J. D. Bischoff for £6,500. Miller & Co., who had been the New Orleans agents of the ship, wrote Capt. Emerson: "So the *Kendrick Fish* has passed over to the land of Sauer Kraut and Zwei Lager. We are pleased to learn that you got a good price. Well! it does seem as though the entire American mercantile marine was passing into the hands of foreigners. We hope to see some steps taken to revive it once more."

Capt. Edward Brown Watts, son of Capt. Alfred Watts and nephew of Samuel Watts, was born in Thomaston in June, 1844, and was schooled there and in college at Portland. He sailed under various captains until taking command of the *Kendrick Fish* in 1867 and continued in her until 1873 when he was transferred to the *Abner I. Ben-*

"LEADING WIND," 1159 TONS, BUILT IN 1874, AT BATH, MAINE.

"M. P. GRACE," 1863 TONS, BUILT IN 1875, AT BATH, MAINE

From a photograph by Swadley, showing her at a wharf in San Francisco

"MANUEL LLAGUNA," 1650 TONS, BUILT IN 1879, AT BATH, MAINE
Courtesy of Edward S. Clark

"MARY L. CUSHING," 1575 TONS, BUILT IN 1883, AT NEWBURYPORT, MASS.
The last full-rigged ship built in Massachusetts. Courtesy of Edward S. Clark

yon. In the latter he served some eight years when he retired from sea life.

Capt. John B. Henry took command of the *Kendrick Fish* in 1877, and died at sea in 1880 at the early age of thirty-six years. The ship was bound to New York when Captain Henry had a severe attack of Bright's disease. A German steamer, bound in the same direction, hove in sight and the Captain was taken aboard her for medical attendance but died the next day. Although the steamer was within twenty-four hours run of her destination, the Captain's body was committed to the deep. Captain Henry was of Irish descent, born in Thomaston. Before taking the *Kendrick Fish* he had been master of the ships *Chimborazo* and *Wm. A. Campbell* and the barks *Etta Stewart* and *Amersham*. The latter vessel had been built in Maine, as the *Annie Hodgman*, but was then under the British flag. While she was lying in port at Penang, a son was born to Mrs. Henry. This son, E. J. Henry, now of Chicago, naturally took up seafaring and continued that life until 1888 at which time he was chief officer of the ship *Joseph S. Spinney*.

Among other shipmasters who commanded the *Kendrick Fish* for short periods were Capt. Henry Mowat, who had previously been her mate, and Capt. John S. Turner.

KING PHILIP

THE *King Philip* was one of the very few full-rigged ships built at Alna, Maine, and was launched from the yard of D. Weymouth in November, 1856. She measured 182 feet, by 36:3, by 24 feet and registered 1189 tons. Her managing owners were Glidden & Williams of Boston, until 1869, after which she belonged to Pope & Talbot of San Francisco.

The *King Philip* was a well-built ship and made fair passages without particular incident while employed in the general carrying trade under her original ownership. In February, 1869, she left San Francisco to load guano at Baker's Island for Hamburg, putting into Honolulu, as was customary, to load necessary equipment, etc. While in port there she was set on fire by members of her crew and damaged to the extent of about $20,000. She was condemned and sold, Pope & Talbot being purchasers, and after temporary repairs were made, she proceeded to her owners' mills at Port Gamble for a thorough overhauling.

After being made ready for sea the *King Philip* loaded wheat for Liverpool and had a five months passage, in heavy weather, during which some 250 tons of her cargo were jettisoned. On return to the Pacific Coast she was operated locally two years, then taking a guano cargo from Howland's Island to Hamburg, subsequently crossing to Baltimore where a cargo of coal, barrels of pitch and bales of oakum was loaded for San Francisco. On May 16, 1874, she sailed from Baltimore with a riotous crew, being followed down the bay by boardinghouse runners in boats. During the morning of the 18th, while the ship was at anchor off Earpe's Island in the Chesapeake, flames were seen issuing from the hatchways, members of the crew having set fire to the cargo. The ship's officers, assisted by those of the crew who were not concerned in the conspiracy, extinguished the fire after two hours of hard labor, and orders were given to weigh anchor and proceed to sea. All the crew except three refused to turn to, claiming that the ship was so badly damaged that she was unseaworthy. After considerable parleying the crew was overawed and the ship was run across the bay to Annapolis Roads, where she was taken charge of by a squad of marines from the Naval Academy who had seen the distress signals set on the ship. The second mate was found to be the leader of the mutineers and so was sent ashore. His associates also wished to be arrested and have the same treatment but as this would mean great detention and expense to the ship they were kept aboard, the guard being in charge until May 23. The next day the ship got under way and passed Fortress Monroe, bound to sea, on the 27th.

The voyage, however, was not to be completed without further incident. While the ship was off Cape Horn, in August, she encountered very heavy gales and received such damage that the pumps could not keep the leak under, there being at times five feet of water in the well. Many spars and sails were lost and on September 8th, when all efforts to continue the voyage were found useless, the ship was put about for Rio de Janeiro where she arrived two weeks later. She was in port repairing four months and finally reached San Francisco in May, 1875, 351 days from Baltimore and 107 days from Rio de Janeiro.

This was the last long-distance voyage of the *King Philip*. She met her end Jan. 25, 1878, by stranding on the ocean beach two miles south of the Golden Gate. She was outward bound in ballast for Port Gamble and had been dropped by her tug just inside the bar, going off with square yards before a light N. E. breeze. This failed her and within a few hours she drifted into the breakers after both anchors had been let go and failed to hold. A boat containing five men succeeded in getting ashore with a line and the rest of the crew then landed safely. The following day the wreck was sold for $1,050 and a month later the hull was blown up, the purchasers realizing several thousand dollars from sails, gear and metal. Capt. Albert W. Keller, who is referred to in account of the ship *Bonanza*, was in command of the *King Philip* when she was lost. Capt. Michael J. Daly had been her first master under Pope & Talbot ownership.

A fine ship of clipper model, of the same name, was built by Isaac Taylor of Quincy, Mass., in 1854, but prior to 1857 she was sold to parties in London, going under the British flag without change of name.

LEADING WIND

THE ship *Leading Wind* was built by Goss & Sawyer at Bath, Maine, and was launched in October, 1874. She measured 186:6 feet, by 37:3, by 22:7 feet and registered 1159 tons. She was owned by William A. Rust and Albert C. Smith of Boston, Goss & Sawyer, and Capt. Francis M. Hinckley, her first commander. Although her hailing port was Bath, Mr. Rust acted as her manager.

The *Leading Wind* was a fine ship in all respects, both in construction, and general appearance of hull, spars and rigging. She had a round stern, a full poop deck to the mainmast and crossed a mainskysail yard. Her first passage was from Baltimore to San Francisco, made in 111 days, and she was always considered a good sailer. Capt. William H. Blanchard, who commanded the ship *Gov. Robie*, said that during the three years he was in the latter she was never out-sailed except by the *Leading Wind*, and the *Robie* was considered quite fast.

The *Leading Wind* made only two passages to San Francisco, the second being from Boston in 123 days, and practically all her voyages were between Atlantic ports and Australia or the Far East. In January, 1891, she was at Auckland, loaded with flax and Kauri gum, for Boston, when fire broke out in the cargo and she was scuttled. She was sold as she lay and after being raised and repaired sailed some two years under the British flag under her original name. She was then purchased by Norwegians who altered her name to *Fjord* and had her rerigged as a bark. As such she was being operated in transatlantic trade as late as 1910, according to registers.

In December, 1877, the *Leading Wind* was one of three ships crossing out over the Columbia River bar, all grain laden. All went ashore near the mouth of the river, the *Nimbus* becoming a total loss. The *Pilgrim* and *Leading Wind* were got off badly damaged, the latter having to discharge all her cargo at Astoria before needed repairs could be affected.

Except for one voyage, when he remained ashore, Capt. Francis M. Hinckley was in command of the *Leading Wind* while she sailed under the American flag. The Captain was a native of Barnstable, Mass., and went to sea at an early age. In 1862 he took command of the ship *Star of Peace*, on a voyage to Calcutta, with ice, from Boston, and on its discharge the ship was loaded with saltpeter and Indian produce all to the value of about $350,000. When 88 days out and in latitude 15° N., in the Atlantic, she was captured and burned by the Confederate privateer *Florida*. Lt.-Com. J. N. Maffitt's log book contains the following entries regarding the occurrence:

"March 6, 1863. At daylight discovered a sail to windward distant about seven miles. Lowered propeller, got up steam and started in chase. When about four miles from her, called all hands to quarters and cast loose the weather broadside guns and pivots, fired a shot across her bow and she immediately hove to. Sent Lt. Boole to board her and found she was the Yankee ship *Star of Peace*, of and for Boston from Calcutta with a valuable cargo, mostly saltpeter. Having taken off her company, thirty-four men all told, we paroled her officers and put her men in single irons. We set fire to her at 4 P.M., having the gratification of knowing that besides being a Yankee ship she contained contraband of war. When she was on fire we beat to quarters and exercised our guns upon her but the roll was so great, our accuracy was not up to expectations and only six shots struck her out of the twenty-two rounds fired. At 9.30 P.M. when about twenty miles from her, the saltpeter ignited and a more beautiful panorama was never witnessed on the ocean. The flames were so high and so brilliant that the focal rays illuminated our sails and the ship did not appear more than five miles distant.

"March 11. Since the capture of the *Star of Peace* no grumbling has been heard among our men, as particular care was taken to divide the mess stores equally.

"March 21. Shipped two of the prisoners of the *Star of Peace*."

The *Star of Peace* was a small but fine ship, 941 tons, built by N. Currier, Jr., at Newburyport in 1858 and owned in Boston. She was valued at $56,000 when destroyed and this, with the value of her cargo, wages of crew, etc., and over $300,000 as interest for ten years at seven per cent, was later paid by the British Government under the rulings of the Geneva Court of Awards.

Captain Hinckley's next command was the new ship *Winged Hunter*, built in 1864 for the owners of the *Star of Peace*, and on leaving her he took the ship *Arabia*, also owned in Boston. In 1869, while on a passage from Cardiff to Hong Kong, in that ship, her coal cargo was found to be on fire when the vessel was in the Indian Ocean 1,000 miles from land. By dint of strenuous exertions the fire was gotten under control and finally extinguished. On arrival of the ship at Hong Kong, Captain Hinckley was presented by underwriters with a handsome gold watch and chain. The Captain retired from sea when the *Leading Wind* was sold and passed the remaining years of his life at home in Barnstable.

LEVI C. WADE

THE ship *Levi C. Wade* was built by William Rogers for Edwin Reed and others and was launched at Bath, Maine, Sept. 7, 1878. She measured 214:2 feet, by 39:8, by 24 feet and registered 1525 tons. The party after whom she was named is said to have been President of the Mexican Central Railroad. During the whole of the short career of the ship she was commanded by Capt. William H. Bagley, except for a passage from Philadelphia to San Francisco in 1883.

The *Wade* was a well built ship and the few voyages she completed were made in fair average time. These numbered two to North Pacific Coast ports and one, her maiden passage, to Shanghai, whence she crossed to British Columbia and then took wheat from San Francisco to the United Kingdom. Starting this voyage she had left New York Oct. 1, 1878, twenty-four days after she had left the ways at Bath, having in that time been metaled and loaded with 54,200 cases of oil.

On July 3, 1884, the *Wade* sailed from Manila with a full cargo of sugar for San Francisco and was never thereafter heard of nor was any wreckage of the ship seen. The day after she left port a series of very heavy gales set in which later developed to hurricane force and lasted several days, it being the supposition that the ship foundered at that time. Accompanying Captain Bagley were his wife and Captain Dickie whose former command, the ship *Florida*, had been burned in Manila Bay a short time before and who was offered a passage to San Francisco as a guest of Captain Bagley.

LEVI G. BURGESS

THE ship *Levi G. Burgess*, built and owned by Samuel Watts, was launched at Thomaston, Maine, Oct. 6, 1877. She measured 217:5 feet, by 41:2, by 24:3 feet and registered 1536 tons. The oak in her frame was purchased from the Brooklyn Navy Yard and other material used in her construction was of the highest class, she being considered as one of the best and strongest vessels ever launched from a Maine shipyard. The party in whose honor she was named was born and raised in Thomaston, and was the son of Capt. Joseph S. Burgess, of Snow & Burgess, New York, who were part owners and agents for many Maine ships.

The *Burgess* was built specially for the California trade but better rates prevailing on the Atlantic, at the time she was ready for sea, she carried cotton cargoes for about the first three years. She then loaded railroad iron at Philadelphia for the Columbia River and after taking wheat to Liverpool, loaded at Hull for San Francisco. On proceeding to sea she took the ground but was pulled off by tugs, losing an anchor and chain and having her keel damaged at the time. She was towed into Plymouth where she was libeled for £500 although the towboat masters had agreed to do the job for £25. R. L. Gillchrest & Co., the Liverpool agents of the ship, had her released under bond and the voyage was resumed. Later the towboats were awarded the amount originally agreed upon.

The passage of the *Burgess* from Plymouth to San Francisco was made in the good time of 115 days, Captain Starrett reporting his run from the Line to port as only 16 days. From San Francisco the ship then went to Queenstown in 117 days, thence to Antwerp to discharge, and then to New York. The following voyage was out to San Francisco in 123 days, thence to Cardiff in 120 days. She then went out to Yokohama in 130 days, crossed to San Francisco in 27 days, and went from there to Havre in 105 days. Then followed the longest passage the ship ever made, 149 days from Baltimore to San Francisco. She started out well, as usual, crossing the Line in 23 days, but thereafter encountered light or contrary winds throughout the remainder of the run, being 42 days in the South Atlantic, 32 days in the South Pacific and 32 days from the Line to port. She arrived at San Francisco July 30, 1887, and was immediately purchased by J. Jensen, Capt. Charles Rock and others for $30,000.

Captain Rock took command and had her rigged with double topgallant yards on the fore- and mainmasts, leaving the main skysail yard crossed as theretofore. When Capt. John A. Youngren took her in 1891 he dispensed with the lower topgallant yards and six years later had her converted into a bark. From 1887 until 1910 she was employed in the coastwise and offshore trades on the Pacific and consistently sustained her reputation of being a fast ship. She made a passage from Callao to Puget Sound in 33½ days, a round between San Francisco and Tacoma in 16 days, and Captain Youngren, who was her master for twelve years, states that during the five years he had her in the coastwise trade between San Francisco and Puget Sound, he was never over 26 days in completing a voyage. He further says that the only ship that could outsail the *Burgess* was the *America*, well known as a fast sailer.

In 1910 the *Burgess* was purchased by the Alaska Portland Packers Association which operated her as a "salmon packer" until 1922 when, after her arrival at Portland from Alaska, she was laid up. In 1928 she was sold to ship breakers who in November had her burned for the metal used in her construction.

Capt. H. A. Starrett of Warren, Me., who had previously been in the first *Frank N. Thayer*, commanded the *Burgess* from 1877 until 1883. Capt. Frank N. Johnson then took the ship and continued in her until she was sold. Captain Johnson lost his life in the *Alfred Watts*, details of whose wreck are contained in "American Merchant Ships," Series I.

Capt. Charles Rock, one of the parties who purchased the *Burgess* in 1887, had been sailing on the Pacific Coast as master some five years in the *Sumatra* and *Detroit*. In 1891 he sold his interest in the *Burgess* to Capt. John O. Youngren and subsequently bought into and commanded the barks *Harvester* and *Roderick Dhu*. Later he sailed for Capt. William Matson in the *Annie Johnson*, and on retiring, made his home in Alameda, Cal., where he died about 1926.

Capt. John O. Youngren, who bought Captain Rock's interest in the *Burgess*, commanded her for twelve years after which he had the bark *Santiago* in the San Francisco-Honolulu passenger and freight service for a short time. He then took command of the steamer *Enterprise*, engaged in the same trade, and served in her as master twenty-five years, a record as to time of service for a shipmaster in one vessel, and during all that time he never had an accident. The Captain retired from sea life in 1927 and now, at the age of seventy-three years, is in good health and living in San Francisco. In 1858, when ten years of age, he had come to this country in the ship *Fleetford*, immediately thereafter shipping as deck boy on the ship *Sumatra*, Capt. John Mullin, and continued in that vessel until Captain Mullin took command of the new ship *Paul Revere* in 1876. Captain Youngren staid with Captain Mullin and after making three voyages in the *Revere*, went from New York to San Francisco as boatswain of the ship *Eureka*. On arrival on the Pacific Coast he determined to remain there and after making a number of voyages in schooners, coastwise, and to Honolulu, bought into the *Burgess*. In that ship he was succeeded by his brother Capt. Jan O. Youngren, who had previously been master of the bark *Gatherer*. When the Burgess was sold to cannery interests, Capt. Jan O. Youngren was given command of the steamer *Hyades*, engaged in the Honolulu trade. During the World War he served in the transport service. He died in the Army Hospital at Livermore, Cal., in 1928 at the age of sixty years.

LIGHTNING

THE circumstances connected with the building of the *Lightning* were peculiar and are said to be as follows: In 1871 her frame was in the shipyard of Robert E. Jackson, East Boston, and work was about to start on construction when a ship carpenters' strike put a stop to all operations. W. F. Weld & Co. of Boston, for whom the ship was to be built, immediately dispatched Mr. Jackson to St. John, N. B., with instructions to rent a yard at that place, and this being successfully accomplished, the frame of the *Lightning* was forwarded by the Weld & Co. ship *George Peabody*, which herself was awaiting extensive repairs. The new ship was built in the Thomas Hilyard yard at St. John and was launched inside of twelve months, the *Peabody* having her repairs attended to at the same time. These operations ended

the great strike. Although owned by Weld & Co. the *Lightning* necessarily had to be put under the English flag and she so continued some
twelve years, with London as her hailing port.

The *Lightning* was 221:7 feet, by 40:3, by 26 feet and registered
1576 tons. Her lines were the same as those of the *Great Admiral* although she was a slightly larger ship. She made no passages from the
Atlantic to North Pacific ports although she called twice at San Francisco, from Melbourne and Callao, respectively. The remainder of her
career, while owned by Weld & Co., was spent in trade with Australia
and the East Indies. Like her sister ship she was a good sailer. Her
last voyage was in 1882-1883, when under command of Capt. James
F. Rowell, she was 81 days from New York to Melbourne, thence
three days to Newcastle, 40 days from there to Hong Kong, thence
17 days to Cebu, and 103 days from that port to New York, a total of
244 sailing days on the round voyage. She subsequently crossed the
Atlantic and was sold to Theo. Ruger & Co., taking the name of the
senior member of that firm and being thereafter employed in the barrel oil trade. In November, 1888, she was run down and sunk in the
English Channel, her captain and twelve of the crew being drowned.

Capt. J. S. Watson, an American shipmaster holding a British cer-
tificate, was given command of the *Lightning* and commanded her
the greater part of her sea life prior to her sale. The Captain was later
in charge of the Cunard pier at Boston and is also said to have been in
command of Pacific Mail Co.'s steamers. Capt. James F. Rowell's
seafaring career is given in account of the ship *Great Admiral*.

LLEWELLYN J. MORSE

THE ship *Llewellyn J. Morse* was built by Joseph Oakes & Son
at Brewer, Maine, and was launched in August, 1877. She measured 198:2 feet, by 36:6, by 24 feet and registered 1325 tons. She
was owned by the party whose name she bore, a lumber merchant of
Bangor, Me., who had interests in a number of vessels. For some ten
years she was employed in trade principally with ports in the Far

East, although in 1882 and again in 1883, she made voyages to San Francisco and there loaded grain for the United Kingdom. In 1888, following her arrival at New York from Calcutta, she was purchased by John Rosenfeld of San Francisco, who operated her between Atlantic ports and San Francisco until 1895 when she was sold to the Alaska Packers Association. She then became a "salmon packer" and made seasonal voyages to Alaska, the last being in 1922. After being laid up for three years she was sold for about $2,500 to Southern California moving picture interests. Her old masts were replaced by show sticks, portholes were cut in the bulwarks and with cannons and cannon balls made of wood she was supposed to represent the *Constitution* in the picture "Old Ironsides." Later on she is said to have been converted into a fishing barge.

While engaged on long distance voyages the *Morse* made good time and met with no mishaps of consequence. The average of the eight passages she made from Atlantic ports to San Francisco is 132 days, two of 121 days each being the shortest and one of 149 days the longest. On the latter she encountered very heavy gales on both sides of Cape Horn, being 18 days from latitude 40° S. in the Atlantic to 50° S. and 34 days from 50° S. in the Pacific to 42° S. She lost a portion of her bulwarks, had her boats smashed and cabins and galley flooded.

The average of the passages made by the *Morse* from San Francisco to New York or the United Kingdom is 118 days, the two shortest being 105 days to Liverpool and 110 days to New York. The longest was 127 days to New York. In 1891 she took nitrate from Iquique to to New York in 88 days.

Capt. Fred B. Ames of Bangor commanded the *Morse* from 1877 until 1881 when he was succeeded by Capt. Samuel Veazie, who had previously been master of the Bangor ship *Florence Treat*. Capt. Benjamin Carver, Jr., of Searsport, succeeded Captain Veazie in 1885 and died on board in August, 1888, while the ship was on a passage from Calcutta to New York. Capt. A. C. Clapp then took the *Morse* for her new owners and continued in the ship until she was sold in 1895. His other commands are mentioned in account of the *Jabez*

Howes and those of Captain Carver in that of the *Oneida,* both of which are in "American Merchant Ships," Series I.

LORETTO FISH

THE ship *Loretto Fish* was built by Samuel Watts at Thomaston, Maine, and was launched in October, 1869. She was 213 feet, by 42, by 29:9 feet, had three decks and registered 1945 tons. She was owned by her builder and his friends among whom was Joseph Fish and the ship was named in honor of the latter's daughter.

While under the American flag the *Loretto Fish* was engaged principally in the coal and guano trades with South American ports. She made two Cape Horn passages to San Francisco and but one or two to the Far East with case oil. Her passages were generally longer than those of other vessels of similar model, that from New York to San Francisco, in 1878, taking 183 days. Two men died from scurvy and the whole crew was affected by the disease due to lack of provisions. The ship was iced up off Cape Horn and a seaman was killed by a fall from aloft. Altogether the voyage was one of the hardest ever recorded in the annals of San Francisco shipping and Captain Hodgman and his officers were tried for cruelty and neglect but through influence they escaped punishment. On one occasion the ship had the extraordinarily long passage of 51 days from Callao to Pabellon de Pica.

The *Loretto Fish* had many mishaps during the course of her voyages. In 1881, while bound from Antwerp to Manzanillo, she put into Rio de Janeiro leaking so badly that part of her cargo had to be discharged before repairs could be made. In completion of this voyage the ship took wheat from San Francisco to Queenstown, arriving out in a damaged condition with about 2,000 sacks of wheat spoiled. She was ordered to Havre to discharge and while about to enter the dock there was damaged by collision with a French steamship. The following year, while on a similar voyage, she made port damaged in hull and rigging, with foremast sprung and ship leaking. Shortly thereafter she was sold for $24,000 and went under the German flag as the *Theodor Fisher* of Bremen. Two years previously Gillchrest & Co., Liverpool agents for Samuel Watts, reported that they had arranged the sale of the *Fish* at the price of £9,750 sterling, but the matter was not brought to a successful conclusion.

Capt. John Watts commanded the *Loretto Fish* prior to 1874 when he was succeeded by Capt. George L. Carney, previously master of the ships *Valley Forge, Wallace,* and others belonging to Thomaston. The Captain was quite an old man on taking the *Fish* and after making a couple of voyages retired to spend the rest of his days at his home in Thomaston. Capt. David J. Hodgman, whose sea career is given in the account of the ship *Alex Gibson,* was in the *Loretto Fish* some five years and Capt. Halver Hyler was her master the voyage prior to her sale. Captain Hyler is more particularly referred to in the account of the ship *Samuel Watts,* "American Merchant Ships," Series I.

M. P. GRACE

THE *M. P. Grace,* one of the most prominent American ships of her time, was built at Bath, Maine, by Chapman & Flint and was launched July 20, 1875. She was a three-decked ship of the same model as the *St. Paul,* a product of the same yard the previous year, and measured 229:9 feet, by 42:1, by 27:8 feet, registering 1863 tons. Following the dissolution of the builder's firm, each partner to continue on his own account, the *Grace* became the property of Benjamin Flint, who, as Flint & Co., maintained an office in New York and had a shipyard at Bath. Mr. Flint died in June, 1891, but the business was continued under the former style of Flint & Co., by his sons Charles R. and Wallace B. Flint, who had been partners from the formation of the firm in 1880. In March, 1898, shortly before Flint & Co. had sold practically their whole sailing fleet to the California Shipping Co. of San Francisco, they disposed of the *M. P. Grace* to Geo. W. Hume & Co., also of San Francisco, who operated salmon canneries in Alaska. The *Grace* was employed in that trade until 1906 when she took a cargo of lumber from Puget Sound to the East Coast and was sold to be converted into a barge. Her career in that capacity was, however, very short as she foundered in November of the same year off Shennecock Light, N. Y. The three men on board were saved.

The *M. P. Grace* was named after Michael P. Grace who, with his brother William R. Grace, as W. R. Grace & Co., was engaged in the shipping, export and import business in New York, with very extensive interests on the West Coast of South America. Prior to the establishment of the firm of Flint & Co., Charles R. Flint had been a partner in the Grace concern, which up to that time acted as agents for Chapman & Flint.

The *M. P. Grace* was built for the California trade and prior to 1898 made twenty passages from New York to San Francisco, the returns being to New York on eleven occasions, to Liverpool on six, to Antwerp once, and by way of the Peruvian guano deposits once. Capt. Robert P. Wilbur was in command during her first eight years, completing seven round voyages in that time. On the first he made San Francisco in 102½ days from New York, beating the celebrated ship *Seminole* ten days. On his third outward passage his time was 102 days and these runs have not since been equalled or eclipsed except by the *S. P. Hitchcock* which in 1887 and again in 1889 covered the course in 101 days. In 1880, Captain Wilbur's time was 107 days and the average of his seven passages is 115 days. The ship covered on her maiden run a distance of 16,250 miles at a daily average of 159.3 miles; best day, 300 miles; best week, 1,454, and poorest week, 804; covered the distance from 50° S., Pacific, to the Line, in 17 days, and again repeated this performance in 1881. On her 102-day run she was only 23½ days from the Line, in the Atlantic, to latitude 50° S., a run which would be considered very good for one of the old-time extreme clippers. Captain Wilbur's slowest passages to the westward were 132 days and 125 days. Returning eastward his average is 112 days, the two fastest being 101 days to New York and 106 days to Liverpool.

Capt. Thomas C. Williams then made six round voyages in the *Grace* but in each instance he reported encountering much adverse weather, mostly prolonged calms and his average for the westward run is 135 days. Going east it is 116 days, the fastest being 106 days to New York, 110 days to Liverpool, and 111 days to Antwerp. On one of his voyages from New York the ship had the foretopmast head and everything above carried away in a violent squall just south of the Line and two seamen who were furling the fore-skysail at the time, were lost overboard. The ship was put into Rio de Janeiro for repairs and was 96 days thence to San Francisco. On another of his westward passages Captain Williams reported the exceptional experience of having very fine weather during all of his nine-day run between the parallels of 50° S., two days being of dead calms.

The voyage in 1890 was made by Capt. M. B. Cook, relieving Captain Williams, and his report of his passage shows so well the conditions old-time sailing ship masters had to contend with that it is quoted in full as follows:

"Sailed from New York, Dec. 12, 1889, passing Sandy Hook at 11 A.M. Had a good chance with favorable winds until the 26th when, in latitude 30°:37′, took the wind east which hauled to S. E. and as far as S. S. E. until we took the N. E. trades. These at times were heavy, too much so for topgallants. Had doldrums from 4° N. to the Line when took the S. E. trades well to the south'ard. Crossed the Line 27 days out. The trades were scant, light and variable both in force and direction; held them 16 days to latitude 26°:30′; then had 15 days of the usual weather and winds for that portion of the ocean until reaching latitude 50° S. which was crossed on the 58th day out. Were 25 days making the Cape Horn passage with almost continual head winds and heavy seas; one gale from N. was very heavy, lasting fifteen hours, with a very low barometer, often under 28°:00′. In latitude 50°, Pacific, took favorable winds lasting eight days, to latitude 30° when they became very strong from S. E. and later from E. until we got to 8° S. when, strange to say, we struck the doldrums with the usual calms, rains and variable changing winds which continued for nine days to latitude 4°:28′ N., where the N. E. trades were picked up. We held these 14 days to latitude 28° N. where we had two days of calms and then scant N. W. and N. winds to port. We had crossed the Line when 24 days from 50° S. and 107 days from New York and then had 27 days to San Francisco."

Capt. John de Winter succeeded Captain Williams at San Francisco in July, 1891, and except for one voyage, continued in the ship until she was sold. He had much the same experiences as to weather conditions on his voyages as had fallen to Captain Williams, on one occasion being 42 days from Cape Henry to the Line, being on the same passage 40 days in rounding Cape Horn. However, on that passage he was only 17 days from the Line in the Pacific to port and then took his ship back to New York in 101 days. The average of the Captain's five passages to San Francisco is 153 days, and of his eastbound runs, 115 days.

An incident out of the usual course of events occurred on the last westward passage of the *Grace* when, shortly after leaving New York, a sailor named Hansen refused to work and was put on a bread and water diet. This infuriated him and he threatened Captain de Winter with a revolver. He was disarmed and put in irons a few days and on being released was not allowed to work but was considered a steerage passenger. He then attempted to incite a mutiny and was told that he would be turned over to the authorities on arrival. He claimed to be acting under orders from God Almighty; that he was answerable to Him only and not amenable to the laws of any country, apparently being insane on the subject. On arrival of the ship at San Francisco he was turned over to the authorities.

Capt. Robert P. Wilbur was a native of Connecticut and prior to taking command of the *Grace* had been master of the Mystic ship *Dauntless*. After leaving the *Grace* he is said to have been associated with an uncle in building small vessels at Mystic. In 1890 he resumed seafaring by taking the ship *St. Frances*, but three years later left the sea for good. The Captain was a thorough gentleman and a fine seaman. He was very religious and on Sundays conducted services on board his ships.

The seafaring career of Capt. Thomas C. Williams is contained in the account of the ship *St. Nicholas*. Capt. M. B. Cook, who relieved

Captain Williams for one voyage, belonged to Friendship, Me., and had been master of schooners on the Atlantic Coast. In 1884 he was offered command of the bark *St. James* but had some doubts about taking a square-rigger and so told the owners of the bark. However, he was persuaded to make the attempt and was successful, continuing in the *St. James* until he went in the *Grace*. The latter is, however, believed to have been the last square-rigged vessel he commanded.

After relinquishing command of the *M. P. Grace*, Capt. John de Winter had the *A. J. Fuller* for a time, after which he retired to spend the last of his days at Sailors' Snug Harbor and died there in August, 1905. The Captain is referred to as being a fine old-time shipmaster, bluff and hale, and his passing was learned of with regret by many friends and acquaintances.

Capt. A. E. Chipperfield was the first master of the *Grace* under her San Francisco ownership. As a young man he had left an English vessel on the Pacific Coast to ship on the old bark *Columbia*, and in her he rose to be mate and later master. He then went as mate on the ship *Invincible*, under Capt. James E. Howland, whose daughter he married. Captain Chipperfield subsequently commanded the *Invincible*, remaining in her until taking the *Grace*. In 1899, while in the last named ship, he had the long passage of 102 days from Sydney to San Francisco and on arrival left her intending to retire from the sea. However, he soon thereafter took command of the ship *Falls of Clyde* and was later in the bark *Newsboy* and the large schooner *Blakely* and subsequently was first officer of a steamer that was captured while running the blockade during the war between Russia and Japan. He had separated from his first wife and subsequently married a lady belonging to New Zealand where he is said to have finally gone to settle down.

Capt. George G. Grant succeeded Captain Chipperfield in the *Grace*. He had previously been in the ship *St. Nicholas* and the bark *Coryphene*, which also belonged to George W. Hume & Co. When that firm purchased the ship *Clarence S. Bement* in 1902, Captain Grant was appointed her master and was in command when she was burned at sea in December, 1903.

McLAURIN

THE ship *McLaurin* was built by Atkinson & Fillmore at New-buryport and was launched in December, 1878. She measured 200:6 feet, by 39, by 21 feet and registered 1312 tons. She was built to the order of Capt. McLaurin F. Pickering of Boston, a shipmaster of the old school who, in early manhood, had commanded ships belonging to William P. Jones of Portsmouth, N. H., and investing his money judiciously in shipping property had retired from active sea life to open offices in Boston and New York to conduct business as a shipowner and operator. The Captain knew practically everything there was to be known about a vessel and her construction and in all his ships the greatest care was taken to the minutest detail and only the best materials and highest class of workmanship were used. His vessels were modeled rather for speed than to carry very large cargoes and all were operated in the China and East India trade. In addition to the *McLaurin*, Captain Pickering owned the *Gov. Goodwin*, *Champlain*, and *Sachem*.

The *McLaurin* was a fine looking ship with an elliptic stern and for a figurehead had a life-size image of her owner. She was well sparred but had no flying kites and was conspicuous as being one of the last ships built to have fidded royal masts. She made but one Cape Horn passage to San Francisco but on a couple of occasions crossed to that port from the Orient to load wheat for Europe. On one of these she was 28 days from Yokohama, then going to Queenstown in 111 days. The outward passage had been 116 days from Cardiff and 37 days from Anjer. During the latter portion of the run she was in a revolving cyclone and sustained heavy damage about decks besides taking in ten feet of water. The mizzenmast had to be cut away to ease her and when the wind subsided the pumps were worked three days and nights before the ship was cleared of water. Bulwarks and boats had been smashed, sails split and lost, everything movable on deck washed overboard and the running rigging was in a terrible mess. Captain Little had a jury mizzenmast rigged and broken spars on the mainmast replaced but on arrival at Yokohama the ship presented a rather dilapidated appearance.

Following the death of Captain Pickering in June, 1890, the business of his firm was carried on for some years by Capt. Samuel Pray, who had previously been master of the *Gov. Goodwin*, and the former office manager Mr. Foster, as Foster & Pray. From 1893 until 1904 the managing owner of the *McLaurin* was Jacob M. Haskell. In March, 1901, the ship arrived at San Francisco, in ballast, from Manila and except for two seasonal voyages to Alaska, under charter, she was laid up until February, 1904, when she was purchased by L. A. Pederson of San Francisco, who operated her in connection with his Alaska salmon cannery interests until 1922. She was then laid up in fresh water, some fifty miles from San Francisco, until October, 1927, when she was sold to ship breakers who later had her burned for the metal used in her construction.

Capt. James H. Little, an old-time shipmaster who had commanded the clipper ship *Flying Dragon* some five years, owned an interest in the *McLaurin* and was her first commander. After serving nearly fifteen years as her master he sold his shares to Capt. Frank L. Oakes and retired from the sea. Captain Oakes was a native of Yarmouth, Me., a son-in-law of Perez N. Blanchard of Blanchard Brothers, and had previously commanded several ships belonging to that firm, among them the *S. C. Blanchard*, *P. N. Blanchard*, and *Sylvanus Blanchard*. He had started seafaring at the age of sixteen sailing in coasting vessels, a number of which he later commanded. He retired from sea life in 1901 to make his home in Boston where he was appointed a Pilot Commissioner and held that position at the time of his death in 1912 at the age of fifty-nine years.

McNEAR

THE ship *McNear* was built for and named after Capt. Baker McNear, an old-time master mariner of Boston who, after retiring from sea life, managed his quite extensive shipping interests. At the time of his death in September, 1887, at the age of eighty years he was one of the directors of the Boston Marine Ins. Co., and was otherwise prominently identified with the business interests of that city.

The ship *McNear* was built at Belfast, Maine, and was launched in December, 1872. She measured 189:9 feet, by 37:7, by 24 feet and registered 1245 tons. She was a good ship and was operated with profit by Mr. McNear for many years. After his death she was purchased by Arthur Sewall & Co. and Capt. Wylie R. Dickinson while in port at New York. Captain Dickinson took her out to San Francisco and sold her there at an advance over the purchase price. H. A. Thompson became managing owner but the ship subsequently changed hands more than once. In 1900, Capt. William H. Marston appears as manager although he was not in command. Towards the end of her career the *McNear* was rigged as a bark.

While owned by Mr. McNear the voyages of the ship were practically all from English coal ports to Hong Kong, thence to the Columbia River or San Francisco to load grain for Europe. While owned in San Francisco she was operated coastwise or offshore on the Pacific.

In June, 1876, while the *McNear* was bound from Antwerp to Newcastle-on-Tyne, in ballast, to load for Hong Kong, she went ashore on the English coast and was abandoned by her crew who landed at Yarmouth in the ship's boats. The ship subsequently floated off unassisted and deserted was picked up by parties who boarded her from a lifeboat and navigated into Deal. Her salvors filed a libel suit in the amount of £3,400 but this was contested as being excessive and the Admiralty Court subsequently decided that £1,460 was ample compensation for the service rendered. The *McNear* was valued at $45,000 at the time.

In November, 1878, the *McNear* arrived off the Columbia River bar from Hong Kong but was unable to cross in for over a week. When at last inside and at anchor, the pilot being still on board, the ship dragged in a gale and went ashore below Tillamook Spit, remaining on the ground several days before being floated. Her keel, forefoot and rudder were considerably damaged and repairs made at Astoria cost $15,000.

During the night of May 14, 1900, the *McNear* was wrecked on Dowsett's Reef, Pacific Ocean, some sixty miles from Leysan Island, whither she was bound from Honolulu with stores and workmen to load back with guano. She was set ashore by treacherous currents and began to fill so rapidly that the pumps had to be manned to keep her afloat until the boats were launched. Her company numbering fourteen and the nineteen Japanese laborers took to three boats at daybreak the next morning but the boats were so crowded that only scant supplies could be taken. A course was steered for Leysan Island but as it sits very low in the water, fears were felt that it might not be sighted. At nightfall of the second day it had not been seen and it was feared that it had been passed, when a light was seen, supposed to be that of a ship. All haste was made to intercept it but it finally proved to be a beacon on the island that had been set to guide the *McNear* which had been anxiously looked for as the guano company's stock of provisions was very low. The *McNear* party landed almost exhausted from the cramped position they had been in for forty hours.

The addition of so many to the population of the island, without a fresh supply of stores, soon practically exhausted all provisions, and everyone subsisted on gull's eggs and fish until the arrival of the bark *Ceylon* on June 10th. This vessel then loaded guano and arrived at Honolulu July 7th with the *McNear's* crew.

A Captain Carter was in command of the *McNear* prior to the stranding incident in 1876, when he was superceded by Capt. William Taylor. Subsequently Captains J. N. Frost and A. C. Larrabee made a voyage or two. While owned in San Francisco she had several different masters including Capt. John Pederson who for some years appears as managing owner.

MAJESTIC

THE ship *Majestic* was built by G. W. Lawrence at Portland, Maine, and was launched in November, 1866. She measured 177 feet, by 36:9, by 23:6 feet and registered 1117 tons. Thayer & Lincoln of Boston were managing owners until following her arrival at San Francisco in January, 1878, she was sold for $31,000 to the Seattle Coal & Transportation Co. Some six years later she was purchased by A. P. Lorentzen and he was owner until the ship met her fate. In December, 1892, she left Seattle with a cargo of coal for San Francisco under command of a brother of her owner and was never thereafter heard from. Heavy gales had occurred shortly after she had passed Cape Flattery and it is supposed that her seams opened up and she foundered before the crew had an opportunity to seek means of escape.

The first two voyages of the *Majestic* were rounds between New York, San Francisco and Liverpool. Thereafter until 1878 she was engaged in the general carrying trade, visiting ports in South America, Europe and the East Indies. She made several passages to Calcutta and was in port there under command of Capt. John F. Pike of Newburyport during the prevalence of the terrific cyclone of 1876 which caused the loss of many lives and ships in the Bay of Bengal.

The *Majestic* was a well built ship, made fair average passages and met with many mishaps although none were of a serious character. While under Eastern management she had many different commanders, the first being Capt. J. Lucas. Capt. Thomas P. Gibbons, who subsequently was in the ship *Triumphant*, was master of the *Majestic* a number of years and took her to San Francisco on her last Cape Horn passage. Capt. John A. Hatfield, who had joined the ship as third mate in 1869, bought into her at the time she was purchased by the Seattle Coal Co. and sailed in her as master about six years. The Captain was born in London and at the age of fifteen years joined the clipper ship *Kingfisher* as deck boy, continuing in that ship until going on the *Majestic*. On retiring from active sea life in 1884 he engaged in the mercantile business in Seattle and subsequently acted as agent for ocean-going and local steamers, owning an interest in one or more of the latter which he at times commanded.

Capt. Adolph Bergman, who bought Captain Hatfield's interest in the *Majestic*, and took over the command, is more particularly referred to in the account of the ship *Big Bonanza*.

MANUEL LLAGUNA

THE ship *Manuel Llaguna*, named after the Chilian resident partner in the important firm of W. R. Grace & Co., was built by Chapman & Flint at Bath, Maine, and was launched in October, 1879. She was 221:3 feet, by 41:5, by 25:5 feet and registered 1650 tons, net. After the dissolution of her builder's firm she was owned by Isaac F. Chapman until September, 1905, when she was sold to Lewis Luckenbach for $20,000. She was converted into a barge and was towed up and down the Atlantic Coast under her new name, *Washington*, some twelve years. During the World War she was purchased by the United States Government.

The *Llaguna* was built for the California trade but on her maiden voyage she took out case oil to Yokohama and she subsequently made two similar voyages. Aside from these all her passages from Atlantic ports prior to 1898 were to San Francisco. These numbered eleven, on two of which she was obliged to touch at ports en route for medical aid. The average of the nine direct passages is 137 days, two of 122 days each being the shortest. This rather poor average for a first class ship is accounted for by her ill fortune in generally meeting with unfavorable weather. However, on one of her outward passages she made port in advance of half a dozen other ships leaving New York with her.

The three passages made by the *Llaguna*, from San Francisco to New York, were made in 126, 102 and 103 days. Four of her passages to Liverpool were made at an average of 116 days and two others were 135 and 141 days but in both these last instances all vessels in the trade at the time had equally long runs. Outside of her performances in the California trade she has to her credit a trip of 102 days from Honolulu to New York, beating the ship *Tillie E. Starbuck*, which had sailed five days ahead of her, fourteen days on the run. On her passage from Hiogo to New York in 1889-1890, her daily average was 157 miles, considered very good for that run. On April 13, 1904, she arrived at Boston, 88 days out from Singapore, 37 days from St. Helena where she had stopped for fresh provisions. From Anjer home she averaged 160 miles daily. Her best day was 285 miles and for several days in the northeast trades she averaged 275. Considering the fact that the *Llaguna* could load 2600 tons dead weight and stowed 6⅝ bales of Manila hemp to the register ton, her sailing record may be regarded as very good. She met with no mishaps worthy of mention on any of her voyages.

The first master of the *Manuel Llaguna* was Capt. Phineas Pendleton, 3rd, but he did not complete the first round voyage, leaving the ship after her arrival at San Francisco from the Orient via British Columbia to exchange commands with Capt. Fred W. Stackpole who had the *St. Nicholas*. Captain Stackpole made one and a half round voyages in the *Llaguna*, turning her over at San Francisco in May, 1884, to Capt. Edwin S. Smalley, an old master in the employ of Chapman & Flint. The Captain's prior commands had been the ships *Frank Flint*, *St. Charles*, *Pactolus*, *St. David*, and *St. John*. On a voyage to San Francisco in 1891 the *Llaguna* put into Callao for medical assistance to Capt. Smalley who had been injured by a fall and on arrival at San Francisco the Captain gave up the command and went home to Thomaston where he passed the remainder of his days. Captain Smalley was a first-class seaman and navigator and was highly respected for his many high personal qualities.

Capt. C. V. Small who had previously been mate of the ship *St. Mark*, succeeded Captain Smalley in the *Llaguna* and continued in her until 1901 when Capt. Daniel C. Nichols took her over and was in command until she was sold. Capt. J. Hovey Kelleran and Capt. Charles W. Bruce each made one voyage as relieving officer of the *Llaguna*. The former had been master of the ship *Andrew Johnson* and was in her when she was sunk by collision in November, 1894, and he later made one passage in the ship *St. Paul*, but he was not successful, although a good seaman. After retiring from the sea he was for a short time superintendent of a salmon cannery but did not make good there either. The Captain belonged to Rockland, Me. Capt. Charles W. Bruce had long been a mate in the employ of Chapman & Flint and did not get a command until late in life. After leaving the *Llaguna* he made a voyage in the *St. Paul* and then retired from the sea. He is said to have then gone to Sailors' Snug Harbor and to have died there. The *Manuel Llaguna* was Capt. C. V. Small's only command.

MARY L. CUSHING

THE *Mary L. Cushing*, the last full-rigged ship built in Massachusetts, was launched at Newburyport in April, 1883, from the yard of George E. Currier. She measured 228:7 feet, by 40:4, by 25:7 feet and registered 1575 tons. She was a fine ship in every respect, presented a handsome appearance and was admired in all ports she visited. As originally rigged she crossed three skysail yards and had double topgallants on the fore- and mainmasts but in later years the skysails were dispensed with and her appearance was further impaired by the substitution of a spike bowsprit. In July, 1902, she was rerigged as a bark.

The *Mary L. Cushing* was built to the order of John M. Cushing of Newburyport and he was her principal owner until December, 1893, when she was purchased by Pendleton, Carver & Nichols of New York. In May, 1900, while she was on a voyage from New York to Hong Kong, she was sold to the California Shipping Co. of San Francisco and they were owners until she was lost.

The *Cushing* was never employed in the Cape Horn trade, all her voyages prior to her purchase on the Pacific Coast being to the Far East. Thereafter she carried lumber from Puget Sound to South Africa or Australia, returning to Honolulu or the Coast with coal. Her last passage was from Newcastle to Mazatlan and was made in the record time of 53 days. So far as can be ascertained this is the only instance in which the ship did better than average work so far as sailing is concerned.

Prior to 1903 the *Cushing* appears to have been fortunate in escaping damage from the elements while on her voyages but thereafter she met with numerous mishaps. In the year stated, while on a passage from Newcastle to San Francisco, she sprung a bad leak and put into Auckland, where a portion of the cargo was discharged and sold. On the passage being resumed she met with further heavy weather, lost spars and rigging and again started to leak so that the pumps had to be kept working steadily until she made port. Two years later, when bound from Fremantle to Newcastle to load for the Hawaiian Islands, she had a number of sails lost and split and returned to Fremantle. After leaving Newcastle she put into Auckland leaky and was repaired but the work done was not effective and the crew had to work the pumps until the ship arrived off Honolulu. On being ordered by her owners to proceed to Elele, which was her destination, the crew refused duty on the ground that the ship was not seaworthy, so new men had to be shipped. A start was then made but in a few days the ship returned to Honolulu where the cargo was discharged. Subsequently she went to Puget Sound and loaded for Australia on what proved to be her last voyage.

The *Cushing* arrived at Mazatlan Aug. 18, 1906, from Newcastle, and soon after coming to anchor a heavy gale blew up causing a strong current to run. During the night of the 20th she dragged her anchors and grounded on a sand bar, becoming a total wreck, but all hands were saved, making shore in their boats.

Capt. Lawrence W. Brown of Newburyport was the first commander of the *Mary L. Cushing* and served in her five years. The Captain's father and his six brothers being shipmasters, he naturally took up a seafaring life. In 1852 he went to San Francisco from New York in the clipper ship *Meteor* and after leaving her was employed on a schooner transporting prisoners to the new State prison at Corte Madera, as the location was then called. Subsequently resuming sea duty he rose to be master and commanded the ships *Sonora*, *Elizabeth Cushing* and *Elcano* before taking the *Mary L. Cushing*. He re-

tired in 1888 and died at Newburyport in December, 1903, at the age
of seventy-two years. For the last fifteen years of his life he was treasurer of the Newburyport Fire Ins. Co. An interesting account of Captain Brown's experiences in the capture of his ship *Sonora*, by the *Alabama*, is given in "American Merchant Ships," Series I.

Capt. James N. Pendleton of Searsport, previously in command of
the *David Brown* and *Nancy Pendleton*, was master of the *Mary L.
Cushing* while she was owned by Pendleton, Carver & Nichols. Capt.
John W. Balch, formerly in the ship *John A. Briggs*, was master of
the *Cushing* during most of the time that she was owned in San Francisco.

MATCHLESS

THE ship *Matchless* was built in 1870 by Curtis, Smith & Cush-
man at East Boston for Capt. James H. Dawes and others, and
measured 180 feet, by 38, by 24 feet, registering 1198 tons. Captain
Dawes was one of the principal owners and is listed as the ship's manager. Except for a voyage made in 1873 by Capt. Walter L. Josselyn,
she was commanded throughout her whole career by Captain Dawes
or his son Capt. John C. Dawes.

Prior to having construction of the *Matchless*, Capt. James H.
Dawes had managed and commanded the *Emma C. Beal*, a fine 600-
ton bark built in 1865, by the firm that constructed the *Matchless*.

The *Matchless* made three voyages to San Francisco, the remainder
of her sea life being spent in trade with Australia or ports in the Far
East. She was a fine looking little ship and made fair passages. Her
principal mishap was at Kobe following her arrival from London via
Yokohama, she being about ready to sail for Victoria, B. C. A heavy
gale sprung up and she was driven ashore but was got off at an expense of $2,500 and the assistance of an American war vessel. Her
hull was considerably damaged and she later proceeded to San Francisco for repairs. Captain Dawes, Jr., was in command at the time and
his wife had a trying experience. The boat in which she was leaving
the ship was stove and all those in her were in the water for some

time before being rescued by Japanese fishermen. Mrs. Dawes was taken to a lighthouse and remained there until her husband rejoined her after the *Matchless* was floated.

On June 15, 1883, while the *Matchless* was on a passage from Iloilo to Boston with a cargo of sugar she drifted, in a calm, on a reef off North Island in the Straits of Sunda and soon commenced to make water. Late the next day she floated off but at 10 P.M. foundered in deep water going down so quickly that the crew had barely time to launch boats and collect a few effects. The next morning they landed at Anjer.

Capt. James H. Dawes was the son of Capt. Abraham Dawes who sailed on the Atlantic in coasting vessels for many years. Capt. James H. was born in Duxbury, Mass., in July, 1826, a descendant of the William Dawes who accompanied Paul Revere on his famous ride. The Captain was in command of the *Matchless* when she was lost and did not go to sea thereafter. He died at Kingston, Mass., in February, 1905. On the maiden voyage of the *Matchless* he had rescued the crew of the ship *Japan*, from Liverpool for San Francisco with coal, having encountered her on fire off Cape Horn.

Capt. John C. Dawes was born in Duxbury in June, 1850, and started a seafaring life at the age of sixteen. Sailing with his father he took command of the *Matchless* in 1875 and thereafter, until 1880, father and son had the ship turn and turn about. Captain Dawes retired from the sea in 1880 to make his home in Kingston and passed away there in August, 1907.

MEROM

THE ship *Merom* was built by C. V. Minott at Phippsburg, Maine, and was launched in March, 1870. She measured 172:9 feet, by 37:6, by 24 feet and registered 1158 tons. Her principal owners were her builder and her first commander, Capt. John S. Lowell. In 1890 she was purchased by the Arctic Packing Co. of San Francisco and spent the rest of her days as a "salmon packer."

The *Merom* was a well-built ship, made fair passages and met with no mishaps of consequence. For a short time during her early career she was in the cotton trade across the Atlantic and she also made a few voyages to the Orient but most of her operations, prior to her sale, were between the Atlantic and San Francisco or the Columbia River, these being eight in number and made without particular incident.

On Oct. 10, 1900, the *Merom* was at anchor off Kodiak Island, Alaska, loaded with 12,000 cases of salmon, when a gale sprung up and her moorings parted, she then being carried against the ship *Santa Clara*. The two vessels were in contact but a few moments when the *Merom* went clear and was blown ashore. The crew started to swim to the beach and all made it except one seaman who was drowned. The ship became a total loss, soon breaking up.

Capt. John S. Lowell was in command of the *Merom* for the first twelve years. Later he had the ship *Gatherer* and is more particularly referred to in the account of that ship. He was succeeded in the *Merom* by Capt. T. B. Glover who continued in her until she was sold. Captain Glover had previously, from 1868, commanded schooners belonging to Phippsburg, operating on the Atlantic. On the purchase of the *Merom* by the Arctic Packing Co., Capt. E. Bjorn was appointed master. He was a native of Denmark and had been sailing along the Pacific Coast from 1875, one of his vessels being the schooner *Enterprise* in which he was shipwrecked in 1883.

MINDORO

THE ship *Mindoro* was built for Silsbee, Pickman & Allen of Salem, Mass., by John and Justin Taylor of East Boston and was launched in November, 1864. In 1884 she was extensively overhauled and practically rebuilt. Throughout her whole sailing career she was owned by the firm for whom she was built or its surviving members who also had a number of other ships named after islands of the Philippine group. Most if not all of these ships were armed with a mounted cannon and also carried stands of arms to repel any pirates that might be met with in the Eastern Seas.

The *Mindoro* was 169 feet, by 38:8, by 23:8 feet and registered 971 tons. She was well built of the best materials and her cost, with outfit ready for sea, was $123,000. She was modeled for a carrier and not for speed, yet her voyages were made in fair time and she was a successful and profitable ship for many years. Completing her last voyage she arrived in Boston in 1893 from the East Indies and after being towed to Salem was laid up some three years. Eventually she was sold to New York parties for conversion into a coal barge.

The maiden voyage of the *Mindoro* was from New York to San Francisco, thence to Hong Kong, Manila and home. This was her only passage around Cape Horn to the westward, the remainder of her career being spent in trade with ports in the Far East or Australia. Many of her cargoes belonged to her owners. Her career appears to have been uneventful.

The first master of the *Mindoro* was Capt. Charles H. Allen, Jr., who had previously commanded the ship *Sooloo* belonging to the same owners. Captain Allen completed three round voyages and after him many different shipmasters had the *Mindoro*. Of these Capt. Stephen P. Bray of Newburyport had her the longest period, some four years, and he had previously been in the ship as chief officer. In 1877, Captain Bray took command of the new ship *Panay*, also belonging to Silsbee, Pickman & Allen, and was in her until she was lost on the island of Samar in 1889, when he retired from the sea to establish himself in the coal business in Newburyport. He passed away there in November, 1897, at the age of fifty-four years, highly respected in his profession and also as to personality. During the last two years of his life he was Treasurer of the Marine Society of Newburyport.

MOGUL

THE ship *Mogul* was built by Capt. N. L. Thompson at Kennebunk, Maine, for J. Henry Sears & Co. of Boston, and was launched in September, 1869. She was 203 feet, by 39, by 24 feet and 1365 tons register. Capt. William Freeman, a relative of Mr.

Sears, was in command during the short career of the ship, owning an interest in her. The Captain was later in the *Ocean King* and is referred to in account of that ship.

The *Mogul* made a couple of transatlantic voyages and then traded to South America or the Far East, her outward cargoes being coal from Great Britain. The last completed voyage was in 1873, Cardiff to Rio de Janeiro, Akyab and Hamburg.

On April 21, 1874, the *Mogul* sailed from Liverpool with coal for San Francisco and the passage was without incident until July 26th when in latitude 18° S. longitude, 100° W., the coal cargo was found to be on fire, due to spontaneous combustion. Large quantities of water were pumped below and for a time it was thought that the fire was under control but after five days of strenuous exertion it was evident that the ship could not be worked into Honolulu, so preparations were made to abandon her. However, the fire was fought for another week until on August 7th, it being deemed unsafe to remain aboard over another night, all hands left in three boats, the position of the ship being then 12° S. latitude, 116° W. longitude. A course was steered for the Marquesas Islands, some 1,300 miles distant to the north and west, and favored by good trade winds, Captain Freeman's boat made a landing August 18th at Resolution Bay, Island of Santa Christiana. The next day chief officer Smith's boat arrived and the day following second officer Deveraux came in with his boat. After a few days stay on the island all hands were taken to Nukahiva in a trading schooner and were cared for by the French Governor. Some two weeks later a San Francisco trading schooner visited Nukahiva and in her the *Mogul's* company went to Tahiti and later to San Francisco, reaching that port four months after the abandonment of the ship. On arrival they were looked on as having arisen from the dead.

A ship named *Mogul*, of 797 tons, built by J. T. Foster at Medford, Mass., in 1859, was sold during the Civil War to parties in Glasgow and went under the British flag without change of name.

•

NEPTUNE

THE ship *Neptune* was built by William H. Webb at New York in 1855 for Charles H. Marshall & Co.'s "Black Ball Line" of Liverpool packets and was 191 feet, by 40, by 28 feet, with a tonnage of 1630. For ten years she was one of the best known ships carrying passengers and cargo across the Atlantic but in common with many other ships in the trade she was forced out by steamers and in 1868 was put on the run between New York, San Francisco and Liverpool. She completed four round voyages, all made in slow time. Her last arrival at Liverpool was in January, 1876, and after discharging her cargo of grain she loaded and sailed for New York.

All went well until April 13th when a dense fog set in and Captain Spencer could get no observation for two days. During the night of April 15th, while under full sail and going eight knots, she went ashore on Sable Island and held on, but rolled in the heavy sea so that both rails were alternately under water. Boats with provisions and nautical instruments were launched but they were immediately stove in. Three other boats were later gotten afloat successfully but by this time the provisions were practically out of reach and only a very small supply could be found. In Captain Spencer's boat were his wife and four children, the eldest seven years and the youngest nine months old. The boats remained alongside the ship during the night and the next morning the chief mate's party was able to make a landing. Nothing was seen of the second mate's boat and Captain Spencer's boat was driven out to sea in spite of all efforts on the part of the crew to get to land. For three days and nights the Captain's party suffered greatly from exposure and frost bites in addition to lack of food, they having nothing but a raw ham and a little water.

During the forenoon of the fourth day Captain Spencer was able to effect a landing and his party crawled along the beach as best they could for about seven miles until the lighthouse was observed. Most of the party were then so exhausted that they could go no further and one man died on the sand. Two of the strongest went ahead for

"MINDORO," 971 TONS, BUILT IN 1864, AT EAST BOSTON

"OCEAN KING," 2516 TONS, BUILT IN 1874, AT KENNEBUNK, MAINE

"PAUL JONES," 1258 TONS, BUILT IN 1877, AT PORTSMOUTH, N. H.
From the oil painting by Charles R. Patterson. Courtesy of Trueman H. Newberry, New York

"RICHARD 3D," 898 TONS, BUILT IN 1859, AT PORTSMOUTH, N. H.

From an oil painting by H. Petersen, 1865. Photograph by George E. Noyes, Newburyport

assistance with the result that an ox team arrived and took the rest of the party to the lighthouse.

There it was found that the occupants of the other two boats had arrived but that provisions were very low, no communication having been had with the mainland for five months. The addition of the thirty-four people belonging to the *Neptune* necessitated all hands being put on the shortest allowance possible to sustain life and prospects were very poor for relief coming when, after several days, an American fishing schooner showed up and arrangements were made by Captain Spencer to have his party taken to Halifax. The schooner's crew numbered fifteen so that the accommodations on the little vessel were overtaxed but the run to Halifax was made safely.

By May 9th the *Neptune* had entirely broken up and disappeared with all her cargo. She was valued at $65,000 and not insured. Her loss followed closely that of the *Harvest Queen*, a former "Black Ball packet," then engaged in the same trade as the *Neptune* and also owned by Marshall & Co., and in addition they had just suffered a severe loss through their ship *Great Western* which was forced to put into Valparaiso damaged and leaking.

Capt. Enoch W. Peabody was in command of the *Neptune* from 1855 until 1871 when Capt. James H. Spencer succeeded. The latter had previously commanded the packet ship *William Tapscott*.

NIMBUS

THE ship *Nimbus*, built and owned by John Patten & Sons of Bath, Maine, was launched in October, 1869. She measured 192 feet, by 37, by 24 feet and registered 1302 tons. She was a well built, handy ship and made fair passages during the course of her brief career. Capt. John R. Kelley was her commander six years and Capt. Robert L. Leonard the remainder of the time.

For about a year the *Nimbus* was engaged in the transatlantic cotton trade and thereafter made two voyages to ports in South America and two to San Francisco. In 1877 she took coal from Cardiff to Hong Kong, thence crossing to the Columbia River where she loaded grain for Queenstown, and left Astoria December 29th in clear weather with favorable winds from northeast. There was a heavy sea on the bar when she crossed out and she was making eight knots when she struck heavily but no damage was apparent and the pilot left her. Captain Leonard squared away on his course but two hours later the ship's carpenter reported three feet of water in the well. This increased rapidly in spite of the pumps being kept going and the ship was then headed back to port but the wind died out. During the course of the afternoon the British ship *Aberystwith Castle*, also outward bound from the Columbia River, hove in sight and stood by the *Nimbus* for two hours when, the water in the latter being above the between decks, she was abandoned, all hands going aboard the other ship in their boats. At midnight the *Nimbus* took a final plunge and went down. The next morning a tug was signaled and took the *Nimbus'* crew to Astoria.

The seafaring career of Captain Kelley is given in account of the ship *John R. Kelley* and that of Captain Leonard in the *Florence*, both of which appear in "American Merchant Ships," Series I.

NORTHERN LIGHT

THE handsome three-skysailyard ship *Northern Light* was built by George Thomas at Quincy, Mass., and was launched in December, 1872. She was 219:7 feet, by 43, by 28 feet, had three decks and registered 1795 tons. Soon after leaving the ways she was purchased by W. F. Weld & Co. of Boston, who, after operating her three years, sold her to W. H. Kinsman & Co. of Boston for $95,000. Following her arrival at Liverpool in August, 1885, from San Francisco, she was sold to go under the Norwegian flag being renamed *Mathilda*. For some twenty years thereafter she was employed in the transatlantic oil and deal trades.

The first four voyages of the *Northern Light* were between New

York, San Francisco and Liverpool, 1873-1877. The westward passages were rather long, averaging 142 days, the shortest being the first made, 128 days from New York. Those from San Francisco were made in much better time, the shortest being 105 days and the average 112 days. Thereafter the ship made four voyages to the Far East, on the last one crossing from Hong Kong to Puget Sound, thence to San Francisco and Liverpool. The last section of this was made in 117 days and this was also the last passage made by the *Northern Light* as an American ship.

The voyage of the *Northern Light*, in 1882-1883, New York to Yokohama, Manila and home, was an eventful one throughout. On leaving New York the rudder was found to be out of order and the ship put into New London, Conn., for repairs. This circumstance offered an excuse for the crew, who had been in an ugly mood when shipped, to refuse further duty and start a mutiny. On an attempt being made to secure the ringleader, he stabbed and mortally wounded the chief officer and both were sent ashore, the mutineer under arrest. Assistance from a Coast Guard steamer was received and the principal malcontents were locked up on board the ship. A new mate was secured and when the ship was ready to sail, Captain Slocum decided to continue with his old crew. This turned out to be an unfortunate venture for more or less trouble was had all the passage to Japan and also on the homeward run from Manila. On the latter passage the ship had the rudderhead twisted off by heavy seas near the Cape of Good Hope and she also started to leak in the topsides so that considerable water got below and melted the sugar in the lower hold. The ship became so crank that a quantity of hemp stowed in the between decks had to be jettisoned to keep her reasonably upright. Under jury steering gear she finally made Port Elizabeth where the cargo was discharged and the ship overhauled, these operations keeping her in port two months. The chief officer was forced to leave the ship on account of severe sickness. The man shipped in his place was, it was ascertained too late, an ex-convict and before signing on he had arranged with some of the crew to murder Captain Slocum and take possession of the ship. On getting to sea he at once started trouble with the final result that he was put in irons and so kept for the rest of the passage.

On the voyage to Yokohama the ship rescued a party of five Gilbert Islanders who were adrift in an open boat, 600 miles from their home. They had been afloat some 40 days and of the original party seven had perished from starvation. Had it not been the rainy season all would have died of thirst. As it was those rescued were barely alive but before reaching Yokohama they had fully recovered their strength. From Yokohama they were given free passage to San Francisco by the Pacific Mail Steamship Co. and later on were sent to their home by way of Honolulu.

A further incident on the passage from Manila to New York, during this voyage, was the passing through the Straits of Sunda two days after the volcano of Krakatoa had blown up. The volcano, however, was still in a state of violent eruption and for many days thereafter the ship sailed through fields of floating pumice stone.

Capt. William H. Nelson, who was master of the *Northern Light* on her two first voyages, had previously been master of Weld & Co.'s ships *Franklin, Sacramento,* and *Golden Fleece.* He was succeeded by Capt. John E. Kenney who completed four round voyages and then, after taking the ship out to Hong Kong, sold his interest to Capt. Joshua Slocum and returned to the States by steamer.

Capt. Joshua Slocum was for a time the best advertised American shipmaster living. He was a native of Nova Scotia and as a boy sailed as cook on a fishing vessel. Later on he became an American citizen and sailing on larger vessels, he rose from seaman to master. In 1877 he purchased the old bark *Amethyst* and for a short time operated her on the Pacific. This vessel, of only 350 tons register, had been built in Boston in 1821 as a full-rigged ship and with her sisters, the *Topaz, Emerald,* and *Sapphire,* was a regular passenger packet between Boston and Liverpool for a number of years. She was then sold and for twenty years was operated as a whaler. Later on she returned to the merchant service and traded along the China Coast. In 1861 she crossed to San Francisco and until being purchased by Captain Slocum was a coasting collier and when the latter sold her to buy into the *Northern Light* she was again outfitted to do duty as a whaler and was operated as such until she went missing on a voyage in 1885.

After disposing of his interest in the *Northern Light*, Captain Slocum took command of the bark *Aquidnet*, but not long thereafter this vessel was wrecked on the coast of Brazil. In 1895-1896 the Captain distinguished himself by sailing alone around the world in a small sloop named *Spray* and his experiences were published in a book which had a large sale. Later he undertook a similar voyage but did not reach his first port of call and just how he met his end will never be known.

Captain Slocum was a first-class seaman and navigator, fearless and courageous, and while a strict disciplinarian, requiring immediate obedience to orders, he was, nevertheless, of a kindly disposition and a fair, just man.

OCEAN KING

THE *Ocean King*, built by Capt. N. L. Thompson at Kennebunk, Maine, and launched in October, 1874, was the first four-masted, square-rigged sailing vessel constructed in this country after Donald McKay's celebrated clipper *Great Republic* left the ways at East Boston in October, 1853. The *Ocean King* was also, when built, the largest sailing ship afloat with the single exception of the *Three Brothers*, which had originally been a steamer. She was 250:5 feet, by 42:3, by 30:1 feet, had three decks and registered 2516 tons. Her manager and principal owner was J. Henry Sears of Boston, others owning interests were her builder, some parties in Boston, Theodore H. Allen of San Francisco, and her first commander, Capt. William Freeman. After the failure of the Sears firm in 1884 its three-quarter interest was sold to William P. Ellison.

The *Ocean King* was what was later called a four-masted bark, being fore and aft rigged on the spanker or jigger mast. On the other masts she crossed skysailyards yet she could not be called a lofty ship nor were her yards as square as those of many old-time clippers half her tonnage, her mainyard being only eighty-six feet long. The foremast was set well forward allowing the bowsprit and jibboom to be quite short. She had wire standing rigging, a flat floor, fairly sharp entrance lines and a good run aft. The poop deck, four feet high, extended forward to midway between the main- and mizzenmasts and on top of this was a trunk cabin. She could not be called a large carrier as later modeled ships of 300 tons less register loaded dead-weight cargoes, for deep water voyages, in excess of her by 500 tons or more. However, when she was later carrying coal along the Pacific Coast she was loaded much heavier and down to a draft of twenty-eight feet and this overloading was given as the cause of her ultimate loss.

During the eight and one-half years prior to June, 1883, the *Ocean King* was continuously employed on the run between New York, San Francisco and Liverpool, completing six round voyages and then returning to San Francisco. It would appear as though she had not been very fortunate in her operations for out of the eight years, fully three and one-half years were spent in ports discharging, loading or awaiting charter. Her passages were made in slow time, the average of those to San Francisco being 145 days, one of 130 days being the shortest. Contrary to the usual schedule, those from San Francisco to the Atlantic were but little faster, their average being 141 days and the shortest 132 days, two days longer than her best westward run. She was, however, quite fortunate in escaping mishaps, the most serious being the loss of her bowsprit by collision with a schooner while proceeding to sea from New York which necessitated her putting back for repairs, and, in another instance, the twisting off of the rudderhead when rounding Cape Horn, but the passage was completed with jury steering gear without further incident.

After her arrival at San Francisco in June, 1883, the *Ocean King* was laid up until March, 1886, when she was chartered for the Coast coal trade. She completed two round voyages between British Columbia and San Francisco and one to San Pedro and was on the way to the latter port with a second cargo when she was lost. She left Nanaimo, April 27, 1887, and three days after passing Cape Flattery met with a succession of southwest gales and sprung aleak. The steam pumps kept the leak in hand for six days when the pump shaft broke.

Hand pumping was then resorted to, the men being lashed to prevent their being swept overboard by the seas which broke over the ship. On May 8th, the ship then having eight feet of water in the hold and the leak continually increasing, it was decided to abandon her. The long boat was crushed in being put over the side, but the sealing schooner *Angel Dolly*, which was standing by, launched one of her boats and rescued the ship's crew. At 6 p.m. the same day the ship went down, her position being then thirty-five miles west of Cape Arago.

Capt. William Freeman was one of the best known American ship-masters of his time. Born in Beverly, Mass., in 1820, he went to sea in early life. One of his first commands was the ship *Maine* and in her he was shipwrecked at the mouth of the Kennebec River in November, 1853, when bound to Bath from Liverpool. His next command was the medium clipper *Undaunted*, built at Bath in 1853, and condemned at Rio de Janeiro ten years later. In 1856, on a voyage from Boston in that ship, part of the crew mutinied and severely wounded Captain Freeman. He, however, with his officers, quelled the malcontents and worked the ship into St. John. The Captain's next command was the fine clipper ship *Kingfisher* which he had some four years. He then took the new ship *Mogul*, belonging to J. Henry Sears, and was her master from 1869 until she was burned in the South Pacific in August, 1874, while bound from Liverpool to San Francisco. The crew took to three boats and all landed safely on the island of Santa Christiana. Captain Freeman made his way home by way of Tahiti and San Francisco and then took command of the *Ocean King*. After arrival of the ship at San Francisco in June, 1883, he sold his interest in her to Capt. L. B. Small and went to New York as master of the ship *Jabez Howes*. Then retiring from active sea life he passed his remaining days at home in Brewster and died there about 1907.

Capt. Loring B. Small, who purchased the interest of Captain Freeman and also that of T. H. Allen, never made a voyage in the *Ocean King*, she being laid up during the term of his ownership. Captain Small had previously been in command of the ships *America* and *Winged Hunter*. After staying in San Francisco a year or so following his purchase of the *Ocean King* he started East on a visit but died en route just before reaching home.

Capt. Charles H. Sawyer was in command of the *Ocean King* while she was employed as a collier along the Pacific Coast. He was a native of Maine, born in 1830, and when fifteen years of age started seafaring. He served three years in the United States Navy during the Civil War, then returning to the mercantile marine. His first command is said to have been the ship *Charmer* which he took in 1884 after having been her chief officer some years. After the loss of the *Ocean King* he was master of several different vessels, among which were the ships *Ericsson* and *Kennebec* and bark *Aureola*.

OLYMPIC

THE *Olympic* was a four-masted vessel having yards on the two forward masts and fore and aft sails on the after two. She was rigged according to the ideas of her managing owner Capt. William H. Besse of New Bedford, who had owned and sailed the *Hattie C. Besse*, similarly sparred, and found her a very satisfactory vessel. There was always a difference of opinion as to what such a rig should be designated, some parties insisting that it was not that of a bark while others thought that "jackass bark" should be the proper term. When she was purchased by merchants of Honolulu and San Francisco in 1899, her new owners incorporated a stock company called the "Bark Olympic Co."

The *Olympic* was designed principally to carry spars and ship timber from Puget Sound to the Atlantic and was modeled to sail at sea without ballast which she successfully did on several short trips. She had a clear deck space of 130 feet between the forward and after houses and could load one and one-half million feet of sawed lumber. She measured 224:4 feet, by 42:1, by 21:3 feet and registered 1402 tons, net. Her fore- and mainmasts were eighty feet and the topmasts sixty feet in length. She had a spike bowsprit. On first coming out she had double topgallant yards and a main skysailyard but was soon altered into a single topgallant and royal yard vessel and in 1917, when she changed hands for the third time, the yards on the mainmast were dispensed with and she became a four-masted barkentine.

The *Olympic* proved to be a good sailer and handled and behaved well both with lumber and such heavy cargo as nitrate of soda which she carried on several voyages. Of the five passages she made from Atlantic ports to those of the North Pacific, the first was to Seattle in 140 days of generally light or unfavorable weather, and the others to San Francisco in 114, 137, 126 and 112 days. Her first timber cargo from Puget Sound was taken to Boston in the fine time of 114 days and as a rule all her passages were made in something better than average time. She took only two lumber cargoes to the Atlantic but many to transpacific ports.

While the *Olympic* was on the Atlantic Coast in July, 1899, she was sold to be operated in trade between San Francisco and Honolulu but was so employed only a few years, then re-entering the lumber carrying business. In 1910 she was purchased by the North Alaska Salmon Co. and for six years was a "salmon packer." She then again changed hands, being purchased by Thomas Crowley for the export lumber trade. On her last voyage as a sailing vessel she left Eureka, Cal., in September, 1920, for Sydney, then going to Callao from Newcastle, thence to San Francisco where she arrived in September, 1921, and was laid up. Four years later she was sold to the Hermosa Amusement Co. and was used in the production of the moving picture "Moran of the Lady Letty." She was subsequently sold to do duty as a fishing barge in Southern California.

On March 17, 1897, the *Olympic* arrived at San Francisco from Philadelphia and was proceeding up the bay without a tug, her sails clewed up but not furled, she being about to drop anchor, when the stern-wheel steamboat *Sunol*, not knowing that she was under headway, attempted to cross under her bows. The *Sunol* was caught and carried ahead by the ship several minutes, during which time her passengers and crew climbed aboard the *Olympic*. The steamer listed so badly that her boilers and safe fell out and went to the bottom of the bay. The safe contained a large shipment of gold bars from upriver smelters but this and the boilers were ultimately recovered by divers.

Capt. S. B. Gibbs took command of the *Olympic* when she was launched and continued in her until 1901 when he retired from the sea to settle in Seattle where he was a marine surveyor until his death several years ago. The Captain had been master of the bark *William H. Besse* for some time prior to her loss in 1896 after which he commanded the ship *William J. Rotch* and bark *Gerard C. Tobey*. He was a son-in-law of Capt. Charles C. Morse, a prominent Pacific Coast shipmaster.

Later commanders of the *Olympic* were Capt. T. H. Evans who served in her nearly ten years and Capt. T. F. Halcrow, her last master. Captain Halcrow's first command was the ship *Alameda*, of which he had previously been chief officer, and later he had the *Louisiana*, *Joseph B. Thomas* and *Alex. Gibson*, operating on the Pacific.

OLYMPUS

THE ship *Olympus* was built at Seabeck, Wash., by Middlemas & Boole of San Francisco, master builder Hiram Doncaster having charge of construction. She was launched in August, 1880, and was built to the order of W. J. Adams for use as a lumber carrier between his mills at Seabeck, Puget Sound, and his yards at San Francisco. An innovation in large ship construction was her being built with but one deck and in this respect she was the largest full-rigged wooden ship afloat. Her knees, breast hooks and other timbers were of immense size and from the top of the keelson to the bottom of the keel there was fourteen and one-half feet of solid wood. The skin was eighteen inches thick at the bilges and sixteen inches elsewhere. Although she was 237 feet long, the outer planking ran the whole length of the ship without any butts. She was most securely fastened and her whole cost was something over $80,000. She had a beam of forty-six feet, and a seventeen-foot depth of hold, being able to stow 1,300,000 feet of lumber under deck. She had good lines, a graceful shear and was neat aloft, crossing three skysail yards. Part of her spars and rigging had previously served on the ship *Frank Jones* which had been wrecked while proceeding to sea from San Francisco in 1877.

During her short career the *Olympus* was very successful. She carried a limited number of passengers on each trip and earned $45,000 net during the first year's operations. Capt. William F. Edwards, who had previously commanded the fine bark *Cassandra Adams*, was her master throughout.

The *Olympus* sailed from San Francisco Sept. 3, 1881, having as cargo a quantity of stores for the Seabeck mill, included in which were kerosene and bales of hay and oakum. Early in the morning of September 14th, when the ship was some 200 miles off the southern coast of Washington, the cargo stowed forward was discovered to be on fire. The hatch, which had been open, was closed with difficulty, the two mates getting hair and eyebrows singed in the operation. Water was then pumped into the hold but the fire ran along the cargo as over a dry brush heap and flames soon burst through the forward and after hatches, at once enveloping the ship and ascending into the rigging. All hands on board, twenty-six in number, including three ladies, were safely embarked in boats, only a few effects being saved. Some hours later the ship *War Hawk*, bound to Port Discovery, hove in sight and rescued the *Olympus'* party. When last seen the ship was a charred wreck and two months later the hull drifted ashore on the California coast.

P. G. BLANCHARD

THE ship *P. G. Blanchard* was built and owned by Blanchard Brothers and was launched at Yarmouth, Maine, in June, 1862. She was a full-bodied, square-sterned cargo carrier and measured 185 feet, by 35:8, by 25 feet, registering 1317 tons. She was named after Paul G. Blanchard, the eldest of three sons of Capt. Sylvanus Blanchard, whose shipbuilding business was continued by the brothers after his death in 1859.

The *Blanchard* was built for the South American coal and guano trade and practically her whole career, while under the American flag, was spent therein. On one occasion she took a coal cargo to Aden and once she went to Australia but these were exceptions to the usual itinerary. She was known as a good and successful ship and made money for her owners. In November, 1883, she was sold to go under the Norwegian flag, without change of name, and thereafter was employed in transatlantic trade. The last report available about her is in 1886 when, on a voyage from Liverpool to Grindstone Island, N. B., she sprung a bad leak and was forced to put into Queenstown.

The first commander of the *Blanchard* was Capt. Eben R. York of Yarmouth, who later was master of the ships *Peru, Columbus, St. John Smith,* and *Wm. G. Davis.* On retiring from the sea Captain York made his home in San Francisco where he was engaged as a ship broker. One of his sons, William, was master of the brig *Don Quixote* and was washed overboard and lost while on a passage across the Atlantic to the eastward. Mrs. York assisted in the subsequent navigation of the ship, but the vessel ran ashore on the Irish coast by her pilot and became a total loss. Fortunately, however, all hands were saved.

Capt. Samuel S. Thomas was master of the *Blanchard* on the Aden voyage, the ship later proceeding to Callao, but having such a long passage, due to continuous calms and light winds, that she was given up for lost. Scurvy broke out and some of the crew died. Captain Thomas himself was very ill but managed to keep the deck and was at the wheel when the ship made Callao. The Captain owned an interest in the ship as also in other vessels built by Blanchard Brothers and the ship *S. S. Thomas* was named in his honor.

Among other masters of the *P. G. Blanchard* were Captains Richard Harding, Henry Newton and Henry McIntyre. Captain Harding was a native of Yarmouth and was for a number of years in command of the ship *Arabia,* built at Brunswick, Me., in 1852. His last ship was the *Grace Sargent,* built at Yarmouth in 1859. He owned interests in a number of vessels and in 1875, on retiring from sea life, had the ship *Alice D. Cooper* built at Cape Elizabeth, Me., and man-

aged her business affairs until she was sold in 1886. Capt. Frank
Harding, son of Captain Richard, was in command of the *Cooper* for
the four years prior to her sale. He later was master of large seagoing yachts and is still living.

Capt. Henry Newton was a native of Liverpool but located in Yarmouth when a young man. In 1856 he took command of the new bark
Priscilla, engaged in the guano trade, and registers of 1858 show him
as managing owner. After leaving the *P. G. Blanchard* he had the
Detroit for the three years prior to 1873, in which year he passed
away at Yarmouth. Capt. Henry McIntyre belonged to Gloucester,
Mass., but sailed for many years for Blanchard Bros. He commanded
the *P. G. Blanchard* some ten years, but during this term of service
made one voyage as relieving officer in the ship *Peru*. Following the
sale of the *Blanchard* he had the ship *Red Cross* and after her loss in
1889 gave up active sea duty. In later years he is said to have been
connected with a salmon cannery in Alaska and to have died there.

PACIFIC

THE ship *Pacific* was built by Blanchard Brothers at Yarmouth,
Maine, J. & A. Seabury, master carpenters, having charge of construction. She was launched May 30, 1869, and was 206 feet, by 41,
by 29 feet, being the deepest vessel ever built in Yarmouth. Her gross
tonnage was 1812 but she loaded 2950 tons of coal or guano on a
draft of twenty-six and one-half feet. As were all the Blanchard ships,
she was built in the strongest manner and of the best materials obtainable. The three lower masts were of iron, taken from a British ship
that had been lost on the coast. In model she was an enlarged *Peru*, a
ship built and owned by Blanchard Brothers and considered by them
as ideal for bulk cargo carrying. The *Pacific* proved to be a good sailer
and sea boat and one of her strong points was ability to work to windward. During her short life she made money for her owners.

The *Pacific* was built for the coal and guano trade with South
America and her whole sea life was spent therein. She had no mishaps

prior to her loss which occurred Nov. 1, 1874, while she was bound in ballast from Antwerp to Cardiff. She was in charge of a pilot in whom Captain Loring had full confidence, but in thick and foggy weather with a strong breeze blowing, land was sighted dead ahead and less than a mile distant, at 9 P.M. Orders were immediately given to wear ship but while the men were squaring the yards the ship struck and within two hours there was ten feet of water in the hold. The masts were cut away but without benefitting conditions and part of the crew began swimming ashore. A boat was launched with great difficulty and those who had remained on the ship got safely ashore. One of the swimmers was drowned. The wreck occurred at Stackpole, on the coast of Wales.

Capt. David W. Blanchard was in command of the *Pacific* the first four years, when he stayed home for a year, being relieved by Capt. David C. Loring. Following Captain Loring's arrival at Antwerp after completing his voyage, Captain Blanchard crossed the Atlantic to resume command but finding the ship a wreck, he took the *Peru* to South America. The *Pacific* was Captain Blanchard's favorite ship. On one occasion she left Mejillones, Bolivia, in company with the Kennebunkport ship *Columbus*, Capt. Eben R. York, and both ships arrived at Antwerp the same day, 84 days out. They had met and spoken each other on several occasions on the passage. Later commands of Captain Blanchard were the ships *Admiral* and *Commodore*. He died in October, 1903, and was buried in Riverside Cemetery, Yarmouth, Maine.

PALESTINE

THE ship *Palestine*, built and owned by W. V. Moses & Son, was launched from their shipyard at Bath, Maine, in January, 1877. She measured 209:9 feet, by 40, by 23:9 feet and registered 1397 tons. In February, 1888, she was sold for $31,000, to Samuel Blair of San Francisco and he continued as owner until she was lost.

Except for a voyage to Singapore, in 1880, the *Palestine* was in the Cape Horn trade with San Francisco until she was purchased there.

The remainder of her sea life was spent in the coal trade between Puget Sound and San Francisco, she completing twenty-two voyages therein. During all of 1883 and 1884 she was laid up at San Francisco with many other vessels which could not get remunerative freights but aside from this she was kept constantly moving and being a good carrier and a very fair sailer, she was considered good property.

On June 27, 1891, the *Palestine* arrived off San Francisco bar with 2500 tons of coal from Tacoma and on crossing in, struck in five and one-half fathoms, soon filling with water. Tugs sent to her assistance took off the crew and started to tow the ship but she sunk so that only her topgallant masts were above water. Until she broke up, a pilot boat patrolled the vicinity. The wreck was sold for $50 but its purchaser made practically nothing out of his bargain.

Prior to her sale in 1888, the *Palestine* was commanded by Capt. S. P. Emmons, one of whose prior ships had been the *Japan*, a fine vessel of 1250 tons, owned by George F. Patten of Bath, built in 1868. In this ship Captain Emmons made a voyage from Baltimore to San Francisco and thence to Liverpool. There she loaded coal for San Francisco but was burned off Cape Horn. On Aug. 20, 1870, suspicions were aroused about the condition of the cargo but that it was on fire was not detected until two days later. For five days the crew did everything possible to smother the fire but without avail and the ship *Matchless*, bound from Boston to San Francisco, heaving in sight, the *Japan* was abandoned. Two weeks later the *Matchless* transferred a portion of the rescued crew to two different vessels bound to Valparaiso and carried the remainder to San Francisco.

Capt. William O. Hayden, whose career as a shipmaster is given in the account of the ship *El Dorado*, in "American Merchant Ships," Series I, commanded the *Palestine* the first two years after she changed hands and Capt. Thomas McCartney the remainder of her career. Captain McCartney had been sailing on the Pacific Coast many years in the *Kate Davenport*, *Two Brothers*, and other ships. He is reported to have been drowned when sailing in a boat on the Amoor River while he was in command of the bark *Wilna*.

PALMYRA

THE ship *Palmyra* was built for F. & E. Reed, of Bath, Maine, by Goss & Sawyer and was launched at that place in January, 1876. She measured 197 feet, by 38:8, by 24:2 feet and registered 1360 tons. She was built to be commanded by Capt. Pearson N. Preble who had sailed for the Messrs. Reed many years as master of the ships *Thomas Lord* and *Ellen Goodspeed*. Captain Preble made two voyages in the *Palmyra* and then retired, being succeeded by Capt. J. P. Minott who continued in her until December, 1891. Captain Minott then took command of the bark *Wakefield* whose master, Capt. Barnabas C. Howes, had died from injuries received by being struck by a San Francisco cable car. On finally giving up sea life Captain Minott was engaged in the coal business at San Rafael, Cal., and passed away there many years ago.

In April, 1887, the *Palmyra* arrived at San Francisco from Newcastle-on-Tyne and shortly thereafter was sold to Pope & Talbot of San Francisco, who operated her in their Puget Sound coastwise and export-lumber business on the Pacific until 1908 when she was purchased by James Griffiths of Seattle, who had her converted into a barge and for a number of years she did duty as such on Puget Sound and British Columbia waters. Eventually she was sold to Southern California parties and was finally burned at Santa Catalina Island.

While employed as a merchantman the *Palmyra* made one voyage to Hong Kong and one to the East Indies, the remainder being between San Francisco and New York or Liverpool. She has no short passages to her credit, the average of those to San Francisco being 149 days and from that port, 129 days. She met with many mishaps such as losing spars and sails and on her passage to Queenstown in 1878, had both topsail yards on the foremast carried away, one man killed outright and several others of the crew badly injured. In 1885, when bound in ballast from Hartlepool to Cardiff, to load for Hong Kong, she struck on the Manacle Rocks but floated off making considerable water. She bore up for Falmouth but having a bad list was practically unmanageable and got embayed near Pendennis Castle Point where

"S. P. HITCHCOCK," 2178 TONS, BUILT IN 1883, AT BATH, MAINE

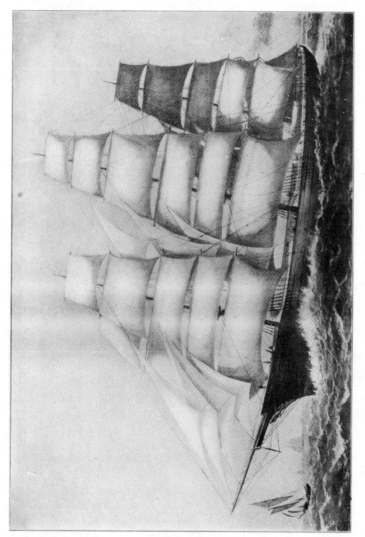

"SACHEM," 1312 TONS, BUILT IN 1875, AT EAST BOSTON

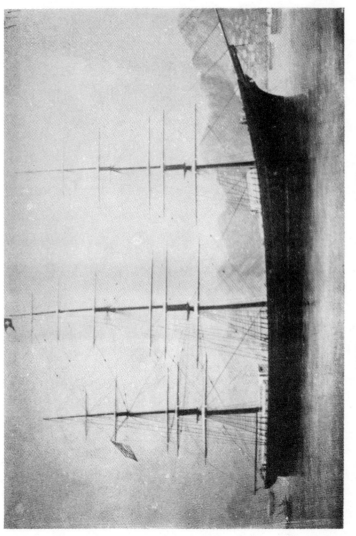

"SACHEM," 1312 TONS, BUILT IN 1875, AT EAST BOSTON

Rig altered to bark in 1897. From a Chinese painting showing the ship off Hong Kong
Photograph by George E. Noyes, Newburyport

"ST. CHARLES," 1166 TONS, BUILT IN 1866, AT THOMASTON, MAINE

Photograph by George E. Noyes, Newburyport

she was forced to anchor close to shore. Tugs were sent to tow her to Falmouth but she again grounded and lost anchor and chain on being pulled off.

That the *Palmyra* was a well-built ship was shown when she was docked at San Francisco in September, 1891, to be recaulked for the first time, her timbers being found as strong as when she was built, while some of the seams were so hard that new oakum could not be driven in.

PARAMITA

THE ship *Paramita* was built by Capt. Enos C. Soule, successor to Soule Brothers, at Freeport, Maine, and was launched in July, 1879. She measured 216:6 feet, by 41:3, by 23:1 feet and registered 1573 tons. Her construction marked the end of operations in the ship-yard which had been established by Capt. Enos Soule, Sr., and two brothers, in 1839. The Soule family owned many of the ships they built and after the *Paramita* was launched, Capt. Enos C. Soule man-aged a fleet of several vessels until his death. Both he and his father, as also other members of the family, were at one time or another, shipmasters engaged in foreign trade.

Prior to 1900 the voyages of the *Paramita*, from Atlantic ports, were about equally divided between those to San Francisco and those to the Far East. In May, 1900, she crossed to Puget Sound from China and soon afterwards was sold to Lewis, Anderson & Co. of San Francisco. For the following four years she was employed on the Pacific in the coal and lumber carrying trade then being purchased by L. A. Pedersen to do duty as an Alaskan salmon packer. In April, 1914, she left San Francisco with supplies and 150 workmen for her owners' Bristol Bay cannery and on May 14th, when near her desti-nation, was driven ashore on Fox Island to become a total wreck. All the people on board were saved.

The *Paramita* was a first class ship in every way and her voyages were made in reasonable time. In February, 1897, she arrived at New York in 99 days from Hong Kong, having on several days made 350 miles. Her shortest passage to San Francisco was 112 days from Leith, in 1884, and the shortest from that port was 113 days to Liverpool, in 1881. The average of all her passages to San Francisco is 129 days and from that port, 128½ days. In this respect her passages are unique as the run around Cape Horn to the eastward was almost invariably made in considerably shorter time than that to the westward.

The *Paramita* met with several mishaps during the course of her voyages, one of which was during her passage from San Francisco to Liverpool, in 1885, when she had bulwarks stove and much damage done about decks in heavy gales off Cape Horn. On subsequently sailing from Liverpool, on return to the Pacific Coast, she was in collision with an unknown vessel at the entrance to St. George Channel, losing her jibboom and head gear and being obliged to put into Queenstown for repairs. In 1902, when bound to San Francisco from Newcastle, N. S. W., she lost all three topmasts in a squall and put into Honolulu after being 82 days at sea. Her coal cargo was discharged and sold and after jury topmasts had been rigged on the fore- and mainmasts she sailed in ballast with a new crew, all her old hands, excepting Captain Backus, having left the ship immediately on her making port.

Prior to her sale in 1900, the *Paramita* had been commanded by Captains Horace B. Soule, M. A. Humphrey, C. D. Prescott, and Claude M. Lawrence. Capt. Charles T. Backus was then appointed master and following him came Capt. B. F. Mohler and several other captains.

PARKER M. WHITMORE

THE ship *Parker M. Whitmore*, or the *P. M. Whitmore*, as she was generally called, was built by A. Hathorn, at Bath, Maine, and was launched Nov. 25, 1883. She measured 239:4 feet, by 43:6, by 28 feet, registered 2104 tons net, and was the largest ship that had been built at Bath up to that time. She was built to the order of Capt. Parker M. Whitmore who, after retiring from active sea life, devoted his time to managing a number of ships in which he was financially interested, among them being the *Gatherer*, *Hagarstown*, *James Ne-*

smith and *George Stetson*. The Captain's last command is said to have been the ship *Italia* in which he served a number of years prior to her loss in 1872.

The sea life of the *P. M. Whitmore* was spent in trade with the North Pacific Coast, she making six passages from Atlantic ports to San Francisco and one, her last, to Tacoma by way of the Orient. All returns were with wheat, five being to the United Kingdom and two to Havre. Her voyages were made in fair time, the shortest being a round between San Francisco and Liverpool in 8 months and 22 days, she being 111 days on the eastward passage and 127 days on the westward. In 1888 she went from San Francisco, in ballast, to Sydney, to load coal for San Pedro and made the whole round voyage in 4 months and 9 days, the downward passage taking 42 days only.

Capt. Dexter Whitmore of Bath was in command of the *P. M. Whitmore* from the time she was built until February, 1890, when Capt. Samuel H. Morrison relieved him for the passage to the Atlantic. Following the discharge of her cargo at Avonmouth, the *Whitmore* sailed in ballast for Philadelphia, where she was to load for the Columbia River. During the night of August 24th she went ashore on the rocky coast near Mizzen Head, Sherburne Harbor, N. S., and became a total loss. The weather was mild and all hands were able to make land in safety. Captain Morrison had been unfortunate in the past, having lost several first class ships, the last being the *Ranier*, in 1883, after which he had retired to live in the interior of California. An interesting account of the wreck of the *Ranier* is given in "American Merchant Ships," Series I.

Capt. Dexter Whitmore was a brother of Capt. Parker M., and prior to taking command of the *P. M. Whitmore* had been master of the ship *Hagarstown*. After the loss of the *Whitmore* he sailed for the California Shipping Co., being for several years master of their ship *Reuce*. He is said to have retired from sea life in 1905 to spend the remainder of his days at his old home.

PAUL JONES

THE ship *Paul Jones* was built by W. F. Fernald, at Portsmouth, N. H., and was launched in August, 1877. She measured 202 feet, by 39, by 23:6 feet and registered 1258 tons. She had somewhat sharper lines than most other ships built at that period and seamen called her the "razor face." She was always painted white and was a handsome ship in every respect. Her managing owner was C. H. Mendum of Portsmouth.

The *Paul Jones* made no Cape Horn passages, her entire sea life being spent in trade with China and the East Indies. She was conceded to be a good sailer but unfortunately it has been found impossible to obtain information about most of her voyages. Those of which figures are available, however, do not show any passages shorter than ordinary. In 1879 she was 103 days from New York to Batavia and the following year made the passage from New York to Shanghai in 105 days. On this run she sailed from New York in company with the ship *Oracle*, bound for San Francisco, and during the course of the first month the two ships met on several occasions, from which it would appear that they were about evenly matched as to sailing qualifications. In 1883 the *Paul Jones* was 83 days from Anjer to New York, on her run from Hong Kong, but made very fair time up the Atlantic, being 38 days from St. Helena and 22 days from the Line to port.

The last voyage of the *Jones* was from New York to Melbourne, in 1885. She was burned shortly after leaving that port for China but her crew were rescued by the British ship *Antiope* and taken to Melbourne.

A ship of about 700 tons, named *Paul Jones*, was built at Medford, Mass., in 1842, for the China trade, and for several years was one of the famous ships so employed. She was a bluff-bowed vessel but made good average passages under command of the well-known shipmasters, Captains N. B. Palmer and John T. Watkins. Capt. R. B. Forbes calls her a fine specimen of the American merchantman of her day. In 1848, while on a passage from Hong Kong to New York, she got ashore in the Gaspar Straits but was floated after considerable of her tea cargo had been jettisoned and the ship heeled over. She arrived at New York safely and that is the last trace that can be learned of her nor is it possible to ascertain her final end. She was not engaged in the China trade in 1850 or thereafter and her name does not appear in registers of 1856.

PAUL REVERE

THE ship *Paul Revere* was built on speculation by Smith & Townsend of Boston, but shortly after being launched, in May, 1876, she was purchased by W. H. Kinsman & Co. who then named her in honor for the famous American patriot of Revolutionary days. Prior to 1886 she was purchased by De Groot & Peck of New York. She measured 221 feet, by 41:2, by 24:6 feet and registered 1657 tons. She was a first class ship in all respects, well built and sparred and presented a handsome general appearance. She had a square stern, a long billet-head and crossed a skysailyard on the mainmast. For many years she set studding sails as high as topgallants. Capt. John Mullin of Salem, who had been in the ship *Sumatra*, as master, for eight years, bought into the *Revere* before she was ready for her first voyage and continued in her until his death, at Manila, in April, 1883. The Captain was not a large man but was very active and energetic and had the reputation of being one of the most efficient shipmasters in the East India and China trade.

The *Paul Revere* appears to have been considered a fast ship but efforts to trace any remarkable fast passages she may have made have been futile. One of her officers is authority for the statement that the best speed she made during a period of four years was twelve and one-half knots while running her easting down. However, on her passage from New York to Hiogo, in 1882, which occupied 132 days, she was 22½ days from the Line in the Atlantic to the meridian of the Cape of Good Hope, having made the prior four days 1,076 miles. For the six days following she logged 1,900 miles, an average of 316 daily, which is a little better than thirteen knots. On Tuesday, Dec. 12, 1882, at 8 P.M. she left Hiogo in ballast for Yokohama, the regular mail steamer *Tokio Maru* having taken her departure for Yokohama at 6:30 P.M. The *Revere* had strong breezes from the start and by 4 o'clock Wednesday morning had overhauled and passed the steamer. By the middle of the afternoon the latter was so far astern that not even her smoke could be seen by the ship. The wind then moderated and soon the steamer began to show herself and rapidly recovered her lost ground. The ship now became second in the race but with the wind freshening all the time she once more stretched away from her competitor which she quickly passed and left astern. The ship had the lower maintopsail split and although a new one was bent as quickly as possible, a little time was lost. The *Revere* arrived at Yokohama at 4 o'clock Thursday morning, her passage of thirty-two hours from Hiogo being the record fast run between the two ports by either steam or sail up to that time. The steamer made port six hours after her, a difference of seven and one-half hours in favor of the ship.

During practically her whole sea life the *Revere* was employed in trade with the East Indies, China, or Japan. Her second voyage was from New York to Yokohama and was made in 116 days. The third was over the same course and took 160 days, she meeting with much light weather in the Indian Ocean, particularly in the vicinity of Madagascar where dead calms were experienced for many successive days. The fresh water supply nearly gave out and scurvy manifested itself so that on nearing the Japanese coast sixteen men were down with the disease. She was fallen in with by the U.S.S. *Ranger* and towed into port.

The *Revere* made but three passages to San Francisco, from Atlantic ports, the first being her maiden voyage, made in 138 days from New York. The second was also from New York, in 130 days, in 1888. She made but one passage back to the Atlantic direct, being 126 days to Queenstown. The other return was by way of Manila.

Capt. Albert T. Whittier of Searsport took command of the *Paul Revere* in 1901 and after making a voyage to the Orient took her from Baltimore to San Francisco in 125 days, and then to Puget Sound where she loaded lumber for Melbourne. Thereafter, she took two cargoes of coal from Newcastle to Manila, being then sold at the latter port for conversion into a barge.

PERU

THE ship *Peru*, built and owned by Blanchard Brothers of Yarmouth, Maine, was launched in June, 1867, and measured 193 feet, by 38, by 26 feet, registering 1457 tons. She was built in the strongest possible manner and was a large carrier, frequently loading as high as 2450 tons of guano. One of her commanders, Capt. Samuel S. Thomas, claimed that she was the best American ship afloat for bulk cargoes. She had full lines, a square stern and crossed a skysail yard on the mainmast.

After leaving Portland, Me., for Liverpool, in July, 1867, the *Peru* was not in any American port for nineteen years except once when she called at San Francisco from British Columbia. All her voyages had originated and also been completed in European ports. Her outward cargoes were coal to South American east and west coast ports and those homeward were guano. She made fair passages; seemed to be in the right place at the proper time; met with no mishaps of consequence and was a money maker. One of her round voyages was made in the short time of nine months.

Following her arrival at San Francisco, the *Peru* took a lumber cargo to Buenos Ayres then going to New York where she was sold to D. & J. Maguire of Quebec, who had her rerigged as a bark and renamed *Kate C. Maguire*. For a short time she was operated in the River Plate trade after which she was purchased by Portuguese parties to run between Rio de Janeiro and the Canary Islands. She was lost on those islands about the year 1894.

Of the masters who commanded the *Peru*, Capt. A. C. Larrabee was in her for the longest period of time. He had joined her as second mate when she was new; was promoted to chief mate on her third voyage and to master in 1875, so continuing until she was sold in 1886. Captain Larrabee then made a voyage in the ship *McNear*,

following which he took the ship *San Joaquin* and was in command
of her when she reached New York, under jury rig, after colliding
with an iceberg off Cape Horn. The ship was then sold for barging
and Captain Larrabee retired from sea life to engage in the fuel business in some town in Massachusetts. He was known as a thorough seaman and navigator and was a man of exceptionally strong character.

Preceding Captain Larrabee, as masters of the *Peru*, were Captains Eben R. York, who is mentioned in account of the ship *P. G.
Blanchard*, Samuel S. Thomas, David C. Loring, and David W.
Blanchard, all of whom are more particularly referred to in "American Merchant Ships," Series I.

PHINEAS PENDLETON

THE ship *Phineas Pendleton* was built in 1866 at Brewer,
Maine, by Dunning & Co. for Capt. Phineas Pendleton, 2nd,
and other members of the Pendleton family of Searsport. She was
185 feet, by 37, by 23:6 feet, and registered 1253 tons. A bark-rigged
vessel of the same name had been built twenty-five years previously
and Captain Pendleton's wife, the former Miss Wealthy Carver, also
had a vessel named in her honor, the *Wealthy Pendleton*. The Captain's family was further represented on the ocean by the barks *Lillias*
and *Delphine*, named after two of his daughters.

The ship *Phineas Pendleton* made two or three guano voyages but
the greater part of her career was spent in trade between England and
ports in India, Australia, and New Zealand. One of these occupied
three years, from July, 1870, to June, 1873, the voyage starting at
London whence the ship went to Melbourne, Calcutta, Bombay, Calcutta, Colombo, and back to London. Her passages were made in fair
average time; she met with no mishaps of consequence prior to her
loss, and she was generally fortunate in her operations. Her end came
in August, 1885. While loading at Manila for New York, she caught
fire from some unknown cause and was scuttled, becoming a total loss.

Capt. Phineas Pendleton, 2nd, managing owner and first commander of the ship, was in her but a short time when he turned her

over to his son Phineas Pendleton, 3rd, and he in turn was succeeded by Captains Alex. H. Nichols, George A. Nichols, and lastly, William H. Blanchard. These three had married daughters of Captain Pendleton, 2nd.

Captain Pendleton was born in Searsport, in 1806, and died there in 1895. Going to sea when very young he was master of a schooner before he had attained his majority. He commanded a large number of small vessels prior to 1842 when he took his first square-rigger, the bark *J. Carver*. In 1854 he became master of his first ship, the *Charter Oak*, and subsequently commanded the *Bosphorus* and *Alice Buck*, from which latter he retired to live ashore and manage his shipping interests. He is said to have commanded a total of twenty-eight different vessels, taking them all when new and, not being very long in any one, he never had to buy a coil of rope or a new sail nor did he ever meet with disaster. He became wealthy through successful management of his shipping property but during the Civil War met with large losses through the depredations of the Confederate privateers. However, after many years and repeated visits to Washington, he received compensation in accordance with the findings of the Geneva Court of Awards. The Captain was kind hearted and generous to a fault and at home was called, by all, "Uncle Phineas."

Captain Pendleton had two sons who were shipmasters, John and Phineas, 3rd. The former was lost with his ship *Solferino*, while yet a young man. The ship was never heard from after leaving India, with rice, for Europe and was believed to have foundered in a hurricane in the Indian Ocean. Phineas, 3rd, was well known in connection with his fine ship, the *Henry B. Hyde*. While in the ship *Phineas Pendleton*, during one of his early voyages and accompanied by his wife and family, three of his small children died of diphtheria while the vessel was on the Peruvian coast. As a token of mourning, Captain Pendleton had the lower masts of the ship painted black.

The seafaring careers of Captains Alex. H. Nichols and George A. Nichols are given in the accounts of the ships *St. Mark* and *Abner Coburn* respectively. That of Capt. William H. Blanchard appears in the history of the *Gov. Robie*, "American Merchant Ships," Series I.

RAPHAEL

THE ship *Raphael* was built by Carleton, Norwood & Co. at Rockport, Maine, and was launched Oct. 28, 1875. She measured 222 feet, by 40, by 24 feet and registered 1542 tons. Her first commander was Capt. Isaac W. Sherman who was later in the ship *Frederick Billings* and whose career as a shipmaster is contained in the account of that ship in "American Merchant Ships," Series I.

Prior to her sale on the Pacific Coast, in 1894, the *Raphael* was employed mainly in trade with ports in Australia and the Far East. She was a first class vessel in all respects and was considered quite smart as a sailer, although the only two passages she made from the Atlantic to San Francisco were rather slow, the first from New York in 138 days and the second from Liverpool in 154 days. On three occasions she passed through the Golden Gate from transpacific ports to load grain or lumber for the United Kingdom and the average of the four passages she so made is 128 days, the shortest of which was 103 days to Queenstown. So far as can be ascertained she met with no mishaps of consequence.

Following the arrival of the *Raphael* at San Francisco, in November, 1893, from Liverpool, she was sold to Capt. A. Y. Trask, the sales price being about $20,000, according to published reports. For a year, thereafter, she was operated in the coal trade between British Columbia and San Francisco, then being chartered for a voyage to Alaska. On July 7, 1895, while she was at Tanglefoot Bay, near Karluk, with some 7,000 cases of canned salmon aboard, she dragged the mooring buoys in one of the worst storms that had ever visited that section and went ashore, becoming a total loss. The crew managed to make land although with great difficulty, the chief mate and some others narrowly escaping being drowned.

Capt. Ed. Harkness succeeded Captain Sherman, in the *Raphael*, and served in her as master about five years when her former mate, Albert Whitney, took command and continued in the ship as master until she was lost.

REAPER

THE ship *Reaper* was built by E. & A. Sewall, at Bath, Maine, and was launched in January, 1876. She measured 211:6 feet, by 39:2 feet, by 24 feet and registered 1469 tons. She was practically a sister ship to the *Granger*, *Harvester*, and *Thrasher*, all built and owned by the Messrs. Sewall and first class vessels in every way.

On her maiden voyage the *Reaper* took deals to Liverpool and coal thence to San Francisco. Her operations thereafter, until she was sold in 1898, were all to Pacific Coast ports from the Atlantic via Cape Horn, these numbering six to the Columbia River; five to San Francisco; three to Acapulco and one to Puget Sound. Her sailing record does not show up as favorably as that of her sister ships but inspection of the memoranda of her passages shows that she was unfortunate in experiencing an undue amount of light weather. The average of her passages to the Columbia River is 149 days; to San Francisco, 162 days; and to Acapulco, 135 days. Her outward cargoes were almost invariably coal. The average of her homeward bound passages from Astoria or Puget Sound, with grain, is 145 days; from San Francisco to New York, with merchandise, 129 days; and from Honolulu, with sugar, 130 days. The only noticeably good runs she made were one of 124 days from New York to Astoria, that being the shortest made over the course in 1893, and a 30-day passage from New London to Newcastle, N. S. W. She made one passage from Astoria to Rio de Janeiro, being 81 days on the way.

In 1898 the *Reaper* was purchased by A. P. Lorentzen of San Francisco and thereafter was employed in the coal and lumber trade on the Pacific. She had all along been exceptionally fortunate so far as escaping mishaps was concerned, the worst damage being received on her passage from Newcastle, Australia, to San Francisco, in 1904, when she lost sails, rigging, and deck fittings, in a gale which lasted 15 days and frequently was of hurricane force.

In July, 1906, the *Reaper* took fire while at Port Ludlow, Wash., and became a total loss. Her last years had been spent under bark rig.

Capt. Edward Poole, who owned a master's interest in the *Reaper*, was in command the first five years. Capt. Robert Bosworth, who had previously been in the *Thrasher*, served six years, after which Captains James A. Sawyer and William Taylor commanded the *Reaper*, each for a period of four years. Captain Sawyer, a younger brother of Capt. Charles H. Sawyer of the *Commodore* and *Ocean King*, was a native of North Yarmouth, Me., and had previously been mate of the *Reaper*. On retiring from the sea he operated a portable sawmill in Maine and died at Yarmouth about fifteen years ago. Captain Taylor is referred to in the account of the ship *Harvester*, in "American Merchant Ships," Series I.

In May, 1895, Capt. Oren C. Young, formerly master of the ship *Robert Dixon*, took command of the *Reaper*, and continued in her until she was sold. Under her new owners she had a number of different masters.

RED CLOUD

THE ship *Red Cloud* was built by George Thomas, for Isaac Taylor of Boston, and was launched from the Taylor & Thomas yard at Quincy, Mass., on Nov. 24, 1877. She measured 230:3 feet, by 43:2, by 29 feet and registered 2208 tons. She had an elliptic stern, a full poop deck 108 feet long and had mounted as a figurehead a carved image of the famous Indian chief after whom she was named. Her mainmast was ninety-two feet long; topmast, fifty-two feet and topgallant, royal and skysail mast, sixty-nine feet. Unlike her sister ships, the *America* and *Triumphant*, which crossed three skysail yards, she had but one, that on the mainmast.

The maiden voyage of the *Red Cloud* was from Boston to Calcutta and Bombay, thence to San Francisco and Liverpool. Her second and third voyages were to San Francisco from Philadelphia and Liverpool, respectively, both returns being to the United Kingdom. This ended the career of the *Red Cloud* as an American ship, she being sold after arriving at Liverpool, in March, 1882, to go under the German flag and renamed *Carl Friedrich*.

The *Carl Friedrich* was operated in trade between Liverpool and San Francisco, between 1882 and 1889, after which her voyages were to the Far East. In December, 1893, while on a passage from New York to Hong Kong, with 74,000 cases of kerosene, she stranded on the Luconia Reef, Java Sea, and became a total loss. She did not immediately break up but efforts to float her were futile and in May, 1894, she was sold by order of court for £780.

While she was under the American flag, the *Red Cloud* was commanded by Capt. John Taylor, a brother of Isaac Taylor. Captain John had previously been in the ships *Dexter*, *Imperial*, and *Star of the West* and the bark *Sea Bird*. He was a large, powerful man of a very nervous disposition, particularly careful about details. When master of the *Sea Bird*, a vessel of 450 tons, he had his crew organized as though they were on a 2000 ton ship and the discipline and routine were similar. Captain Taylor died at an advanced age in Chatham, Mass., in June, 1886.

RED CROSS

THE ship *Red Cross*, built and owned by T. J. Southard & Son, was launched at Richmond, Maine, in September, 1877. She measured 185:3 feet, by 38, by 23 feet and registered 1236 tons. She was built for the Cape Horn trade but her first voyage was to London, better freight rates in transatlantic trade than those to the Pacific Coast, then prevailing. Thereafter, however, all her voyages were to San Francisco or the Columbia River except one from Cardiff to Hong Kong. Her voyages were without particular incident and averaged rather long.

The last voyage of the *Red Cross* was from Philadelphia to San Francisco, Puget Sound, Sydney and Newcastle where she loaded for San Francisco. Sailing from the latter port, Dec. 12, 1888, she was dismasted in a hurricane towards the end of January, 1889, and put into Roratonga in distress. The crew refused further duty on the ground that the ship could not be made seaworthy and following a survey, she was sold for $2,500. On March 16th she was driven on the rocks during a hurricane and became a total wreck.

Capt. James E. Howland was in command of the *Red Cross* the first six years. For the eight years prior to 1877 he had been master of the clipper ship *Gov. Morton* and on giving up the *Red Cross* sailed along the Pacific Coast five years in the *Kate Davenport* and six years in the *Invincible* after which he retired from the sea. He had turned the *Red Cross* over to Capt. John Sparks of *Gatherer* notoriety who committed suicide by jumping overboard on the passage to Queenstown. Capt. John P. Reed then took the *Red Cross* back to San Francisco from Philadelphia, where Capt. Henry McIntyre succeeded and continued in command until the ship was condemned. During the 60's Captain Reed was owner and master of the brig *Marine* of Belfast, Me., and subsequently commanded the ship *Bullion* during the eight years she sailed under the American flag. The sea career of Captain McIntyre is given in the account of the ship *P. G. Blanchard.*

REPUBLIC

THE ship *Republic* was built by Crawford & Perkins, at Kennebunkport, Maine, and launched in June, 1869. She measured 193:6 feet, by 39:6, by 23:7 feet and registered 1203 tons. She was owned by George C. Lord & Co. of Boston, until 1889, when shortly after sailing from Caleta Buena for New York, she was badly damaged by colliding with another vessel during a storm and put into Valparaiso in distress. There she was condemned and sold to local parties who had her repaired and placed under the Chilian flag without change of name. She was then operated in the off-shore lumber trade on the Pacific. In November, 1897, while bound from Puget Sound to Port Pirie, she put into San Francisco leaking badly. She was repaired and after a windmill and a steam pump had been installed, the voyage was resumed. Subsequently, being badly damaged in heavy gales, she put into Sydney where she was sold to local parties and put under the British flag. She was repaired and again proceeded but was forced to put into Melbourne leaking and in bad condition generally. She was condemned and not being considered worth repairing further, was sold for conversion into a coal barge. She was renamed *Geographe* and did duty as a barge, at Melbourne, until January, 1930, when she was broken up.

Prior to 1889 the *Republic* was employed mainly in the coal trade, making voyages to South America, the North Pacific Coast and to the Orient. She was a good carrier and her passages averaged fairly well. In 1872 she was 114 days from San Francisco to Liverpool, making port the same day as the fast ship *Swallow* which had passed through the Golden Gate two days before her. In 1871 she was 232 days from Newport, Wales, to San Francisco, having put into Port Stanley to repair damages sustained during a month of battling very heavy gales and seas off Cape Horn.

In 1883 the *Republic* arrived at Wilmington, Cal., after a good passage of 127 days from Liverpool. When just north of the Line in the Pacific she sighted a boat and rescued five men who proved to be part of the crew of the Nova Scotia ship *Novarro*, Shields for San Francisco, burned at sea a week previously. Although the boat contained an ample supply of bread and water its occupants had no compass and their being picked up was considered little short of a miracle. They had suffered only from exposure and heat.

During practically all the time the *Republic* sailed under the American flag she was commanded by Captains John W. McGilvery and Jacob H. Holmes.

REUCE

THE ship *Reuce* was built for Capt. George H. Theobald of Bowdoinham, Maine, by N. L. Thompson, and was launched at Kennebunk in November, 1881. She measured 229:2 feet, by 41, by 27:1 feet and registered 1829 tons. She was well built, classed A1 for fifteen years. While on a passage from Hong Kong to New York, in 1900, she was sold to the California Shipping Co. of San Francisco, who sent her to the Pacific Coast, by way of Yokohama, and she was then operated in the lumber trade between Puget Sound and Australia. In December, 1908, she arrived at San Francisco after a long passage from Newcastle via Sydney, where she had put in to have a bad leak stopped. She was then laid up nearly three years when she was purchased by the Columbia River Packers Association of Astoria, who operated her to Alaska through the season of 1922. The following year she was sold to parties in Portland, Ore., who sent her to Japan where she was wrecked.

Prior to 1896 the *Reuce* was operated continuously in trade between Atlantic ports and San Francisco and made eleven such round voyages. She then completed three voyages between New York and China or Japan. She was a good carrier and made fair passages, the average of those to San Francisco being 146 days, the shortest, 120 days and longest, 178 days. Those from San Francisco averaged 128 days; shortest, 110 days and longest, 161 days. One of these was to New York and the others to the United Kingdom. During the course of these voyages she met with no mishaps of consequence.

In November, 1889, the *Reuce* arrived at San Francisco after a fair-weather passage of 150 days from New York. On making port, seventeen of the twenty men before the mast were more or less seriously ill with scurvy and were sent to the Marine Hospital. Suit was entered against Captain Adams and the owners of the ship on the ground that the food furnished was poor and insufficient and after a hard-fought case, the defendants were found at fault and they finally compromised by paying the claimants $1,650.

In October, 1883, the *Reuce* sailed from Astoria for Nagoya, Japan, and soon after getting to sea met with heavy gales from the westward which continued for weeks. The food supply became low and all hands were placed on short rations. When the ship was 62 days out the fresh water was entirely exhausted and thereafter dependence was had upon occasional rain squalls. The ship finally made the Japanese coast but was driven far offshore by hard gales. When 110 days out from Astoria she again made the coast and took refuge in Suruga Bay. Four days later a gale of hurricane force blew up and in an endeavor to work the ship out to sea, she was driven ashore near

"ST. DAVID," 1536 TONS, BUILT IN 1877, AT BATH, MAINE
From the oil painting by Charles R. Patterson. Courtesy of R. H. Beaton, Esq.

"ST. FRANCES," 1898 TONS, BUILT IN 1882, AT BATH, MAINE

Photograph by L. S. Slevin, Carmel, California

"ST. MARK," 1870 TONS, BUILT IN 1860, AT THOMASTON, MAINE

"ST. NICHOLAS," 1723 TONS, BUILT IN 1869, AT BATH, MAINE

From an oil painting photographed by George E. Noyes, Newburyport

Omaesaki and soon bilged, with tremendous seas breaking all over her. A life line thrown overboard was washed ashore and being picked up by native fishermen, a rude breeches buoy was rigged. Over this all hands were dragged through the breakers to safety.

Prior to her sale in 1900 the *Reuce* was commanded by Capt. Benjamin Adams except for a couple of voyages when he stayed ashore and was relieved by other masters. The Captain was a native of Bowdoinham and had previously sailed for Captain Theobald in his ships *Theobald* and *Sea King*. Subsequent masters of the *Reuce* included Capt. Dexter Whitmore and Capt. Fred B. Dinsmore who are further referred to in accounts of the ships *Parker M. Whitmore* and *E. F. Sawyer* respectively.

RICHARD 3RD

THE ship *Richard 3rd* was built at Portsmouth, N. H., in 1859, for Capt. Richard Holbrook Tucker of Wiscasset, Me., and the circumstances attending her being given the name she received were unique. When the ship was built, Capt. Richard Hawley Tucker, father of Capt. Richard Holbrook Tucker, was still living, and on the day the ship was to be launched a son was born to Mrs. Tucker, Jr., and was named Richard H. The new ship was thereupon called after the recent arrival, who is now a distinguished astronomer residing in California.

The *Richard 3rd* was 175 feet, by 34, by 23:6 feet and 898 tons register. She was a good carrier, loading 1300 tons of coal on passages around Cape Horn. During her later years, as a coal drogher on the Pacific Coast, she often carried 1700 tons.

The early years of the *Richard 3rd* were spent principally in the transatlantic cotton trade. Following her arrival at San Francisco, in November, 1882, from Liverpool, she was purchased by Middlemas & Boole and subsequently changed hands several times during the fifteen years she was running coastwise and offshore on the Pacific. In 1897 she was converted into a barge for operation in British Columbian waters, subsequently making some trips to Alaska. In January, 1907, she went ashore in Clarence Straits and became a total loss.

During the time the *Richard 3rd* was owned in Wiscasset she was commanded by Captains John K. Greenough, who had a one-eighth interest in the ship, Joseph Tucker Hubbard and Edward H. Wood, all Wiscasset shipmasters. Among her commanders, while owned in San Francisco, were Captains James McIntyre and T. J. Conner, both of whom had been on the Pacific Coast many years. Captain McIntyre had arrived at Victoria, B. C., in 1854, as second mate of a ship from England and left her to go in South Sea Island trading schooners. He started coasting in 1859, in the old bark *Ann Perry*, and was master of the bark *Revere* from 1866 until she was wrecked near Cape Flattery, in September, 1883, after which he took the *Richard 3rd*. Captain Conner was for many years master of the bark *Glimpse* which had the reputation of being a fast sailer, and subsequently of the bark *Mary Glover*. The Captain died at the Marine Hospital, San Francisco, in 1904.

RINGLEADER

THE ship *Ringleader* was built by Pierce & McMichael, at Chelsea, Mass., and launched in October, 1868. She measured 185 feet, by 37:6, by 22:9 feet and registered 1145 tons. Her original owners were Howes & Crowell of Boston. While in port at Hong Kong, in December, 1881, she was reported sold for $35,000 to parties in Boston and was thereafter managed by Edward Lawrence, Jr. In 1894 she was sold and converted into a coal barge, continuing as such until 1902 when she was lost near Sandy Hook.

The maiden voyage of the *Ringleader* was from Boston to San Francisco, thence home by way of Manila. Within the next ten years she made five other passages from the Atlantic to San Francisco and one to the Columbia River. The rest of her career as a sailing ship was spent in trade with China, the East Indies and Australia. She was a fine looking ship, of good model and had the reputation of being quite a good sailer but there is no evidence to show that she ever did any remarkable work in this respect. In 1878 she went over a course seldom made by sailing vessels, Shanghai to San Francisco, and her run of 30 days was the fastest that had been made up to that time, although it was subsequently eclipsed by two days. The distance covered by the *Ringleader* was 5,340 miles. Her shortest passage to San Francisco was 117 days from Boston. She sailed in company with the *Southern Cross*, but the latter passed through the Golden Gate five days in the lead. In 1871, the *Ringleader* and the *Frolic* had a "race" from New York to San Francisco, which the former won by 17 days, but as her passage was 147 days the contest would appear to have been anything but a race. One of the *Ringleader's* passages from Hong Kong to New York was made in 107 days, one from Manila in 144 days, and one from New York to Sydney in 104 days, so that her sailing record may be considered as fair to average.

Among the early commanders of the *Ringleader* were Captains Edmund B. Hamblin, who had previously been master of the ship *Regent*, Edwin Thacher, who subsequently had the ships *Ericsson* and *Glendon*, and B. Bray, formerly in the *Comet*.

A clipper ship named *Ringleader* had been built for Howes & Crowell, at Medford, Mass., in 1853, and had many fast passages to her credit. She was lost on the Formosa Banks in May, 1863, while bound from Hong Kong to San Francisco, with Chinese coolies, but there was no loss of life.

ROBERT L. BELKNAP

THE ship *Robert L. Belknap* was built by Carleton, Norwood & Co. at Rockport, Maine, and launched in June, 1884. She measured 264:8 feet, by 43:8, by 29:3 feet and registered 2251 tons. She was conspicuous through her rig of three sets of double topgallant yards and three skysail yards, being, so far as can be ascertained, the only American ship so sparred. Throughout her whole career she was commanded by the two Staples brothers, Horace and Everett, the later, however, making but one voyage in the ship.

The *Belknap* made six round voyages during her sea life of which five were between Atlantic ports and San Francisco and one to Japan, on which latter she crossed to San Francisco and loaded for Liverpool. Her passages were made in good time, the average of those to San Francisco being 132 days and those from that port, which were mostly to Liverpool, being 122 days. The shortest to the latter port was 110 days. In February, 1890, she left New York for San Francisco and made the run out in 120 days; thence to Liverpool in 113 days; and then back to San Francisco in 121 days, the three passages occupying only one year, two months and four days, including detentions in port discharging and loading cargo. The only passage she made from San Francisco to New York was in 1889 when she loaded 1300 tons of barley and filled up with miscellaneous merchandise. On getting to sea she was found to be very crank and for the first twenty-four hours all hands were on deck tacking or wearing ship in baffling airs. She then took good winds but later had no trades at all and her time to the Line, 32 days, was the longest and most tedious ever experienced by Captain Staples. Just before crossing, the head of the foremast was badly sprung in a sudden squall, necessitating the upper yards being sent down and the head fished. In spite of these handicaps the ship took her pilot when 114 days out but a dense fog then setting in, she did not make New York until four days later.

In September, 1892, the *Belknap* arrived at Yokohama after the long run of 163 days from New York. Captain Staples had gone out around Australia instead of by way of Anjer, as was understood. The result was that many underwriters lost considerable sums through reinsuring their risks at advanced figures. In continuation of this voyage the *Belknap* left Yokohama early in January, 1893, for New York, and towards the end of the month went ashore on a reef near Natunas Island, the vessel and cargo becoming a total loss. All hands made Singapore in the ship's boats.

Capt. Horace Staples belonged to Stockton, Me., and prior to taking command of the *Belknap* had been in the schooner *Hannah* and the barks *Henry Flittner* and *Adolph Obrig*, taking the latter when new, in 1881. He was usually accompanied on his voyages by his wife, and two sons were born aboard the *Henry Flittner* who were named John Neptune and Henry Seaborn Staples. The Captain retired from sea life when the *Belknap* met her end. He was a thorough navigator but was said to be a man rather hard to get along with so he deemed it best to spend his days ashore at the Sailors' Snug Harbor and passed away there in 1928.

S. P. HITCHCOCK

THE ship *S. P. Hitchcock* was built in the yard of Isaac F. Chapman at Bath, Maine, and launched in October, 1883. She was 247:4 feet, by 44:3, by 28:6 feet and 2178 tons register. She was named in honor of Samuel P. Hitchcock, Mr. Chapman's master builder and also his brother-in-law. Mr. Hitchcock had at one time been in the shipbuilding business as a partner in the firm of Adams & Hitchcock and also later with Zina Blair, another brother-in-law, although the latter was not a practical mechanic. Antecedently Mr. Hitchcock had been associated with his brother in building and operating schooners. The ship *S. P. Hitchcock* was owned by Mr. Chapman until her loss at Hong Kong in September, 1906. She was dragged down on, during a typhoon, by the ship *I. F. Chapman* and parting her moorings was set against the breakwater and became a total loss. The anchors of the *Chapman* held and she brought up with but slight damage.

Capt. Joshua B. Nichols of Searsport commanded the *Hitchcock* for the first six years. On the maiden voyage of the ship Captain Nichols left New York, Dec. 22, 1883. The new ship *John R. Kelley* had left New York on November 29th and her master, Capt. Thos. P. Gibbons, had then promised to assist in mooring the *Hitchcock* on her arrival at San Francisco. The latter, however, ran out in 108 days, making port on April 4, 1884, while the *Kelley* did not get in until two days later. Captain Nichols had skysails set all the way from latitude 42° south to port and his run up from the Line was made in the fast time of 19 days.

Captain Nichols made four subsequent passages in the *Hitchcock*,

from New York to San Francisco, and the average of her five runs is
111 days. Two of them were made in 101 days each and since that
time these have never been approached in point of time. One of the
Captain's return passages was from the West Coast of South America,
with nitrate, the other four being from San Francisco to Liverpool
and averaging 116 days.

Capt. Frank L. Carver, a nephew of Captain Nichols, then made
a voyage in the *Hitchcock* from New York to San Francisco and
Liverpool, being 107 days on the latter run. Capt. E. V. Gates succeeded Captain Carver, at New York, in 1891, and except for one
voyage made by Capt. Orris H. Fales, in 1901, Captain Gates was
continuously in command of the *Hitchcock* until his death at Liverpool in December, 1905. The Captain was a thorough navigator and
a great man for carrying sail, but due to the fact that his departures
from New York, when bound for San Francisco, were invariably during the unfavorable season, his passages were much longer than those
of Captain Nichols. While the latter's averages from New York to
the Line was 24½ days and of rounding Cape Horn 12½ days, those
of Captain Gates were 40 days and 33 days respectively. The average
of Captain Gates' seven passages from New York or Baltimore to San
Francisco is 143 days, the shortest being 130 days. Of return passages
two were to Liverpool in 119 and 110 days, three to New York, 129,
113 and 119 days, one in 1897, from Honolulu to New York, in 92
days, and one in 1899, from Hilo to the Delaware Breakwater, in
106 days. During the Japanese-Russian war the ship took case oil to
Yokohama and Captain Gates entered the port during the night.
When seen by Japanese officers the next morning it was marvelled
how the Captain had managed to get in. The harbor was mined and
it was said that no pilot would have ventured to take a ship to the
position where the *Hitchcock* was anchored.

The voyage made by Captain Fales was from New York to Sydney, in 1901, and took 97 days. The ship later proceeded to San
Francisco where Captain Gates resumed command. Before leaving
Sydney Captain Fales said he would make the Golden Gate inside
of 60 days and he did so, beating that figure by eight days.

After the death of Captain Gates at Liverpool, the chief officer of the *Hitchcock*, Mr. Zerks, took command and after crossing to New York, took her out to Hong Kong where she met her fate.

The seafaring careers of Captains Joshua B. Nichols, Frank L. Carver and E. V. Gates are given in "American Merchant Ships," Series I. That of Captain Fales appears in the account of the ship *St. Joseph*.

SACHEM

THE ship *Sachem* was built to the order of M. F. Pickering & Co. at East Boston, and was launched in April, 1875. She measured 194 feet, by 39:4, by 23:8 feet and registered 1312 tons. She was well built, her frame being diagonally iron strapped and like all of Captain Pickering's vessels, was first class in every particular. She had a round stern and for a figurehead bore an image of an Indian Chief in full war dress. In general appearance she closely resembled the ship *Paul Jones*, both being quite sharp forward and in model what might be called medium clippers.

While the *Sachem* was in course of construction her builders failed and Captain Pickering took charge of affairs resulting in his having to defend half a hundred law suits for labor and material. The future career of the ship was not much more satisfactory. In 1890, on her homeward passage from Singapore, a considerable portion of her cargo was damaged and a series of law suits followed. The ship was a small carrier in comparison to others of her tonnage and is said not to have been a financial success.

The *Sachem* was conceded to be a fast sailer but unfortunately it has been found impossible to obtain details of her passages to or from ports in the Far East and it was in that trade that she was employed practically all her sea life. She made but three Cape Horn voyages, all being to San Francisco from New York or Boston, in 130, 126 and 148 days. The returns were to Havre or Antwerp in 111, 112 and 127 days. On the passage from Antwerp to New York she was 20 days from the Scilly Islands and arrived ahead of some twenty vessels that had sailed in company with her. On one of her outward passages to San Francisco she crossed the Line in 20 days from New York and on the following voyage ran from 50° S. in the Pacific to 20° N., less than 1,000 miles from San Francisco, in 33 days, which was very fast sailing.

M. F. Pickering & Co. were managing owners of the *Sachem* until 1898 when Abram Pigeon succeeded. About this time the rig of the vessel was changed to that of a bark and Capt. Henry T. Lancaster of Searsport bought a master's interest and the *Sachem* became his first command. In 1899, while on a voyage from Philadelphia to Hong Kong, the ship encountered a typhoon near Formosa, during the course of which she was struck by lightning and lost her foremast. Captain Lancaster had died some time previously and the mate navigated the ship into Hong Kong. Capt. Sewall L. Nickels of Searsport, father-in-law of Captain Lancaster, went to China to look after his daughter who was aboard the ship, and also to take command of the vessel. He made two additional voyages, after which the ship was condemned at New York and in May, 1903, was sold and converted into a barge named *Holton*.

The first master of the *Sachem* was Capt. N. G. Reed who was in command about five years. Later masters included Captains J. C. Bartlett and William H. Gould. The *Sachem* was the last vessel Captain Nickels commanded. After she was sold he lived several years in Sailors' Snug Harbor and died there. He was a brother of Capt. James Nickels of the ships *Frank Jones* and *Alameda*.

ST. CHARLES, 1st

THE ship *St. Charles* was built by Chapman & Flint, at Thomaston, Maine, and was launched in September, 1866. She was 188 feet, by 38, by 23 feet, and of 1166 tons register. She was of the same model as the ship *Pactolus*, built by Chapman & Flint the year before, both having considerably sharper ends than later-day ships and both proved to be of good sailing qualifications.

During the first eleven years of her career the *St. Charles* was employed in the California trade, making ten passages to San Francisco, eight of which were from New York and two from Liverpool. Returning eastward, six runs were to the United Kingdom, two to New York and one each by way of Valparaiso and Manila. In 1872 she made a side voyage from San Francisco to Newcastle, N. S. W., and return. The average of her passages to San Francisco from eastern ports is 128 days, the three shortest being 116 and 119 days from New York and 118 days from Liverpool. The average of those from San Francisco to the Atlantic direct, is 118 days, the shortest being 101 days to New York, in 1873, she being then commanded by Capt. E. S. Smalley. Her gross time on the round between San Francisco and Newcastle was 4 months, 11 days, the return being made in the fast time of 52 days, Capt. William Tobey then in command. Her voyages were remarkably free from mishaps, the most serious one being in 1872 when, on a passage from New York, her rudderhead was twisted off and she was forced to put into Rio de Janeiro.

In September, 1876, the *St. Charles* loaded wheat at Martinez, near San Francisco, and being the first vessel to arrive at the new warehouses there, the occasion of her tying up at the docks was duly celebrated. There was an elaborate banquet, guns were fired and great enthusiasm prevailed among local people and the large committee of prominent merchants and shipping men who had arrived from San Francisco.

In 1879, following the arrival of the *St. Charles* from Manila, she loaded case oil for Hiogo and sailed October 10th. She was reported as arriving out prior to March 1, 1880, and not long thereafter was burned, it being evident that the fire had been started by some disaffected member of her crew. In March, 1882, the steamship *City of Tokio* arrived at San Francisco from the Orient having among her passengers one James O'Neill, a former seaman on the *St. Charles*, who was en route to San Quentin prison, under a sentence imposed by the United States Consular Court at Kobe. He had been found guilty of killing James King, second mate of the *St. Charles*, at that port. The prisoner's defense was that Mr. King went to the forecastle at midnight and accused him of setting fire to the ship. A fight ensued and two hours afterwards King was found dead from knife wounds. A sentence of twenty years was imposed but this was commuted to ten years, by President Hayes, on the ground that the original term was excessive for the crime.

The first master of the *St. Charles* was Capt. William S. Colley of Thomaston. Captain Colley, who was born in 1829, was a brother of Capt. James Colley and father of Edward S. and Lewis S. Colley, both of whom afterwards became well-known shipmasters. Capt. William S. Colley had commanded the clipper ship *Crest of the Wave*, built at Thomaston in 1854. After serving some six years in the *St. Charles* he had the *St. Joseph* a short time and then took command of the new ship *Isaac Reed*, in which he owned a considerable interest. He sailed in her from 1875 until about 1882 when he turned her over to his son Edward S. and retired from sea life.

Capt. William Tobey, formerly in the *Pactolus*, was the second master of the *St. Charles*, but only made one voyage in her when he was succeeded by Capt. Edwin S. Smalley who was in the ship some four years. The last master of the *St. Charles* was Capt. E. V. Gates. Captain Smalley is more particularly referred to in account of the ship *Manuel Llaguna*, while the seafaring career of Captains Tobey and Gates are given in "American Merchant Ships," Series I.

A ship named *St. Charles*, of 800 tons, built at New York in 1847, arrived at San Francisco from New York in 1864, under command of Capt. Joseph Higgins of Brewster, Mass. She then went to Johnston's Island to load guano but was cast ashore on the reef and became a total loss.

ST. CHARLES, 2ND

THE ship *St. Charles*, built and owned principally by C. V. Minott, was launched at Phippsburg, Maine, in October, 1883. She was 225 feet, by 41:6, by 25 feet and registered 1662 tons. She had but a short life, completing six round voyages and being lost before the termination of the seventh.

She was built for the California trade and all her passages from the Atlantic were to San Francisco, six from Philadelphia and one from Swansea, Wales. The six returns were to the United Kingdom or the Continent with grain. In 1887 she made a round voyage between San Francisco and British Columbia. Her passages were made in fair average time, the fastest to the westward being 120 days and to the eastward 103 days. On her passage to San Francisco she spoke the ship *Charmer*, in the South Atlantic, and the two ships were in company 20 days, then parting but arriving at their common destination on the same day. The *Charmer's* passage was 118 days from New York, two days shorter than that of the *St. Charles* from Philadelphia. Completing this voyage the *St. Charles* spoke at different places on her passage to Hull, the British ships *Anaurus*, *Thalatta* and *Glenbreck* which had passed through the Golden Gate bound to the United Kingdom, 10 days, 13 days and 17 days respectively ahead of her. On her arrival at Hull, a pleasure steamer with a large crowd on board steamed around the *St. Charles* with a band playing "Yankee Doodle" as a welcome on her appearance at the port.

The *St. Charles* met with two serious mishaps before her final loss. The first was on the passage from Swansea to San Francisco in 1885. She was off Cape Horn 19 days in variable weather, three days being practically of dead calms. However, she had several days of very heavy weather and during one squall of great violence the mainmast was broken off at the head, all the yards, sails and gear above going overboard. The falling wreckage broke the upper foretopsail yard in the slings and also the mizzen topgallant mast in the sheave hole. Captain Purinton was several days in setting up jury spars and under this rig completed the passage, arriving at San Francisco 58 days after the disaster, a good run under these conditions. In February, 1889, she arrived at Queenstown and was ordered to Waterford for discharge. On making that port she got aground and sprung a bad leak, having nine feet of water in the hold on being floated. Later she again went aground and her cargo had to be discharged into lighters. Steam pumps were put aboard and the ship went to Liverpool for repairs.

On April 2, 1892, the *St. Charles* arrived at San Francisco from Philadelphia and on the 20th sailed for British Columbia to load a return cargo of coal. She left Nanaimo May 14th and early in the morning of the 17th the second mate, who had just come on watch, and a sailor, opened the fore hatch to get some potatoes for the cook. The sailor carried a lighted lantern and on the hatch being opened there was a terrific explosion which blew the decks of the ship open. The chief mate, who had just turned in, was thrown from his bunk to the cabin ceiling by the lifting of the deck but he was not injured. Captain Chapman was pinned under falling timbers and was extricated from his stateroom with great difficulty. The mate had two boats launched immediately and all hands made shore safely but Captain Chapman was so badly injured that he died three days later. The day after the disaster the *St. Charles* was fallen in with by the schooner *Hayes*, whose captain boarded the derelict. She was found to be in a badly wrecked condition with the rudder unshipped and eleven feet of water in the well. As she would be a menace to navigation, the schooner captain had her set on fire before returning to his vessel.

The first commander of the *St. Charles* was Capt. Frank H. Purinton of Bowdoinham, Me., and he completed five round voyages in the ship, then turning her over to his nephew, Martin Chapman. Captain Purinton owned an interest in the *St. Charles* and on relinquishing command he retired from the sea. He was a nephew of Samuel Merritt of Oakland, Cal., and after the death of the latter the Captain attended to some affairs connected with the estate. He did not prove a good manager, however, and after about a year returned to his eastern home. Captain Chapman had sailed with his uncle a number of years and was mate of the *St. Charles* before becoming her master. He was an able officer and had many friends.

ST. DAVID

THE ship *St. David* was built for Benjamin Flint in the ship-yard of Chapman & Flint at Bath, Maine, by masterbuilder John McDonald and although Mr. Flint was then in partnership with his brother, Isaac F. Chapman, the latter had no interest in the vessel and it is said that her construction was one of the causes that led to the dissolution of the firm some two years later. The *St. David* was launched in October, 1877, and was 213:4 feet, by 40:6, by 25:2 feet and registered 1536 tons. She was named after Capt. David B. Scribner, brother of the second Mrs. Benjamin Flint, and was built to be commanded by him, but he being absent on a voyage in the *St. John* when the *St. David* was ready to sail on her first voyage, Capt. Edwin S. Smalley took the latter to San Francisco from New York. Mr. Flint, with his sons, did business as Flint & Co. and were owners of the *St. David* until October, 1899, when they sold her and the rest of their large sailing fleet to the California Shipping Co. of San Francisco. Her new owners operated her in the lumber and coal trades on the Pacific until December, 1909, when she was sold to James Griffiths of Seattle and converted into a barge. For some eight years she was towed between Puget Sound and Alaska and on Oct. 31, 1919, was lost by stranding in Yakutat Bay, Alaska.

The *St. David* was one of the famous three skysailyard Cape Horn traders of her day. Leaving Bath, Nov. 24, 1887, she arrived at New York three days later; discharged ballast, was docked and metaled, loaded 3100 tons of general cargo, cleared and was ready to sail for San Francisco on December 14th, only 20 days after she had left Bath. Prior to 1901 she completed ten round voyages between Atlantic ports and San Francisco and made seven to the Orient on four of which she returned to the Atlantic by way of San Francisco. The average of her passages to the latter port, via Cape Horn, is 146 days, the shortest being 122 days from New York and the longest 160 days. The average of her passages from San Francisco to New York or the United Kingdom is 122 days, 110 days to Queenstown being the shortest and 139 days to New York the longest. Completing two of her voyages to the Orient she loaded wheat at Tacoma for Havre and made the runs in 137 and 142 days respectively. In 1888 she went in ballast from San Francisco to Sydney in 45 days and then took coal from Newcastle to San Pedro in 63 days. Her voyages in the Far East trade were also made in fair average time, that in 1893-1894 being 171 days from New York to Yokohama and 110 days from Kobe to Portland, Me. During this period she met with no mishaps of consequence.

In November, 1901, the *St. David* loaded lumber at Puget Sound for Adelaide and had the long passage of 100 days and then another long one of 62 days from Newcastle to Manila. At the latter port her master, Capt. M. H. Harrington, had to leave the ship on account of sickness and Capt. Cyrus Ryder was sent from San Francisco to take the ship. She left Manila, Oct. 23, 1902, in ballast, for Puget Sound, in good and seaworthy condition and Captain Ryder was assured that there was a sufficiency of provisions on board. For the first month nothing but calms and light, baffling winds were met with and it was then discovered that supplies were running very short and all hands had to be put on short rations. Early in December stormy weather was encountered and on the fifth of the month a typhoon of only a few hours duration stripped the ship of everything on the mainmast above the lower masthead — carried away the mizzen topgallantmast, smashed the deck house and did other damage. The pounding of the floating wreckage against the sides of the ship caused her to leak and all hands were forced to the pumps. Captain Ryder steered for Yokohama but winds continued unfavorable and the ship, disabled and with a weak crew, made but slow progress. Finally the steamship *America Maru* was sighted and supplied the *St. David* with a liberal quantity of stores, besides taking off a sick seaman. Another man had died a week previously, unable to stand the hard labor and lack of sufficient food. A month or so subsequently the ship was fallen in with by the steamship *Glenogle* and towed to Yokohama where she arrived Jan. 26, 1903, 110 days from Manila.

Capt. David A. Scribner was a native of Brunswick, Me., and without having the advantage of much schooling, took to seafaring at an early age, sailing in ships belonging to Chapman and Flint. He was very painstaking and methodical and when he became a third mate, thought he had reached the summit in his profession. However, he kept hard at work, was careful and persevering and in 1870 was given command of the ship *St. Lucie* and four years later, the much larger ship *St. John*. After taking the *St. David* from San Francisco to New York he completed two round voyages in her and then took the new ship *St. Frances* which had been built for him to command. The *St. David* had been named in his honor and the *St. Frances* for Mrs. Flint, second. Captain Scribner was in the *St. Frances* some ten years when, having sufficient means, he decided to retire from sea life, but after living ashore for some time he made two voyages in the famous *Henry B. Hyde*. His experiences on one of these is recounted in account of that ship in "American Merchant Ships," Series I.

Early in the present century Captain Scribner became connected with the Sailors' Snug Harbor, as manager of their New York office, and later made his home at its Long Island place, passing away there something over ten years ago. The Captain was a genial, kindly man, a competent navigator but not a "driver," and did not make fast passages. However, he met with no disasters and only a few minor mishaps. He always took a great interest in young men, assisting them in making headway in the world. In 1874 he met a Chinese boy born in Singapore who was then twelve years old, and taking a fancy to him, shipped him and had him as steward of his various ships until just previous to his retiring from sea, this "boy" was adopted by the Captain and legally named Bennie David Scribner. He is now steward on a San Francisco pilot schooner and expects to spend the last of his days at the "Harbor." Captain Scribner's widow was living at Freeport, Me., at a recent date. .

Other commanders of the *St. David*, while she was owned by Flint & Co., were Captains William Wallace Frost, Fred H. Pearson and William Lyons. Captain Frost had previously been master of the ship *Hoogly* and other vessels belonging to Boston. On retiring from the sea he was Port Warden at Boston. Captain Pearson had been in the employ of Flint & Co. as mate and later was master of the barks *Wal-*

lace B. Flint and *St. Katherine.* Captain Lyons started sea life on a Nova Scotia fishing schooner at the age of thirteen. Three years later he shipped on a schooner bound for the West Indies. The vessel was capsized in a hurricane but she was righted after the masts were cut away. Three days later her crew was rescued by a Norwegian bark and following his arrival home, Captain Lyons sailed on vessels engaged in transatlantic lumber and oil carrying. In 1883 he joined the first four-masted schooner built in this country and in 1887 went as mate on the *Wallace B. Flint,* becoming her master in 1890. He took command of the *St. David* in 1892 and except for a voyage he made in the *A. J. Fuller,* in 1894-1895, was in her until 1900. He then joined the American-Hawaiian Steamship Co.'s steamer *Californian,* as mate, and in May, 1901, was appointed her master. He has continued in the employ of that company ever since and now, at the age of seventy years, is Commodore of their fleet and commander of their motorship *Californian.*

Captain Lyons was in command of the steamer *Missourian* which, while being used as a horse transport, was torpedoed and sunk in April, 1917, while returning to New York from Genoa. Captain Lyons and his crew took to their boats and were picked up by a patrol boat. On return home the Captain was given command of the steamer *Montanan,* but in October, 1918, she also was attacked and sunk by a submarine, her crew being rescued by the yacht *Noma* which was then acting as an American destroyer. Undismayed by these experiences Captain Lyons then took the steamer *Texan* and made six transatlantic voyages in her after which he superintended the building of the motorship *Californian,* in 1922, and on her completion became her commander.

Capt. M. H. Harrington belonged in Appleton, Me., and before taking command of the *St. David* had the *Gov. Robie.* He died within a year after leaving the *St. David.*

"ST. PAUL," 1824 TONS, BUILT IN 1874, AT BATH, MAINE

From a photograph taken in San Francisco in September, 1880, showing the ship as originally rigged. Courtesy of Fireman's Fund Insurance Co.

"SANTA CLARA," 1474 TONS, BUILT IN 1875, AT BATH, MAINE

Courtesy of Edward S. Clark

LOOKING AFT ON THE DECK OF THE SHIP "SEA WITCH,"
1233 TONS, BUILT IN 1872, AT EAST BOSTON

"SERVIA," 1773 TONS, BUILT IN 1883, AT BATH, MAINE

Photograph by George E. Noyes, Newburyport

ST. FRANCES

THE three skysailyarder *St. Frances* was built in the shipyard of
Benjamin Flint, by his master builder John McDonald, and was
launched at Bath in May, 1882. She measured 231:4 feet, by 41:8,
by 25:9 feet and registered 1898 tons. She was named after the second wife of Mr. Flint. She was well built and cost $105,600. Mr.
Flint, who, with his sons, did business in New York as Flint & Co.,
was owner of a trifle less than a half interest in the ship, the remaining shares being held by Eastern and San Francisco parties. While
the *St. Frances* was on a passage from Philadelphia to San Francisco
in October, 1899, she was sold to the California Shipping Co. who,
ten years later, resold her to the Alaska Fisherman's Packing Co. of
Astoria, and she was operated as a salmon packer until May 14, 1917,
when she was wrecked, without the loss of any lives, in Unimak Pass,
Alaska.

Except for a voyage from Norfolk to Honolulu, in 1898, the *St.
Frances* was operated between Atlantic ports and Japan or San Francisco during the time she was owned by Flint & Co. While owned by
the California Shipping Co. she was employed in the offshore lumber
and coal trade on the Pacific.

So far as can be ascertained the voyages of the *St. Frances* were
made without incident; she met with no mishaps of consequence and
her passages were made in fair time. The average of the eight made
to San Francisco is 146 days, the shortest being 136 days from New
York in 1893, when Captain Wilbur was master. Captain Wilbur
then had the good run of 106 days back to Liverpool and this is the
shortest eastward passage made by the ship. Her second shortest, 110
days to Queenstown, was also made by the same captain. The average
of the eight passages made by the ship to the eastward is 120 days.

On one occasion the *St. Frances* caught fire while lying at Dutch
Harbor, Alaska, but was saved by the united efforts of her crew and
that of the revenue cutter *Manning*, who flooded her with water.

The *St. Frances* was built to be commanded by Capt. David A.
Scribner, brother-in-law of Benjamin Flint, and aside from a voyage

made by Capt. R. P. Wilbur, he was in the ship ten years. His other commands are mentioned in the account of the ship *St. David*. Capt. Robert P. Wilbur was relieving master of the *St. Frances* on two different occasions. His seafaring career is mentioned in the account of the ship *M. P. Grace*. Capt. W. W. Winn took command of the *St. Frances* in 1894 and continued in her until she was sold. He then took the ship *R. D. Rice* and was in ommand when she was burned in Japan in 1901. Later he had the *Henry Failing* for a short time.

ST. JOHN

THE ship *St. John* was built by Chapman & Flint, at Bath, Maine, and was launched in October, 1870. She was 216 feet, by 42:7 feet, by 28:9 feet, had three decks and registered 1820 tons. She was owned by her builders until the dissolution of the firm after which she was the property of Isaac F. Chapman.

The maiden voyage of the *St. John* was from New York to San Francisco and was made in 117 days, a good run for a ship modeled to carry large cargoes. Capt. James F. Chapman was in command and after his ship was discharged he distinguished himself and made a name for his ship by making three round voyages between San Francisco and Australia in spaces of time that were never thereafter equalled. Including detention in loading at Australia these voyages were accomplished in 4 months and 11 days; 5 months and 4 days; and 4 months and 12 days, respectively. The ship was only 44 days on one of the downward passages. On the completion of these voyages she took wheat to Liverpool in 110 days.

This series of voyages brought the *St. John* into prominence in the shipping world and thereafter she was one of the best-known ships engaged in the New York-San Francisco-Liverpool trade. Prior to 1897 she made seventeen passages from Atlantic ports to San Francisco and fifteen direct returns; the other two were via the Chincha Islands and Japan respectively. Her passages averaged well though none came up to her first voyage, the fastest subsequent run from New York being 136 days and from San Francisco to Liverpool, 111 days. After 1897 she completed two voyages to the Orient, on the last outward passage being 212 days from Philadelphia to Hiogo.

The voyage of the *St. John* from New York to San Francisco, in 1878, when Capt. Theodore P. Colcord was relieving officer, was replete with incidents somewhat out of the ordinary. When the ship was seven days out the patent steering gear broke; a spare tiller and steering ropes were rove and used the rest of the passage. Two seamen were lost on the run, one from a fall overboard from aloft and the other from disease. At 2 A.M., July 25th, when the ship was off Cape Horn, in a light wind from southwest, braced sharp up on the port tack, she was struck on the port bow by an unknown iron bark which was running free. The bark swung alongside and then went astern. After getting clear she kept away before the wind and the *St. John* did the same but after a couple of hours, no signals for assistance being shown by the bark, the ship hauled to the northwest again and the vessels soon lost sight of each other. While they were in contact a seaman on the bark attempted to jump into the mizzen chains of the ship but fell and was crushed between the two vessels. The *St. John* had rails, bulwarks and some of the planking of the port bow cut down but the damage was slight and the ship did not start a leak.

In February, 1876, the *St. John* sailed from San Francisco for Liverpool; crossed the Line 17 days out and hove to off Pitcairn Island seven days later, Captain Scribner having on board a large quantity of miscellaneous supplies donated by San Francisco merchants to the islanders. Included in these was an organ and Captain Scribner was quite overcome by the welcome he received. The Captain had stopped at the island on several previous occasions and was considered by the people as their best friend and most generous benefactor.

In October, 1899, the *St. John* sailed from New York with case oil for Yokohama and all went well until she reached Lombok Straits when, during a pitchy dark night, in squally weather with rain, thunder and lightning, the ship was discovered to be on fire in the between decks forward. The fire had already gained such headway that the apparatus on board for fighting it was wholly insufficient. It was fought, however, for two hours when the boats were hoisted out and the ship was abandoned. The coast was only some five miles distant so a landing was soon made in a cove on the island of Bali, whence the ship's company of twenty-six men made their way to the nearest place of white residence. Later all hands were taken to Singapore.

Capt. James F. Chapman was born at Damariscotta, Me., in 1830, to the second wife of Robert Chapman, therefore being a half brother of Isaac F. and Benjamin Flint Chapman. Capt. James F. followed the trade of his father, a ship caulker, and when working on the *Ionian*, being built in 1849, at Thomaston, he pounded his hand with a mallet. He then and there threw down his tools and when the *Ionian* was finished shipped on her with seven other Thomaston boys, one of whom was Samuel C. Jordan, for whom the ship *Joseph H. Spinney* was built. Capt. Charles Ranlett, who lived to be 101 years old, was master of the *Ionian*, and her first voyage was from Boston to San Francisco, Calcutta, London and home, occupying nearly two years. James F. Chapman continued following the sea and was appointed master of the ship *I. F. Chapman* when she was built in 1855. Later he commanded the *St. Lucie*, leaving her to take the *St. John*.

After serving as master of the *St. John* four years Captain Chapman went to San Francisco, in 1873, and established the firm of J. W. Grace & Co. After a few months his partner, Mr. Grace, arrived and all went well for several years when Mr. Grace went to South America to join his brother in the firm of Grace Brothers. Mr. George L. Duval went out to San Francisco from New York to become a partner in J. W. Grace & Co. but Captain Chapman withdrew from the firm, in 1880, to establish himself in business as James F. Chapman & Co., and for many years he represented most of the New England shipowners besides being himself financially interested in a number of ships. Until his death at Oakland, in 1897, he was one of the most prominent shipping merchants of San Francisco, a gentleman held in the highest esteem and his passing was universally regretted. He died of pneumonia after a sickness of only four days.

Later commanders of the *St. John* were Captains David H. Rivers, David A. Scribner, Edwin S. Smalley and Orris H. Fales, the latter being in command when the ship met her fate.

ST. JOHN SMITH

THE ship *St. John Smith* was built by Capt. N. L. Thompson, at Kennebunk, Maine, and was launched in April, 1874. She measured 236 feet, by 42:6, by 29:8 feet and registered 2220 tons. She was named after a prominent resident of Portland, Me., and was owned by J. S. Winslow, also of that place. Mr. Winslow was owner of a large fleet of vessels, mostly schooners engaged in the coasting trade, and was not much interested in ships sailing deep water but owned several. During the World War his vessels were disposed of at large figures.

In 1880 the *St. John Smith* made a voyage between Liverpool and Bombay and Calcutta. Aside from this, her short career was spent in trade between San Francisco, New York and Liverpool, one of her outward passages being by way of Rio de Janeiro, whence she had taken a cargo of coal from Cardiff. She completed six round voyages in all, most of which were made in rather slow time although her second run from New York to San Francisco was made in 107 days. In July, 1882, she left Liverpool with coal for San Francisco and was never thereafter heard of.

The *Smith* met with several mishaps, the principal one being on her passage from San Francisco to Liverpool in 1879. Off Cape Horn she sprang a bad leak and on putting into Rio de Janeiro divers failed to discover its cause. She continued to make considerable water even in the harbor so her cargo was all discharged when a large portion of it was found to be badly damaged. Repairs occupied two months and underwriters had large claims to pay. On her arrival at San Francisco, in 1881, she was surveyed and ordered docked for additional strengthening, so that on the whole her career does not appear to have proved very successful.

Capt. E. R. York, whose seafaring life is given in account of the ship *P. G. Blanchard*, commanded the *St. John Smith* the first three years after which Capt. John Waterhouse was master until her arrival at Liverpool, in May, 1882. The former mate of the ship, John Fritz, of Brewster, Mass., then took command and was lost with the ship.

Captain Waterhouse left the *St. John Smith* to take command of the *Benjamin F. Packard* which had been built for him. He made three voyages in that ship and then retired from sea life. He died at his home in Portland, Me., in 1890.

ST. JOSEPH

THE ship *St. Joseph* was built by Samuel P. and James Hitchcock, at Bath, Maine, and was launched in August, 1865. She measured 184 feet, by 36, by 21 feet and registered 1138 tons. Her principal owners were her builders and some friends. She was employed in the general carrying trade but the majority of her voyages were with South American West Coast ports, taking coal out and guano home. As a rule her passages were made in quite slow time.

When the tidal wave of May, 1877, swept the Peruvian Coast, the *St. Joseph* was at Pabellon de Pica, nearly loaded with guano. Through collision with other vessels she was damaged to the extent of $20,000, having the bowsprit, cutwater and figurehead carried away, port and starboard bulwarks, stanchions and channels smashed, deck houses started and being otherwise seriously injured. Prior to the disaster the sound value of the ship had been estimated at only $32,000. She was repaired at Callao and then took a cargo of guano to Valencia.

In September, 1881, while the *St. Joseph* was at San Francisco, in the stream at anchor, ready to sail with a cargo of wheat for Falmouth, she was run into by a ferry steamer and had to discharge before going on drydock for repairs, which cost $10,000. Following her arrival out, she proceeded to Cardiff and loaded coal for San Francisco. Then, after taking wheat to Dublin, she was sold to William Murphy of that place and went under the British flag without change of name.

Capt. Orris H. Fales of Thomaston, best known as Capt. Harvey Fales, was in command of the *St. Joseph* eight years, after which he was in the ship *St. John* an equal length of time and until she was burned. He then served as master of the *S. P. Hitchcock* for a short time and on relinquishing her command, retired from a seafaring life.

ST. LUCIE

THE ship *St. Lucie* was built by Chapman & Flint, at Bath, Maine, being the first vessel they constructed after having given up their shipyard at Thomaston. She was also the first vessel built under the superintendence of the firm's master carpenter, John McDonald. She was the fourth ship her builders and owners had named "Saint," which prefix, contrary to general belief, did not necessarily refer to a calendar Saint. The term was often used in honor of relatives or friends of the owners and the *St. Lucie* was so called after the wife of J. W. Elwell, whose firm acted as New York agents for Chapman & Flint for many years. The "Saint" ships were celebrated the world over for their fine lines and trim and beautiful appearance of hull and rig. The *St. Lucie*, although one of the smallest of the fleet, was no exception to the rule. Her dimensions were 194 feet, by 37, by 24 feet, and she registered 1264 tons.

During most of her sea life the *St. Lucie* was employed on the run between New York, San Francisco and Liverpool, exceptions being two voyages to the Far East, one to the Columbia River and one to the Gulf of California with coal for the United States Naval Station at Pichlinque. She has no fast passages to her credit but generally made fair time and was fortunate in escaping damage from the elements.

Capt. James F. Chapman was in command of the *St. Lucie* on her first voyage, leaving her on its completion to take the new and much larger ship, *St. John*. A short biography of the Captain is contained in account of that ship. Capt. Walter Carney and Captains William Tobey, David A. Scribner, and J. J. Humphrey each made a voyage in the *St. Lucie* until, in 1875, she was taken over by Capt. David H. Rivers who continued in her as master until he took the ship *Santa Clara*, in 1882. Captain Rivers was later in the ship *A. G. Ropes* and is more particularly mentioned in account of that ship in "American Merchant Ships," Series I.

Capt. E. V. Gates had relieved Captain Rivers for one voyage to Japan, from whence the ship proceeded to the Philippines to load for home. On being ready to leave Japan Captain Gates was strongly urged to have his papers forwarded by steamer but he refused, taking them with him in the ship. The steamer that would have taken the documents was disabled and had to return to port, while the *St. Lucie* arrived at Manila ahead of the following steamer and having her papers all ready and in order she was able to start loading ahead of other vessels that were in port awaiting orders. The matter caused considerable comment at the time.

The last master of the *St. Lucie* was Capt. John Williams, a brother of Capt. Thomas C. Williams. Captain John was transferred from the *Santa Clara*, in May, 1882, while both ships were on the Pacific Coast and after taking the *St. Lucie* from San Francisco to Liverpool he made a voyage from New York to the Columbia River and thence to Havre and Philadelphia. He left the latter port in August, 1884, for San Francisco and that was the last ever heard of the *St. Lucie* or her crew. Two theories were advanced as to her end, the most plausible one being that she was struck by lightning and burned. The other was that she had been in collision with another vessel, both foundering with all hands. The Nova Scotia ship *Vice Reine*, from Calcutta for New York, was spoken about that time north of the Line in the Atlantic and she also was never thereafter heard from. No bad weather having been reported, the collision theory was advanced.

ST. MARK

T HE ship *St. Mark* was built by Hitchcock & Blair, at Bath,
Maine, and was launched in September, 1877. She measured
239:9 feet, by 42:5, by 27:3 feet and registered 1896 tons. She was
owned by Isaac F. Chapman, Rufus Hitchcock, J. W. Elwell and
others. She was managed in turn by Mr. Chapman and Mr. Elwell
until 1900 when she took a cargo of coal from Norfolk to Manila for
the United States Government who had her converted into a barge
after arrival.

The *St. Mark* was built for the California trade and the first sixteen years of her career were spent on voyages between New York or
Liverpool and San Francisco. Her passages to the Pacific Coast port
numbered eleven from New York and two from Liverpool, the latter being made in the excellent time of 111 and 116 days. The shortest from New York was 120 days and the average of the whole thirteen is 132 days. The shortest of the eight passages made to the
United Kingdom was 111 days to Bristol and the shortest of the four
to New York, 101 days, the average of all the eastbound runs being
118 days. By this it will be seen that the *St. Mark* had a good sailing
record for a Down East cargo carrier. During the course of these voyages the only mishap she met with was when entering port at Bristol,
in June, 1886, she took the ground. Some four hundred tons of her
wheat cargo was discharged into lighters after which she was floated
without having sustained any damage.

In 1894 the *St. Mark* was diverted from the Cape Horn run to
take case oil to the Orient and made three such voyages in fair time
except that during the course of that made in 1899 she had the very
long passage of 101 days from Newcastle to Manila with coal. Re-
insurance on the vessel had risen to fifty per cent although no grave
fears had been felt for her safety, it being thought that she was de-
layed by long spells of calm weather, which proved to be the case.

Capt. P. D. Whitmore, who was in command of the *St. Mark* on
the two first voyages, died in April, 1879, while the ship was at
Liverpool, as the result of injuries received while assisting to move

an anchor by hand. Capt. James Colley was sent over to take the ship to New York where the command was given to Capt. Alex. H. Nichols of Searsport, and he continued in her until his death at San Francisco in November, 1889, from injuries received by a fall at night into an unguarded excavation in a sidewalk. The Captain was only forty-seven years of age at the time but was well known in all the principal world ports. His first command had been the bark *Henry Buck*, after which he was in the ships *Phineas Pendleton* and *M. P. Grace*. He was a thorough navigator as well as a good business man and had hosts of friends. He was a brother of Capt. Joshua B. Nichols for whom the ship *S. P. Hitchcock* had been built.

Capt. A. E. Work, who was sent to San Francisco to assume command of the *St. Mark* after the death of Captain Nichols, had been master of the ship *Thomas M. Reed* for six years. During the passage of the *St. Mark* from Hong Kong, in 1894, the Captain was stricken blind and shortly after the arrival of the ship at home, in January, 1895, he passed away of pneumonia.

The last master of the *St. Mark* was Capt. Benjamin Dudley who had been a shipmaster for over forty years prior to his death at Dallas, Texas, in May, 1930, at the advanced age of ninety-three years. The Captain was born in Lyman, Me., but for most of his life made his home in Kennebunk. He had sailed in all parts of the world and during the Civil War served in the United States Navy.

A ship named *St. Mark* was built by Chapman & Flint, at Thomaston, Me., in 1860, to be commanded by Capt. James Colley who had previously been master of the *St. James*, also built for him and named in his honor. This *St. Mark* had an elliptic stern and was of 1870 tons register. She made several passages to San Francisco, the first being in 1861 and the second in 1867, when commanded by Capt. Aaron H. Wood, but most of her career was spent in the coal and guano trade with ports in South America. During her later years she was unfortunate. In 1873 while bound from San Francisco for Liverpool she put into Cadiz with pumps choked and fourteen feet of water in the hold, having met with very heavy weather and been obliged to jettison five hundred tons of wheat. She then went out to the West Coast to load guano and after waiting her turn over a year, finally got away from Callao in July, 1876, but was wrecked on the coast a short time later.

ST. NICHOLAS

THE ship *St. Nicholas* was built by Chapman & Flint, at Bath, Maine, and was launched in October, 1869. She measured 206:9 feet, by 42:8, by 29 feet and registered 1723 tons. She was owned by her builders until they dissolved partnership in 1880 and on their vessel property being distributed, the *St. Nicholas* went to Benjamin Flint. In December, 1896, she was sold to Geo. W. Hume & Co. of San Francisco who, some six years later, resold her to the Columbia River Packers Assn. to be operated in connection with their salmon canneries in Alaska. Her last voyage as a "salmon packer" was the season of 1922 when, on her return to the Columbia River, she was laid up at Portland for four years. She was subsequently sold to ship breakers and in September, 1927, was burned in a slough near Portland for her metal. Her masts and yards up to royals were standing at the time and made a spectacular scene as they fell.

The *St. Nicholas* made two voyages in the coal and guano trade with the West Coast of South America and two with case oil to China prior to her sale in 1896. During this period the remainder of her operations were with San Francisco. On a couple of occasions she made a voyage in the coal trade on the Pacific Coast and in 1871 went to Australia for a return cargo of coal to San Francisco. Her passages to San Francisco, by way of Cape Horn, were twelve from New York, two from Liverpool and one from Philadelphia. Those from San Francisco were eight to Liverpool, three to New York and one to Antwerp. On two occasions she returned East by way of the Orient and on one via the Peruvian guano deposits.

The *St. Nicholas* proved to be a good sailer for a ship of her class, her passages to San Francisco averaging 130 days and those from that port directly to the Atlantic, 127 days, the shortest being 125 days on the outward and 106 days on the homeward runs. On her first passage to Liverpool she sailed in company with the *Pactolus*, a ship well known as a fast sailer, and both made port the same day, 119 days out. In 1873 she left San Francisco the same day the *Ericsson* sailed and made Liverpool in 119 days, six days in the lead. The *Ericsson* was a wooden ship of clipper model, converted from a steamer, and had the reputation of being a very fast sailer. In 1892 the *St. Nicholas* was only 19 days from latitude 50° South, in the Pacific, to the Line and but 20 days thence to port.

Prior to 1896 the *St. Nicholas* had but one mishap of consequence, that being in 1874 when bound from Liverpool with coal for San Francisco. All had gone well until the ship was in latitude 23° South, in the Pacific, when the cargo was discovered to be on fire. Captain Williams bore up for Callao and arrived there seven days later. Holes were bored in the hull by divers and the hold was flooded, after which the cargo was discharged and sold. The voyage to San Francisco was abandoned and the ship loaded guano at Lobos de Tierra for Europe.

In December, 1897, while bound from Seattle to San Francisco, the *St. Nicholas* was badly strained and had spars and rigging damaged in heavy weather. New main- and mizzenmasts were put in while the ship was being repaired.

The *St. Nicholas* was built to be commanded by Capt. Thomas C. Williams who had been for the prior eight years master of the Chapman & Flint full-rigged ship *St. James*. In 1876 he was transferred to the ship *St. Paul* and in 1883, on turning that ship over to his son, Capt. Herbert H. Williams, he went in the *M. P. Grace*. Leaving the latter, in 1891, he retired from the sea to spend the remainder of his days at his home in Thomaston. Captain Williams was one of the best known and most efficient of American shipmasters.

Capt. William Tobey was the second master of the *St. Nicholas* and made two voyages in her. The Captain's career as a shipmaster is given in the account of the ship *Pactolus*, in "American Merchant Ships," Series I. In the *St. Nicholas* he was succeeded by Capt. Frederick W. Stackpole who is more particularly referred to in the account of the ship *Joseph Fish*. Captain Stackpole made two voyages in the *St. Nicholas*, she being then taken by Capt. Phineas Pendleton, 3rd, later of the *Henry B. Hyde*. Captain Pendleton took the *St. Nicholas* at San Francisco, in July, 1880, and turned her over to Capt. William P. Joy, at New York, in June, 1882.

Capt. William P. Joy was a native of Nantucket, son of Capt. Samuel Joy, a famous whaling skipper who followed the slogan "a dead whale or a stove boat." Captain Joy made three voyages in the *St. Nicholas*, passing away while the ship was in port at Hong Kong, in July, 1885, from what was called the black fever. The Captain ranked high in his profession and on three occasions had been the recipient of tokens in recognition of bravery displayed by him at sea, the last being the presentation by the British Government of a silver tea and coffee service for his rescue of the officers and crew of the bark *Lennox* of Glasgow. On his arrival in the *St. Nicholas*, at San Francisco, in December, 1882, Captain Joy furnished the following details of this affair:

"Oct. 17, 1882, in latitude 46° S., longitude 62° W. fell in with the bark *Lennox*, Captain Doughty, from Dundee for San Francisco, with coal, who hoisted the signal 'I am on fire.' I kept away for him, boarded him and found his crew discharging coal from the main hatch; the donkey engines pumping water into the hold and all spare hands drawing water with buckets. Dense volumes of smoke were rising from the main hatch. Captain Doughty requested me to stay by his ship all night, it then being four P.M., and this I consented to do. We arranged signals to communicate with each other during the night and I went back on board my own ship. At seven P.M. the *Lennox* was observed to blow the main hatch off, flames ascending nearly to the mainyard. At two A.M. a signal from the bark indicated that they were leaving her. Shortly after, Captain Doughty and his crew, 25 in number, were received on board the *St. Nicholas*. At 3:30 A.M. the mainmast of the *Lennox* went over the side. A bark heaving in sight astern, I tacked and stood back and asked the captain to relieve me of some of the *Lennox's* crew. The other vessel proved to be the British bark *Hindostan*, Liverpool for Valparaiso, and her captain took ten of the *Lennox's* men. At ten A.M. I kept away on my course, having lost 18 hours in fresh N.N.W. winds."

The fire on the *Lennox* had been discovered at 5 A.M. the day the *St. Nicholas* was sighted. The foremast of the ship fell shortly after the mainmast went and when last seen the *Lennox* was a roaring furnace with only the mizzenmast standing, the spanker being still set.

Captain Joy's brother, Capt. B. W. Joy, served as mate of the *St. Nicholas*, *Invincible*, *Triumphant*, and other vessels, and in 1886 was given command of the bark *Richard Parsons*. After making several successful voyages in that vessel Captain Joy was caught in a typhoon off the coast of Mindoro and the *Parsons* went down with twenty members of her crew. Captain Joy and six men clung to a yard that had got adrift and were washed ashore where they found friendly natives. The Captain then gave up sailing vessels to go into steam and passed away at Nantucket, in January, 1931, at the age of seventy-one years.

At the time of Capt. William P. Joy's death at Hong Kong, Benjamin Flint's ship *St. Frances* was in the Orient and instead of a captain for the *St. Nicholas* being sent out to take the ship, Capt. David A. Scribner was notified by cable to select a man if possible. He thereupon put his chief officer, C. H. Crocker, in the *St. Nicholas*, but the latter, after making three voyages, retired from the sea to make his home in one of the western states. Following Captain Crocker's retiring in 1888 Capt. Caleb F. Carver served in the *St. Nicholas* six years, then taking the *R. D. Rice*, the history of which is recorded in "American Merchant Ships," Series I. The last commander of the *St. Nicholas*, under her original ownership, was Capt. David McIntosh who was subsequently master of the bark *St. Katherine* for a time. Captain McIntosh died in China, from cholera, when quite a young man.

During the time the *St. Nicholas* was owned by George W. Hume & Co. she was employed in the coasting and off-shore trades on the Pacific and was commanded by Capt. George C. Grant, who later was in the ship *M. P. Grace*, and by Capt. Henry Olsen, who died in Alaska, supposedly through having eaten poisonous mussels.

ST. PAUL

THE ship *St. Paul* was built by Chapman & Flint, at Bath, Maine, and was launched in September, 1874. She measured 228 feet, by 42, by 27:5 feet and registered 1824 tons. When Chapman & Flint dissolved partnership and the firm's assets were divided, the *St. Paul* became the property of Isaac F. Chapman and he and his estate continued her owners until 1901 when she was sold to the Pacific Packing and Navigation Co. of Seattle. Several years later she was purchased by the Northwestern Fisheries Co. and in 1918 she again changed hands becoming the property of the Booth Fisheries Co. In 1924, after serving as a salmon packer for twenty-three years, she was laid up near Seattle. In 1927 she was purchased by the Pacific Cement Co. who proposed to convert her into a barge for service between Alaska and Puget Sound but these plans were not put into effect and she was sold to the Pacific Coast Engineering Co. who expected to dismantle her and have her burned to recover the metal used in her construction. She remained, however, with all her masts and spars intact until March, 1930, when C. Arthur Foss, an operator of tug boats and barges on Puget Sound, purchased her to be kept for exhibition purposes, a specimen of the once famous American wooden sailing ship, now obsolete. Reconditioned throughout and apparently ready to start on another voyage as of old, she also is used as a museum for the display of relics and curios pertaining to the history of the Pacific Northwest.

When the *St. Paul* first came out she had double topgallant yards on fore- and mainmast, a main skysail yard on the main and single topgallants on the mizzen, but for the greater part of the time while she was employed on long distance voyages she had single topgallants and three skysail yards. In 1888 the wooden fore- and mizzenmasts were replaced by iron masts, the mainmast which had been sprung and scarfed while the ship was at Philadelphia, being allowed to remain and this is still in the ship.

Prior to 1895 the *St. Paul* made one round voyage between Philadelphia and Liverpool. All the rest were from New York to San

Francisco and return to Liverpool or New York. The outward passages numbered fifteen on one of which the ship had very heavy weather in the South Atlantic, the rudderhead was twisted and a leak developed causing Captain Bruce to put into Callao for repairs. The average of the other fourteen passages is 141 days, the two shortest being 115 and 116 days. From San Francisco eastbound she made ten passages to the United Kingdom, three to New York and one each by way of the Peruvian guano deposits and via Manila. Those made direct to Atlantic ports averaged 120 days, the two shortest being 103 days to New York and 107 days to Liverpool. On Feb. 28, 1891, she sailed from Liverpool with a part cargo of salt as ballast and arrived at New York on March 19th. She had put into Queenstown when four days out, proceeding the same day. A fine easterly breeze sprung up and Captain Ford crowded on every inch of canvas including some studding sails. The breeze held fresh for three days during which she logged three hundred miles or upwards daily. No head winds were met with and the sea was comparatively smooth throughout. The run from Queenstown to New York occupied 16 days, a very short passage. As the *St. Paul* generally loaded 2800 tons of wheat her sailing record may be considered as quite good for a cargo carrier.

Between 1895 and the time she was sold, the *St. Paul* was engaged in trade with the Far East. In March, 1898, she sailed from New York with case oil for Kobe and had the fair passage of 140 days. She sailed from Kobe, September 22, with part cargo and was proceeding to Hong Kong to complete lading when she was caught in a typhoon off the south end of Formosa and was hove down for twelve hours. The rudderhead was twisted off and some five hundred sheets of copper stripped from her port side by wind and sea. She went on dry dock for repairs and later made the run to New Orleans in 102 days. From there she took cotton and molasses to New York. In 1901 she took coal from Newcastle to Manila thence going to Seattle in ballast and it was during the course of this voyage that she was sold. The *St. Paul* suffered damage on several of her voyages, on four different occasions having her rudderhead twisted but only on the occa-

"SOUTH AMERICAN," 1694 TONS, BUILT IN 1876, AT EAST BOSTON
Courtesy of Fireman's Fund Insurance Co.

"SOVEREIGN OF THE SEAS," 1443 TONS, BUILT IN 1868, AT EAST BOSTON

Courtesy of Edward S. Clark

"SUMATRA," 1073 TONS, BUILT IN 1856, AT CHELSEA, MASS.

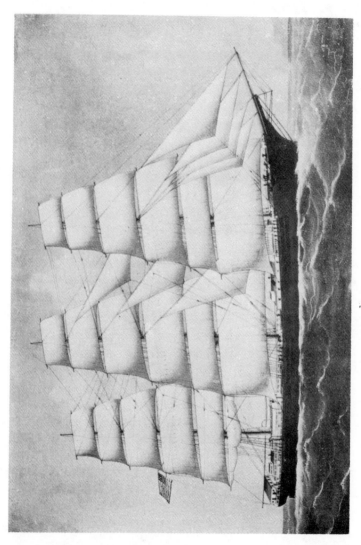

"TACOMA," 1739 TONS, BUILT IN 1881, AT BATH, MAINE
Courtesy of Capt. Frederick William Wallace

sion of her putting into Callao as previously referred to, was it found necessary to have her enter a port for repairs.

The first commander of the *St. Paul* was Capt. Albert D. Wood who had been master of the Chapman & Flint ships, *Oracle*, first, and *Oracle*, second. Capt. Thomas C. Williams and his son, Capt. Herbert H. Williams, had the *St. Paul* some fourteen years except for a couple of voyages when relieving masters were in command. Later commanders were Captains Alanson Ford, Charles W. Bruce, Albert G. Thomson and Forest W. Treat. Captain Treat, whose seafaring career is given in "American Merchant Ships," Series I, retired from sea life on relinquishing command of the *St. Paul* and died a number of years ago at his home in Searsport. While owned on the Pacific Coast the *St. Paul* changed masters too frequently for listing.

Capt. "Bert" Williams gave the following interesting report of his experiences in rounding Cape Horn on the passage to San Francisco in 1889:

"Having been ten days with heavy southwest gales and high seas, on the morning of June 6th I was close under Cape Horn and about six miles west of it. A heavy gale coming on from west-southwest, I concluded to make one of the good harbors in that vicinity. At ten o'clock kept the ship away and ran up into the Middle Cove, which is on the northeast side of Wollaston Island, twenty miles north of Cape Horn, and let go anchor in seventeen fathoms, sand and clay, good holding ground. Hoisted out the boats and went on shore. Perfectly smooth water and no tide. Met with several of the natives and found them very inoffensive people, speaking no English. They were, however, very filthy. The men and women had no European garments and the children were naked. Their food consisted of shag, a species of duck which they catch and keep for eating until rotten. The smell in their huts is such that to a seasick person would be unbearable and a well person would soon become sick.

"The natives are low in stature and of a copper color, have black, coarse hair and not bad features. After we lay at anchor two days the wind came out from the north and I got under way and came out at midnight. Made 200 miles straight to the west during the next twenty-four hours. During the two days we lay at anchor it blew a regular screetcher from west-southwest but the high land breaks the wind off and there is no great strain on the anchors. There were plenty of wild geese and ducks but we could catch no fish.

"Middle Cove is easy of access and there is nothing to prevent a vessel from going in or out in the night. We saw a number of whales right at the mouth of the harbor. Although it was June, the mid-winter month, there was no frost on the ground. The grass was all of six feet long; the trees green and numerous singing birds were about. These harbors ought to have more attention paid them. In case of a vessel sustaining damage she could find no better place than one of them.

"I took a boat and went to the place where the *P. R. Hazeltine* was lost. Took the lead and searched diligently for the rock that she was supposed to have struck and which is marked on the chart as 'Hazel-tine Rock' but could not find it. There is a rock marked on the chart as 'Dedalus Rock' which I had no difficulty in finding and which I think she struck on, although possibly there may be another rock there. I should very much like to see a harbor or refuge made in one of these places and I think that all mariners would agree with me that it would do a great deal of good and save many lives."

SAMARIA

THE *Samaria*, built and owned by Houghton Brothers, was launched at Bath, Maine, in September, 1876. She measured 217:6 feet, by 39:1, by 24:1 feet and registered 1509 tons. Like all Houghton productions she was well built and modeled and presented a fine appearance, although she had no flying kites and crossed no yards above the royals.

Aside from three voyages made between New York and Australia the *Samaria* was in the Cape Horn trade with San Francisco until May, 1896, when, following her arrival from Baltimore under command of Capt. Charles H. Reed, she was sold to S. B. Peterson. She was then put in the Coast coal trade and completed four round voyages between San Francisco and Puget Sound. In prosecution of the fifth she sailed from Seattle, March 21, 1897, and five days later was seen in moderate weather under short sail but apparently in good condition. The next day a strong gale blew up and a heavy cross sea ensued during which the *Samaria* is supposed to have foundered as a life buoy subsequently found washed up on the beach just north of the mouth of the Columbia River was all that was ever seen or heard of her. Captain McRae, who had been appointed master of the ship shortly after her purchase on the Coast, had his wife and two minor children accompanying him.

The passages of the *Samaria* were made in good average time but the fastest were her first four when commanded by Capt. Charles E. Patten, the outward runs to San Francisco averaging 121 days. Two rounds were made in excellent time, New York to San Francisco in 119 days, thence to Liverpool in 114 days, Philadelphia to San Francisco in 115 days and thence in 118 days to Havre.

Capt. Charles E. Patten was born in Bath, in January, 1835, and starting a sea life at the age of sixteen, he was appointed master of the ship *Brittania* at twenty-two years. Taking command of the *Moravia*, on her being launched in 1863, he served in her nine years. On completing his fourth voyage in the *Samaria*, in 1882, after thirty-one years of sea life he purchased the former Guy C. Goss residence in Bath and lived there the rest of his days. He was mayor of Bath for a time.

Capt. David Gilmore succeeded Captain Patten in the *Samaria* and after making two voyages, took command of the new ship *Servia*. Capt. J. H. Snow then served as master of the *Samaria* until 1896, a period of twelve years.

SANTA CLARA

THE ship *Santa Clara* was named for one of the most fertile valleys of California and was launched from the yard of Chapman & Flint at Bath, Maine, in January, 1876. She was owned by her builders until the dissolution of the firm in 1880, after which she was the property of Isaac F. Chapman. In August, 1896, she was purchased by the Alaska Packers Association of San Francisco and for many years was operated in connection with their salmon canneries in Alaska. In June, 1926, she was sold to the Metro-Goldwyn Co. for moving picture purposes and was used in making the picture "Captain Salvation," which was adapted from the novel of that name written by Capt. Frederick Wm. Wallace. Later, she is said to have been sold to do duty as a fishing barge in Southern California waters.

The *Santa Clara* measured 209:5 feet, by 40, by 25:5 feet and registered 1474 tons. She was a first class ship in all respects and for many years was one of the best known vessels engaged in the California trade. She made a few voyages in the case oil trade to the Orient but most of her career as a merchantman was spent on the run between Atlantic ports and San Francisco. Over this course she made ten voyages and in addition, one between New York and the Columbia River. Her shortest outward passage was 122 days from New York and the average is 138 days, which high figure is due to the two long runs she had, 158 and 172 days. The average of returns to the Atlantic is 117 days, one of 107 days to Havre and two of 111 days each to Liverpool being the shortest. On her passage from Philadelphia to San Francisco in 1878 she spoke the ship *Sachem*, off Cape Horn, and when just north of the Line, in the Pacific, met and passed the *America*. These ships were well known as fast sailers but the *Santa Clara* led the *America* into port by one day and the *Sachem* by three days. One of her first voyages, after being purchased in San Francisco, was a round between that port and British Columbia, made in 26 days, and in 1899 she made the run from Karluk, Alaska, to the Golden Gate in 12 days.

During the first twenty years of her career the *Santa Clara* met with but two mishaps. The first was in January, 1885, when, after discharging her wheat cargo at Liverpool, she loaded salt for New York and shortly after sailing came into collision with the Dublin steam packet *Admiral Moorsom*. The latter went down with the loss of several lives but the *Santa Clara* was but little damaged aside from having the head gear carried away. The ship was libeled and the decision of the Admiralty Court was that both vessels were to blame, the steamer for not having a proper lookout and the ship because her lights were burning but dimly. The steamer's owners appealed to the House of Lords who decided in favor of the ship and ultimately her owners were reimbursed the amount spent in repairing their vessel. Capt. Robert K. Dunn was making his first passage in the *Santa Clara* at the time.

In April, 1890, the *Santa Clara*, when making the Japanese Coast, bound to Hiogo from Philadelphia, got jammed into a small bay or bight during a dense fog. She touched bottom but was not damaged to any extent and did not leak. Captain Fuller went to Hiogo in one of the ship's boats and chartered the German steamer *Ingo* to go to the assistance of his ship. On reaching her, the next day, she was found to be afloat but the bay was so narrow that the steamer was obliged to back in to get a line to the ship, which being done, she was towed to her destination. Both her anchors and cables were lost.

Capt. David H. Rivers took command of the *Santa Clara*, at San Francisco, in May, 1882, and made the passage to Queenstown in 125 days, and thence to Liverpool, after which the ship crossed to New York in 26 days. She then loaded for Yokohama and as Captain Rivers had never been "Out East," he conferred with several veterans in that trade as to the best route to be taken during the season of northeast monsoons which would be prevailing when he would reach the China Seas. Contrary to all the advice he received, the Captain got into the Pacific by way of the Ombay Pass and arrived at his destination in the shortest passage made about that time. A number of the old timers were skeptical on hearing the report of the *Santa Clara's* arrival and all were considerably discomfited. Captain Rivers was a "driver" and it used to be said that he needed no mates. He was very particular about details and had a motto painted on the boatswain's locker "A place for everything and everything in its place" and woe be to the one who did not carry out his suggestions.

On his return from the Yokohama voyage, referred to, Captain Rivers took the *Santa Clara* to San Francisco, from New York, and then went East, overland, to take command of the new ship *A. G. Ropes*. His career as a shipmaster is given in more detail in the account of the last-named ship which appears in "American Merchant Ships," Series I.

Capt. William J. Tobey, Jr., who had previously been master of the ship *Pactolus*, commanded the *Santa Clara* during the first six years of her career. Capt. Robert K. Dunn followed Captain Rivers and completed two round voyages, the second being to the Orient. His third was from New York to San Diego, Cal., after which the ship went to Tacoma and loaded wheat for Queenstown. On the latter passage the *Santa Clara* put into San Francisco with Captain Dunn too ill to continue, so he was relieved by Capt. R. W. Fuller, the former chief mate of the ship *E. B. Sutton*, and Captain Fuller continued master until the ship was sold in 1896. Captain Dunn recovered his health and during his later years was Marine Superintendent for the U. S. A. Transport Service at San Francisco. He passed away at his home in Oakland, Cal., a number of years ago.

SEA WITCH

THE ship *Sea Witch* was built by Robert E. Jackson, at East Boston, and was launched in July, 1872. She measured 197 feet, by 37:8, by 24:2 feet and registered 1233 tons. She was built to the order of W. F. Weld & Co. of Boston, and after the death of Richard Baker, Jr., and the segregation of the assets of the firm, she became the property of the Baker estate in 1875. Some years later she was purchased by Edward Lawrence, Jr., and others, of Boston, and they continued owners until 1901 when she was sold at San Francisco to the North Alaska Salmon Co. In December, 1906, she was abandoned off Cape Flattery in a sinking condition but all hands were saved.

Early in her career the *Sea Witch* made three voyages between New York, San Francisco and Liverpool; thereafter, until she was sold, she was operated in trade with Australia and the Far East and was one of the best known American ships visiting India, China, the Philippines and Madagascar. Her passages were made in fair average time and so far as can be ascertained she met with no serious mishaps.

The best known commanders of the *Sea Witch* were Captains John H. Drew and Henry T. Howes. Captain Drew was a native of Chelsea, Mass., and started a seafaring life at the age of eleven years. In 1863, when twenty years old, he was chief officer of the clipper ship *Fearless*, under Capt. George W. Homans, and on the following voyage was her master. Four years later he took the *Franklin*, also belonging to Weld & Co., and was in her until 1876 when he was transferred to the *Sea Witch*. He retired from the sea in 1889 and lived at his home at Farmingdale, Me., in the Kennebec Valley, until his death in 1900 at the age of fifty-eight years.

Captain Drew was one of the most prominent American merchant shipmasters of his time, a thoroughly competent navigator and as a master, firm but kind. He was very proud of the *Sea Witch*, calling her his "Witch of the Sea" and being quite an artist, he painted many pictures of her, his home containing a large collection of marine paintings, flags and other marine curios. During the time he was in the *Sea Witch* he contributed many articles on maritime subjects to Boston journals under the pen name of "Kennebecker." A brother of the Captain was second mate of the ship *Peruvian*, one of Weld & Co.'s fleet, when she was lost, with all hands, on Peaked Hill Bar, in 1872.

Capt. Henry T. Howes was the last master of the *Sea Witch* prior to her purchase by San Francisco parties after which he retired from sea to become superintendent of Sailor's Snug Harbor and died there. The Captain gained considerable renown through running the blockade off Delagoa Bay in the *Sea Witch*. The ship had been chartered at Melbourne, by an English firm, to take a cargo of flour from Wollaroo to the Portuguese port of Lourenzo Marquez where 800 tons was to be discharged, the ship then to proceed to Natal to finish unloading. The *Sea Witch* arrived off Delagoa Bay, just at dark, one evening, and the Captain saw the lights of the British war ships blockading the harbor, but as his presence did not appear to have been observed by them, he stood boldly in and came to anchor, without molestation, about midnight. The next morning the *Sea Witch* was boarded by officers from the British fleet who were much chagrined over the incident and particularly so on discovering the nature of the ship's cargo. However, they could do nothing except put obstacles in the way of the ship getting quick dispatch in unloading and departing and this they successfully accomplished. At last Captain Howes got away and after discharging at Natal, proceeded to Australia where a cargo of coal was laden for Manila. At that port the ship took fire in the lazarette and was damaged to quite an extent. She subsequently proceeded to Hong Kong and after a long stay there was ordered to San Francisco to be repaired or sold. Arriving at the latter port in October, 1901, she was put up at auction in December and after changing hands and being repaired, was rerigged as a bark.

SERVIA

THE ship *Servia* was built at Bath, Maine, by Houghton Brothers, and was launched in December, 1883. She measured 234:1 feet, by 41:1, and 26:7 feet and registered 1773 tons. She was built to be commanded by Capt. David Gilmore and aside for a few voyages made by relieving masters Charles H. Reed and A. C. Otis, Captain Gilmore was in command during the sixteen years preceding the sale of the ship.

The *Servia* made three or four voyages to the Orient and nine rounds between Atlantic ports and San Francisco prior to her sale. Towards the end of 1899, on completing her tenth outward passage to the Pacific Coast, she was sold to San Francisco parties among whom was Capt. Henry Nelson, formerly master and owner of the ship *Columbia*. Captain Nelson then took command of the *Servia* and on his becoming her sole owner appointed Captain Anderson as master. The latter was in the ship when she was lost.

The voyages of the *Servia* were made in fair time and without unusual incident or important mishap. The average of her passages to San Francisco was 138 days, two of 120 days each, from New York and Baltimore respectively, being the shortest. She made seven passages with grain to European ports at an average of 125 days, of which the shortest was 113 days, to Liverpool, and two to New York in 97 and 106 days. On the 97-day run she was in ballast and sailed four days after the *Parthia*, another Houghton ship, also in ballast. The latter made New York five days in the lead, thus beating the *Servia* one day. Captain Reed was in command of the *Servia* at the time and also on the following voyage, New York to Kobe in 153 days, thence nine days to Manila and 103 days from that port to New York. On the latter run the ship made 273 miles in one day, which being given prominence, is possibly the best sailing done by the ship during the three years Captain Reed was in command.

Following her sale at San Francisco, the *Servia* was operated on the Pacific and made a number of voyages to Alaska under charter. On Nov. 6, 1907, while she was at Karluk loading canned salmon for San Francisco, an unusually heavy gale sprung up at midnight causing a very high sea to run almost immediately. The ship's anchor chains parted and she was driven on a rock about 75 feet from shore where she held fast. The masts went by the board and soon she was on beam ends. Three men were drowned in attempting to swim ashore but the rest of the ship's company were able to make land over a sort of floating bridge composed of cargo and wreckage from the vessel. The ship was completely broken up within a few hours after striking.

Captain David Gilmore was born in Woolwich, Me., in 1840, and in early life shipped on the *Assyria* of which his uncle John P. Delano was master. In 1874 he was appointed commander of the *Austria* and after eight years service in her he took the *Samaria*. After the sale of the *Servia* he was master of the bark *Guy C. Goss* and the ships *Parthia* and *St. Paul*. In 1905 he retired from the sea to make his home with a brother at Auburn, Washington. He died in August, 1916, from a heart shock superinduced by an automobile accident. His remains were sent East for interment.

Captain Gilmore was one of the prominent American merchant shipmasters of his time, of a quiet unassuming disposition yet smart and active and successful as a manager. While a strict disciplinarian he was just to his subordinates and never in trouble with his crews. His great grandfather had come to this country, in 1699, from England.

SOUTH AMERICAN

THE ship *South American* was built to the order of Henry Hastings of Boston, by Smith & Townsend, and was launched from their East Boston yard in September, 1876. In model she closely resembled the *North American* which had been built for Mr. Hastings three years before but was about 100 tons larger. The Hastings' fleet was composed of first class ships and each one built excelled its predecessor. The *South American* was considered the acme of shipbuilding and in her early life was regarded as the finest wooden sailing ship afloat. Only the best materials and workmanship entered into her construction and her cost was $130,000. She was 245 feet long from knighthead to taffrail, with a beam of 41:6 and depth of hold of 25:2 feet. She registered 1694 tons. She had moderately sharp ends, a bold, raking bow with lines slightly concave as they ascended and carried as a figurehead a finely carved image of an Amazon. A full poop deck extended aft from just abaft the mainmast. The main truck was 167 feet above the deck; the mainyard 87 feet long and the mainskysail yard, 34 feet. The bowsprit and jibboom extended 91 feet outboard from the knightheads.

The *South American* was a good carrier, loading 2600 long tons of wheat, yet her sailing record is very good. The following list of her passages was compiled from log books in possession of her owners.

1876-77	New York to San Francisco,	109 days.	San Francisco to Manila,	45 days.
1877	Manila to Boston,	110 "		
1878	New York to San Francisco,	123 "	San Francisco to Cork,	99 "
1879	Cardiff to Hong Kong,	114 "	Hong Kong to San Francisco,	43 "
1879-80	San Francisco to Cork,	105 "		
1880	Cardiff to Hong Kong,	103 "	Hong Kong to San Francisco,	61 "
1881	San Francisco to Liverpool,	115 "		
1882	Liverpool to San Francisco,	114 "	San Francisco to Liverpool,	100 "
1882-83	Liverpool to San Francisco,	121 "	San Francisco to Cork,	117 "
1883-84	Liverpool to San Francisco,	130 "	San Francisco to Liverpool,	100 "
1884	Cardiff to Hong Kong,	89 "	Hong Kong to San Francisco,	42 "
1884-85	San Francisco to Dublin,	120 "		
1885	Cardiff to Hong Kong,	100 "	Hong Kong to New York,	89 "
1886-87	New York to Calcutta,	106 "	Calcutta to New York,	89 "
1887	New York to Colombo,	104 "	Colombo to Hong Kong,	28 "
1887-88	Hong Kong to New York,	102 "		
1888	New York to Sydney,	88 "	Sydney to San Diego, Cal.,	53 "
1889	San Diego to Nanaimo, B.C.,	13 "	Nanaimo to San Francisco,	8 "
1889	San Francisco to Iloilo,	57 "	Iloilo to Cape of Good Hope,	55 "

On her maiden voyage she left New York, December 3, 1876, with
3500 tons of weight and measurement goods, under command of
Capt. Gorham B. Knowles and with 24 men before the mast. She
crossed the Line 19 days out and passed Rio de Janeiro on the 26th
day; was in the latitude of the Plate 33 days out and in 50° S. on the
43rd day; was around the Horn 12 days later but meeting with very
light trades was not up with the Line until 85 days out; thence was
24 days to port. Had skysails set all the way from latitude 30° N. in
the Atlantic except for four days off Cape Horn. Beat the *Seminole*
16 days and by a greater margin all other ships going over the course
about that time. On her second voyage she again made the run from
New York to 50° S. in the Atlantic in 43 days.

It will be seen that the list of her passages included some very fast
runs. That from Sydney to San Diego was the shortest on record up to
that time. On one day she covered 353 miles according to good ob-
servations. When 18 days out she met and passed the British ship
Slieve Bawn which had sailed ten days before her. On her passage
from Hong Kong to San Francisco, in 1879, she made the Farallons
in 39 days. In November, 1883, she left San Francisco and arrived

back there in October, 1884, after being absent 10 months and 17 days, during which time she had gone to Queenstown, Liverpool, Cardiff, and Hong Kong and this record has never been approached.

On Nov. 29, 1884, the *South American* sailed from San Francisco, bound for Dublin, and on December 8th the *R. D. Rice* left port for Liverpool. They met each other just north of the Line, in the Atlantic, and Capt. Newell B. Jordan of the *Rice* was greatly elated at having caught up with the famous Boston ship, writing friends that she "could not sail for sour apples" and that he had no trouble in getting away from her. However this may be, the ships were in company some two weeks and the *South American* arrived at Dublin five days before the *Rice* made Liverpool.

The only serious mishap met with by the *South American*, prior to her loss, was in 1881, when bound from Hong Kong to San Francisco. Leaving port on September 30th she encountered a typhoon in the Bashee Straits and lost the mizzenmast with everything attached and a number of yards on the mainmast, in addition to which nearly all the sails and rigging were damaged. She put back to Hong Kong and was two months undergoing repairs.

On July 22, 1889, the *South American* sailed from Iloilo with 2700 tons of sugar for Boston and was wrecked September 15th in Struy's Bay, near Cape Agulhas. She struck a reef two miles offshore and soon went on beam ends. On attempts being made to launch the boats they were all stove. Captain Connolly, his wife, the chief officer and two seamen lashed themselves to an improvised raft and drifted ashore. Of the nineteen others remaining on the ship, two were drowned and the others got safely to land on the break of the poop deck which had become separated from the rest of the ship. The vessel was valued at the time at $80,000 and was insured for $60,000. When sold at auction it brought only $400.

The commanders of the *South American* were Captains Gorham B. Knowles, B. C. Creelman and Frank Fowle, all of whom are more particularly referred to in "American Merchant Ships," Series I, and Capt. James Connolly. The latter had originally been employed by Mr. Hastings as mate and later had commanded his ships *Pilgrim* and

Charger. He was a native of East Dennis, Mass., and after the *South American* was lost engaged in the real estate business at San Diego, Cal., in partnership with Capt. A. H. Dunbar, formerly master of the ship *Grecian.*

SOVEREIGN OF THE SEAS

THE ship *Sovereign of the Seas* was built by Donald McKay at East Boston and was launched in November, 1868. She measured 199:5 feet, by 41, by 23:9 feet and registered 1443 tons. She was owned by Lawrence Giles & Co. and hailed from New York. Her last voyage as an American ship was in 1883-1884, New York to Astoria, in 160 days and thence to Queenstown in 141 days. She was ordered to Antwerp to discharge and was subsequently sold to go under the German flag, being renamed *Elvira*, hailing from Vegesack. She was operated in transatlantic trade until 1898 when she was sold to Lewis Luckenbach who had her converted into a barge. Her original name was restored but her further career was short as in 1902 she foundered off New York.

The *Sovereign of the Seas* was a good looking ship with an elliptic stern and fair lines which would seem to have allowed her a better sailing record than what she has. She was built for the California trade and except for her last voyage, as previously referred to, all her passages were between New York, San Francisco and Liverpool or the European continent. Of such she completed eleven voyages of which the average of those to San Francisco is 150 days for ten. On the other passage, leaving New York March 1, 1872, she met with heavy gales the second day out and lost a number of her principal sails besides having the rudderhead twisted off. After much difficulty Captain Johnson managed to get her put about for return to New York but was ten days in making port. Gales and high seas had continued; more sails were blown away; the decks were full of water most of the time, with the ship iced up badly and practically unmanageable with the temperature down to fourteen degrees. On repairs being completed the voyage was resumed and all went well until latitude 33°

S. was reached when the mainmast was seriously damaged and the ship was put about for Rio de Janeiro. A new mainmast was put in and after a delay of six weeks the ship again proceeded and after a hard passage around the Horn, during which a number of sails were blown away, she finally arrived at San Francisco in 215 days from New York, 100 days from Rio de Janeiro.

The shortest passage made by the *Sovereign of the Seas* to San Francisco was 138 days. The shortest of those from that port to the Atlantic was 114 days and the average of all such was 127 days. During the course of her Cape Horn voyage she was fortunate in escaping damage from the elements except in the instance stated.

The first commander of the *Sovereign of the Seas* was Capt. Nathaniel C. Johnson who, after serving as her master seven years, was succeeded by Capt. Aaron H. Wood who continued in the ship until she was sold. Captain Wood had previously been master of the ship *St. Mark*, built at Thomaston by Chapman & Flint, in 1860, but owned at the time by J. D. Fish and others.

In 1852 Donald McKay had built an extreme clipper ship named *Sovereign of the Seas* which established a record as a very fast sailer. In 1854 this ship was sold to merchants of Hamburg and five years later was lost on the Pyramid Shoal, Straits of Malacca.

STORM KING

THE ship *Storm King*, built and owned by Theobald & Harward, was launched at Richmond, Maine, in July, 1874. She measured 189:6 feet, by 37, by 24:2 feet and registered 1206 tons. Her capacity for dead weight cargoes was 1900 tons. Her mainmast was 80 feet long, mainyard, 72 feet, and royal yard, 33:6 feet. She had wire rigging. Towards her later years she was not well kept up, her copper was in poor condition and ragged and spars and rigging had been allowed to deteriorate. In August, 1892, she was sold to Boston parties who had her converted into a barge. Ten years later she foundered in a gale.

The following is a complete list of the voyages made by the *Storm King*: 1874-1875.Wiscasset to Liverpool, 19 days. Liverpool to Rangoon, 110 days. Rangoon to Queenstown, 108 days. Queenstown to Bremerhaven, 7 days. 1875-1876. Bremerhaven to Galveston via Tybee, 71 days. Galveston to Liverpool, 40 days. Liverpool to Wilmington, Cal., 134 days. Wilmington to Astoria, 12 days. 1877-1878. Astoria to Liverpool, 123 days. Liverpool to Bombay, 110 days. Bombay to Moulmein, 38 days. Moulmein to Bombay, 36 days. Bombay to Astoria, 77 days. Astoria to Victoria, 2 days. 1879-1880. Victoria, B. C., to Callao, 60 days. Callao to Victoria, 53 days. Departure Bay to San Francisco, 8 days. San Francisco to Queenstown, 143 days. Queenstown to Havre, 6 days. Havre to Cardiff, 7 days. Cardiff to Rio de Janeiro, 44 days. Rio de Janeiro to San Francisco, 65 days.

1881-1882. San Francisco to Queenstown, 120 days. Queenstown to Avonmouth, 2½ days. Avonmouth to Newport, Wales, 3 hours. Newport to Guaymas, 140 days. Guaymas to Victoria, B. C., 26 days. Victoria to Astoria, 5 days. Astoria to Queenstown, 134 days. Queenstown to Liverpool, 2 days. Liverpool to New York, 51 days.

1883. New York to San Francisco, 139 days. San Francisco to Queenstown, 133 days. Queenstown to Fleetwood, 3 days. Fleetwood to Cardiff, in tow, 35 hours.

1884-1885. Cardiff to Hong Kong, 120 days. Hong Kong to Honolulu, 88 days. Honolulu to Victoria, 33 days. Victoria to Port Gamble, 15 hours. Port Gamble to Montevideo, 97 days. Montevideo to Buenos Ayres, 3 days. Buenos Ayres to New Orleans, 59 days.

1886. New Orleans to Havre, 56 days. Havre to New York, 44 days.

The passage of the *Storm King* from Rio de Janeiro to San Francisco in 65 days, has been equalled or excelled only by the *Witchcraft*, in 1851, and *Spitfire*, in 1854, their time being 62 and 65 days respectively. Both those ships were of extreme clipper model but were loaded deep with cargo while the *Storm King* was in ballast. The latter had fair winds as a rule and made the 16-mile run through the Straits of Le Maire in 65 minutes. She made no high speed during the passage, her best day being only 232 miles. To offset this short passage she had the very long run of 88 days from Hong Kong to Honolulu, in 1884, when under command of Capt. Charles J. Carter, who was relieving Captain Reed. She had left Hong Kong during the height of the northeast monsoon and for two months made so little progress that Captain Carter knew his provisions would not hold out until he reached Victoria, so he made for Honolulu for additional supplies.

Capt. Charles H. Reed of Woolwich, Me., sailed as chief officer of the *Storm King*, under Capt. A. P. Boyd, when the ship started on her maiden voyage and was promoted to command her at Liverpool, in January, 1876. Aside from the voyage to Hong Kong and Victoria in 1884, Captain Reed continued as master of the ship until she was sold. He subsequently served for a short time in the ships *Servia*, *Samaria* and *Berlin* and on retiring from the sea, in 1898, he bought a home in Richmond, Me., and engaged in the grain business. He passed away in November, 1919, at the age of seventy-four years. Captain Reed had a clear record as a shipmaster and while he always maintained strict discipline on his ships, he was a just man and was well thought of by his crews. He had started a sea life at the age of seventeen and before joining the *Storm King* was mate of the ships *Crescent City* and *James A. Wright*.

SUMATRA

THE ship *Sumatra* was built by John Taylor, at Chelsea, Mass., in 1856, and was 180 feet, by 36, by 23:5 feet and registered 1073 tons. She was owned by B. W. Stone & Bro., wealthy Salem merchants who frequently owned outright the cargoes carried in their ships. For the first twenty-five years of her career she traded principally with Hong Kong and was one of the best known vessels visiting that port.

"TAM O'SHANTER," 1522 TONS, BUILT IN 1875, AT FREEPORT, MAINE

From a Chinese painting, showing the ship at Hong Kong. Photograph by George E. Noyes, Newburyport

"TENNYSON," 1246 TONS, BUILT IN 1865, AT NEWBURYPORT

Photograph by George E. Noyes, Newburyport

"TWILIGHT," 1303 TONS, BUILT IN 1866, AT MYSTIC, CONN.

"VALPARAISO," 1158 TONS, BUILT IN 1863, AT NEWBURYPORT
Courtesy of Fireman's Fund Insurance Co., San Francisco

The *Sumatra* was a fine looking vessel of medium clipper model but does not appear to have any fast passages to her credit. At quite widely separated intervals she made four voyages from New York to San Francisco, returning East by way of China. The outward runs averaged 140 days, the shortest being 121 days. The last of these voyages was in 1869 and thereafter, for 13 years, she was steadily employed in trade between San Francisco and Hong Kong, making about one round voyage a year and being generally between 50 and 60 days on the passages each way. In 1874, while she was in port at Hong Kong, a typhoon came on and to prevent her from being driven ashore, her masts were cut away. New spars were sent out from Boston and it was something over two years before she was again put into commission.

The *Sumatra* met with a number of other mishaps. In 1867, repairs at San Francisco cost $10,000, the ship having sprung a leak in heavy gales off Cape Horn. In 1870, while bound from Hong Kong to San Francisco, she again became leaky and put into Yokohama where all her cargo had to be discharged. On repairs being completed she crossed to Puget Sound and while bound to sea, with a coal cargo for San Francisco, struck a sunken rock and was seriously damaged. On being towed into Esquimault, she sunk but was raised and taken to San Francisco for a thorough overhauling. This cost $16,000 and as her sound value had been estimated at only $20,000, underwrighters were sorry they had not allowed her to remain under water at Esquimault.

The *Sumatra* was then sold to Jacob Jensen, Capt. Charles Rock and other San Francisco parties and was operated in the coastwise and offshore coal and lumber trades on the Pacific until 1891 when she was laid up at San Francisco. Later on she was sent to Honolulu to do duty as a store hulk but her usefulness was about over and in November, 1895, she was sold for $750 to be broken up.

TACOMA

THE handsome three-skysailyard ship *Tacoma* was built for Charles Davenport of Bath, Maine, and was launched at that place from the yard of Goss & Sawyer on July 21, 1881. She measured 222:2 feet, by 41, by 25:9 feet and registered 1739 tons. She was one of the finest ships ever built in Maine, an excellent specimen of an American merchantman and was equipped with all the latest improvements of the time, including a condensing apparatus with a capacity of 500 gallons daily. Her cabins and saloons were as elegantly fitted up as those of first class passenger steamships of the day; she had six spare staterooms, bath rooms and a dispensary. She was built to be commanded by Capt. John R. Kelley, owner of an interest in the ship, but after making one voyage in her he retired from active sea life. The interesting career of the Captain as shipmaster, owner and builder is given in the account of the ship named in his honor, the history of which appears in "American Merchant Ships," Series I.

Prior to 1897 the *Tacoma* made from Atlantic ports two voyages to the Orient and eleven to San Francisco. In 1897-1898 she made a passage from Philadelphia to Seattle and after arrival was sold for $40,000 to the Alaska Packers Association who continued owners until her loss.

The sailing record of the *Tacoma* may be considered as good, the average of ten of her passages from Atlantic ports to the North Pacific Coast being 138 days. The other two were very long, 178 days from Cardiff and 204 days from New York, but both were accomplished in the face of great difficulties. On the first mentioned she had heavy weather for the first ten days during which she made no progress and then met with light winds and calms to the Line which was crossed 48 days out. She fell to leeward of Cape St. Roque, had to beat a long spell before she could clear the land, and was 40 days from the Line to Cape St. John. The passage around the Cape occupied only 18 days but the weather was freezing cold and the ship was much iced up. In the Pacific unfavorable winds were met with and the ship was 51 days from the Line to San Francisco. While she was in

the South Atlantic the coal cargo was found to be on fire but by sealing ventilators and hatches and the use of plenty of water, the fire
was kept under control and finally extinguished without any damage
having been done to the ship.

On her 204-day passage the *Tacoma* had the good run of 26 days
to the Line but had either strong head winds and gales or calms in
the South Atlantic and did not cross latitude 50° S. until 86 days out.
She was 63 days in getting around Cape Horn, losing many new sails
and being thrown on beam ends on two occasions. In one very severe
gale she was struck by an electric ball which, on exploding with a loud
report, scattered sparks of fire in all directions but fortunately no
damage resulted. The remainder of the passage was uneventful and
made in fair time. The day before the ship made port 95 per cent re-
insurance had been quoted as she had been practically given up as lost.

Eastbound from San Francisco, the *Tacoma* made six passages to
the United Kingdom and five to New York, the average of all of
them being 118 days. The shortest was 105 days to New York and
longest, 137 days to Liverpool.

Shortly after her sale at San Francisco the *Tacoma* was chartered
to the United States Government to transport horses to Manila. The
main and between decks were fitted up with stalls containing portable
mangers and canvas slings to support the animals when the ship was
rolling; the condensing plant was enlarged to a capacity of 2000
gallons of water daily; electric fans and two huge windsails, for ven-
tilating purposes, were set up and nothing was omitted to protect and
give comfort to the living cargo of the ship. A false deck, flush with
the topgallant forecastle, was laid to the break of the poop as a roof
over the animals stowed on the main deck. Pessimists expressed grave
doubts as to the success of the plan to ship horses by sailing vessel
but results showed that their fears had been groundless. The *Tacoma*
landed her first cargo at Honolulu and later took two cargoes from
San Francisco to Manila. On the second she was in a typhoon of fifty-
two hours duration and although the members of the Fourth Cavalry
had to perform strenuous duty to prevent their frightened charges
from being injured, through stampeding or by broken beams, not one

of them was hurt. When the ship arrived at Manila the horses were in such fine condition that inside of thirty-six hours they were in actual service. The steamship *Siam*, also from San Francisco, with horses for Manila, passed through the same typhoon and lost all her live cargo so that an important expedition planned by General Otis would have been impossible but for the arrival of the *Tacoma*.

On return from Manila, early in 1900, after her third voyage as a transport, the *Tacoma* became a "salmon packer" and so continued until May, 1918, when she was lost in the ice pack. She had sailed from San Francisco, April 10th, with cannery supplies and laborers for Nushagak, Alaska, but when nearing her destination, on May 3d, met with ice fields. After manoevuring several days, a clear lane, some fifteen miles wide, was observed between the ice floe and the land and the *Tacoma* was tacked up the passage. The ice subsequently closed in and crushed her so badly that on May 19th the bowsprit and masts were broken off, the mainmast disappearing through the bottom of the ship. She then filled with water and went down, the ice closing over her. Life boats had previously been launched on the floe and provisioned and all hands made camp. They were finally able to reach other vessels that were fast in the ice within a radius of a few miles, but one man perished from exposure while trying to make his way to the ship *St. Nicholas*.

Capt. William B. Sheldon succeeded Captain Kelley, as master of the *Tacoma*, and was in her some eight or nine years. Capt. William H. Starkey, who is referred to in the account of the ship *Belle of Bath*, succeeded Captain Sheldon and two years later Capt. B. Gaffry assumed command and continued in the *Tacoma* until she was purchased in San Francisco. He then made a voyage in the *Berlin*, after which he took the *Arthur Sewall* and was her master in 1907 when she was lost, with all hands, near Cape Horn, while bound from Philadelphia to Seattle.

TAM O'SHANTER

THE ship *Tam O'Shanter*, built and owned by the Soule family of Freeport, Maine, was launched at that place Sept. 18, 1875. She measured 213:8 feet, by 41:7, by 24:3 feet and registered 1522 tons. She was considered one of the best built ships ever constructed in Maine and was the pride of the Soule fleet. Her sailing record is good and she lived up to her reputation of being a fast ship.

Prior to 1894 the *Tom O'Shanter* was engaged in trade principally with San Francisco, making ten round voyages between that port and the Atlantic, one round to the Far East, and three passages to Japan from whence she returned East by way of the North Pacific Coast. From 1894 until her loss in 1899 in the Gaspar Straits, all her voyages were between New York and China or Japan.

In 1882 the *Tam O'Shanter*, bound from New York to San Francisco, made Staten Island after an average run of 55 days, but then met with adverse gales and could not get through the Straits of Le Maire. She was 43 days in getting around Cape Horn and then meeting with light and contrary winds, did not arrive at her destination until 163 days out. This was the only long passage made by the ship and makes the average of her ten passages to San Francisco 130 days, which otherwise figures 126 days. Her shortest run was 110 days, in 1892, when she beat the ships *S. D. Carleton* and *Shenandoah* in a race, the interesting particulars of which are given in the account of the *Shenandoah*, "American Merchant Ships," Series I.

The *Tam O'Shanter* made one passage from Tacoma to Queenstown, her time being 122 days, a smart trip. She made twelve passages from San Francisco to Atlantic ports of which three were to New York and nine to the United Kingdom or Continental Europe. The average of the nine in the grain trade is 115 days and the average of the whole twelve is 117 days. The shortest was 107 days to Queenstown. In 1895 she left Hong Kong in company with the fast ship *Wandering Jew*, Capt. Daniel C. Nichols, and both arrived at New York on the same day, 95 days on the passage, so the race which had been arranged between Captain Peabody and Captain Nichols was declared a draw. The ships met on several occasions during the passage, sailing at times nearly side by side, day after day, showing that they were quite evenly matched.

Among the commanders of the *Tam O'Shanter* were three members of the Soule family, Captains Horace B., Julius, and Wallace Soule. Other masters were Captains Alfred T. Small, C. D. Prescott, Henry T. Waite, Thomas Peabody and —— Ballard, the latter having the ship when she was lost. Captain Peabody was in command for the longest period, some ten years, and he was the most conspicuous of her masters. In 1866 he made his first visit to the Pacific Coast in the old ship *Raduga* and a few years later was mate of the ship *Reunion*. His first command was the bark *C. O. Whitmore* and after her he was in the *Antelope*, *Tam O'Shanter*, *New York*, *Willscott*, *Cyrus Wakefield*, and the Army Transport *Sheridan*, running between San Francisco and Manila. He lost the *New York*, formerly the *T. F. Oakes*, built of iron at Philadelphia, in 1883, south of the Golden Gate while bound to San Francisco with a very valuable cargo from Hong Kong, and was also unfortunate in having the *Sheridan* go ashore on one of the Hawaiian Islands. She was, however, soon gotten off. He subsequently had a large schooner in the Honolulu trade but was forced to retire from sea, broken in mind and body, and passed away at San Francisco some twenty years ago.

Captain Peabody was regarded as a high class navigator and was a driver. A strict disciplinarian, he was not well regarded by his crews. He attained much notoriety in 1876 when in command of the *C. O. Whitmore*, on a passage from Cardiff to Hong Kong, the second mate of the vessel died as a result of starvation and abuse while under confinement during the greater part of the voyage. Captain Peabody and his chief officer, John H. Snow, were accused of murder and the feeling against them at Hong Kong was very bitter. They were able to get away from that port, however, and nearly three years later, when Captain Peabody was brought to trial at Boston and his mate prosecuted at San Francisco, both were acquitted for lack of evidence.

The *Tam O'Shanter* was the second ship of that name owned by the Soule family, the first having been built in 1850 by Capt. Enos

Soule and his two brothers. This ship was commanded by Capt. Enos
C. Soule, who, on retiring from sea life, took over the business of his
father and uncles and constructed many fine ships besides the second
Tam, his last being the *Paramita*. The first *Tam* had but a short
career, completing only two voyages. In March, 1853, she arrived at
San Francisco from Boston, thence going to Calcutta where a valuable
cargo was loaded for Boston. On Dec. 28, 1853, when close to her
destination, she was abandoned with fifteen feet of water in her hold
and hull and spars badly damaged. The crew took to their boats and
were picked up by a passing vessel. The ship was of medium clipper
model and of about 800 tons burden.

TENNYSON

THE ship *Tennyson* was built by John Currier, Jr., at Newburyport, Mass., and launched in May, 1865. She was 1246 tons
register and was a well-built ship having cost more than any vessel
that had been built at Newburyport up to that time. Her owners were
William Graves & Co., merchants of Newburyport, who were extensively engaged in trade with India.

The maiden voyage of the *Tennyson* was from Bangor to Liverpool, with lumber, thence to Calcutta, Bombay, Point de Galle, Penang, Singapore, Hong Kong, San Francisco and Liverpool, the
whole round taking nearly two years. On the passage from Hong
Kong to San Francisco she had 565 coolie passengers and that was her
only appearance at a port on the North Pacific Coast. She made the
run from San Francisco to Liverpool in 118 days. The second voyage
she made was a round between Liverpool and Calcutta and thereafter she was employed in trade with the Far East, principally with
ports in India.

On her last voyage the *Tennyson* took ice from Boston to Madras
and Calcutta and on the return she left Calcutta with a large cargo of
Indian produce for Boston, in January, 1873. On February 22d, she
encountered a hurricane of exceptional violence, south of Mauritius,

during the course of which her wood-ends were sprung and she made water rapidly, soon taking a plunge and going down bow first with all hands except the second mate, one seaman and a boy. When the ship went down the after house was lifted off and the three survivors were able to reach this and climb aboard. Later they secured some bales of jute which had floated out of the ship's hold and making a buttress of them, along the sides of the house, managed to keep from being washed overboard from their refuge. They were nine days on their frail support during which their only food was a few sea birds they managed to catch, while their drinking water was a meagre supply of rain caught in oilskins. On the ninth day they were sighted and picked up by the bark *Warren Hastings*, but were nearly dead from hunger, thirst and exposure.

The first commander of the *Tennyson* was Capt. Alex. Graves of Newburyport, who had previously been master of the ships *Castillian* and *Kenmore*. The Captain made only one voyage in the *Tennyson*, retiring on account of ill health and in May, 1869, he passed away at the early age of forty-six years. Capt. Edward Graves succeeded in command and except for one voyage made by a relieving master, continued in the ship until her end, losing his life when she foundered. He also belonged to Newburyport and had been master of the bark *Washington Allston* and the ships *Josiah L. Hale* and *Kenmore*. He was only forty-two years of age when he was lost.

TWILIGHT

THE ship *Twilight*, built and owned by Charles H. Mallory of Mystic, Conn., was launched at that place in October, 1866. She measured 188:5 feet, by 39, by 23:3 feet and registered 1303 tons. She had sharper ends than most other ships of her period, crossed a main skysail yard and was in every way a fine appearing vessel. A full poop extended nearly to the mainmast.

Aside from a couple of cotton voyages across the Atlantic, the *Twilight's* first twelve years were spent in trade with San Francisco.

The following six years were passed in voyages between the Atlantic and Australia or the Far East. In 1885 she was sold to go under the Austrian flag without change of name.

The *Twilight* was a well-known and favorite vessel turning out her cargoes in good condition and making fair passages although there is no evidence to show that she lived up to her reputation of being a fast sailer. She made eight passages from New York to San Francisco at an average of 147 days, the shortest being 136 days. However, her log books show that she generally met with unfavorable weather, which accounts for the high figures in some degree, at least. Her shortest time from San Francisco to New York was 109 days and to Liverpool, 135 days. Records show that her work in the Far East trade was only fair, she having one passage of 107 days from Anjer to New York and one of 102 days from New York to Melbourne. On one of her passages from New York to San Francisco she was 35 days making 14 degrees of latitude in the South Pacific.

In January, 1880, while on a passage from Manila to New York, the *Twilight* was dismasted in a typhoon and it was at first reported that she would prove to be a total loss, being at the time far distant from a repair port. However, she was able to reach Hong Kong where repairs were made.

Capt. Peter E. Rowland, the first commander of the *Twilight*, had sailed for Mr. Mallory a number of years previously, being in his fine clipper ship *Mary L. Sutton* on two occasions and when she was lost on the reefs of Baker's Island, in November, 1864. Capt. George W. Gates of Mystic was master of the *Twilight* for the eight years prior to 1877. His prior commands had been the steamer *Nevada* of New York, a vessel of 900 tons, plying on the Atlantic Coast, and the fast sailing bark *Galveston*, belonging to Mystic. The Captain was a brother of Capt. Gurdon Gates, master of Mr. Mallory's first *Twilight*, and of Capt. Charles H. Gates who lost his life when his ship *Cremorne* was posted as missing in 1870.

Capt. W. C. Warland was the last commander of the *Twilight* and after she was sold, he took the new ship *Hotspur*. His seafaring career is given in account of that ship.

A medium clipper ship named *Twilight* was built by Mr. Mallory in 1857 and made many passages which compared very favorably with those of the out-and-out clippers. This ship was sold at San Francisco in 1865, to carry coolie laborers from China to the Peruvian guano deposits, later being in the lumber trade between Puget Sound and South America. She sailed under different names and flags until 1887 when, as the Costa Rican ship *Hermann*, she arrived at San Francisco, leaky and badly strained on the passage from Callao. This was her last voyage, she then being condemned and burned for her metal.

VALPARAISO

THE ship *Valparaiso* was built by John Currier, Jr., at Newburyport, Mass., and was launched in June, 1863. She was 190 feet, by 37, by 24 feet and registered 1158 tons. During her career as an American ship she was very successful and made money for her owners. She was a good carrier and a fast sailer.

The *Valparaiso* was built for the California and East India trade but made only one passage from an Atlantic port to the Far East, that being from Cardiff to Hong Kong in 1880. The remainder of her outward runs were all to San Francisco and year after year she made round after round as regular as clock work. During the year 1882 she passed twice through the Golden Gate on passages from Europe, an unusual occurrence. One series of voyages was remarkable. Leaving San Francisco in August, 1868, she made the run to New York in 96 days, thence back to San Francisco in 116 days, then to New York in 117 days, back again to San Francisco in 108 days, then to New York in 111 days, and back to San Francisco in 114 days, then to Liverpool in 110 days and back to San Francisco from Newport, Wales, in 107 days. The total gross time taken on these four rounds was three years, five months and eleven days. One of her voyages from New York to San Francisco and return was accomplished in eight months and fourteen days, and two others in less than nine months each, gross. In

1882 she was 111 days from San Francisco to St. Nazaire, then going back in 106 days.

On her last passage as an American ship the *Valparaiso* left San Francisco in March, 1883, for New York, but was forced to put into Rio de Janeiro to have a leak stopped. This was done by divers and she proceeded, but later a worse leak developed and on arrival at New York she had six feet of water in the hold. On her first passage, which was from New York to San Francisco, in 1863-1864, she put into Montevideo, damaged in spars and rigging by gales off Cape Horn, but the expense incident to this was not great, some $3,400. On the whole she was fortunate in escaping mishaps on her voyages.

The *Valparaiso* was built for Fabri & Chauncey of New York who, in 1865, sold her to George Howes & Co., of New York and San Francisco. Following the liquidation of that firm, in 1880, she was purchased by John Rosenfeld of San Francisco and he sold her shortly after her arrival at New York, in 1883, to go under the German flag. She was renamed *Caroline* and hailing from Bremen, passed the remainder of her sea life in transatlantic trade.

The best known master of the *Valparaiso* was Capt. John L. Manson who was in command some ten years, leaving her to take the clipper ship *Young America*. Later, Captain Manson had the American iron ship *Mariposa* which, as the British ship *Jessie Osborne*, had been sold and refitted after stranding near the entrance to San Francisco harbor. Captain Dwight Goff, formerly master of the ships *Edith* and *Derby*, belonging to the Messrs. Howes, was in command of the *Valparaiso* for two voyages, leaving her to take the ship *Jabez Howes*.

INDEX

INDEX

A CATALOG OF SELECTED
DOVER BOOKS
IN ALL FIELDS OF INTEREST

A CATALOG OF SELECTED DOVER
BOOKS IN ALL FIELDS OF INTEREST

DRAWINGS OF REMBRANDT, edited by Seymour Slive. Updated Lippmann, Hofstede de Groot edition, with definitive scholarly apparatus. All portraits, biblical sketches, landscapes, nudes. Oriental figures, classical studies, together with selection of work by followers. 550 illustrations. Total of 630pp. 9⅛ × 12¼.
21485-0, 21486-9 Pa., Two-vol. set $25.00

GHOST AND HORROR STORIES OF AMBROSE BIERCE, Ambrose Bierce. 24 tales vividly imagined, strangely prophetic, and decades ahead of their time in technical skill: "The Damned Thing," "An Inhabitant of Carcosa," "The Eyes of the Panther," "Moxon's Master," and 20 more. 199pp. 5⅜ × 8½. 20767-6 Pa. $3.95

ETHICAL WRITINGS OF MAIMONIDES, Maimonides. Most significant ethical works of great medieval sage, newly translated for utmost precision, readability. Laws Concerning Character Traits, Eight Chapters, more. 192pp. 5⅜ × 8½.
24522-5 Pa. $4.50

THE EXPLORATION OF THE COLORADO RIVER AND ITS CANYONS, J. W. Powell. Full text of Powell's 1,000-mile expedition down the fabled Colorado in 1869. Superb account of terrain, geology, vegetation, Indians, famine, mutiny, treacherous rapids, mighty canyons, during exploration of last unknown part of continental U.S. 400pp. 5⅜ × 8½. 20094-9 Pa. $6.95

HISTORY OF PHILOSOPHY, Julián Marías. Clearest one-volume history on the market. Every major philosopher and dozens of others, to Existentialism and later. 505pp. 5⅜ × 8½. 21739-6 Pa. $8.50

ALL ABOUT LIGHTNING, Martin A. Uman. Highly readable non-technical survey of nature and causes of lightning, thunderstorms, ball lightning, St. Elmo's Fire, much more. Illustrated. 192pp. 5⅜ × 8½. 25237-X Pa. $5.95

SAILING ALONE AROUND THE WORLD, Captain Joshua Slocum. First man to sail around the world, alone, in small boat. One of great feats of seamanship told in delightful manner. 67 illustrations. 294pp. 5⅜ × 8½. 20326-3 Pa. $4.50

LETTERS AND NOTES ON THE MANNERS, CUSTOMS AND CONDITIONS OF THE NORTH AMERICAN INDIANS, George Catlin. Classic account of life among Plains Indians: ceremonies, hunt, warfare, etc. 312 plates. 572pp. of text. 6⅛ × 9¼. 22118-0, 22119-9 Pa. Two-vol. set $15.90

ALASKA: The Harriman Expedition, 1899, John Burroughs, John Muir, et al. Informative, engrossing accounts of two-month, 9,000-mile expedition. Native peoples, wildlife, forests, geography, salmon industry, glaciers, more. Profusely illustrated. 240 black-and-white line drawings. 124 black-and-white photographs. 3 maps. Index. 576pp. 5⅜ × 8½. 25109-8 Pa. $11.95

THE BOOK OF BEASTS: Being a Translation from a Latin Bestiary of the Twelfth Century, T. H. White. Wonderful catalog real and fanciful beasts: manticore, griffin, phoenix, amphivius, jaculus, many more. White's witty erudite commentary on scientific, historical aspects. Fascinating glimpse of medieval mind. Illustrated. 296pp. 5⅜ × 8¼. (Available in U.S. only) 24609-4 Pa. $5.95

FRANK LLOYD WRIGHT: ARCHITECTURE AND NATURE With 160 Illustrations, Donald Hoffmann. Profusely illustrated study of influence of nature—especially prairie—on Wright's designs for Fallingwater, Robie House, Guggenheim Museum, other masterpieces. 96pp. 9¼ × 10¾. 25098-9 Pa. $7.95

FRANK LLOYD WRIGHT'S FALLINGWATER, Donald Hoffmann. Wright's famous waterfall house: planning and construction of organic idea. History of site, owners, Wright's personal involvement. Photographs of various stages of building. Preface by Edgar Kaufmann, Jr. 100 illustrations. 112pp. 9¼ × 10. 23671-4 Pa. $7.95

YEARS WITH FRANK LLOYD WRIGHT: Apprentice to Genius, Edgar Tafel. Insightful memoir by a former apprentice presents a revealing portrait of Wright the man, the inspired teacher, the greatest American architect. 372 black-and-white illustrations. Preface. Index. vi + 228pp. 8¼ × 11. 24801-1 Pa. $9.95

THE STORY OF KING ARTHUR AND HIS KNIGHTS, Howard Pyle. Enchanting version of King Arthur fable has delighted generations with imaginative narratives of exciting adventures and unforgettable illustrations by the author. 41 illustrations. xviii + 313pp. 6⅛ × 9¼. 21445-1 Pa. $5.95

THE GODS OF THE EGYPTIANS, E. A. Wallis Budge. Thorough coverage of numerous gods of ancient Egypt by foremost Egyptologist. Information on evolution of cults, rites and gods; the cult of Osiris; the Book of the Dead and its rites; the sacred animals and birds; Heaven and Hell; and more. 956pp. 6⅛ × 9¼. 22055-9, 22056-7 Pa., Two-vol. set $20.00

A THEOLOGICO-POLITICAL TREATISE, Benedict Spinoza. Also contains unfinished *Political Treatise*. Great classic on religious liberty, theory of government on common consent. R. Elwes translation. Total of 421pp. 5⅜ × 8½. 20249-6 Pa. $6.95

INCIDENTS OF TRAVEL IN CENTRAL AMERICA, CHIAPAS, AND YUCATAN, John L. Stephens. Almost single-handed discovery of Maya culture; exploration of ruined cities, monuments, temples; customs of Indians. 115 drawings. 892pp. 5⅜ × 8½. 22404-X, 22405-8 Pa., Two-vol. set $15.90

LOS CAPRICHOS, Francisco Goya. 80 plates of wild, grotesque monsters and caricatures. Prado manuscript included. 183pp. 6⅜ × 9⅜. 22384-1 Pa. $4.95

AUTOBIOGRAPHY: The Story of My Experiments with Truth, Mohandas K. Gandhi. Not hagiography, but Gandhi in his own words. Boyhood, legal studies, purification, the growth of the Satyagraha (nonviolent protest) movement. Critical, inspiring work of the man who freed India. 480pp. 5⅜ × 8½. (Available in U.S. only) 24593-4 Pa. $6.95

ILLUSTRATED DICTIONARY OF HISTORIC ARCHITECTURE, edited by Cyril M. Harris. Extraordinary compendium of clear, concise definitions for over 5,000 important architectural terms complemented by over 2,000 line drawings. Covers full spectrum of architecture from ancient ruins to 20th-century Modernism. Preface. 592pp. 7½ × 9⅝. 24444-X Pa. $14.95

THE NIGHT BEFORE CHRISTMAS, Clement Moore. Full text, and woodcuts from original 1848 book. Also critical, historical material. 19 illustrations. 40pp. 4⅝ × 6. 22797-9 Pa. $2.25

THE LESSON OF JAPANESE ARCHITECTURE: 165 Photographs, Jiro Harada. Memorable gallery of 165 photographs taken in the 1930's of exquisite Japanese homes of the well-to-do and historic buildings. 13 line diagrams. 192pp. 8⅝ × 11¼. 24778-3 Pa. $8.95

THE AUTOBIOGRAPHY OF CHARLES DARWIN AND SELECTED LETTERS, edited by Francis Darwin. The fascinating life of eccentric genius composed of an intimate memoir by Darwin (intended for his children); commentary by his son, Francis; hundreds of fragments from notebooks, journals, papers; and letters to and from Lyell, Hooker, Huxley, Wallace and Henslow. xi + 365pp. 5⅜ × 8. 20479-0 Pa. $5.95

WONDERS OF THE SKY: Observing Rainbows, Comets, Eclipses, the Stars and Other Phenomena, Fred Schaaf. Charming, easy-to-read poetic guide to all manner of celestial events visible to the naked eye. Mock suns, glories, Belt of Venus, more. Illustrated. 299pp. 5¼ × 8¼. 24402-4 Pa. $7.95

BURNHAM'S CELESTIAL HANDBOOK, Robert Burnham, Jr. Thorough guide to the stars beyond our solar system. Exhaustive treatment. Alphabetical by constellation: Andromeda to Cetus in Vol. 1; Chamaeleon to Orion in Vol. 2; and Pavo to Vulpecula in Vol. 3. Hundreds of illustrations. Index in Vol. 3. 2,000pp. 6⅛ × 9¼. 23567-X, 23568-8, 23673-0 Pa., Three-vol. set $36.85

STAR NAMES: Their Lore and Meaning, Richard Hinckley Allen. Fascinating history of names various cultures have given to constellations and literary and folkloristic uses that have been made of stars. Indexes to subjects. Arabic and Greek names. Biblical references. Bibliography. 563pp. 5⅜ × 8½. 21079-0 Pa. $7.95

THIRTY YEARS THAT SHOOK PHYSICS: The Story of Quantum Theory, George Gamow. Lucid, accessible introduction to influential theory of energy and matter. Careful explanations of Dirac's anti-particles, Bohr's model of the atom, much more. 12 plates. Numerous drawings. 240pp. 5⅜ × 8½. 24895-X Pa. $4.95

CHINESE DOMESTIC FURNITURE IN PHOTOGRAPHS AND MEASURED DRAWINGS, Gustav Ecke. A rare volume, now affordably priced for antique collectors, furniture buffs and art historians. Detailed review of styles ranging from early Shang to late Ming. Unabridged republication. 161 black-and-white drawings, photos. Total of 224pp. 8⅜ × 11¼. (Available in U.S. only) 25171-3 Pa. $12.95

VINCENT VAN GOGH: A Biography, Julius Meier-Graefe. Dynamic, penetrating study of artist's life, relationship with brother, Theo, painting techniques, travels, more. Readable, engrossing. 160pp. 5⅜ × 8½. (Available in U.S. only) 25253-1 Pa. $3.95

HOW TO WRITE, Gertrude Stein. Gertrude Stein claimed anyone could understand her unconventional writing—here are clues to help. Fascinating improvisations, language experiments, explanations illuminate Stein's craft and the art of writing. Total of 414pp. 4⅜ × 6⅜. 23144-5 Pa. $5.95

ADVENTURES AT SEA IN THE GREAT AGE OF SAIL: Five Firsthand Narratives, edited by Elliot Snow. Rare true accounts of exploration, whaling, shipwreck, fierce natives, trade, shipboard life, more. 33 illustrations. Introduction. 353pp. 5⅜ × 8½. 25177-2 Pa. $7.95

THE HERBAL OR GENERAL HISTORY OF PLANTS, John Gerard. Classic descriptions of about 2,850 plants—with over 2,700 illustrations—includes Latin and English names, physical descriptions, varieties, time and place of growth, more. 2,706 illustrations. xlv + 1,678pp. 8½ × 12¼. 23147-X Cloth. $75.00

DOROTHY AND THE WIZARD IN OZ, L. Frank Baum. Dorothy and the Wizard visit the center of the Earth, where people are vegetables, glass houses grow and Oz characters reappear. Classic sequel to *Wizard of Oz*. 256pp. 5⅜ × 8. 24714-7 Pa. $4.95

SONGS OF EXPERIENCE: Facsimile Reproduction with 26 Plates in Full Color, William Blake. This facsimile of Blake's original "Illuminated Book" reproduces 26 full-color plates from a rare 1826 edition. Includes "The Tyger," "London," "Holy Thursday," and other immortal poems. 26 color plates. Printed text of poems. 48pp. 5¼ × 7. 24636-1 Pa. $3.50

SONGS OF INNOCENCE, William Blake. The first and most popular of Blake's famous "Illuminated Books," in a facsimile edition reproducing all 31 brightly colored plates. Additional printed text of each poem. 64pp. 5¼ × 7. 22764-2 Pa. $3.50

PRECIOUS STONES, Max Bauer. Classic, thorough study of diamonds, rubies, emeralds, garnets, etc.: physical character, occurrence, properties, use, similar topics. 20 plates, 8 in color. 94 figures. 659pp. 6⅛ × 9¼. 21910-0, 21911-9 Pa., Two-vol. set $14.90

ENCYCLOPEDIA OF VICTORIAN NEEDLEWORK, S. F. A. Caulfeild and Blanche Saward. Full, precise descriptions of stitches, techniques for dozens of needlecrafts—most exhaustive reference of its kind. Over 800 figures. Total of 679pp. 8⅛ × 11. Two volumes. Vol. 1 22800-2 Pa. $10.95
Vol. 2 22801-0 Pa. $10.95

THE MARVELOUS LAND OF OZ, L. Frank Baum. Second Oz book, the Scarecrow and Tin Woodman are back with hero named Tip, Oz magic. 136 illustrations. 287pp. 5⅜ × 8½. 20692-0 Pa. $5.95

WILD FOWL DECOYS, Joel Barber. Basic book on the subject, by foremost authority and collector. Reveals history of decoy making and rigging, place in American culture, different kinds of decoys, how to make them, and how to use them. 140 plates. 156pp. 7⅞ × 10¾. 20011-6 Pa. $7.95

HISTORY OF LACE, Mrs. Bury Palliser. Definitive, profusely illustrated chronicle of lace from earliest times to late 19th century. Laces of Italy, Greece, England, France, Belgium, etc. Landmark of needlework scholarship. 266 illustrations. 672pp. 6⅛ × 9¼. 24742-2 Pa. $14.95

ILLUSTRATED GUIDE TO SHAKER FURNITURE, Robert Meader. All furniture and appurtenances, with much on unknown local styles. 235 photos. 146pp. 9 × 12. 22819-3 Pa. $7.95

WHALE SHIPS AND WHALING: A Pictorial Survey, George Francis Dow. Over 200 vintage engravings, drawings, photographs of barks, brigs, cutters, other vessels. Also harpoons, lances, whaling guns, many other artifacts. Comprehensive text by foremost authority. 207 black-and-white illustrations. 288pp. 6 × 9.
24808-9 Pa. $8.95

THE BERTRAMS, Anthony Trollope. Powerful portrayal of blind self-will and thwarted ambition includes one of Trollope's most heartrending love stories. 497pp. 5⅜ × 8½. 25119-5 Pa. $8.95

ADVENTURES WITH A HAND LENS, Richard Headstrom. Clearly written guide to observing and studying flowers and grasses, fish scales, moth and insect wings, egg cases, buds, feathers, seeds, leaf scars, moss, molds, ferns, common crystals, etc.—all with an ordinary, inexpensive magnifying glass. 209 exact line drawings aid in your discoveries. 220pp. 5⅜ × 8½. 23330-8 Pa. $3.95

RODIN ON ART AND ARTISTS, Auguste Rodin. Great sculptor's candid, wide-ranging comments on meaning of art; great artists; relation of sculpture to poetry, painting, music; philosophy of life, more. 76 superb black-and-white illustrations of Rodin's sculpture, drawings and prints. 119pp. 8⅜ × 11¼. 24487-3 Pa. $6.95

FIFTY CLASSIC FRENCH FILMS, 1912–1982: A Pictorial Record, Anthony Slide. Memorable stills from Grand Illusion, Beauty and the Beast, Hiroshima, Mon Amour, many more. Credits, plot synopses, reviews, etc. 160pp. 8¼ × 11.
25256-6 Pa. $11.95

THE PRINCIPLES OF PSYCHOLOGY, William James. Famous long course complete, unabridged. Stream of thought, time perception, memory, experimental methods; great work decades ahead of its time. 94 figures. 1,391pp. 5⅜ × 8½.
20381-6, 20382-4 Pa., Two-vol. set $19.90

BODIES IN A BOOKSHOP, R. T. Campbell. Challenging mystery of blackmail and murder with ingenious plot and superbly drawn characters. In the best tradition of British suspense fiction. 192pp. 5⅜ × 8½. 24720-1 Pa. $3.95

CALLAS: PORTRAIT OF A PRIMA DONNA, George Jellinek. Renowned commentator on the musical scene chronicles incredible career and life of the most controversial, fascinating, influential operatic personality of our time. 64 black-and-white photographs. 416pp. 5⅜ × 8¼. 25047-4 Pa. $7.95

GEOMETRY, RELATIVITY AND THE FOURTH DIMENSION, Rudolph Rucker. Exposition of fourth dimension, concepts of relativity as Flatland characters continue adventures. Popular, easily followed yet accurate, profound. 141 illustrations. 133pp. 5⅜ × 8½. 23400-2 Pa. $3.50

HOUSEHOLD STORIES BY THE BROTHERS GRIMM, with pictures by Walter Crane. 53 classic stories—Rumpelstiltskin, Rapunzel, Hansel and Gretel, the Fisherman and his Wife, Snow White, Tom Thumb, Sleeping Beauty, Cinderella, and so much more—lavishly illustrated with original 19th century drawings. 114 illustrations. x + 269pp. 5⅜ × 8½. 21080-4 Pa. $4.50

SUNDIALS, Albert Waugh. Far and away the best, most thorough coverage of ideas, mathematics concerned, types, construction, adjusting anywhere. Over 100 illustrations. 230pp. 5⅜ × 8½. 22947-5 Pa. $4.00

PICTURE HISTORY OF THE NORMANDIE: With 190 Illustrations, Frank O. Braynard. Full story of legendary French ocean liner: Art Deco interiors, design innovations, furnishings, celebrities, maiden voyage, tragic fire, much more. Extensive text. 144pp. 8⅞ × 11¼. 25257-4 Pa. $9.95

THE FIRST AMERICAN COOKBOOK: A Facsimile of "American Cookery," 1796, Amelia Simmons. Facsimile of the first American-written cookbook published in the United States contains authentic recipes for colonial favorites— pumpkin pudding, winter squash pudding, spruce beer, Indian slapjacks, and more. Introductory Essay and Glossary of colonial cooking terms. 80pp. 5⅜ × 8½. 24710-4 Pa. $3.50

101 PUZZLES IN THOUGHT AND LOGIC, C. R. Wylie, Jr. Solve murders and robberies, find out which fishermen are liars, how a blind man could possibly identify a color—purely by your own reasoning! 107pp. 5⅜ × 8½. 20367-0 Pa. $2.00

THE BOOK OF WORLD-FAMOUS MUSIC—CLASSICAL, POPULAR AND FOLK, James J. Fuld. Revised and enlarged republication of landmark work in musico-bibliography. Full information about nearly 1,000 songs and compositions including first lines of music and lyrics. New supplement. Index. 800pp. 5⅜ × 8¼. 24857-7 Pa. $14.95

ANTHROPOLOGY AND MODERN LIFE, Franz Boas. Great anthropologist's classic treatise on race and culture. Introduction by Ruth Bunzel. Only inexpensive paperback edition. 255pp. 5⅜ × 8½. 25245-0 Pa. $5.95

THE TALE OF PETER RABBIT, Beatrix Potter. The inimitable Peter's terrifying adventure in Mr. McGregor's garden, with all 27 wonderful, full-color Potter illustrations. 55pp. 4¼ × 5½. (Available in U.S. only) 22827-4 Pa. $1.75

THREE PROPHETIC SCIENCE FICTION NOVELS, H. G. Wells. *When the Sleeper Wakes, A Story of the Days to Come* and *The Time Machine* (full version). 335pp. 5⅜ × 8½. (Available in U.S. only) 20605-X Pa. $5.95

APICIUS COOKERY AND DINING IN IMPERIAL ROME, edited and translated by Joseph Dommers Vehling. Oldest known cookbook in existence offers readers a clear picture of what foods Romans ate, how they prepared them, etc. 49 illustrations. 301pp. 6⅛ × 9¼. 23563-7 Pa. $6.00

SHAKESPEARE LEXICON AND QUOTATION DICTIONARY, Alexander Schmidt. Full definitions, locations, shades of meaning of every word in plays and poems. More than 50,000 exact quotations. 1,485pp. 6½ × 9¼. 22726-X, 22727-8 Pa., Two-vol. set $27.90

THE WORLD'S GREAT SPEECHES, edited by Lewis Copeland and Lawrence W. Lamm. Vast collection of 278 speeches from Greeks to 1970. Powerful and effective models; unique look at history. 842pp. 5⅜ × 8½. 20468-5 Pa. $10.95

THE BLUE FAIRY BOOK, Andrew Lang. The first, most famous collection, with many familiar tales: Little Red Riding Hood, Aladdin and the Wonderful Lamp, Puss in Boots, Sleeping Beauty, Hansel and Gretel, Rumpelstiltskin; 37 in all. 138 illustrations. 390pp. 5⅜ × 8½.   21437-0 Pa. $5.95

THE STORY OF THE CHAMPIONS OF THE ROUND TABLE, Howard Pyle. Sir Launcelot, Sir Tristram and Sir Percival in spirited adventures of love and triumph retold in Pyle's inimitable style. 50 drawings, 31 full-page. xviii + 329pp. 6½ × 9¼.   21883-X Pa. $6.95

AUDUBON AND HIS JOURNALS, Maria Audubon. Unmatched two-volume portrait of the great artist, naturalist and author contains his journals, an excellent biography by his granddaughter, expert annotations by the noted ornithologist, Dr. Elliott Coues, and 37 superb illustrations. Total of 1,200pp. 5⅜ × 8.
Vol. I 25143-8 Pa. $8.95
Vol. II 25144-6 Pa. $8.95

GREAT DINOSAUR HUNTERS AND THEIR DISCOVERIES, Edwin H. Colbert. Fascinating, lavishly illustrated chronicle of dinosaur research, 1820's to 1960. Achievements of Cope, Marsh, Brown, Buckland, Mantell, Huxley, many others. 384pp. 5¼ × 8¼.   24701-5 Pa. $6.95

THE TASTEMAKERS, Russell Lynes. Informal, illustrated social history of American taste 1850's-1950's. First popularized categories Highbrow, Lowbrow, Middlebrow. 129 illustrations. New (1979) afterword. 384pp. 6 × 9.
23993-4 Pa. $6.95

DOUBLE CROSS PURPOSES, Ronald A. Knox. A treasure hunt in the Scottish Highlands, an old map, unidentified corpse, surprise discoveries keep reader guessing in this cleverly intricate tale of financial skullduggery. 2 black-and-white maps. 320pp. 5⅜ × 8½. (Available in U.S. only)   25032-6 Pa. $5.95

AUTHENTIC VICTORIAN DECORATION AND ORNAMENTATION IN FULL COLOR: 46 Plates from "Studies in Design," Christopher Dresser. Superb full-color lithographs reproduced from rare original portfolio of a major Victorian designer. 48pp. 9¼ × 12¼.   25083-0 Pa. $7.95

PRIMITIVE ART, Franz Boas. Remains the best text ever prepared on subject, thoroughly discussing Indian, African, Asian, Australian, and, especially, Northern American primitive art. Over 950 illustrations show ceramics, masks, totem poles, weapons, textiles, paintings, much more. 376pp. 5⅜ × 8.   20025-6 Pa. $6.95

SIDELIGHTS ON RELATIVITY, Albert Einstein. Unabridged republication of two lectures delivered by the great physicist in 1920-21. *Ether and Relativity* and *Geometry and Experience*. Elegant ideas in non-mathematical form, accessible to intelligent layman. vi + 56pp. 5⅜ × 8½.   24511-X Pa. $2.95

THE WIT AND HUMOR OF OSCAR WILDE, edited by Alvin Redman. More than 1,000 ripostes, paradoxes, wisecracks: Work is the curse of the drinking classes, I can resist everything except temptation, etc. 258pp. 5⅜ × 8½.   20602-5 Pa. $3.95

ADVENTURES WITH A MICROSCOPE, Richard Headstrom. 59 adventures with clothing fibers, protozoa, ferns and lichens, roots and leaves, much more. 142 illustrations. 232pp. 5⅜ × 8½.   23471-1 Pa. $3.95

PLANTS OF THE BIBLE, Harold N. Moldenke and Alma L. Moldenke. Standard reference to all 230 plants mentioned in Scriptures. Latin name, biblical reference, uses, modern identity, much more. Unsurpassed encyclopedic resource for scholars, botanists, nature lovers, students of Bible. Bibliography. Indexes. 123 black-and-white illustrations. 384pp. 6 × 9. 25069-5 Pa. $8.95

FAMOUS AMERICAN WOMEN: A Biographical Dictionary from Colonial Times to the Present, Robert McHenry, ed. From Pocahontas to Rosa Parks, 1,035 distinguished American women documented in separate biographical entries. Accurate, up-to-date data, numerous categories, spans 400 years. Indices. 493pp. 6½ × 9¼. 24523-3 Pa. $9.95

THE FABULOUS INTERIORS OF THE GREAT OCEAN LINERS IN HISTORIC PHOTOGRAPHS, William H. Miller, Jr. Some 200 superb photographs capture exquisite interiors of world's great "floating palaces"—1890's to 1980's: *Titanic, Ile de France, Queen Elizabeth, United States, Europa,* more. Approx. 200 black-and-white photographs. Captions. Text. Introduction. 160pp. 8⅞ × 11¾. 24756-2 Pa. $9.95

THE GREAT LUXURY LINERS, 1927–1954: A Photographic Record, William H. Miller, Jr. Nostalgic tribute to heyday of ocean liners. 186 photos of Ile de France, Normandie, Leviathan, Queen Elizabeth, United States, many others. Interior and exterior views. Introduction. Captions. 160pp. 9 × 12. 24056-8 Pa. $9.95

A NATURAL HISTORY OF THE DUCKS, John Charles Phillips. Great landmark of ornithology offers complete detailed coverage of nearly 200 species and subspecies of ducks: gadwall, sheldrake, merganser, pintail, many more. 74 full-color plates, 102 black-and-white. Bibliography. Total of 1,920pp. 8⅝ × 11¼. 25141-1, 25142-X Cloth. Two-vol. set $100.00

THE SEAWEED HANDBOOK: An Illustrated Guide to Seaweeds from North Carolina to Canada, Thomas F. Lee. Concise reference covers 78 species. Scientific and common names, habitat, distribution, more. Finding keys for easy identification. 224pp. 5⅜ × 8½. 25215-9 Pa. $5.95

THE TEN BOOKS OF ARCHITECTURE: The 1755 Leoni Edition, Leon Battista Alberti. Rare classic helped introduce the glories of ancient architecture to the Renaissance. 68 black-and-white plates. 336pp. 8⅜ × 11¼. 25239-6 Pa. $14.95

MISS MACKENZIE, Anthony Trollope. Minor masterpieces by Victorian master unmasks many truths about life in 19th-century England. First inexpensive edition in years. 392pp. 5⅜ × 8½. 25201-9 Pa. $7.95

THE RIME OF THE ANCIENT MARINER, Gustave Doré, Samuel Taylor Coleridge. Dramatic engravings considered by many to be his greatest work. The terrifying space of the open sea, the storms and whirlpools of an unknown ocean, the ice of Antarctica, more—all rendered in a powerful, chilling manner. Full text. 38 plates. 77pp. 9¼ × 12. 22305-1 Pa. $4.95

THE EXPEDITIONS OF ZEBULON MONTGOMERY PIKE, Zebulon Montgomery Pike. Fascinating first-hand accounts (1805–6) of exploration of Mississippi River, Indian wars, capture by Spanish dragoons, much more. 1,088pp. 5⅜ × 8½. 25254-X, 25255-8 Pa. Two-vol. set $23.90

A CONCISE HISTORY OF PHOTOGRAPHY: Third Revised Edition, Helmut Gernsheim. Best one-volume history—camera obscura, photochemistry, daguerreotypes, evolution of cameras, film, more. Also artistic aspects—landscape, portraits, fine art, etc. 281 black-and-white photographs. 26 in color. 176pp. 8⅜ × 11¼. 25128-4 Pa. $12.95

THE DORÉ BIBLE ILLUSTRATIONS, Gustave Doré. 241 detailed plates from the Bible: the Creation scenes, Adam and Eve, Flood, Babylon, battle sequences, life of Jesus, etc. Each plate is accompanied by the verses from the King James version of the Bible. 241pp. 9 × 12. 23004-X Pa. $8.95

HUGGER-MUGGER IN THE LOUVRE, Elliot Paul. Second Homer Evans mystery-comedy. Theft at the Louvre involves sleuth in hilarious, madcap caper. "A knockout."—Books. 336pp. 5⅜ × 8½. 25185-3 Pa. $5.95

FLATLAND, E. A. Abbott. Intriguing and enormously popular science-fiction classic explores the complexities of trying to survive as a two-dimensional being in a three-dimensional world. Amusingly illustrated by the author. 16 illustrations. 103pp. 5⅜ × 8½. 20001-9 Pa. $2.00

THE HISTORY OF THE LEWIS AND CLARK EXPEDITION, Meriwether Lewis and William Clark, edited by Elliott Coues. Classic edition of Lewis and Clark's day-by-day journals that later became the basis for U.S. claims to Oregon and the West. Accurate and invaluable geographical, botanical, biological, meteorological and anthropological material. Total of 1,508pp. 5⅜ × 8½.
21268-8, 21269-6, 21270-X Pa. Three-vol. set $25.50

LANGUAGE, TRUTH AND LOGIC, Alfred J. Ayer. Famous, clear introduction to Vienna, Cambridge schools of Logical Positivism. Role of philosophy, elimination of metaphysics, nature of analysis, etc. 160pp. 5⅜ × 8½. (Available in U.S. and Canada only) 20010-8 Pa. $2.95

MATHEMATICS FOR THE NONMATHEMATICIAN, Morris Kline. Detailed, college-level treatment of mathematics in cultural and historical context, with numerous exercises. For liberal arts students. Preface. Recommended Reading Lists. Tables. Index. Numerous black-and-white figures. xvi + 641pp. 5⅜ × 8½.
24823-2 Pa. $11.95

28 SCIENCE FICTION STORIES, H. G. Wells. Novels, *Star Begotten* and *Men Like Gods*, plus 26 short stories: "Empire of the Ants," "A Story of the Stone Age," "The Stolen Bacillus," "In the Abyss," etc. 915pp. 5⅜ × 8½. (Available in U.S. only)
20265-8 Cloth. $10.95

HANDBOOK OF PICTORIAL SYMBOLS, Rudolph Modley. 3,250 signs and symbols, many systems in full; official or heavy commercial use. Arranged by subject. Most in Pictorial Archive series. 143pp. 8⅜ × 11. 23357-X Pa. $5.95

INCIDENTS OF TRAVEL IN YUCATAN, John L. Stephens. Classic (1843) exploration of jungles of Yucatan, looking for evidences of Maya civilization. Travel adventures, Mexican and Indian culture, etc. Total of 669pp. 5⅜ × 8½.
20926-1, 20927-X Pa., Two-vol. set $9.90

CATALOG OF DOVER BOOKS

DEGAS: An Intimate Portrait, Ambroise Vollard. Charming, anecdotal memoir by famous art dealer of one of the greatest 19th-century French painters. 14 black-and-white illustrations. Introduction by Harold L. Van Doren. 96pp. 5⅜ × 8½.
25131-4 Pa. $3.95

PERSONAL NARRATIVE OF A PILGRIMAGE TO ALMANDINAH AND MECCAH, Richard Burton. Great travel classic by remarkably colorful personality. Burton, disguised as a Moroccan, visited sacred shrines of Islam, narrowly escaping death. 47 illustrations. 959pp. 5⅜ × 8½. 21217-3, 21218-1 Pa., Two-vol. set $17.90

PHRASE AND WORD ORIGINS, A. H. Holt. Entertaining, reliable, modern study of more than 1,200 colorful words, phrases, origins and histories. Much unexpected information. 254pp. 5⅜ × 8½. 20758-7 Pa. $4.95

THE RED THUMB MARK, R. Austin Freeman. In this first Dr. Thorndyke case, the great scientific detective draws fascinating conclusions from the nature of a single fingerprint. Exciting story, authentic science. 320pp. 5⅜ × 8½. (Available in U.S. only) 25210-8 Pa. $5.95

AN EGYPTIAN HIEROGLYPHIC DICTIONARY, E. A. Wallis Budge. Monumental work containing about 25,000 words or terms that occur in texts ranging from 3000 B.C. to 600 A.D. Each entry consists of a transliteration of the word, the word in hieroglyphs, and the meaning in English. 1,314pp. 6⅜ × 10.
23615-3, 23616-1 Pa., Two-vol. set $27.90

THE COMPLEAT STRATEGYST: Being a Primer on the Theory of Games of Strategy, J. D. Williams. Highly entertaining classic describes, with many illustrated examples, how to select best strategies in conflict situations. Prefaces. Appendices. xvi + 268pp. 5⅜ × 8½. 25101-2 Pa. $5.95

THE ROAD TO OZ, L. Frank Baum. Dorothy meets the Shaggy Man, little Button-Bright and the Rainbow's beautiful daughter in this delightful trip to the magical Land of Oz. 272pp. 5⅜ × 8. 25208-6 Pa. $4.95

POINT AND LINE TO PLANE, Wassily Kandinsky. Seminal exposition of role of point, line, other elements in non-objective painting. Essential to understanding 20th-century art. 127 illustrations. 192pp. 6½ × 9¼. 23808-3 Pa. $4.50

LADY ANNA, Anthony Trollope. Moving chronicle of Countess Lovel's bitter struggle to win for herself and daughter Anna their rightful rank and fortune—perhaps at cost of sanity itself. 384pp. 5⅜ × 8½. 24669-8 Pa. $6.95

EGYPTIAN MAGIC, E. A. Wallis Budge. Sums up all that is known about magic in Ancient Egypt: the role of magic in controlling the gods, powerful amulets that warded off evil spirits, scarabs of immortality, use of wax images, formulas and spells, the secret name, much more. 253pp. 5⅜ × 8½. 22681-6 Pa. $4.00

THE DANCE OF SIVA, Ananda Coomaraswamy. Preeminent authority unfolds the vast metaphysic of India: the revelation of her art, conception of the universe, social organization, etc. 27 reproductions of art masterpieces. 192pp. 5⅜ × 8½.
24817-8 Pa. $5.95

CHRISTMAS CUSTOMS AND TRADITIONS, Clement A. Miles. Origin, evolution, significance of religious, secular practices. Caroling, gifts, yule logs, much more. Full, scholarly yet fascinating; non-sectarian. 400pp. 5⅜ × 8½.
23354-5 Pa. $6.50

THE HUMAN FIGURE IN MOTION, Eadweard Muybridge. More than 4,500 stopped-action photos, in action series, showing undraped men, women, children jumping, lying down, throwing, sitting, wrestling, carrying, etc. 390pp. 7⅞ × 10⅝.
20204-6 Cloth. $19.95

THE MAN WHO WAS THURSDAY, Gilbert Keith Chesterton. Witty, fast-paced novel about a club of anarchists in turn-of-the-century London. Brilliant social, religious, philosophical speculations. 128pp. 5⅜ × 8½.
25121-7 Pa. $3.95

A CEZANNE SKETCHBOOK: Figures, Portraits, Landscapes and Still Lifes, Paul Cezanne. Great artist experiments with tonal effects, light, mass, other qualities in over 100 drawings. A revealing view of developing master painter, precursor of Cubism. 102 black-and-white illustrations. 144pp. 8¾ × 6⅜.
24790-2 Pa. $5.95

AN ENCYCLOPEDIA OF BATTLES: Accounts of Over 1,560 Battles from 1479 B.C. to the Present, David Eggenberger. Presents essential details of every major battle in recorded history, from the first battle of Megiddo in 1479 B.C. to Grenada in 1984. List of Battle Maps. New Appendix covering the years 1967–1984. Index. 99 illustrations. 544pp. 6½ × 9¼.
24913-1 Pa. $14.95

AN ETYMOLOGICAL DICTIONARY OF MODERN ENGLISH, Ernest Weekley. Richest, fullest work, by foremost British lexicographer. Detailed word histories. Inexhaustible. Total of 856pp. 6½ × 9¼.
21873-2, 21874-0 Pa., Two-vol. set $17.00

WEBSTER'S AMERICAN MILITARY BIOGRAPHIES, edited by Robert McHenry. Over 1,000 figures who shaped 3 centuries of American military history. Detailed biographies of Nathan Hale, Douglas MacArthur, Mary Hallaren, others. Chronologies of engagements, more. Introduction. Addenda. 1,033 entries in alphabetical order. xi + 548pp. 6½ × 9¼. (Available in U.S. only)
24758-9 Pa. $11.95

LIFE IN ANCIENT EGYPT, Adolf Erman. Detailed older account, with much not in more recent books: domestic life, religion, magic, medicine, commerce, and whatever else needed for complete picture. Many illustrations. 597pp. 5⅜ × 8½.
22632-8 Pa. $8.50

HISTORIC COSTUME IN PICTURES, Braun & Schneider. Over 1,450 costumed figures shown, covering a wide variety of peoples: kings, emperors, nobles, priests, servants, soldiers, scholars, townsfolk, peasants, merchants, courtiers, cavaliers, and more. 256pp. 8⅜ × 11¼.
23150-X Pa. $7.95

THE NOTEBOOKS OF LEONARDO DA VINCI, edited by J. P. Richter. Extracts from manuscripts reveal great genius; on painting, sculpture, anatomy, sciences, geography, etc. Both Italian and English. 186 ms. pages reproduced, plus 500 additional drawings, including studies for Last Supper, Sforza monument, etc. 860pp. 7⅞ × 10¾. (Available in U.S. only) 22572-0, 22573-9 Pa., Two-vol. set $25.90

THE ART NOUVEAU STYLE BOOK OF ALPHONSE MUCHA: All 72 Plates from "Documents Decoratifs" in Original Color, Alphonse Mucha. Rare copyright-free design portfolio by high priest of Art Nouveau. Jewelry, wallpaper, stained glass, furniture, figure studies, plant and animal motifs, etc. Only complete one-volume edition. 80pp. 9⅜ × 12¼.   24044-4 Pa. $8.95

ANIMALS: 1,419 COPYRIGHT-FREE ILLUSTRATIONS OF MAMMALS, BIRDS, FISH, INSECTS, ETC., edited by Jim Harter. Clear wood engravings present, in extremely lifelike poses, over 1,000 species of animals. One of the most extensive pictorial sourcebooks of its kind. Captions. Index. 284pp. 9 × 12.
23766-4 Pa. $9.95

OBELISTS FLY HIGH, C. Daly King. Masterpiece of American detective fiction, long out of print, involves murder on a 1935 transcontinental flight—"a very thrilling story"—NY Times. Unabridged and unaltered republication of the edition published by William Collins Sons & Co. Ltd., London, 1935. 288pp. 5⅜ × 8½. (Available in U.S. only)   25036-9 Pa. $4.95

VICTORIAN AND EDWARDIAN FASHION: A Photographic Survey, Alison Gernsheim. First fashion history completely illustrated by contemporary photographs. Full text plus 235 photos, 1840–1914, in which many celebrities appear. 240pp. 6½ × 9¼.   24205-6 Pa. $6.00

THE ART OF THE FRENCH ILLUSTRATED BOOK, 1700–1914, Gordon N. Ray. Over 630 superb book illustrations by Fragonard, Delacroix, Daumier, Doré, Grandville, Manet, Mucha, Steinlen, Toulouse-Lautrec and many others. Preface. Introduction. 633 halftones. Indices of artists, authors & titles, binders and provenances. Appendices. Bibliography. 608pp. 8⅜ × 11¼.   25086-5 Pa. $24.95

THE WONDERFUL WIZARD OF OZ, L. Frank Baum. Facsimile in full color of America's finest children's classic. 143 illustrations by W. W. Denslow. 267pp. 5⅜ × 8½.   20691-2 Pa. $5.95

FRONTIERS OF MODERN PHYSICS: New Perspectives on Cosmology, Relativity, Black Holes and Extraterrestrial Intelligence, Tony Rothman, et al. For the intelligent layman. Subjects include: cosmological models of the universe; black holes; the neutrino; the search for extraterrestrial intelligence. Introduction. 46 black-and-white illustrations. 192pp. 5⅜ × 8½.   24587-X Pa. $6.95

THE FRIENDLY STARS, Martha Evans Martin & Donald Howard Menzel. Classic text marshalls the stars together in an engaging, non-technical survey, presenting them as sources of beauty in night sky. 23 illustrations. Foreword. 2 star charts. Index. 147pp. 5⅜ × 8½.   21099-5 Pa. $3.50

FADS AND FALLACIES IN THE NAME OF SCIENCE, Martin Gardner. Fair, witty appraisal of cranks, quacks, and quackeries of science and pseudoscience: hollow earth, Velikovsky, orgone energy, Dianetics, flying saucers, Bridey Murphy, food and medical fads, etc. Revised, expanded In the Name of Science. "A very able and even-tempered presentation."—The New Yorker. 363pp. 5⅜ × 8.
20394-8 Pa. $5.95

ANCIENT EGYPT: ITS CULTURE AND HISTORY, J. E Manchip White. From pre-dynastics through Ptolemies: society, history, political structure, religion, daily life, literature, cultural heritage. 48 plates. 217pp. 5⅜ × 8½.   22548-8 Pa. $4.95

SIR HARRY HOTSPUR OF HUMBLETHWAITE, Anthony Trollope. Incisive, unconventional psychological study of a conflict between a wealthy baronet, his idealistic daughter, and their scapegrace cousin. The 1870 novel in its first inexpensive edition in years. 250pp. 5⅜ × 8½.　　　　24953-0 Pa. $4.95

LASERS AND HOLOGRAPHY, Winston E. Kock. Sound introduction to burgeoning field, expanded (1981) for second edition. Wave patterns, coherence, lasers, diffraction, zone plates, properties of holograms, recent advances. 84 illustrations. 160pp. 5⅜ × 8¼. (Except in United Kingdom)　　24041-X Pa. $3.50

INTRODUCTION TO ARTIFICIAL INTELLIGENCE: SECOND, EN-LARGED EDITION, Philip C. Jackson, Jr. Comprehensive survey of artificial intelligence—the study of how machines (computers) can be made to act intelligently. Includes introductory and advanced material. Extensive notes updating the main text. 132 black-and-white illustrations. 512pp. 5⅜ × 8½.　　24864-X Pa. $8.95

HISTORY OF INDIAN AND INDONESIAN ART, Ananda K. Coomaraswamy. Over 400 illustrations illuminate classic study of Indian art from earliest Harappa finds to early 20th century. Provides philosophical, religious and social insights. 304pp. 6⅜ × 9⅜.　　　　25005-9 Pa. $8.95

THE GOLEM, Gustav Meyrink. Most famous supernatural novel in modern European literature, set in Ghetto of Old Prague around 1890. Compelling story of mystical experiences, strange transformations, profound terror. 13 black-and-white illustrations. 224pp. 5⅜ × 8½. (Available in U.S. only)　　25025-3 Pa. $5.95

ARMADALE, Wilkie Collins. Third great mystery novel by the author of *The Woman in White* and *The Moonstone*. Original magazine version with 40 illustrations. 597pp. 5⅜ × 8½.　　　　23429-0 Pa. $7.95

PICTORIAL ENCYCLOPEDIA OF HISTORIC ARCHITECTURAL PLANS, DETAILS AND ELEMENTS: With 1,880 Line Drawings of Arches, Domes, Doorways, Facades, Gables, Windows, etc., John Theodore Haneman. Sourcebook of inspiration for architects, designers, others. Bibliography. Captions. 141pp. 9 × 12.　　　　24605-1 Pa. $6.95

BENCHLEY LOST AND FOUND, Robert Benchley. Finest humor from early 30's, about pet peeves, child psychologists, post office and others. Mostly unavailable elsewhere. 73 illustrations by Peter Arno and others. 183pp. 5⅜ × 8½.　　　　22410-4 Pa. $3.95

ERTÉ GRAPHICS, Erté. Collection of striking color graphics: *Seasons, Alphabet, Numerals, Aces* and *Precious Stones*. 50 plates, including 4 on covers. 48pp. 9⅜ × 12¼.　　　　23580-7 Pa. $6.95

THE JOURNAL OF HENRY D. THOREAU, edited by Bradford Torrey, F. H. Allen. Complete reprinting of 14 volumes, 1837–61, over two million words; the sourcebooks for *Walden*, etc. Definitive. All original sketches, plus 75 photographs. 1,804pp. 8½ × 12¼.　　20312-3, 20313-1 Cloth., Two-vol. set $80.00

CASTLES: THEIR CONSTRUCTION AND HISTORY, Sidney Toy. Traces castle development from ancient roots. Nearly 200 photographs and drawings illustrate moats, keeps, baileys, many other features. Caernarvon, Dover Castles, Hadrian's Wall, Tower of London, dozens more. 256pp. 5⅜ × 8¼.

24898-4 Pa. $5.95

AMERICAN CLIPPER SHIPS: 1833–1858, Octavius T. Howe & Frederick C. Matthews. Fully-illustrated, encyclopedic review of 352 clipper ships from the period of America's greatest maritime supremacy. Introduction. 109 halftones. 5 black-and-white line illustrations. Index. Total of 928pp. 5⅜ × 8½.
25115-2, 25116-0 Pa., Two-vol. set $17.90

TOWARDS A NEW ARCHITECTURE, Le Corbusier. Pioneering manifesto by great architect, near legendary founder of "International School." Technical and aesthetic theories, views on industry, economics, relation of form to function, "mass-production spirit," much more. Profusely illustrated. Unabridged translation of 13th French edition. Introduction by Frederick Etchells. 320pp. 6⅛ × 9¼. (Available in U.S. only)
25023-7 Pa. $8.95

THE BOOK OF KELLS, edited by Blanche Cirker. Inexpensive collection of 32 full-color, full-page plates from the greatest illuminated manuscript of the Middle Ages, painstakingly reproduced from rare facsimile edition. Publisher's Note. Captions. 32pp. 9⅜ × 12¼.
24345-1 Pa. $4.50

BEST SCIENCE FICTION STORIES OF H. G. WELLS, H. G. Wells. Full novel *The Invisible Man*, plus 17 short stories: "The Crystal Egg," "Aepyornis Island," "The Strange Orchid," etc. 303pp. 5⅜ × 8½. (Available in U.S. only)
21531-8 Pa. $4.95

AMERICAN SAILING SHIPS: Their Plans and History, Charles G. Davis. Photos, construction details of schooners, frigates, clippers, other sailcraft of 18th to early 20th centuries—plus entertaining discourse on design, rigging, nautical lore, much more. 137 black-and-white illustrations. 240pp. 6⅛ × 9¼.
24658-2 Pa. $5.95

ENTERTAINING MATHEMATICAL PUZZLES, Martin Gardner. Selection of author's favorite conundrums involving arithmetic, money, speed, etc., with lively commentary. Complete solutions. 112pp. 5⅜ × 8½.   25211-6 Pa. $2.95

THE WILL TO BELIEVE, HUMAN IMMORTALITY, William James. Two books bound together. Effect of irrational on logical, and arguments for human immortality. 402pp. 5⅜ × 8½.   20291-7 Pa. $7.50

THE HAUNTED MONASTERY and THE CHINESE MAZE MURDERS, Robert Van Gulik. 2 full novels by Van Gulik continue adventures of Judge Dee and his companions. An evil Taoist monastery, seemingly supernatural events; overgrown topiary maze that hides strange crimes. Set in 7th-century China. 27 illustrations. 328pp. 5⅜ × 8½.   23502-5 Pa. $5.00

CELEBRATED CASES OF JUDGE DEE (DEE GOONG AN), translated by Robert Van Gulik. Authentic 18th-century Chinese detective novel; Dee and associates solve three interlocked cases. Led to Van Gulik's own stories with same characters. Extensive introduction. 9 illustrations. 237pp. 5⅜ × 8½.
23337-5 Pa. $4.95

Prices subject to change without notice.
Available at your book dealer or write for free catalog to Dept. GI, Dover Publications, Inc., 31 East 2nd St., Mineola, N.Y. 11501. Dover publishes more than 175 books each year on science, elementary and advanced mathematics, biology, music, art, literary history, social sciences and other areas.